I0092599

WHITE WOMEN, GET READY

HOW HEALING POST-TRAUMATIC
MISTRESS SYNDROME LEADS TO
ANTI-RACIST CHANGE

AMANDA K GROSS

© 2024 by Amanda K Gross
ALL RIGHTS RESERVED

CREATIVE DIRECTOR: Saeah Wood
EDITORIAL & PRODUCTION MANAGER: Amy Reed
EDITORIAL: Amy Reed, Taia Pandolfi, Margaret High, Christa Evans
DESIGN: Ivica Jandrijević
EDITORIAL & PRODUCTION ASSISTANTS: Elizabeth Evey & Terri Welch

"The Wicked Webs of Patriarchy, Capitalism, & Racism" was developed in partnership by YogaRoots On Location and Mistress Syndrome in 2018. Shoelace Metaphor, a component of "The Wicked Webs of Patriarchy, Capitalism, & Racism" was created by Mistress Syndrome in 2018. The FRubric was developed in partnership by YogaRoots On Location and Mistress Syndrome.

YOGAROOTS ON LOCATION
Felicia Savage Friedman
yogarootsonlocation.com
FACEBOOK: https://www.facebook.com/yogarootsonlocation
INSTAGRAM: https://www.instagram.com/yogarootsonlocation/
LINKEDIN: https://www.linkedin.com/in/felicia-savage-friedman/

MISTRESS SYNDROME
mistresssyndrome.com
SHOELACE METAPHOR: https://mistresssyndrome.com/2020/08/26/shoelace-metaphor/
BOOK: https://www.mistresssyndrome.com/book
FACEBOOK: https://www.facebook.com/MistressSyndrome/
INSTAGRAM: https://www.instagram.com/mistresssyndrome/

This book was made with love by humans and does not contain any AI generated content.

PAPERBACK ISBN: 978-1-955671-43-9
E-BOOK ISBN: 978-1-955671-44-6

OTTERPINE
otterpine.com

For Cyrus, Alioune, Remix, Sophia Mae,
Maya Cusi, and all the niblings yet to come

TABLE OF CONTENTS

PART II: NAMING OURSELVES

PART III: UP CLOSE AND PERSONAL

PART IV: POST-TRAUMATIC GROWTH

FOREWORD

by Felicia Savage Friedman

They said, the white supremacist said
that you were better than me,
that your fair brow should never know the sweat of slavery.
They lied.
White womanhood too is enslaved,
the difference is degree.

They brought me here in chains.
They brought you here willing slaves to man.

—Beah Richards, from "A Black Woman Speaks"

Dearest precious human cousins who wish to heal from having to break your pretty gold, silver, and platinum chains, I am honored and deeply humbled to shout from the rooftops—*White Women, Get Ready: How Healing Post-Traumatic Mistress Syndrome Leads to Anti-Racist Change* is Amanda K Gross's epic opportunity to share herself intimately, motivated by the intense desire to heal herself and our cousins. I am delighted that she genuinely did the damn thing. In this book, she has stated the historical facts and has told on herself through telling her story.

Amanda and I worked, played, and lived together during the height of our organizing work in Pittsburgh from 2013 to 2020. I call her family because of our close bond, which reaches back to other lifetimes. I credit Amanda for assisting me in doing the intense work of looking at and identifying my personal and business experiences, as a Black, cisgender woman, with white people, particularly white women. This work enabled me to expand my heart (like the Grinch!) to include white folx and, yes, to even see white cisgender men as dating options, which I had never done before. This soul work made me recognize the love of my life, Martin, so I could see his humanity.

Amanda is a weaver of fabrics and people. Her request that I write this foreword was another opportunity to continue to grow by being uncomfortable, looking back while moving forward, and reflecting, as the Sankofa bird reminds me, to remember my history to contextualize my present and future.

I was Amanda's convener, and she was my history mentor. We developed many tools together, including the Wicked Webs of Patriarchy, Racism, and Capitalism workshop. She was my "ride or die" during my first four years running my AntiRacist Raja Yoga Teacher Training, handling and recording the collection of monies.

But we had dysfunction in our relationship as well. There was mammy-fication of me by Amanda, and protectionism and infantilizing of her by me, just to name a few. The lines were often blurred between our private lives, our community organizing, and my business, so we experienced various forms of enmeshment. Now, in 2024, four years after Amanda and I paused working, playing, and living together, I am delighted to emerge healthier and with a little more wisdom from this time of self-reflection. And I know Amanda is committed to continuing her healing journey as well.

Amanda continues to do her "soul work" of self-introspection, as witnessed in her sharing her story with us all. I can only pray that other white women will follow her example and consistently do this work of unpacking how we have all been oppressed and how we have all simultaneously been oppressors. There is something peculiarly powerful—both painful and cleansing—in telling our truths. These are stories we can all share once we are ready.

Amanda is ready and supports other white women in getting ready, too.

Yours in solidarity,

Felicia Savage Friedman
Founder, YogaRoots On Location

Born and raised on unceded Indigenous lands of the Monongahela culture, Haudenosaunee (Iroquois), Shawandasse Tula (Shawanwaki/Shawnee), and Wahzhazhe Manzhan (Osage) peoples.

Written from Boca Raton, Florida, on the unceded Indigenous lands of the Tequesta, Taino, and Seminole.
May 2, 2024

INTRODUCTION

*Native women stay ready. Black women
be ready. White women get ready.*

—2017 Women's March protest sign

The hardest thing about writing is telling the truth.

—Sue Monk Kidd

I have always known I was white. Born and raised in the heart of Atlanta, Georgia in the 1980s, I knew even as a young child that Atlanta was a Black city. Andrew Young was mayor. John Lewis was my congressman (my father had worked on his first campaign). Afrocentrism was emerging from recent popularity in academia and had descended on the Atlanta Public Schools with brilliant performances, music, and rhythms that week after week danced across my elementary school stage. At school every day we would noisily push back from our desks to stand and sing "Lift Every Voice" followed by a folksy rendition of "This Land Is My Land." In Atlanta in the 1980s, the post–civil rights era activists had successfully integrated public education and we were on our way to a multicultural utopia. Or at least that's one story I could tell you about my childhood.

Another story is this: I have always known I was white. When I was six weeks old, my parents hired a Black woman, Ms. Sylvia, to help raise me. She surprised my mother when she started cleaning the house too—so they gave her a raise. Somewhat oblivious to the racial dynamics they were calling upon with this domestic arrangement, my parents saw Ms. Sylvia as the answer to their Swiss German Mennonite prayers. As I got older, Ms. Sylvia would take me on the bus downtown and sneak me junk food. We would go on epic excursions to the park and to the neighborhood library. I don't remember if there were other Black nannies with white charges, but I was happy to hold her hand. She would read me book after book and tell me stories from her childhood, such as the time when the mean white boys bullied her. "Don't be like them," she would say.

In early grade school, the classroom walls were bordered with images of the heroes and sheroes of African American history. I breezed through reading group after reading group until I was permitted to go upstairs and take certain subjects with the big kids. But the playground was another story. My classmates used words I didn't know and language my puritanical upbringing had taught me was sinful. They played by rules I didn't think I could win by. Here, in this new context, the assertiveness and aggression I had developed by dominating my younger brother at home was not nearly as effective as cultivating my good little white girl. So, cultivate I did.

My first memory of the gold-star chart was in first grade. A white 3x5-inch index card was taped on each desk to collect the stars, and we got a fresh card every week. Being quiet during quiet time: gold star! Raising your hand before you speak: gold star! Giving the answer the teacher wanted to hear at the time she wanted to hear it: gold star! *I can play this game*, I thought.

And I did and mostly won. When my classmate called me a "cracker" in the stairwell when scrambling to library hour, when the fifth grader angrily pushed me up against the bathroom door, when the science teacher wasn't actually teaching the content in the syllabus, I told my mom, and with our whiteness combined, things were immediately remedied. I was moved up and out of those situations. Or, in the case of the science teacher, people were moved out to make way for me. Even within the proudly Black school system that is Atlanta Public, my good little white girl bubble grew as I did, granting me both distance and protection from Blackness and the consequences of being Black in America. As I got older, my classrooms and my teachers got whiter too. My white girl bubble followed me around the halls and into the locker rooms, into the magnet programs and through the Advanced Placement course curricula, eventually walking me across the stage to deliver my high school's valedictory address.

I may have always known I was white, but I haven't always known what my whiteness meant.

The 2016 US presidential election offered a wake-up call for many white liberals. The multicultural illusion of a diverse, equitable, race-neutral America was always just that: an illusion. And with over half of white women casting votes in 2016, 2020, and 2024 for an overtly bigoted candidate, we white women have been offered a particularly hard lesson about what our whiteness has meant. We have had over eight years of continued glaring examples, and we have yet another opportunity to dig deeper and do the soul-searching work that can lead, that will lead—no, that *must* lead—lasting, real, and significant change.

While I have spent the past decade as an intersectional anti-racist organizer and educator, and the past two decades studying and working within social justice movements, peacebuilding, and the arts, my sensitivity to this need for change first developed as I navigated the internal politics of my childhood home.

Throughout the course of my life, I have spent buckets of brain power and heart sweat unpacking the mystery of my father's ideological conversion. Although much of it remains lost in the translation of worldviews, what I do know is that sometime between my parents' move to Atlanta in the 1970s and the year of my birth, my father had a political and religious conversion that caused him to withdraw from his left-leaning social work world and propelled him into the throes of Christian conservatism. While my quest to understand his allegiance to systemic oppression has been a source of much pain and confusion in my life, it has also been the force that led me to anti-racism and to writing this book. And for that I am grateful.

Ultimately, looking at him has meant looking at myself, which is why this book doesn't focus on the rise of the Christian Right or point fingers at the evils of toxic white masculinity. Instead, it tells an interconnected story—the story of how a good little white girl grew up to be a status quo white lady and what that has to do with upholding racism. It wades into the complex and sometimes problematic waters of how whiteness does violence to white people. It insists upon a level of vulnerability that already has me squirming in my seat—and perhaps you in yours. And it is written from a place of determination and passion to divest from whiteness, restore my humanity, and contribute to our collective liberation, which gets me up in the morning and motivates me to keep on being. Doing this work has helped me get clearer about the ways I am harmed and about the ways I also harm. It has supported me in feeling and grieving collectivized trauma and has supported me in reclaiming my agency to make different choices, because the choices made from a positionality of white womanhood have drastic impact.

I offer *White Women, Get Ready* as one way of grappling with such choices and impact. As you follow my trajectory of learning and unlearning the ways of white womanhood, I invite you to pay attention to what resonates for you, to tune in to your body as a way of knowing, to notice when you may be nodding your head or feeling a sharp pang in your gut. I invite you to move slowly and to take breaks when you need to. At the same time, I encourage you to come back after breaks and not wait too long. I invite you to call upon courage when you notice fear, to gift yourself with curiosity when you feel frustration, and to lend compassion to spaces of grief. I invite you to bring as much of yourself as you are able. Because—real deal—this book will not be a checklist of white-lady dos and don'ts.

As much as I have looked for an anti-racist rulebook to replace the Christian dogmas of my youth, this work is not neat and simplistic. Rather, the work of healing and transformation is messy and collaborative. I am asking you to show up, to contribute, and to co-create with me because there are at least as many takes on what it means to heal from Post-Traumatic Mistress Syndrome as there are humans who have had to contend with white girlhood and/or white womanhood. There are at least as many ways to divest from whiteness as there are humans on whom it's been imposed. There are at least as many stories of learning and unlearning as there are humans who are interested in change.

I offer *White Women, Get Ready* as one way of engaging with our interconnected stories. I unpack my stories here so that we might clarify our interconnectedness. In that way, this book is both incredibly personal and expansively collective.

Of course, you don't have to take my words for it. In fact, you shouldn't. There are countless books and articles and bodies of work by Indigenous folks, people of the African diaspora, and other People of the Global Majority* that describe the multigenerational devastation, lasting emotional and psychological effects, and enduring legacies of these collective, historical, cultural, and structurally induced traumas, alongside brilliant resources chronicling resilience, asserting resistance, sharing culture, and promoting healing. I highly recommend reading—often and frequently—works that outline the many varied experiences of Black, Indigenous, and other People of Color written by Black, Indigenous, and other People of Color, and I recommend reading with vulnerability and listening to learn. And while *White Women, Get Ready* will certainly weave in histories of and resources by many Black, Indigenous, and other People of Color, the focus of this book is to touch down where those histories and legacies intersect with white womanhood. I use my stories as examples with the goal of unpacking, healing, and ultimately dismantling its foundation. Reading *White Women, Get Ready* is not a substitute for learning about the impact of racism directly from the people whom it impacts the most; it is a complement.

---

* People of the Global Majority is a term used to describe people of Indigenous, African, Asian, and Latine descent, and other People of Color, who collectively make up the large majority of the earth's population.

MISTRESS SYNDROME DEFINED

Dr. Joy DeGruy's book *Post Traumatic Slave Syndrome* was one of the first places I learned about the interlocking traumas of victims and perpetrators, the oppressed and the oppressors:

> These crimes are perpetuated in a seemingly never-ending cycle…For who can be truly human under the weight of oppression that condemns them to a life of torment, robs them of a future, and saps their free will? *Moreover, who can become truly human when they gain so much from the pain and suffering of those whom they oppress and/or take advantage of?*[1] (emphasis added)

Her groundbreaking work describes Post Traumatic Slave Syndrome as "a condition that exists when a population has experienced multigenerational trauma resulting from centuries of slavery and continues to experience oppression and institutionalized racism today."[2] Dr. Joy builds off the more popularly known diagnosis of post-traumatic stress disorder (PTSD) to unpack a pattern of behaviors and beliefs impacting those who were enslaved, their communities, and their descendants today. She later posits that white people have also been impacted by this traumatic legacy of multigenerational violence, racial superiority, and the justification of "500 years of trauma and dehumanization [that Europeans and their descendants] and their institutions produced."[3]

To paraphrase Dr. Joy, if there is a Post Traumatic Slave Syndrome, then there must also be a Post-Traumatic Master Syndrome. Or, to apply social psychologist Rachel M. MacNair's[*] concept of Perpetration-Induced Traumatic Stress,[4] Post-Traumatic Master Syndrome speaks to the "psychological consequences of violence against human beings"[5] on the people perpetrating the violence.

---

[*] While I do not agree with MacNair's anti-choice stance and political activity, I felt it was important to attribute her work on Perpetration-Induced Traumatic Stress because it was where I was first introduced to the idea that those complicit in causing harm can experience lasting negative psychological consequences. Throughout this book, I will take a similar approach in attributing sources while also problematizing them when I have that information.

When I asked a friend and colleague where I could find the book on Post-Traumatic Master Syndrome, he told me it was mine to write.

This book and related bodies of work are me accepting his challenge, with one important modification. Post-Traumatic Master Syndrome—the ways in which the multigenerational enactment of physical and structural violence, the internalization of superiority based on the racial designation of "white" and its corresponding belief system that afflicted and continues to afflict the racial descendants of slave masters—is not entirely mine to write about. But a very interconnected piece of it — Post-Traumatic *Mistress* Syndrome—most definitely is.

Long before Julia Roberts starred in the psychological thriller *Sleeping with the Enemy*, white women have been doing just that. White women have been in bed with "imperialist white-supremacist capitalist patriarchy"* for a good long while. That historical legacy is a collective struggle at the intersection of race, gender, and class that is both specific to white womanhood and also entirely connected to toxic white masculinity in an interlocking and overlapping partnership that has kept violence unnamed, normalized, and securely in place, both inside and outside the White House. With so many white women casting votes for white supremacy in recent US elections, with a climate crisis, with ongoing genocides in Gaza, the Democratic Republic of the Congo, and the Sudan among many other global atrocities, with the growing repression of trans rights and abortion access, the continued normalization of police brutality, militarization, and the rise of fascism, understanding Post-Traumatic Mistress Syndrome is as urgent as ever.

WHY MISTRESS SYNDROME?

This book focuses on healing from Post-Traumatic Mistress Syndrome from the perspective of status quo and passing white ladies for three main reasons:

---

* According to hooks, "imperialist white-supremacist capitalist patriarchy" describes "the interlocking political systems that are the foundation of our nation's politics" ("Understanding Patriarchy," 1). I will reference this term throughout the book.

1. This is the perspective I am most qualified to speak from.

2. We are everywhere.

3. I am committed to practices of solidarity.

This is the perspective I am most qualified to speak from

I am a nondescript status quo white lady. To see me is often not to see me, because in my status quo white-ladyness, I blend into the most nonthreatening of middle-class, middle-age white woman archetypes. My long brown hair is straight with natural highlights in the summer months. I am on the tall side of average, with blue-greenish eyes, a face that I've been told is pleasant to look at, and teeth that testify both to my parents' commitment to orthodontic insurance and their ability to afford it. My skin is fair, though not usually pasty, and even when my skin is tanned by the sun, I am still undeniably racialized as white.

Like many other status quo and passing white ladies, my appearance has allowed me to float seamlessly through most of life unquestioned and unpoliced. When people see me walking down the grocery store aisle, my ponytail swinging and hips swaying, they see a straight status quo white lady with straight hair, straight teeth, and a straight back—unthreatening to the patriarchy and no one to worry about. I know this because time and time again institutions and the people who run them respond to me in this way. I don't have to go out of my way to sleep with a culture of white supremacy. The system has been set up for me to comfortably and conveniently do just that.

* * *

With the possible exception of a very small minority of white Americans, nobody grows up planning on becoming a racist. It is not the answer children give to that annoyingly persistent question that plagues our childhoods: What do you want to be when you grow up? At the age of five, my personal plan was to become the first woman to play Major League Baseball. But instead, like other white people in the US, I grew up to support, maintain, and benefit from racist system after racist system.

When I was summoned to the Allegheny County Courthouse in downtown Pittsburgh for jury duty one late-winter month, I was slightly irritated yet ready to redeem centuries of white folks jurying for white supremacy—or at the very least, cast one vote against it. The holding pen for potential jurors was long and uncomfortable with lots of two-dimensional old white men sternly looking down from portraits as we waited listlessly. Five hours later my juror number got selected for the final pool. When I was called up front for questioning, I answered honestly and to the best of my ability. I said that I had lots of experience with the topic at hand and had known people personally who had been negatively impacted by it. When asked if I could be objective, I responded frankly that I didn't believe in objectivity. The white folks at the table didn't bat an eye and politely thanked me. Fully expecting to be dismissed, I returned to my seat. What seemed like several decades later, my jury number was in fact selected. Later, when I shared this story with a friend, she noted that it must have been my cardigan and ponytail. The meaning of my words couldn't reach their ears because their whiteness and mine had already made up their minds.

Two decades before my selection at jury duty, I had spent a year in a math class being confused with the other smart white girl. In a high school with a majority Black student body, I can hear my father's peers calling it reverse discrimination, but in this case the geometry teacher was white like me. Between the other white girl and me, we had few things in common other than being white. She had short blond hair; mine was butt-long and brown. She was at least five inches shorter than me. Our names started with letters at the opposite ends of the alphabet. And besides, I made incredibly elaborate artwork during class time. But all of our differences didn't matter, because at the end of the day, the teacher had typecast us into the very safe yet unglamorous unit of smart white girl. Our collectivization as white people has its perks and its disadvantages, too.

When I went off to college, smart white girl came along with me. Classes had just let out in the rural Virginian town where I attended school. The sun was bright and the sky was blue and I was on a mission to visit a friend and start summer out right. I took a back road, which also passed through a school zone. The speed limit was 25 but I zoomed through at 50, windows down and music blaring. It wasn't until I arrived at my friend's house that the police officer pulled me over. He must have followed me for a full two miles. I was caught white-handed, which meant he let me off with a warning. I didn't even have time to apologize or resort to sneaky white-lady tears. He ran my plates and that was that.

My point is this: please don't be alarmed by my repetitive use of *us* and *we*. You, of course, get to decide the specificities of when, if, and how *us* and *we* apply to your personal experience. However, I have chosen to use *us* and *we* deliberately in order to make more transparent the ways systems group us together based on race. Notably, whiteness has been normalized such that white people don't usually have to acknowledge the racial aspects of our identities. In the silencing of my voice at jury duty, in the erasure of my identity in geometry, in the dismissal of accountability after my joyride, the bubble of whiteness has collectivized me while simultaneously dehumanizing others. Whether I like it or not, my white-lady bubble surrounds me everywhere I go, just as the threat of racism follows Black folks around in stores, while crossing the street, and while driving on the highway. These systems have not asked for our consent. Consent is implied.

There is a personally specific way I have been colluding with whiteness that comes out of my own unique human story yet cannot be detached from the story of other white folks. Individualism maintains white supremacy by keeping white folks from seeing ourselves as connected, belonging to, and shaped by our racial group. But being seen as an individual is an exception, not the rule. Unlike other racialized groups, all white people, especially straight, cisgender, able-bodied white men, are allowed to be fully individual, unadulterated by the impacts of *racial* socialization, acting and making decisions out of distinct character, inventing from original genius, and operating from an individual moral compass. That we can be fully individual without being white is a myth racism has fed us from a very young age.

I'm a status quo passing white Swiss German Mennonite lady who grew up in Atlanta. Chances are, you're not. But if you've been racialized as white and navigated white girlhood or white womanhood at any point in your life, then Post-Traumatic Mistress Syndrome (or Mistress Syndrome for short) has something to say about your story. I use the term "status quo and passing white lady" because it offers both a specificity and expansiveness that is helpful for our work of unpacking the labels put on us while acknowledging that we are more than those labels. I also use "passing" as a nod to the legacies and ongoing organizing led by Black femmes and queer folx* that have informed my consciousness.

There are many ways to "pass," a term I first learned growing up through stories of how light-skinned Black people in the Jim Crow era used their ability to pass for white to increase access and safety on behalf of their families and communities. Within queer spaces, "passing" is commonly used to refer to queer folx who might be read as "straight"† or "cis."‡ As I began to become more involved in anti-racist organizing and more deeply consider how systems and strangers saw and treated me, I realized that I, too, could "pass" in many ways. If I didn't open my mouth and reveal my politics, I could be welcomed among conservatives. If I acted like I knew where I was going, I could walk past security. If I didn't disclose the details of my dating life at church, no one questioned my heteronormativity. If I didn't give the police officer the middle finger, I would be seen as someone to be protected.

Rather than something to be ashamed of or something to angrily defy, my ability to pass as a status quo white lady is an asset I can use to disrupt status quo harm. As a specific, historical, and intersectional identity, my access to white womanhood is something that has both harmed me and given me advantages. So it is important that even

---

* "Folx" is a gender-inclusive term for "folks," meaning a group of people.

† Interestingly, use of the term "straight" to refer to someone who is heterosexual comes from mid-century gay slang as a way to describe someone who was "re-closeting themselves" (PBS, "Why Does 'Straight' Mean Heterosexual?," 3:19).

‡ "Cis" refers to someone who identifies with the gender they were assigned at birth.

as I acknowledge its harm and leverage its access, I don't become so strongly identified with it that I neglect the many other parts of who I am and who I want to become. These are some of the themes we will be investigating throughout these pages.

You too might pass for status quo. You might pass for white. You might pass for lady. You might also reject all of those labels, even as you still have access to them. I invite you to consider your specific experiences in order to add to our collective work of healing from Mistress Syndrome. I also encourage you to get curious about the intersections as much as those points of divergence. Within white womanhood we have had lots of practice in comparing and competing, in jockeying for best, better, or at least "not her." But what are the overlaps, the connections, the relatedness between your stories and mine? And what might that tell us about healing, growing, and building toward something beyond the limitations of white womanhood?

We are everywhere

When I was offered the position in 2014 as local program director for a peace and justice nonprofit, I suspected there were white women in the nonprofit world, but it wasn't until our program focused on disrupting racism in the education system that I realized the extent of white-lady overrepresentation in the fields of helping and "doing good." The robust cohort of young people I worked with ranged in age from thirteen to early twenties and was mostly, though not entirely, composed of Black youth. No matter their school structure, whether it be private, public, or charter, magnet program, or International Baccalaureate, these students' classrooms, administrative offices, and counseling services were dominated by white women.

And it didn't stop there. As I began outreach to other after- and out-of-school programs and student support services, I ran into white woman after white woman. Mirrors of myself, give or take fifteen years, were everywhere. Another colleague (also a white lady) and I began to realize our work in youth organizing was as much in educating and organizing the white women who served as institutional gatekeepers as it was in directly supporting the youth. As our calendars became crowded with coffee dates and white-lady meetings, White Women's Group (WWG) was born, an affinity group* for status quo white ladies, and those who passed for such, to continue our own education using a BIPOC-led anti-racist analysis and with accountability to local and national organizers.

This call for white affinity-based anti-racist organizing has been a long-standing request by Black organizers exhausted from the double burden of fending off racial violence while simultaneously having to teach the oppressor about our harmful ways. White people educating other white folks also makes good strategic organizing sense.

What I also realized within the radical white anti-racist spaces of Pittsburgh's Left was that a disproportionate amount of labor was being shouldered by queer white anti-racist organizers. So I asked: How could I contribute to the important work already being done? Who was I as an organizer? And whom could I organize who wasn't already tapped in? Reflecting on those questions led me to lean in to the aspects of my identity that passed for status quo, to recognize that we white ladies are everywhere and to begin to realize the incredible collective power white women have within institutions, within social circles, within culture, and within homes.

As I began to apprentice as a facilitator for anti-racism trainings, I noticed that we were overrepresented in racial justice spaces too, though we weren't always having the specific intersectional conversations that would help us to strategically disrupt the status quo. Despite our white-lady conditioning of helping others and looking good, I believe that we are overrepresented in social services and anti-racism because we really do care. I know I do.

---

* Affinity spaces (sometimes called "caucusing") are commonly used in anti-racist organizing. For those unfamiliar with race-based affinity work, the idea of racially segregating on purpose can come as a surprise. Affinity spaces help facilitate more honest conversation than often happens in multiracial spaces. Affinity spaces around dominant identities also aim to transfer the work of education from those with marginalized identities and onto those with shared dominant identities.

In his book *How to Be an Antiracist*, historian and anti-racist scholar
Ibram X. Kendi notes that we uphold racist systems by default unless
we are putting forth ideas, policies, and solutions that are explicitly
against racism, or in other words, anti-racist. Others, such as author
Justin Michael Williams, challenge anti-racist frameworks to shift
toward the language of ending racism, as part of embracing the possibility of oppression's end and imagining the beyond.

I am all for conceptualizing anti-racism in these ways. I approach
anti-racism as a practice, an active and dynamic expression that holds
the potentiality of ending racism in our lifetimes, and I believe that we
white women can contribute to this potentiality in significant ways. As
more than one Black woman in my life has confided to me: If white
women would get their act together, oppression wouldn't stand a chance.

I am committed to practices of solidarity

As I will share in this book, sustained organizing relationships with
fellow white women have not always come easily for me. I don't want
to be associated with the white women who voted for 45 in 2016, or
2020, for that matter. Yet, the everyday aspects of my life continually
shove me into this specific racialized and gendered category, with or
without my consent.

Likewise, when white people begin the lifelong process of recognizing the extent of racism, our tendency has been to move away
from other white people and lean toward the racial other. The reality
is that most white people mostly grow up around other white people,
which insulates us from seeing the realities and impacts of racism on
Black, Indigenous, and other People of Color. We don't know what we
don't know. Perhaps you were once sitting in a classroom and realized
that People of Color are suffering en masse. Maybe for you, like me,
this information led to outrage. And inspiration. Maybe your sense
of justice kicked in. Inequality should not be tolerated! Of course it
shouldn't.

Often our first urge is to go directly to those communities suffering
from racial inequities. We go directly to the symptoms of racism.

Once we're aware there are gaping wounds, we helicopter in, thinking we'll bandage them up (never mind that many of us don't know what effective bandages are, where to find them, or how to dress a gaping wound). This makes sense, because if you're bleeding, it's a natural reaction to stop the blood flow. It is a very human response to see suffering and want to stop it. But unfortunately, our metaphorical band-aids, much like the literal ones, are ineffective for the size of the gaping wound. Most importantly, we fail to recognize how we may have been part of inflicting those wounds in the first place.

As white people, this dynamic is a setup. We have been taught that we should have the answers. But the hard truth is that within these simulated first responder moments, we can cause more harm while also not having to make any meaningful changes in our own lives. Middle-class whiteness grants the option of dipping in and out. We can drive home to "safer" neighborhoods after a long, hard day of work. We can pick up our children from schools that are different from the ones we work in. We can fly back to comfort after volunteering for disaster relief. It is possible to leave these communities with a false sense of having done good, incentivizing us to repeat the pattern.

I name this dynamic not to blame or shame us for trying to alleviate suffering, but so we can become more effective. There is a paradox in white folks addressing racial disparity by working in communities of color. Not only can we make things worse for those we are trying to help, but we end up undermining and ignoring the position, power, and influence we *do* have in white communities with real live white people and white institutions, which is precisely where we have the capacity to make lasting, real, and significant change. We don't have to parachute into communities of color to end racism. We just have to address it at its source: us. That is why we white women are important to this work. It requires the hard, vulnerable, intimate work of knowing ourselves.

As I will continue to point to in this book, white womanhood has been historically and is still today centered in very harmful ways. So why center white womanhood here in a pursuit to end racism?

In short, healing from Mistress Syndrome is solidarity work. Along with my lineages in peace traditions, Southern civil rights organizing, and anti-racism, this book has been influenced by healing justice, transformative justice, and abolitionist movements, all of which ask us to dig into the roots of harm and healing to get radical about our paradigm shifts and our collaborations. As solidarity work, healing from Mistress Syndrome means understanding how our oppressions are interconnected. Since Post-Traumatic Slave, Master, and Mistress Syndromes were manufactured as a package, so too is our liberation work interdependent. The fight for my humanity is part of the fight for the humanity of us all. Honoring our mutual humanity is part of honoring the living, breathing ecosystems of which we are also a part.

As I will continue to explore throughout this book, solidarity work is not saviorism. It is not martyring ourselves on behalf of others or indiscriminately following anti-racist rules. Solidarity is not using the master's tools to dismantle the master's house,* replacing one abuse of power with another. Solidarity is a living, breathing, imperfect messy practice and one we need to work on both alone and together.

For status quo and passing white ladies, this solidarity work means recognizing the masks we've been given, the masks we've worn, and those we've come to accept as parts of ourselves. It means peeling back the masks and reconnecting with our humanity. Mistress Syndrome has been built upon lies. This book will work to illuminate why we've been nursed on these lies, why we act upon these lies, and how we've learned to tell them to ourselves and each other so that we will stop exhausting ourselves with lying and use our valuable energy instead for work that benefits us all.

This book will help explain why we white women seem to care more about keeping up appearances rather than addressing what is happening inside us. It will investigate why we starve ourselves for thinness, suppress our emotions for politesse, and silence ourselves to keep the peace.

---

* In *Sister Outsider: Essays and Speeches*, writer and intersectional feminist Audre Lorde says: "For the master's tools will never dismantle the master's house. They may allow us temporarily to beat him at his own game, but they will never enable us to bring about genuine change. And this fact is only threatening to those women who still define the master's house as their only source of support" (112).

In unpacking Mistress Syndrome, this book will disentangle how our worth has been tied to our relationship to white maleness, how we've wagered our souls for the toxic pseudo-protection of whiteness, and how we've bartered our human value in between his white sheets. Within Mistress Syndrome, we've exchanged our agency for the psychological paranoia that the cognitive dissonance of racism commands. Our identity, value, and sense of self-worth are directly relative to our ability to meet the inhumane demands of a dominant white culture. This toxic dynamic conditions us to be hypersensitive to what we think other people need and want without ever knowing ourselves or questioning our own motives. It allows us to function in the daily overwhelm of never being enough. Sacrificing ourselves at the altars of white culture, we are exhausted, stressed, anxious, inundated, fraught, and cloaked in the false self-protection of good intentions. As one such recovering self-sacrificial white lady, I am no longer willing to be martyred for such an unjust cause.

This book will critically examine how even the movements that were supposed to be about our liberation have failed us, how white women have sought to advance our gendered positions by proving to white culture that we play a necessary role. For poor and working-class white women, this middle-class aspiration has provided a link to affluence, a thin thread of superiority that enables a separation from neighbors of color—if not in material substance, in a sense of superiority, because at least in whiteness we are not them. For middle-class and affluent white women (a middle-class experience is the one I'm most qualified to speak on), white feminism has been a way out of the psychological doldrums of being valued for our bodies, an intellectualized pursuit while being imprisoned behind the walls of patriarchy.

This book will delve into the ways white womanhood does not keep white women safe. We have had Black men lynched and Black communities terrorized and burnt to the ground on behalf of keeping our (perceived) sexual purity intact, but we can't keep wealthy white college athletes from gang raping us on video, with entire institutions and court systems cosigning on their right and innocence in doing so. To quote poet, playwright, and award-winning actor Beah

Richards in "A Black Woman Speaks," white womanhood, with its denial and complicity in one's own oppression, is a fate "worse than death."[6] The cruel joke is on us, which is precisely what women of color—sometimes in love, sometimes in rage, sometimes in desperation, and sometimes in all of the above—have been trying to tell us since the inception of white womanhood.

Moreover, this book will describe the false path that we white women have inherited. We are both victims of these systems and active perpetrators of their harm. This book will consider how we white ladies are (and historically have been) complicit in our own oppression as well as in the oppression of others, how we have dedicated our waking hours to helping, fixing, and saving others so that we won't have to do the difficult work of helping, fixing, or saving ourselves—even though helping, fixing, and saving ourselves is exactly what we need to do with this information.

As Dr. Joy writes, "Those who have been the perpetrators of these unspeakable crimes and those who continue to benefit from those crimes, have to honestly confront their deeds and heal from the psychic wounds that come with being the cause and beneficiaries of such great pain and suffering."[7]

White Women, Get Ready: How Healing Post-Traumatic Mistress Syndrome Leads to Anti-Racist Change is my attempt to honor Dr. Joy's call to action: to confront and to heal. It is my hope that this book will help equip those of us who have been conditioned as white ladies to engage with the complexities of our identities, traumas, and harms. I want us to know that our fight for gender equality is not separate from the fight for racial justice. I want us to realize we have a responsibility to heal from and to transform the legacies of whiteness in our communities, workplaces, and homes. I want us to understand that compassion does not necessitate comfort, that commitment does not mean martyrdom, that health and well-being for us is not separate from the health and well-being of us all.

I dream that white women will read this book alone and together, that it will spark mobilizing conversations, that it will help us to change and heal. I dream that it will support us in divesting from whiteness and building healthier, more authentic relationships, cultures, and communities. I hope this book will inspire, motivate, and equip you to contribute to lasting, real, and significant change, that you will more deeply understand how these systems don't serve you, that you will *feel* it and commit to a lifelong practice of solidarity.

Likewise, I dream that this book will serve as a resource for those who have been most impacted by the violence of white womanhood. For every Black woman and femme who has asked me to talk to their "white lady," I dream of a stack of these books for you to hand out.

This book is structured into four main sections with breaks in between to support the integration and embodiment of the material. "Part I: Deep Cuts" provides a foundational analysis and historical context. "Part II: Naming Ourselves" traces white-woman archetypes as they've developed in the US context at the intersections of race, gender, and class. "Part III: Up Close and Personal" goes deeper into my story as I share about family, chosen family, intimate partnerships, and organizing relationships. "Part IV: Post-Traumatic Growth" further integrates the book's analysis, history, and archetypes with my stories and seeks to move in a solutionary direction*; that is, toward the co-creation of revolutionary alternatives.

This book can be read alone, but it is intended to be discussed together. I suggest finding a reading buddy or forming a group. On the Mistress Syndrome website† there are support materials to help you go deeper in reflection and use the book as a resource for discussion and action.

While grounded in research, this book is also a memoir. It may not seem so at first, with my focus on history, analysis, and references. But

---

* According to author and social activist Grace Lee Boggs, in an article titled "Solutionaries are Today's Revolutionaries": "True revolutionaries…are about redefining our relationships with one another, to the Earth and to the world; about creating a new society in the places and spaces left vacant by the disintegration of the old; about hope, not despair; about saying yes to life and no to war; about finding the courage to love and care for the peoples of the world as we love and care for our own families."

† https://www.mistresssyndrome.com/.

the book's trajectory from heady analysis, to relational adversities, to embodied agency, mirrors that of my own. The journey of the book follows the journey of my own healing work, from intellectualizing within the safety of my head to unlearning through trying, failing, and feeling, and doing so within the messiness of relationship, family, and community.

Awesomely, there are so many books out there today (several of which I reference in these pages) that chronicle the whats and hows of racism, offering detailed critique and tactical solutions. While you will certainly find aspects of those approaches in this book, my goal is to align the vision with the resource. Really, this book is grounded in story. I hope that the stories will model transformation and embody healing.

Culture can be medicine. Art can be medicine.* In these pages, I offer the story as medicine. May these stories contribute to our healing.

---

* I was first introduced to this idea of arts and culture as medicine through work collaborations with several Indigenous art therapists through the Winnipeg Holistic Expressive Arts Therapy Institute, including Fyre Jean Graveline. See Resources for Further Support at the end of this book for links to their work.

PART I
DEEP CUTS

CHAPTER ONE

WE ARE LIVING IN A TRAUMATIZED WORLD AND I AM A TRAUMATIZED GIRL

The story is seeking a witness.

—Arlene Ardegon

We violate our own dignity by wronging others.

—Donna Hicks

In early 2016, I was sitting alone in my partner's VW Jetta at a public park in Lancaster County, Pennsylvania, land where my ancestors had been some of the earliest European colonizers.

It was spring, but not the kind I grew up with. Unlike southern springtime, which gloriously announced its arrival and then stuck around to play, Pennsylvania spring teased like a cat tormenting its prey. It drifted back and forth between blue skies and gray slush, redbuds and snowflakes. I remember the season because I was cold and grouchy about it. Stubbornly refusing to put my winter coat back on, I sat in the front seat at a public park trying to absorb the late day's waning rays. Other much more appropriately dressed park-goers walked by with their dogs. Some talked with friends. I tilted my head down as they passed, hoping they wouldn't notice the tears or how my face was turning magenta with anger.

I was on the phone with my mother who was expressing her displeasure with my latest blog post. It was the first time I had written about family matters. The blog was a new venture for me. Though I had authored plenty of term papers and grant applications, never before had I written so publicly *and* so personally. Perhaps a more methodical person would have thought this through, but the hurt and anger in her quivering voice had honestly taken me by surprise.

My mother was not one to express discord. On the contrary, with the exception of consumer advocacy and protecting her children, she was one of the most accommodating and supportive people I knew. She was so accommodating that when I announced at the age of nine that I was never again going to eat meat, she responded by teaching me to cook and ensuring I had enough vegetarian protein. She was equally as supportive on the day I announced I was going to school in France (I was fifteen) and later, to live in Germany (at eighteen).

I had expected backlash from my father, since we argued regularly about politics. Besides, in this particular blog post, I was writing about what had happened at his father's funeral. Or more accurately, I was writing about what hadn't happened, how the words that could have been said to describe my grandfather weren't, how the unspoken norms weighed heavily on my body, how my name got erased from the program, and the real reasons why my husband hadn't accompanied me.

The rarity of my mother's offense made it that much more distressing. I wanted, and naively, had expected her support in this, my latest creative endeavor. But in speaking in a public way about "private" family dynamics, it seemed I had violated an unspoken cultural norm, a boundary I had not previously tested or entirely knew existed.

When I saw her number on my phone, I picked it up and asked how she was doing. "Not very well," she said, sounding angry and concerned. She said she was uncomfortable with me sharing details about our family. She was especially concerned about how what I had written would impact my relationships with my father's family, relationships that I'd mostly neglected as an adult as my cousins had married and had children.

I was upset that she was upset. Really, I was afraid. In hearing her list her concerns, a jolt of fear went up my spine.

"That's what I honestly felt. I'm just writing my truth," I responded defensively. She repeated her concerns about what this might do to my relationships.

"I don't really have relationships with them anyway," I said, denying the consequences. I paused for a response. I could hear her skepticism through the silence.

"Besides," I began to bargain, "there's not much relationship there to lose."

"I'm still upset," was her simple reply. Then she let out a long slow sigh.

With my arguments failing to win her over, I pivoted toward false harmony. I changed the subject to something less volatile, perhaps the weather or planning an upcoming gathering.

I probably chose the weather.

But underneath my attempt at false harmony was the extreme discomfort of discord and deeper fears of what alienating my mother might mean for me. None of our previous challenges—my childhood temper, bullying my younger brother, spending much of my adolescence abroad, or that one time when she wouldn't let me housesit for my aunt—had tested our relationship the way my blogging about our family and white Christian patriarchy had.

I don't remember the exact way we ended our call, the precise words we used, or how we left it, but I do remember a deep unsettling that shook me to my core. I drove back to Pittsburgh wavering between shock and grief. The tears muddled my glasses as I tried to stay between the lines on the PA Turnpike.

I've filed this memory away in the imaginary filing cabinet where I store emotionally charged moments and things I find difficult to accept. In my mind the filing cabinet is tall and metallic. Its long drawers are cool to the touch and hard and fixed in their function. At the top of the folder where I store the memory of this cold spring conversation with my mother, I notice that I've cross-listed it. The first label says: The Moment the Pain I've Been Carrying Begins to Be Shared by Others. The second: When I Began to Feel the Isolation of Anti-racism.

I think it was also the moment when I began to do the work in earnest.

It was one thing to call out a racist act in the workplace like I had been practicing in my new nonprofit job, but a whole other to bring that same information home. It was one thing to argue with my dad about his harmful politics as I had for years, but another to challenge the very cultural fabric of my family all while staying invested in being part of the change. It was one thing to critique loosely held family relationships like cousins I hadn't seen since childhood, yet entirely different to potentially risk my most foundational one.

As a family truth teller, I guarded myself against the inevitable rejection that happened when speaking up. Of course, I felt hurt when it happened. Here I was, taking a risk being honest. Here they were, hurt that I had been brave enough to name my pain. And here I was once again, not feeling seen or heard, left to tend to my wounds alone, left to guard myself against future inflictions.

Defensiveness. Denial. Deference. Distancing. These words describe some of the ways I've shielded myself against the hurt; the ways I shield myself when others name their pain to me. On that uncomfortable spring day, I responded to my mother's concerns about my public confessions in those ways too, shifting between a defensive posture and denying responsibility, ultimately settling on the superficial harmony of the weather.

I could get into the weeds sorting through my pattern of family systems truth-telling/rejection/righteous pain (and I will, eventually), but for now I want to return to that memorable spring day, in which my defensiveness and denial did not offer the soothing balm that they had perhaps offered me in the past. No, that moment with my mother felt different. I didn't feel solace in a sense of righteousness as I sacrificed family relationships for anti-racist actions. Instead, I felt a sharp unease as a new reality began to settle in between my connective tissue: this process of working with my family was going to be slow, painful, scary, and not at all guaranteed to result in lasting relationship or unconditional love.

THE 4DS

Defensiveness. Denial. Deference. Distancing. The 4Ds have become a framework I use for noticing, sensitizing, and tending to deeper wounds. They have helped me go below those initial reactions, get curious and, when I'm ready, learn from them. The 4Ds have become a foundational tool I use for developing self-awareness as a white person committed to ending racism. As I was taught in anti-racism spaces, reactions like defensiveness and denial are ways an internalized sense of racial superiority can show up for those of us who are white.*

Notably, these 4Ds can be blocks to going deeper. A defensive stance prevents a white woman from investigating her urge to control a situation in which weaponized tears shift sympathies back on her. Denial lets us avoid the historical harm our ancestors caused as we uncritically proclaim the struggles they faced. Deference allows me to perform anti-racism. My boundaryless support for a Black colleague's perspective protects me from potentially saying a problematic thing, having to take responsibility for that thing, and getting to learn and grow as a consequence of being corrected. Distancing (or dissociation) shuts the whole system down. Our bodies may go through the motions, but we are not connected to their wisdoms. Disconnected, we are unable to fully engage, to feel, or to activate our agency.

In working with these 4Ds within myself and with other white ladies, I have noticed how they run parallel to the trauma responses of fight, flight, fawn, and freeze. Though trauma responses show up in our bodies in the present, they are informed by our histories. They come from deep wounds that want to be witnessed.

These 4Ds (or 4Fs) exist for a reason. We have learned them over generations and within our lifetimes as ways to keep ourselves safe. Wanting to be safe and responding in ways that ensure safety is not

---

* I learned about internalized racial oppression and its manifestations through the People's Institute for Survival and Beyond (PISAB). Since 1980, PISAB has supported the development of anti-racist organizers. I was first introduced to PISAB in 2014 and spent several years as a trainer-in-training and collaborating through bringing their analysis and workshops to Pittsburgh. For more information, see https://pisab.org.

bad or wrong; those are brilliant and important survival skills. It's just that with all these unaddressed multigenerational patterns and deep cultural wounds, we may react out of our coping mechanisms when other wiser options are actually available.

I want to be very clear that there are moments when we might need to use them to keep ourselves safe and it is appropriate in those situations to do so. The dangers of having a feminized body persist even for those of us who may be able to access the added buffers of whiteness and cis, class, and able-bodied privilege. But in my experience there have also been many times when I had more safe options than my trauma responses let on, especially because of those added buffers of whiteness and cis, class, and able-bodied privilege.

Left over generationally from our ancestry and from our childhoods, these 4Ds are embodied strategies that have been passed down culturally in the customs we uphold and through the silences we keep. As I will unpack further, these coping mechanisms have likewise been physiologically encoded in our DNA and somatically transferred via geography, space, and habitual movement. They have shaped our pathways for resilience, resistance, and continued oppression.

WHAT IS TRAUMA?

I was born into white-ladydom, given a race and a gender in an Atlanta hospital in the early 80s. Along with my name, pink dresses (which I still love), and Cabbage Patch dolls, there were immediate references to dating, jokes that boys better stay away, and hypothesizing about how my future (white) feminine sexuality would be fortified and kept pure while waiting for the one right (white) man to come along. I grew up a good little white girl, groomed to play by the rules and win, or at least maintain the flawless and effortless appearance that I was. And when occasionally I wasn't winning, my white-lady mama would go remind the system that I was supposed to.

At the same time that I was being conditioned to win at the perfect grade, the perfect body, and the perfect attitude, I was also conditioned to help, support, defend, and ultimately defer my self-interest to God (the Father), men (almost always white, including my actual father), and the (church) Family (if not actually white in the pews, the dominant cultural norms, elevated history, and power seat of Mennonites* in the US and Canada remains steeped in whiteness).

There is a 1,100-page book to this effect titled *Martyrs Mirror*, an important Mennonite text that outlines approximately seventeen centuries of dying for the cause…with illustrations! These stories of persecution and sacrifice became part of my cultural and religious vocabulary during congregational children's story hour when I was first introduced to the martyred stories of my ancestors. I was four.

And yet my Anabaptist ancestors weren't the only Europeans with tales of historical traumas. Many North Americans of European descent have likewise been connected to traumatic legacies, whether or not we have personal access to those specific stories. Groups often left Europe for a variety of life-threatening reasons. Many of us either have ancestry in the peasantry and indentured servants who were expelled as class prisoners from England, or in Jewish and other religious communities who faced widespread terror and extermination from hundreds of years of state-sanctioned violence through pogroms, Inquisitions, and the Holocaust, or in European indigenous people groups who had been colonized for generations like the Irish or the Catalans, or in more recent immigrant communities fleeing poverty, the World Wars, and fascism of twentieth-century Europe.

Much of the collective and historical trauma for people of European descent happened as a result of that dangerous social norm of European-on-European crime. Unlike the narrative of triumph that I learned in my Eurocentric world history course, Europe has been far from

---

* The Mennonite tradition comes out of a revolutionary communal political movement in Europe. As historian Silvia Federici outlines: "It was through the prism of the Peasant War and Anabaptism that the European governments, through the 16th and 17th centuries, interpreted and repressed every form of social protest. The echoes of Anabaptist revolution were felt in Elizabethan England and in France, inspiring utmost vigilance and severity with regard to any challenge to the constituted authority. 'Anabaptist' became a cursed word, a sign of opprobrium and criminal intent, as 'communist' was in the United States in the 1950s, and 'terrorist' is today" (*Caliban and the Witch*, 119).

utopic. It has historically been a terribly violent place for the people living there. For thousands of years, Europeans brutalized each other, kicked each other out of their homes, and sent each other to perish oceans away. No wonder we have culturally internalized so much fear.

My high school textbooks conveniently forgot to mention that thousands of years of normalized violence in Europe is what built America. That fancy timeline in the textbook's centerfold, with its black-and-white photographs of factory workers and Ford Model Ts, cheerfully proclaimed the linear progress of the American Dream, but didn't show how generations of European traumas were key ingredients in the cocktail of whiteness. Even when war and violence in Europe was explicitly named, those books didn't say much about where the aftereffects went. Did they evaporate over the waters of the Atlantic Ocean like some sort of reverse baptism? Did they magically disappear the moment our European ancestors arrived on Turtle Island*? Those history texts most certainly left out how the traumas traveled within the *bodies* of Europeans, in muscle memory, through DNA, and in dreams. Imagine all that unmetabolized historical multigenerational trauma filling up boat after boat as Europeans set sail for what they later classified as the Americas, as well as the continents of Africa, Asia, and Australia.

The word "trauma" calls up images of soldiers coming home from war, witnesses to mass shootings, survivors of sexual assault, and people who experienced childhood abuse. Occasionally, the word invokes a more collective dynamic—communities that survived natural disasters or experienced prolonged armed conflict. But in general, trauma in the narrative of dominant American culture indicates an individual's experience based on a traumatic event that is over and done with, in which there was normalcy before the incident occurred, and healing will result in some sort of normalcy afterward.

This one-and-done model is *not* how trauma usually happens, and yet this is the predominant way most people in the US think about

---

* Turtle Island is an Indigenous name for what has come to be called North America and is used by several Indigenous groups native to the continent.

it because we've been greatly influenced by things like individualism and meritocracy and other myths that can mainly be attributed to white hierarchical culture (which we will continue to unpack in these pages…along with our perceptions of normalcy).

That is not to dismiss how traumatic experiences impact us at the individual level* (we've got the science to prove it), but human experiences with trauma tend to be layered and recurring as collective and societal rather than individually isolated—even though trauma often *feels* individually isolating. Our experience of it in our physical, emotional, and psychological landscapes is intricately connected to wider historical, cultural, and structural ecologies.

Church tales of martyrs introduced me to collective trauma stories from a very young age, but it was my graduate studies in Conflict Transformation that gave me the language to describe them as such. Since my time at graduate school, the field of trauma healing has grown expansively. But despite the many new resources, the foundational frameworks I was first introduced to still ground my understanding of collectivized trauma. The "STAR: Strategies for Trauma Awareness and Resilience" manual, an early text in my graduate program, offers:

Collective or Societal Trauma – traumatic events that affect specific groups or entire societies.

Historical Trauma – the cumulative emotional and psychological wounding over the lifespan and across generations emanating from massive group trauma.

Cultural Trauma – the effect created when attempts are made to eradicate part or all of a culture or people.

Structurally-Induced Traumas – trauma created by policies that result in unjust, abusive, racist, or unsafe systems that cause

---

* This is also not to discount the importance and seriousness of PTSD as an individualized medical diagnosis. I use a collective trauma framework because individual experiences with trauma do not exist in isolation, and in fact are informed and compounded by these collective and historical influences.

hardship often on a long-term, continuous basis. These include situations of conflict and/or poverty that result in the inability to meet basic needs such as adequate food or health care.[1]

Most of us humans living on this earth encounter a combination of the traumas listed above in one way or another. Tragically, we don't have to travel farther than the United States for horrific, large-scale examples that have had long-term impact on many communities. The transatlantic slave trade, chattel slavery, and their racist legacies invoke layers of collective, historical, cultural, and structurally induced trauma for generations of people of African descent. The attempted genocide of Indigenous peoples of this land through armed conflict, displacement, sexual abuse, attempted erasure, and disease, calls upon many interconnected forms of collective trauma, both historical and ongoing.

If you are white and reading this book, you most likely have some awareness that racism has caused—and still causes—trauma for people who have been racialized as Black, Indigenous, Asian, Pacific Islander*, and other racial categorizations the US system has imposed on humans not racialized as white. You may even have reflected on what it means for you, as someone who has been racialized as white, to be connected to the traumas of racism, both past and present. But it is less likely that you have considered how the collective trauma of racism also harms you as a white person.

Personally, I was thirty years old before I seriously considered how racism, and specifically whiteness, harms me. My childhood field trips included days at the King Center, and we had civil rights activists as school assembly speakers. I knew racism was a thing. I knew it was still a thing. I knew racism was bad for Black and Brown people. White racial justice activists weren't just children's book characters, they were my friends' parents and attended my parents' house church.

---

* White; Black or African American; Native American/Alaska Native; Asian; Native Hawaiian/Other Pacific Islander; and Some Other Race were the racial categories offered on the 2020 US Census. Race is considered separate from the concept of Hispanic origin (United States Census Bureau, "Race").

But for all the racialized harm I learned about and witnessed, not one adult ever suggested that racism was something that concerned my well-being or that of my (white) family.

What would it mean if we white people approached conversations about race and racism aware not only of our complicity in perpetrating racist violence, but also of our own psychological harm? What decisions might we change if we saw how our daily choices contribute to racism? If we viscerally felt its damage to our well-being in return? How might we develop more grace and compassion for ourselves and each other? How might acknowledging, and moreover, *feeling* our interconnected traumas alter the choices we make with our bodies and in our social justice movements? How might it help us to heal?

This is why understanding racism through the lens of trauma is so helpful: Trauma is not just a static thing that individual victims experience, but a collective dynamic that whole societies and communities navigate, including those responsible for the traumatic events. We are all connected. MacNair's work on Perpetration-Induced Traumatic Stress (PITS), draws attention to the impact on the perpetrator of violence. In examining PITS, MacNair names active participation in causing trauma (including in the line of duty) as a main cause of PITS. In the foreword of *Perpetration-Induced Traumatic Stress*, Professor Harvey Langholtz writes:

> But it may not at first be so easy to understand why a perpetrator might also suffer from symptoms that are similar to PTSD. After all, wasn't it the perpetrator who brought about the stress-inducing situation in the first place? Why should we feel sympathy for the perpetrator and how can he or she claim to be suffering from anything remotely like PTSD? And even if the perpetrator is suffering, isn't that perhaps some fair justice?[2]

MacNair notes studies revealing that a high percentage of soldiers in war either avoid shooting or intentionally shoot off-target when in close physical contact with the assigned enemy, especially when eye contact is involved. In an effort to adjust for this, the US Army altered training methods to desensitize and condition soldiers with denial and defense mechanisms. While this adjustment resulted in more efficient shooting, according to MacNair, it "also contributed to greater psychological costs in the long run."[3]

As we will continue to examine throughout this book, such desensitizing mechanisms have been built into structural racism and the culture of whiteness, and at great psychological costs. Denial and defense mechanisms may have developed as survival strategies to keep us safe, but as US Army training demonstrates, they can be used to keep us from empathizing with the humanity of others. Especially over the past several decades, denial and defensiveness have enabled more covert forms of racism to flourish (and more overt forms of racism to make a comeback).

Before we continue, I want to invite you to begin to consider how the 4Ds may show up for you. Often there are one or two that come up more frequently, depending on the moment, who you're with, and how safe you feel. In the groups I facilitate, I ask people to draw four capital letter Ds, each one nested within the other. The outermost D represents how you most often respond in moments of heightened stress, conflict, fear, and shame. Many of us white ladies have been rewarded for our deference: the please and appease response. Historically deferring to the (white) men in power has been a way to keep ourselves and our children (relatively) safe. But is deference to white masculinity serving us today? And moreover, is it actually keeping us safe?

As I continue to unpack Mistress Syndrome, I offer the 4Ds as a tool. As you read this book, you might practice noticing moments when defensiveness, denial, deference, or distancing is present for you. When those arise, can you get curious about what might be underneath?

This initial noticing is an important place to start because denial is one of racism's favorite tricks.

THE POWER OF DENIAL

In the book *Deep Denial*, anti-racist organizer and minister Rev. David Billings chronicles how racism has continued despite the gains of the Civil Rights Movement. As the title points out, denial for white folks, especially for white liberals and progressives, has supported a myth that systemic racism is largely over and that, in the exceptional cases where racism still exists, we good white people are not responsible for it.

Denial has us celebrating the diversity of our workplace and ignoring that there are now more Black people incarcerated in the US prison system than were once enslaved. Denial has us correcting our racist relative's bigotry while overlooking how our choice of neighborhood or children's school is part of systemic racism. Denial has me so exhausted identifying institutional racism on the job that I disregard how my self-care routines keep me walking the same worn-out paths in the same affluent neighborhood day after day. At some point, I became so attuned to other white people's racism that I have become neglectful of my own.

Just as it has for the US Army, denial serves a purpose. Denial is embodied, a self-protective mechanism that traps past traumas in our bodies so that we can continue to function within dysfunctional realities.

I may have always known I was white, but as a Mennonite of Swiss German ethnicity, my unique cultural religious identity has given me a way to opt out when identifying with whiteness made me feel too uncomfortable. This is not to deny how differences shaped the experiences of previous generations. With their distinct clothing, communal farming practices, low German language, and general avoidance of "worldly things," my ancestors most certainly experienced being othered. But once my grandma unpinned her head covering and retired her cape dress to the cedar trunk, my family line pretty seamlessly waded into the segregated swimming pool of white Americans.

Historically speaking, and even with these cultural distinctions, legal whiteness was granted to my ancestors upon their arrival on Lenape land. For those entering the colony of Pennsylvania in the

1700s, whiteness proved a systemic advantage that allowed them to practice their quirky religious and ethnic customs. This racial advantage invited their existence in Pennsylvania, while at that same time, Indigenous people on the same lands were experiencing a colonial policy of genocide. Mennonite and Amish cultural practices may have seemed strange to other European colonists, but as strange as those customs were, they were not only allowed to coexist, in some instances they were invited as "loyal foreign Protestants" for the explicit purpose of settling Indigenous land.

Yet, these celebrated aspects of identity (as a peace church, as a persecuted minority, as über godly) have prevented me and much of my community from fully reckoning with our whiteness. A cultural identity of Mennonite has offered me a qualifier, a place of psychological respite, an "I'm white, *but...*" But really, there's no "but." Actually accepting that I have also been racialized as white frees up my energy to do something about it.

Denial requires a whole lot of bandwidth—take the efforts to deny the 2020 election results. That particular denial required the spread of multiple conspiracy theories; the public consent of politicians, religious leaders, and social media outlets; and continuous dog-whistling lies in order to fuel and maintain the momentum leading up to the January 6th insurrection. What if all that energy had been redirected to dealing with the pandemic instead? What if, since then, all the organizing geared toward election denial had been channeled into building cooperative economics or reducing carbon emissions or providing affordable housing? What if we redirected our resistance to accepting our whiteness toward healing our traumas, ending violent systems, and uplifting humanity?

Alongside the brutal violence of cultural oppression for enslaved African people, alongside the attempted erasure and eradication of Indigenous peoples and so many people's languages and cultures, also stands the cultural trauma of white folks. I name this not to equate these traumas, nor to justify or minimize the atrocities that Black, Indigenous, and other People of Color face; I name it to deepen and complexify our understanding of the role of racism as trauma and its interrelated impact on communities of European descent. I name it to help us contend with how unaddressed trauma reinforces the continuation of violence hundreds of years later.

So how do these unaddressed traumas continue to perpetrate violence? And how does that show up for those of us who have been racialized as white? For one, the stories we tell ourselves about our histories and identities matter. Staying in denial about our historical complicity keeps us from feeling and grieving. Denial desensitizes us to harm and suffering, both to that of ourselves and of others.

But we are not without options. We can reckon with our denial as part of the grieving—and healing—process. Reckoning with the denial of whiteness may not be easy. It may be uncomfortable and painful, but the disconnect and desensitization that comes from denial has consequences as well. Among many harmful consequences, denial gets in the way of co-creating the communities that could help us to do the courageous work of acknowledging, feeling, and grieving the pain that comes with being the beneficiary of someone else's harm.

ASSIMILATION AND LOSS

The first time I was challenged to consider the cultural loss for white folks was while sitting in a circle of chairs at a PISAB workshop. The trainer asked the white folks in the room, "What did your people have to give up in order to assimilate into whiteness?"

This question got my wheels turning.

But, you may be saying, I don't know much about my ancestry. It's true that many white people aren't able to trace their European ancestry as specifically as I can. Thanks to cultural insularity, centuries of a limited genetic pool, settler colonization, and some very problematic religious nationalist tendencies, I have a level of genealogical access that most people do not. While some white folks have a vague idea of belonging to one ethnicity or another, others may not know their specific roots much better than the descendants of those who were enslaved.

For many white people, becoming white has meant a profound loss of cultural and historical identity. Yet even for white people who have been able to stay connected to the threads of our ancestry, assimilation into North American whiteness has ultimately erased much of our cultural ways of knowing as well. So I ask you: How much of your ancestral cultures are part of your day-to-day living? Do you speak the languages of your ancestors fluently? Do you celebrate cultural holidays and are you connected to the communal and spiritual reasons those holidays exist? Does your ancestral culture shape your worldview, your spirituality, your home, and your everyday way of being in this world?

I can trace my ancestry directly to Switzerland and Germany. I know English is not the native tongue of my ancestry, yet English is the language my parents spoke to me. It's the language their parents spoke to them. It's the language I think in and write in. It's the only language I have fluency in. Even though I am a person of European descent, my tongue and mind have been infiltrated by American English.

What did your ancestors sacrifice for this assimilation? Most did not pass down languages so that their children would succeed in an English-speaking world. Many Europeans changed their names and acquired a certain "American" accent so that their descendants could pass for Anglo-Saxon, Nordic, or American (as Nell Irvin Painter outlines in *The History of White People*, "white" has been coded differently at different times in order to include and exclude depending on the politics of the time). Henry Ford, among other robber barons and corporate bosses, established schools to condition European immigrants into white American middle-class cultural norms, replicating reforms of earlier eras such as early nineteenth century prisons and poorhouses geared toward reforming impoverished Scots, English, and Irish into middle-class Protestant whiteness. Such "Americanizing" schools ensured a more compliant industrial workforce and are the predecessors of our contemporary public education system.

The consequences of these cultural losses were not unintended. Our European ancestry was slowly bought off as they bought into the material and identity-based advantages of whiteness. In exchange for a seat at the whiteness table, our families sold the depth of our diverse cultural legacies. But (and I'm hopeful this is beginning to change), we typically don't talk about our cultural losses as a racialized transaction. A legacy of silence insulates the loss that whiteness has demanded.

CHOSEN TRAUMA/CHOSEN GLORY

Evening dinner time was an important staple in my family of origin's diet. No matter the day's activities, after school and soccer practice, piano lessons or homework, in the evenings we came together around the oval oak kitchen table to enjoy my mother's home-cooked meals. Before we were allowed to dig in, we prayed over the food. Occasionally (and these were my favorite) singing a song counted as saying grace. At some point, we began to end family dinner time with another type of religious ceremony in the form of family devotions.

I have a hazy memory of a badger illustration on the front of a white booklet. Several booklets fit vertically into a standing box. Each one had an animal paired with a story and a thematic virtue like purity or chastity for my little brother and me to aspire to. While I don't remember them specifically (sorry Dad), I do remember that my mother wasn't as into them as my father and that eventually they stopped, and we went back to ending family dinner by asking for permission to leave the table and clearing our dishes.

In many ways, our family dinner and devotion rituals are a story about whiteness, specifically about its silence. In the roughly 3,983 family dinners of my childhood, there were many conversations about what it meant to be a Christian and some about our Mennonitism in particular. Rarely were there conversations about race and racism. But never in my recollection were there conversations about how our ancestors became white and what had been given up in the process.

To borrow a concept from *The Little Book of Trauma Healing*, this "conspiracy of silence"[4] not only maintains a dominant white culture throughout our extended families, but also prevents the "grieving and mourning [that has] never taken place"[5] for those of us who have come to be called white. At the intersection of denial and Perpetration-Induced Traumatic Stress sits a cultural pattern that "STAR" describes as "chosen trauma."[6] Even as silence discourages family conversations about how whiteness has historically harmed us, like the tales of my martyred ancestors, there are specific traumas we effortlessly repeat.

According to "STAR," a chosen trauma may prevent victimized groups from moving forward in healthy ways so that they develop a fixed identity narrative that reinforces "a sense of entitlement about what they are owed" and that "justify acts of aggression/violence against others"[7] as a way of reclaiming what was lost. On the other hand, a "chosen glory" is marked by "High points, often victories in a group's history and story that are a source of pride for a group, often but not always won at the expense of another group."[8] The manual goes on to note, "A chosen trauma and chosen glory may be the same event(s)."

Like the legacy of the Confederacy in the South and its ongoing symbols of flags and monuments, like the pervasive rituals to remember 9/11, like the lasting effects of the Holocaust on the identity of Ashkenazi Jewish communities, European Mennonites uphold our loss and persecution as a cornerstone of our collective identity. The problem is not in remembering or honoring our traumas. The problem is that our chosen trauma/chosen glory has become a monolithic narrative around which our identities revolve.

This overidentification with our chosen trauma/chosen glory prevents us from learning the full scope of our histories, which includes the history of our assimilation into whiteness, our role as settlers on Indigenous land, and our contributions to US imperialism, capitalism, and militarism. At its roots, this overidentification with victimhood/heroism prevents us from healing and prevents us from working to repair the harm we've helped cause.

Like denial, keeping our chosen trauma/chosen glory in place requires a tremendous amount of energy. It blocks us from getting specific about the harm we are connected to and forestalls curiosity about what is in our power to change.

Like many European settlers, in the case of European Mennonite migration, we contributed to violence toward Indigenous peoples through the acquisition, displacement, and colonized cultivation of Indigenous land—land that we still occupy. Yes, we were suffering, dying, and landless (an added impotence to an agrarian people), but that doesn't justify, excuse, or erase the role that we have played (and maintained) in creating structurally violent systems in what is now the US and Canada. The problem is that in the telling and retelling of our chosen traumas/chosen glories we have become generational martyrs. In the dominant narrative of European Mennonite suffering, we solely occupy the role of victim and thus have no responsibility for our impact. Harmless and righteous, in a martyr narrative this suffering supposedly brings us closer to God.

What, then, is the psychological impact of this victim mindset for people who have come to be called white? As "STAR" puts it, this impact includes "the inability of individuals of ethno-national groups, as a direct result of its own historical traumas, to empathize with the suffering of others," leading to "little guilt about committing retaliatory violence."[9] With racism already institutionalized, many communities of European descent arriving in eighteenth-, nineteenth-, and twentieth-century North America accepted the categorization of white along with its complicity with violence. Our chosen trauma/chosen glory stories erase the history of how European immigrants used deliberate and strategic admission into the police force, union organizing, land grabs, and segregated neighborhoods to prove allegiance to whiteness through direct violence toward Black, Asian, and other communities of color.

In reading this book, you are opening yourself up to considering these ancestral questions, too. I invite you to get as specific as you can in investigating your own family's stories, in examining your own cultural legacies, in holding the traumas of your lineage tenderly, vulnerably, and courageously. I am extremely grateful for your openness to engage with my stories. Thank you for reading this and for grappling along with me. It can be an uncomfortable and lonely road, but ultimately one I believe is in the service of our collective healing; that is, if we are willing to turn and (re)turn toward the pain.

As Catholic priest Richard Rohr stated, "If we do not transform our pain then we will most assuredly transmit it."[10] We cannot transform that which we do not grieve, and we cannot grieve that which we have not acknowledged. Unacknowledged, ungrieved, and unmetabolized, the lasting collective psychological effects of Perpetration-Induced Traumatic Stress and Post-Traumatic Master/Mistress Syndrome linger on. We pass it down and we pass it down. Cycles of trauma repeat.

Trauma expert Dr. Gabor Maté differentiates between trauma and traumatic events in a way I haven't necessarily so far. Dr. Maté says, "Trauma is not terrible things that happen from the other side—those are traumatic. Trauma is that very separation from the body and emotions. So, the real question is: How did we get separated and how do we reconnect? Because that's our true nature—our true nature is to be connected."[11]

That is the work that this book aims to do, to be with these questions: How have collective and historical traumas separated us? How have they forced a separation of mind from body? Of individual from community? Of human from earth? Moreover, how do we—as humans with bodies, as people racialized as white, as status quo and passing white ladies—begin the process of (re)connection?

These are the questions that have been with me over the past decade: How has multigenerational trauma served to separate? How has it served to disconnect my mind from my body, me from my community, from spirituality, from a deeper connection with this earth? How do I begin practices of reconnection? How can I do that with other white people, with other white women?

How might you?

Defensiveness. Denial. Deference. Distancing. We store such coping mechanisms in our bodies. Which also means that information is there for us to work with in the here and now. You don't have to know the details of your exact lineage in order to engage with this healing work; you just need to have a body.

EMBODIED TRAUMA

At the close of the workshop in which I was first asked what my people gave up for whiteness, I eagerly approached the facilitators with my questions. Where could I read more? Where was the book on Mennonites and whiteness? And also, the one on Post-Traumatic Master Syndrome?

While none of those particular resources existed, the facilitation team provided me with an extensive bibliography. Their list of over eighty books, articles, and documentaries began to help supplement what my US public school education had omitted.

And I dove in.

I read voraciously, determined to absorb facts and commit to memory the most recent statistics. I fell asleep at night with stacks of records of structural violence beside my bed. The more I read, the more I realized I had more to learn. And with contemporary books about race and racism becoming popularized in the 2010s, my stacks of books grew faster than I could consume them. They definitely grew faster than I could emotionally process and physiologically metabolize their many, horrific, and vast accounts of violence.

In that era of driven intellectual pursuit, I certainly learned and unlearned a lot of history. I honed my analysis and sharpened my scalpel. But after returning from my bookshelves and browser tabs, I was left with a sense of emptiness, of numbness, and most likely some depression. My body was struggling to keep up with the endless word stream of brutality.

But, I told myself, these were just words. It wasn't as if I was actually enduring the horrors I read about, ones that actual humans had endured—were still enduring. Witnessing other people's pain was the least I could do, I thought. I forced myself to return and read again, shutting down my sensitivities to get through book, chapter, and page. To do this I was shutting down parts of my humanity, too.

Distancing. Another one of those Ds that was trying to protect me. I think about how my ancestors must have had to disconnect from their bodies to embrace martyrdom, must have had to dissociate in order to watch their loved ones suffer and die. And if I dig deeper, below my distancing are the messages I've been taught about suffering for a just cause: that it will bring me closer to God, that it is to be celebrated, that martyred suffering means I'm doing the right thing. Distancing was a rationalization that helped my ancestors face great suffering.

But my body, thank God, is not about to step onto the fire pyre. With many generations of distance and with the added buffers of whiteness, and cis, class, and able-bodied privilege, I find myself with the spaciousness to engage with healing work that my ancestors weren't able to do. Perhaps I can retrieve those emotional files that my ancestors couldn't. Perhaps I am safe enough to be able to extend (self)compassion.

It took several months and a shift in seasons for me to reemerge from the depressive slog and move toward a different energy, but slowly, and when I did, I began to wonder if anesthetizing myself wasn't actually helping extricate my whiteness. Maybe the work of anti-racism was less about shutting myself down in order to know every historical fact. Maybe it wasn't about having all the info. Maybe the more supportive, deeper—and much scarier—question was: Could I stay present and *feel*?

Often, the overwhelming accounts of atrocities seem to lodge permanently in my left brain and refuse to ground in my body. Like a wash/rinse cycle perpetually set to repeat, the long fancy words and analytical jargon, though important, sooner or later has sanitized the bloody realities.

Besides, memorizing the dates and details of history didn't leave me with much new information about *me*. As in, specifically, how have these multigenerational traumas been passed down through *my* body?

How have they been passed down through yours?

In *My Grandmother's Hands*, Resmaa Menakem writes about trauma as an embodied—and racialized—experience. Menakem acknowledges that communities who have not been racialized as white have long understood this embodied response to trauma. "Bodies of culture," as Menakem collectivizes nonwhite folks, have resourcefully created in-body collective cultural responses to preserve survival and to thrive within the harmful context of "white-body supremacy." White-body supremacy, Menakem says, affects white bodies too, numbing us to violence, causing us to deny reality, and distract with hyperactivity.

To briefly touch on the language of neuroscience, polyvagal theory helps to explain this embodied disconnection. Polyvagal theory emphasizes the role of the vagus nerve (which Menakem calls the "soul nerve"[12]) in helping to regulate our nervous systems and respond to traumatic events. The vagus nerve connects to almost all the organs of the body including the gut. However, Menakem writes, "One of the organs your soul nerve does not connect to is your thinking brain."[13]

So, when a traumatic event occurs, we humans are wired to disconnect from critical thinking and rely on our fight, flight, fawn, or freeze instincts. As Menakem and others have pointed out, it is our collective, cultural, and embodiment practices that can support us in (re)integrating the critical thinking parts of the brain, especially during and after experiences of trauma. Collective, cultural, and embodiment practices help us to (re)connect.

Notably, being racialized as white has separated white-bodied humans from many collective, cultural, and embodied healing practices that belonged to our ancestors, which helps us answer the question: What did our ancestors give up to assimilate into whiteness? Whiteness has disconnected us from our ancestral healing practices and diminished our access to embodied wisdom. We have lost many of the cultural practices that would help us with collective acknowledgment, feeling, and grieving and to do so in an embodied way.

As studies of epigenetics show, the lasting effects of these multigenerational traumas have literally shaped our physiology, imprinting on our brains and DNA. With the embrace of their chosen traumas/chosen glories, my ancestors must have had to desensitize themselves in order to acquire Indigenous lands. In order to do something so contrary to the beliefs they died for in Europe, they would have had to distance themselves in some way from the suffering of Indigenous people and their humanity.

Dr. Michael Yellow Bird uses the term "colonial brain disorder" to describe how settler colonization has physiologically suppressed the critical thinking part of the brain through limiting brain plasticity and by shaping DNA, microbiomes, and gene expression. This research points to how the traumatic legacies of racism and colonization have actually altered our brain waves, neurotransmitters, and modulators. According to Dr. Yellow Bird, colonial brain disorder

> biases us to have an overstated evaluation of ourself and our skills, and our intelligence…and we don't really evaluate our "true" capacities."[14]

To further paraphrase Dr. Yellow Bird's work, the more we see ourselves through rose colored glasses, the less we can access our critical thinking and the less we are able to see ourselves as interconnected to our fellow humans.

White-body supremacy and colonial brain disorder are embodied manifestations of the collectivized and historical trauma of racism and colonization, ones that we've inherited through bodies that have been racialized. These symptoms get at the ways we as white settlers have learned to numb, to distance, to deny, to shut off the pain, to see ourselves as separate. They point to how whiteness has facilitated a mind-body split, reinforcing a sense of either/or, perpetuating, among other things, the good guy/bad guy narratives that pervade our children's books, the local news, and movie scripts.

In a culture of dualistic thinking, we are forced to choose between being either the victim or the perpetrator, acting as either the hero or villain. In the trap of good guy/bad guy, we can only be one and not the other. It is no wonder then, that we want to see ourselves as the good guys, to uplift our chosen traumas/chosen glories, to be righteous victims. It is quite distressing to imagine ourselves as evil or bad.

Dualism is also the focus of Leonard Shlain's work, *The Alphabet Versus the Goddess*. Shlain proposes that a historical and cultural imbalance in left-brain overdevelopment, associated with masculine, linear, and literary ways of thinking, being, and acting in the world, is in part responsible for historical and present-day patriarchy including the suppression of goddess worship, spiritual disconnection with the earth, and demonizing feminine cyclical, circular, and holistic ways of thinking and being. Shlain posits that this collective imbalance has led to dualism, misogyny, competition, and violent domination throughout our economic and social systems. Not so coincidentally, dualism, misogyny, competition, and violent domination are all aspects of white supremacy.

Much of Shlain's case centers European history (although not with an explicitly anti-racist lens) and offers a framework for considering one of this book's main pursuits: What was going on in Europe that created such a receptive environment for white to become right, normal, and good? What made Europeans so eager to take up an ideology based on dualism and superiority at the cost of forfeiting their souls?

Shlain's approach offers a helpful thread for tracing the history of Post-Traumatic Mistress Syndrome. It tells us something about how the traumas of European patriarchy readied brains for colonial brain disorder and bodies for white-body supremacy.

As we begin to trace some of the threads of European patriarchy, I invite you to honor your body. We each experience different levels of safety in being able to tune in to bodily sensation. Sometimes embodiment might not be available. As I shared above, distancing and dissociation is often what first happens for me when I feel overwhelmed, but usually, with some time and compassion, I can bring myself back online. Noticing the 4Ds is one place to start and may help you tune in to what's happening in your body. As you consider how your people became white, what was lost, and who was harmed in the process, you may also want to use the 4Ds. You might practice noticing where defensiveness shows up in your body, how you feel when deference is present, or when feeling seems difficult.

While delving into this history of European patriarchy, as we are about to do, has at times felt incredibly affirming, there have also been moments when I feel its pain in my bones. As we move forward, please continue to take courageous care.

CHAPTER TWO

A SEASON FOR WITCH HUNTS

Only bad witches can be ugly.
—Glinda the Good Witch

Glinda: Are you a good witch, or a bad witch?
Dorothy: I'm not a witch at all. I'm Dorothy Gale from Kansas.
—The Wizard of Oz

O nce upon a time in a land not so far away, I found myself sitting in the elegant conference room of a local private school. Across the posh, well-lit space, I recognized an equity officer from one of the old-money schools. Making eye contact, I briefly nodded in their direction before hunkering down in my corner with a social worker I knew from youth organizing. A trio of principals huddled on the other side, looking unsure. After ten minutes of obligatory mingling, a middle-aged white lady stepped to the front of the room, projector remote in hand. She began her presentation by introducing the "Big 8."

Chances are, if you've ever attended a diversity and inclusion workshop, you've heard of the Big 8, too. They are the main social identity markers that include "race, ethnicity, sexual orientation, gender identity, ability, religion/spirituality, nationality, and socio-economic status."[1] (Sometimes age makes the list.) The "social" part of "social identity" means that all of us—whether we want to or not—contend with all of these markers as we navigate our lives.

As I was listening to her presentation, vigorously doodling on the fancy agenda, I began to notice my frustration. Of course, I valued diversity awareness. I felt strongly about supporting these schools in building inclusive learning environments, but this repetitive conversation about identity markers hadn't done much to reduce instances of institutional racism for the students I worked with. It hadn't stopped principals from punishing students who spoke up about racism, nor had it inspired school faculty to drastically alter classroom norms. These and other diversity and inclusion frameworks were proving extremely limited in their helpfulness, like using a mouse trap when you're trying to catch a tornado.

Don't get me wrong—it's not all trash. These frameworks do call attention to parts of our identities that society discourages us from seeing, as is typically the case when our social identity markers reflect dominant identities. Like white people in an all-white space (or a mostly white school), generally we are not thinking about our race or talking about our racism. At the very least, diversity and inclusion frameworks help us to notice and acknowledge our specific differences.

But these frameworks fall short because they aren't functionally real. These markers compartmentalize our human experience into silos. In the real world, we can never isolate aspects of our identities. They are in relationship to each other and to power structures all the time. This interdependency is known as "intersectionality," a term first coined by Black feminist scholar Dr. Kimberlé Williams Crenshaw in 1989 to describe the specific intersection of oppression that Black women were experiencing in the workplace. Intersectionality has been further developed by Black, Indigenous, and other women of color, offering an important critique to white feminism and Black resistance movements, both of which have historically marginalized Black women and queer folx. Intersectionality makes visible the relationships among aspects of our identities, which is how I've come to understand that my conditioning into white middle-class womanhood cannot be universalized as the experience of all women. As in hooks' "imperialist white-supremacist capitalist patriarchy," intersectionally speaking, imperialism cannot be removed from capitalism, nor white supremacy extracted from patriarchy.

* * *

A few years before attending that elite school's diversity day, I was a self-employed artist and grad student searching for community in a city where white culture saturated day-to-day life just like its gray skies made one forget about the possibility of sunshine. As a young adult, three years into making Pittsburgh home, I first visited my neighborhood's community center thinking I would mainly swim laps at the pool.

When I was greeted by the warm welcome of the front desk attendant and a thriving eight-foot monstera plant, the community center[*] felt like my hometown neighborhood Y. After swimming for a few months, I decided to try out a yoga class. The first class was me and two other students in a beautiful space with a 270-degree view. The instructor's smile was genuine and inviting. There was jazz and dancing to warm up, unapologetic Blackness, an acknowledgment of yoga's East Indian roots, (more) happy tropical plants, and an enthusiastic consensual group hug at the end. I breathed a sigh of gratitude; maybe this could be home.

I don't remember the first time I talked with my yoga teacher, Felicia Savage Friedman, after a class, but I do remember how her curiosity, excitement, and warmth came through in our increasingly frequent interactions. When I pull out the thick memory file from those early years when we were getting to know each other, I leaf through page after page of scenes of us talking: Felicia sharing about her studies with monks providing hospice care; me telling about my latest organizing endeavor (we were knitting a bridge[†]); us giggling in

---

[*] The Kingsley Association, located in the Larimer neighborhood of Pittsburgh, has a 130-year history and continues to provide services to the community.

[†] I was the lead artist and codirector of Knit the Bridge, which brought over two thousand people together to create the largest fiber art installation of its kind. As a community-led project, our goal was to knit together stronger communities and bridge disparate ones across the southwestern PA region: https://knitthebridge.wordpress.com.

the corner or lingering by the door as the front desk attendant gave us five more minutes before kicking us out. These long conversations about love, life, and justice eventually migrated to a late-night meal at the restaurant around the corner. And then another. And many more.

As someone who's frequently had older women as mentors, friends, and aunts in my life, I was not uncomfortable with our twenty-year age difference. As a transplant and someone passionate about social justice issues, I was excited to get input from someone who called Pittsburgh home. I had been doing my practicum with a peace and justice organization and helping to coordinate a listening project* in the community in which Felicia had grown up. We were collaborating with youth to listen to the stories of elders in a place where gentrification was rapidly encroaching.

When my supervisor asked me if I knew anyone who might be interested in participating, I immediately thought of Felicia. She and I scheduled an afternoon time to talk. As I entered the yoga studio, I was nervous to make the ask. I sat down on one of the two chairs she had strategically positioned in the momentary sunlight.

"So…I've come to ask if you would consider participating in this project I'm working on—"

"Absolutely!" She answered immediately, before knowing any of the details.

In the year that followed, Felicia would become more than my yoga teacher and close friend. She would become a key advisor, collaborator, and accountability partner in anti-racist organizing. When I asked her to be on the (almost all-white) advisory committee at the nonprofit where I was newly employed, she replied "Absolutely!" again, without any hesitation.

In my naiveté, I had very little idea of the hardships ahead as we would try to make anti-racist changes in the organization. I sensed her support would be critical and felt grateful she was willing to give so generously of her energy, wisdom, and time. As a longtime yoga

---

* Listening projects train people to listen deeply, gathering oral histories, and identifying community needs in order to support community-based resourcing that can lead to community organizing and action.

practitioner and Black cis woman in America, she must have had a hunch about the fights ahead.

While there were highs and lows, as is often the case in social justice organizing, one of the many valuable outcomes of our growing collaboration was a workshop we initially called "The Wicked Webs of Racism, Patriarchy, and Capitalism."* We wanted a way to talk about intersectionality while also getting specific about how and why these intersections formed. Rather than a two-dimensional crossroads of equal paths of oppression, we saw these wicked webs as having been deliberately constructed into interlocking layers over time. The wicked webs were less like your basic four-way stop and more like Atlanta's Spaghetti Junction,† with its multidimensional layered highways of aggressive traffic and winding on- and off-ramps.

Or, to use a more ubiquitous (and less Atlantan) example, the wicked webs are much like the tied knots keeping your sneaker laces in place.

I learned how to tie a shoe in preschool (a shout out to Ms. Martha). I have vague memories of practicing on a shoe box, but more clearly remember trying to teach my little brother: "You cross one string over the other and then pull tight. But not too tight!" Learning this first knot took time and many tries. Usually, one lace would end up tangled in the other, but rarely would that knot be stable enough for the next step.

Like the tedious repetition of a preschooler learning to tie their shoes, it took patriarchy over seven thousand years to get its foundational knot in place.

Centuries before white ladies began selling our souls to whiteness, we were fighting patriarchy in our own communities and our own homes. How did we get from patriarchy to whiteness? And what do I mean when I use the word patriarchy?

---

* Later called "The Wicked Webs of Patriarchy, Capitalism, & Racism" due to the concept's historical construction. See the copyright page for the full attribution.

† Situated north of the city of Atlanta, the Spaghetti Junction is a stack interchange of highways and on-ramps that connect several main traffic arteries in and out of Atlanta, so called because it resembles a bunch of spaghetti noodles.

SEX VS. GENDER

In our wicked webs workshops, Felicia and I defined patriarchy* as a historically established process that takes all of humanity and divides us into two separate groups based on the biological categories of male and female. After being assigned a biological sex, patriarchy gives each sex a gender. This categorizing happens to most humans shortly after birth, often in the hospital delivery room and sometimes even earlier in utero due to ultrasound technology, impatient parents, and an upswing in the popularity of gender-reveal parties.

(For those of you following along, it might be helpful to take out a paper and pen and draw a big circle. This circle represents all of humanity. Next, draw a line down the middle, from top to bottom.)

Humans with the anatomy of penis, testicles, scrotum, prostate, and XY chromosomes are given the biological sex, "male." (Write "male" on the left side of your circle.) Those humans with the anatomy of vagina, vulva, uterus, ovaries, and XX chromosomes are given the biological sex, "female." (Write "female" on the right.)

Biological sex may inform a human being's reproductive capacities and what they can do anatomically with their body. But regardless, that human is assigned a corresponding gender, which is socially described and enforced and has to do with things like power, behavior, appearance, identity, norms, and weird associations like colors, deodorant scents, and toy genre. In the world of patriarchy, the sex categories of male/female neatly line up with the gender categories of man/woman or boy/girl and also with all sorts of other English words such as he/she, hero/heroine, god/goddess, John/Jane, and blue/pink to name a few.

(Now fill in the left side of the circle with the words "man/boy/he" and other masculine gender associations you have learned. Write "woman/girl/she" along with feminine gender associations under "female" on the right.)

---

* The way we conceptualized European patriarchy was influenced by several of the resources cited here and also by our colleagues, Cavanaugh Quick and Cole Parke-West.

Like zooming in on a low-resolution jpeg, the hard lines that establish and keep male = men and female = women get fuzzier the closer you look. For example, as much as 1.7 percent of children are born intersex and do not fall neatly into the patriarchal-ascribed male or female categories.[*] Intersex is a term used to describe a range of anatomical and genetic variations that don't fit a binaried categorization of sex. As poet, comedian, speaker, and author Alok Vaid-Menon notes in one of their phenomenal Instagram book reports, "definitions of sex change drastically over time."[2] Vaid-Menon highlights historian Dr. Thomas Laqueur's book, *Making Sex: Body and Gender from the Greeks to Freud*, which outlines "how the west transitioned from a 'unisex' model to a 'binary sex' model in the late 18th/early 19th century."[3]

In Western society, it's been common medical practice for doctors to alter a child's anatomy at birth to fit more neatly into a clearly defined female or male sex category, sometimes without the informed consent of the child's parents. Beyond being born intersex, there are many other reasons why an individual's anatomy might not neatly fit into sex box one or sex box two, including a wide range of medical procedures like hysterectomies, getting one's tubes tied, or receiving hormones and gender-affirming surgeries.

(Shoot, now what are you going to do with that middle line?! Did you write it in ink?)

Gender, like race, is socially constructed and enforced. And while there are plenty of examples of societies throughout the world and throughout history that have multiple and overlapping genders outside of and beyond a man/woman gender binary,[†] patriarchy's

---

[*] The UN Office of the High Commissioner for Human Rights notes, "In some cases, intersex traits are visible at birth while in others, they are not apparent until puberty. Some chromosomal intersex variations may not be physically apparent at all" (https://www.unfe.org/know-the-facts/challenges-solutions/intersex).

[†] Some historical and contemporary examples of this include being Two-spirit, which within some North American Indigenous communities refers to a person who identifies as having aspects of both feminine and masculine spirits; a third gender identity in Thailand (which is now also officially recognized in the country's constitution); and other nonbinary gender identities in various South Asian and Pacific Islander traditions.

strict binary depends on the initial subjugation of people gendered men. Or as bell hooks states:

> The first act of violence that patriarchy demands of males is not violence toward women. Instead patriarchy demands of all males that they engage in acts of psychic self-mutilation, that they kill off the emotional parts of themselves. If an individual is not successful in emotionally crippling himself, he can count on patriarchal men to enact rituals of power that will assault his self-esteem.[4]

(At this point, I usually draw mad arrows surrounding the left side of the circle, but however else you want to represent the ritual of emotionally harming boys will work too.)

The ritual of emotionally harming boys prepares them to be grown men who dominate women and girls; compete with and command weaker, less masculine, and younger men; and police that gender binary with violent aggression. The performance of violent homophobia and transphobia is one example of gender-binary policing that patriarchy demands.[*]

(Sometimes I illustrate this violence by compelling the circle to tilt 90 degrees to the right and then folding it into a pyramid shape, with men at the top.)

THE BIRTH OF PATRIARCHY

One could say I was pissed about patriarchy from the moment my mother pushed me out of her womb. Upset about gender rules and the whole female submission thing, I spent much of my childhood proving I could compete by being better, stronger, smarter, and more

---

[*] According to a 2021 UCLA law study, trans people are more than four times likelier to be victims of violent crime than cisgender people, and trans women of color suffer the highest rates of violence (https://williamsinstitute.law.ucla.edu/press/ncvs-trans-press-release/). Sue Kerr chronicles these tragedies and honors those who have tragically lost their lives to transphobia at https://www.pghlesbian.com.

dominant than the boys around me. Unfortunately for my kid brother, he was the one boy typically at hand. My heart hurts to recall how he received intensive round-the-clock training in emotional harm from my misdirected rage. I coparented my brother into the ways of toxic masculinity. When he cried, I pushed him to push down his emotions. I modeled domination, brute force, and psychological manipulation. I realize now that in order to do this, I had to push down my own tenderness too.

bell hooks could just have well been talking about our sibling dynamic when she said, "Patriarchy has no gender."[5] In fact, reinforcing toxic masculinity has proven a key contribution of white womanhood. This helps explain why some of the most vocal proponents of white Christian patriarchy are women. Some of the most well-positioned proponents of US imperialism and violent warfare have been, too.*

But I am getting ahead of myself. We are still learning how to tie our shoes, beginning with patriarchy. It turns out that the racial and economic disparities we have today are a direct result of European patriarchy's reorganizing of human relationships away from cooperation and collaboration and into control and domination.

Which brings up a heap of questions that somehow never made my school's history curriculum, like: Where did patriarchy come from? Why did we reject cooperation and collaboration? And in Europe, from which patriarchy spread via colonization, was there ever a time when patriarchy wasn't the main (or)deal? (I want this so badly to be the case.)

It is hard for me not to paint an idealistic pre-patriarchy picture. In my linear thinking, I wish for there to be something to return

---

* There is a long history of white women championing sexism. Antifeminist Phyllis Schlafly organized against gay rights and abortion access and successfully campaigned against the Equal Rights Amendment, which would have constitutionalized legal rights for US citizens regardless of sex. Many white women have been at the forefront or organizing for abortion restrictions at the state and federal levels. US politicians such as Hillary Clinton consistently voted to support US imperialist militarized policy.

to, something before, some time, some culture, some historic utopia where my ancestry cultivated enoughness and collaboration rather than contributing to hierarchies and violence. I want documentation so I can prove that those of us who descended from Europeans have cultures that precede and transcend our oppressive legacies. I look to historical records for proof of my humanity. And while no such perfect written documentation exists, there are both living and archaeological records that attest to a time in Europe when patriarchy did not dominate as the inevitable way of organizing social economic relationship.

I am flooded with relief.

There was a time in Europe, as it has been and still is in many parts of the world, where patriarchy was not the only option. Across the majority of the globe, and even in Europe, throughout the Paleolithic era (before 10,000 BCE) and in the Neolithic era (between 10,000 and 4000 BCE), there were societies that prioritized values of interconnectedness, revolved around cooperative economics, and celebrated the role of mothers and elders—grandmothers in particular, whose wisdom was central to the politics of the community.

(If you're still taking notes, draw a second circle, to represent all of humanity. Here, you could draw spirals or loopy circles to indicate interconnectedness and cooperation.)

Although globally the pervasiveness of nonpatriarchal societies began to dwindle, especially with the rise of monotheism, all over the world—from the banks of West Africa to the Haudenosaunee Nation of what is now the northeastern US—cooperative societies were prevalent, that is until the invasion of Europeans. Many of these cultures still vibrantly exist in spite of European invasions and are as diverse in culture as they are in their forms of resistance.[*]

Of course, there are problems with describing nonpatriarchal societies within the limits of patriarchal thinking. "Nonpatriarchal,"

---

[*] According to the UN, "There are over 476 million indigenous people living in 90 countries across the world, accounting for 6.2 per cent of the global population. Of those, there are more than 5,000 distinct groups" (United Nations, "Indigenous Peoples"). See Resources for Further Support for Indigenous-led groups that are organizing to resist colonization and oppression.

"matriarchal," and "matricentric" still describe ways of being on patriarchy's terms: as in, not patriarchy, -rule and -centrism. There is also
the risk that in collectivizing pre- or nonpatriarchal societies, I will
flatten out the nuances of many Indigenous peoples and cultures,
erasing diversities and histories. (Again, this resource is a complement, not a substitute.)

As we consider what was going on in Europe twelve thousand or
eight thousand or four thousand years ago, there is also the risk of
accepting the assumptions of a patriarchal frame, of assuming that
progress happens as we move forward in time with the evolution of
our species and technologies. I am reminded of George Lakoff's book,
Don't Think of an Elephant!, in which he shows how facts bounce off
frames.* It's not that facts are irrelevant, it's just that as humans we
pick and choose the ones that support our understanding of the world.

A progress trajectory was the lens through which (white male)
scholars viewed the history of European civilization until Lithua-
nian American archeologist Marija Gimbutas asked, circa 1950,
(and I paraphrase): What if patriarchy hadn't always been the rule
in Europe? What if pre-patriarchal European societies were actually
happier and healthier and less obsessed with violence?

During her research and archaeological excavations in the
following decades, that's more or less what she found.

Gimbutas's Kurgan theory posits that the shift from indigenous
European cultures to patriarchy was a violent transition attributed in
part to increased land scarcity and climate change. According to scholar
Cristina Biaggi, circa 6600 BCE, climate change caused glaciers to
melt, which rapidly flooded the Black Sea region, prompting whole
communities to seek dry land.† In the millennia that followed, lands

---

* Shoutout to my sociology professor, Dr. Terry Jantzi.

† This flood corresponds to the biblical story of Noah. In *The Rule of Mars*, Biaggi
cites Bill Ryan and Walter Pitman's book *Noah's Flood* in describing the cataclysmic
event. According to Biaggi, "These events left such an impression on the psyches
of the people surrounding the Black Sea that legends filled with dramatic images
of floods arose in the mythologies of Southeastern Europe and the Middle East"
(*The Rule of Mars*, 79).

became overgrazed, drying up and pushing nomadic tribes to invade neighboring societies. Other factors such as advances in weaponry and the domestication of the horse helped these nomadic groups travel greater distances. Loosely known as the Kurgans*, these invading tribes spread across Europe, infiltrating nonpatriarchal agricultural societies, killing, raping, enslaving, stealing, and replacing earth Goddess worship with masculine sky gods.

My goal here is not to lay out all the arguments for the Kurgan theory or to dig into studies on Eurasian linguistics or DNA, nor is it to go into depth about the theory's skeptics. Instead, it is to emphasize the power of Gimbutas's questions. Their possibilities resonated so much for me: What if European patriarchy hadn't always been the case? What if we white women actually had lineages in cooperative societies that treated the feminine as sacred and were less obsessed with violence?

I think this is why Gimbutas's work has been so important for feminists searching for something before and beyond the violence of European patriarchy.[†] We are looking for alternatives to the violence that came from our homelands. We, too, want to belong to societies, cultures, and spiritual traditions where we are seen as sacred.

Perhaps Gimbutas's pre-Kurgan Europe offers us comfort within the dualism. I am tempted to overidentify with those pre-patriarchal societies, to claim the people who inhabited the mountains and forests of current-day Switzerland, France, and Germany as my true ancestors, to sympathize with their historical plight, and to reject the injustices that caused such a tragic loss of their cultures. My orientation toward victimhood (perhaps you're noticing a theme?) confuses the uncomfortable complexities of my history and DNA.

---

* The Kurgans were not one people group but a term used to describe a number of peoples with shared cultures and traditions who lived in and around the Pontic-Caspian steppes extending from Eastern Europe to Central Asia, "between the Don River and southern Urals" (Biaggi, 80).

† Riane Eisler's *The Chalice and the Blade* and other writings emerged in the late-twentieth century and sought to reclaim sacred goddess archetypes as well as the history of nonpatriarchal society as part of a lost European lineage.

Why am I so ready to identify with the suffering of colonized foremothers and so quick to dismiss the pastoral invaders as part of my ancestry, legacy, and DNA? Why do I want to opt out of my connection to the oppressor? Their blood runs in me, too.

This is the work of healing from Mistress Syndrome: to see both oppressor and oppressed as parts of me, to accept the histories I am eager to claim and those I loathe, to realize more fully how my inheritance into "imperialist white-supremacist capitalist patriarchy" has both advantaged and harmed me, to recognize that these systems have deliberately created a false dichotomy that has fooled me into thinking I have to choose between my mother and my father.

As one of my early readers pointed out, this false dichotomy brings up questions of opting out. Am I denying my whiteness in order to identify with the victimhood of being a woman? Who gets to claim which parts of an identity? Which parts do we try to hide from? Like the white nationalists who seek to cover up their Jewish ancestry, like the one-drop rule for people of African descent, our relationship to ancestral identity has also been framed by the power structures of today.

But before we can discuss the power structures of today, we need to finish the painful story of how patriarchy got that initial knot in place. Shlain posits that a shift into linear, abstracted written communication paralleled a shift toward patriarchy. Whether correlation or causation, as soon as the technology of writing emerged, it was used to subjugate women via written laws and creation mythology.*

Perhaps most devastating was the way patriarchy found its way into cosmology, the creation stories of our universe. During the 1700s BCE, *The Seven Tablets of Creation* radically altered the spiritual worldview, for the first time featuring, and even celebrating,

---

* In 2350 BCE, the first Mesopotamian written code codified domestic violence and paved the way for male-centric polygamy. Hammurabi's Code (1792–1750 BCE) followed, one-fourth of which was devoted to curbing women's rights, e.g., "The women of the former days used to take two husbands, but the women of today (if they attempt to do this) must be stoned" (Shlain, *The Alphabet Versus the Goddess*, 52).

misogyny and death. *The Seven Tablets of Creation** tells a tale of matricide, in which a mother—resembling a woman in her late term of pregnancy—is murdered and dismembered by her male children. Her body parts are strewn about to create the earth's topography. As Shlain writes, in radical contrast to the standard cosmology of its day, "An allegory of death has replaced the metaphor of birth."[6]

Versions of this story were later adopted by Hittites, Aryans, and East Indians and set the tone for the emergence of the monotheistic male sky god and a spiritual lineage of male clergy and patriarchs. Shlain theorizes that the Hebrew Ten Commandments marked the invention of the alphabet, furthering the written word as both a reflection and a tool of patriarchy.[7]

Sadly, this decline in feminine power reverberated throughout the Eastern hemisphere and was especially embraced by the empires of civilization. By the eighth century BCE, the Greeks institutionalized warfare along with the idea of "polis" as a civilization exclusively made of male citizens.[8] From 27 BCE to 476 CE, the rule of the Roman Empire was based on military might, patriarchy, and enslavement.

On the European subcontinent, where the soil of patriarchy had been cultivated for the past five thousand years, an intensely patriarchal form of Christianity took hold. Once Constantine decriminalized Christianity in AD 313, it began its ascent as the dominant religion throughout Europe. Both western (Holy Roman) and eastern (Eastern Orthodox) Christianity established patriarchal institutionalized church-state rule.† The doctrine of the Trinity a century earlier established divinity as Father, Son, and Holy Spirit, replacing any maternal aspect of the divine with an emphasis on paternity and elevating the role of the male savior. Only the Holy Spirit, derived

---

* *The Seven Tablets of Creation* was a Babylonian creation myth and the earliest written cosmology. It is considered by scholars to be primary source material for the Book of Genesis.

† The Christian Church institutionalized patriarchy despite evidence that women participated in the priesthood in early Christianity, going to such lengths as covering up artwork depicting women in leadership, as this article reports: https://www.thedailybeast.com/did-vatican-hide-art-that-depicted-female-priests.

from the Greek "Sophia" meaning "wisdom," retained any female connotations, although English translations are often gender-neutral.

In Europe, that first tangled knot of patriarchy and economic exploitation was further tightened through what historian Silvia Federici describes in *Caliban and the Witch* as the "devaluation and feminization of reproductive labor,"*[9] better known as the witch hunts.

WITCH HUNTS AND THE LIBERATION OF CAPITAL

I first learned about witch hunts on my elementary school playground. It was second grade. My two best friends and I had formed an inseparable trio. Visiting each other's homes, we bonded over a shared disgust of our younger lizard-loving brothers and a fascination with My Little Ponies (my friends had them; I didn't). And then one day, the mutual likefest ended. I don't remember what happened; I'm not even sure I knew at the time. But it felt like just as soon as our second-grade white girl threesome began, it was over, and I was the odd girl out. I remember feeling hurt and confused. I remember loneliness and looking in with a mix of envy and shame. I was angry and also old enough to begin doubting myself: Why wasn't *I* good enough? There was power in their exclusion of me, as if my social loss gave them status and emboldened their bond. After excommunicating me, they linked arms and walked mockingly away.

The next day at recess I noticed an opportunity. One of my two former best friends was standing alone at the edge of the crumbling asphalt. It was my chance to get back in. I joined her in pulling up the wild onions that surrounded the worn-out basketball court and we both decided that actually it was us who were best friends. That other girl had been so mean. Now *she* was out.

---

* The term "reproductive labor" refers to not only the work of bringing children into the world, such as conception, pregnancy, and childbirth, but all care that supports our existence as humans, including feeding and nutrition; housing; supporting mental, emotional, and physical well-being; caring for social relationships; raising children; and caring for elders.

This frenemy triangle continued off and on for weeks. In our spats, we practiced mean-girl attitudes and finger-pointing reflexes. We rehearsed envy and practiced projecting it onto to each other. But most skillfully, we trained in blame and malicious gossip. At some point, each of us got to play innocent, and each of us got to play witch. Eventually the dynamic worked itself through our mini–social system. But in retrospect, developmentally speaking, we were playing a kind of witch hunt, acting and reenacting the insider-outsider exclusionary tactics we inherited from the divide-and-conquer strategies of our great great-great-great-great-great-great-great-great-great-great-great-great-great-great-great-great-great-great-grandmothers. According to Federici, before the witch trials, the word "gossip" in Middle English was synonymous with friendship. It is only after the witch hunt era that it morphed into the negative, divisive, gender-stereotyping term that we have today.

The witch hunts of the fifteenth through the eighteenth centuries targeted at least tens of thousands (some estimates reach into the millions) of women, men, and even children. Similar to later projected social fears of terrorism, super-predators, and slave revolts, the witch hunt frenzy came out of a historic context in which the ruling classes used fear to keep the lower classes in check. Federici points to the class dynamics of who was called witch and who got to hunt: "The majority of those accused were poor peasant women—cottars, wage laborers—while those who accused them were wealthy and prestigious members of the community, often their employers or landlords."[10]

While feudal Europe certainly had its sexism, the witch hunts further fragmented communal social fabric by targeting its key weavers—women—in order to undermine lower class solidarity. This era also saw the restructuring of Europe into a lineup of nation-states. The male-headed state was replicated in its citizens' male-headed households and reinforced by male-headed religious institutions.

Before the witch hunts, peasants in feudal Europe had access to land that was passed down generationally and farmed for subsistence in exchange for being bonded to a landlord. In addition, peasants had access to communal land and woods. It was in these commons that

European women maintained a connection to the land by growing herbs, cultivating gardens, and nurturing social ties. In the commons, women cultivated community cooperation in a realm largely free of the influence of men, encouraging female solidarity and fortifying women's resistance to sexist Canonic law.[*]

Lest you think the Middle Ages were a feminist utopia, a peasant woman's social, sexual, and family life was ultimately dictated by the authority of her landlord. However, a peasant woman was not locked into a nuclear family unit or dependent on male relatives or a husband for subsistence. Instead, her strength was in the strength of the community.

Access to land meant peasants could feed themselves even while organizing against their landlords. At that time, lower classes all over western Europe were revolting—and winning. In the fourteenth century, after the Black Death wiped out one third of the population, peasants' work was in demand.[†] In the cities, workers' guilds began to revolt with increasing frequency.[‡] The heretic movement, which included my own lineage of Anabaptism, arose, seeking to create a new society while denouncing the hypocrisy of the Church, economic, and social orders. The Peasant War erupted in Germany. And the ruling classes responded.

This was a time of land grab as entire economies shifted from the feudal system to wage labor for currency—silver and gold that flowed via the blood of colonization and into the pockets of the greedy European elite. In the newly emerging economic system of mercantilism (more about this in the next chapter), a predecessor to contemporary capitalism, women's work fetched a much lower price than that of their male counterparts, increasing women's dependence on male relatives, devaluing their reproductive labor, and disconnecting them

---

[*] Such as laws that gave husbands the right to beat their wives and backed a religious doctrine of feminine submission.

[†] In the wake of the Covid-19 pandemic, there have been echoes of this post-plague dynamic including increased organizing for worker's rights. See chapter three.

[‡] Soon organizing at the exclusion of women, workers' guilds were the predecessors to trade unions today.

from communal networks. Widows and older women, who could no longer farm to feed themselves, were made even more dependent at a time when the price of food grew eightfold while wages only increased threefold.[11] These women were scapegoated as a target for working-class anger alongside Jewish people, who, in their prescribed role as money lenders, became symbols for the resentment of the indebted peasants toward the rich.

In campaign after campaign to root out evil, the witch became the criminal of her day, a convenient scapegoat whose torture, trial, and burning fueled religious, political, and social institutions. Priests and ministers were back in demand, called to exorcise the demons.* Mayors platformed off of purifying their towns. New courts were established, and expert judges and attorneys were required to legitimize fear and its antidote: law and order.

According to historian Lyndal Roper, a lucrative system emerged in "housing and feeding the children [awaiting trial] and paying guards to watch over them."[12] Men known as "witch finders" made a business out of hunting down and accusing witches. The wage employees of these newly expanded legal systems used torture techniques learned from the Inquisition, persecution of European Jewish populations, and failed religious crusades. We persecuted our grandmothers to the fullest extent of the law.

Sound familiar? The modern resurgence of the law-and-order candidate, the juvenile justice system, Native American boarding schools, detention of immigrant children, child abuse in religious institutions, and misogynistic rape culture all have origins in the several hundred years of terror in which our mothers, grandmothers, and aunts were targeted. Indeed, it is no huge leap to connect the roots of today's toxic (white) masculinity to the feelings of entitlement, expectations of control, and the use of spiritual, physical, sexual, and emotional violence that European men further internalized at this pivotal point in history.

---

* While the Roman Catholic Church was defending its political and economic base in the midst of the Protestant Reformation, the social purging of those accused of witchcraft was something both Christian sects enthusiastically agreed on.

The fear propaganda of the witch hunts was especially spread by religious authorities as the Church began to name sexual desire as a dangerous power that women had over men. Just as it had in *The Seven Tablets of Creation* and especially in its association with older women, the iconography of the witch trials was such that sexual activity was morphed into a tool of death rather than a means of life-giving regeneration. All nonreproductive sexual activity was criminalized. Sexual activity such as cunnilingus and anal sex, along with collective sex, nudity, and dances that had held a place in communal customs of the Middle Ages were rebranded as forms of devil worship. Homosexuality, which had been quietly accepted and publicly celebrated in several parts of Europe*, became increasingly demonized and fatally punished.

Sexuality connected to nature became a threat. Tortures, interrogations, rapes, and executions by fire or drowning in water, recently tested on heretics, used the natural elements to usurp matriarchal authority. In fact, the witch hunts proved that theological disagreements could be overcome for the greater goals of torturing women and pillaging the world. Or as Federici puts it, "The witch-hunt was the first unifying terrain in the politics of the new European nation-states, the first example, after the schism brought about by the Reformation, of a European unification."[13]

The large majority of those accused of witchcraft were women accused of crimes against fertility.† As a consequence, women were no longer trusted in the delivery room, especially ironic since many accused of witchcraft were healers knowledgeable about women's health during pregnancy and birth. Increasingly, male doctors replaced midwives as those giving birth became specimens in the emerging

---

* In *Same-Sex Unions in Premodern Europe,* John Boswell chronicles many examples of same-sex unions being tolerated and integrated into the social fabric of the day, from ancient Greece to fourteenth-century Europe. Federici notes that even in the time leading up to fifteenth-century Florence, "homosexuality was an important part of the social fabric" (58).

† The severest penalties were levied against reproductive crimes such as contraception, abortion, and infanticide (Federici, 88).

theater of medicine, which was set up like an actual theater with men as the spectators and performers and the pregnant, sick, or dead as subjects to be acted upon.

These theaters of medicine later mutated across the Atlantic Ocean* into increasingly horrific experimentation on (mostly Black) women's bodies—or what's more commonly known as the history of modern gynecology. These are the many knots that bring us to today's campaigns to criminalize abortion, the movement to control feminized and queer bodies and reproductive labor, and the entitlement to do so.

By the 1700s, the witch hunts had served their purpose, breaking the solidarity of European peasants and ushering in a new divide-and-conquer strategy that would be used in the creation of race. A campaign of terror originally meant for us was ultimately deflected onto racialized others. The violent exorcism of powerful feminine leadership from European peasant communities prepared a multitude of people groups with diversity in customs, languages, and cultures to become white. The witch hunts were the final tug that secured that initial shoelace knot of European patriarchy firmly in place.

WE ARE THE WITCHES

I feel the pangs of survivor's guilt as I think about how the atrocities originally meant for my foremothers morphed and compounded to oppress others. My heart beats faster. The trauma gets louder in my bones the closer we get to the present. I sense a complicity I hadn't felt before. Where exactly does my responsibility lie? What have I learned through no fault of my own? What have I continued to teach?

While oppression's tactics are not entirely surprising, it's the main-tenance of the divide by those who are being divided that seals the

---

* Although the witch hunts helped lay the foundation for colonialization and chattel slavery, attempts to use gendered divide-and-conquer strategies proved less successful in the colonies than among the European peasantry. In both Peru and Mexico, European colonists tried (and largely failed) to use the witch-hunt model to undermine Indigenous resistance. Instead, those Indigenous communities flipped the script by embracing the witch symbolism and using it to propel their resistance.

deal. The witch hunts proved especially serviceable in convincing the lower classes to enact psychological warfare on themselves.

Like my second-grade playground drama, envy and projected envy appear thematically throughout the witch hunt era. What started with accusations by the ruling class spread like wildfire among tight-knit communities. Neighbors told on neighbors. Friends insinuated about former friends. Children outed parents. And while we know patriarchy had been around the European block a few times already, during the witch hunts we played right into its hands. In case after case, it was the peasant classes' betrayal of each other that gave the enemy their proof. It is the betrayal of ourselves and each other today that keeps the webs of imperialist white-supremacist capitalist patriarchy wicked strong.

The mean girl. The gold digger. The gossip. The backstabber. *They must want what we have.* As long as the enemy is an other, then it can't be us—except that patriarchy was set up so we white women are also an other. The historical memory of our collective trauma lies forgotten in the back of our walk-in closets, hidden beneath high heels and business suits and passports that mark our race as white. Centuries later, how have we been fooled into believing that our right to play the whiteness game protects us from the violence of misogyny?

The painful truth of our legacy is that we told on each other. We took our unchecked personal vendettas straight to the ears of those who could do us harm. We whispered our dissatisfactions and accusations and they traveled. The negativity and rumors repeated and mutated into the hands of the men in power, who inflicted institutionalized terror in God's name and washed their hands of responsibility. Some of the dead were buried. Others burned.

The fallouts are deep. The communal social networks that predated the witch hunt era were destroyed. Now adultery and bearing children outside of wedlock could provoke the death penalty.[14] Infanticide and abortion, even when unintended, became punishable by death. Five hundred years later, what are the impacts on our psyches? How might we have begun to believe in our culpability? In the culpability of each other?

* * *

I wish I could tell you differently, but the first iterations of White Women's Groups replayed our witch hunt inheritance as my co-facilitator (another white woman) and I struggled to share leadership.

Our initial work together was pretty badass. In collaboration with several colleagues of color, we developed a citywide strategy for intersectional anti-racist youth organizing. My cofacilitator at the time and I supported each other as we leveraged our institutions to resource BIPOC leadership. We questioned white culture within local coalition networks. As white-aware white ladies clear about our institutional power, we were poised to infiltrate the worlds of nonprofits and philanthropy and to clue other white ladies in on the strategy. Together we founded the first two iterations of WWGs.

Sure, there were some bumps in those initial months. Early on, a couple of people left in ways that I later realized was emblematic of white people opting out. Yet overall, we co-created space for conversations that weren't happening at that time around white womanhood. Around my dining room table, we discussed Robin DiAngelo's article "White Women's Tears and the Men Who Love Them"[15] and considered our historic relationship with Black men. We delved into how whiteness and womanhood intersected in our lives. We looked at our family systems and wondered about how familial ruptures had been widened by whiteness. Our early work together deeply influenced future iterations of WWGs and the ways I approach white affinity organizing today.

The first dominoes began to fall in our organizing outside of the WWG space, and then the drama overflowed into it. Unfortunately, WWG members found themselves in between. When my cofacilitator brought an outside conflict into the WWG space, it was reminiscent of a witch hunt era power grab. Some of the white ladies closest to her had been requesting a shift in our structure, advocating for more of a support group and less of a facilitated space. Felicia, as our accountability partner, had disagreed. "If anything," she said, "they need more facilitation. They don't have the analysis yet. They think they're ready, but they're not."

To try to resolve the messy stalemate, my cofacilitator and I met to figure out how we would move forward. We accused one another. We both were angry and hurt. At one point I offered a compromise. "We could split the groups. You take one and I the other?" I deferred even though I wanted to continue to work with both, but she didn't seem that interested in taking on either group alone.

Then it was my turn to make a witch hunt era power grab. I emailed the white ladies to communicate that she and I were at an impasse and wouldn't be continuing our work together. If they wanted, I wrote, they'd be welcome to continue with me at our meeting next week. She found out about the email, felt betrayed, and blasted an email back. Already mired in my own feelings of betrayal, I responded to the group that the offer to meet still stood. Unfortunately for us, we hadn't yet embraced a curriculum that highlighted the witch hunts, which might have clued us in on how they undermined efforts at solidarity.

Eventually, Felicia, as our accountability partner, suggested a reset. And eventually, there was another cohort of WWG. And then another. And then another, all without my former cofacilitator.

* * *

I was named for my great-great-aunt Amanda. A conservative Mennonite woman born in the late 1800s in eastern Pennsylvania, she never married or had children of her own. Yet, she was known for her reproductive labor and for attending to mothers and their newborns after birth. Aunt Amanda wove her community's women's social networks like her ancestors did in the Middle Ages, carrying news from house to house, privy to the intimate inner workings of the homes. Whether she would have seen connections to her life and the witch hunts, I will never know. She passed before I was born. But for me, my namesake has become a powerful example of a woman who resisted the patriarchal norms of her day, a bridge between my life and those of my Swiss German ancestors at the advent of the witch hunts. The story I tell myself is that in light of her options, she made a conscious choice to live independently, cultivate ancient wisdoms, and nurture the community's well-being.

One time, when we were sitting at the kitchen table, I shared my Aunt Amanda thesis with my mother, even suggesting that Aunt Amanda might have been gay. I was unprepared for her response, a pin in my safely cultivated bubble of symbolic admiration. I heard pity and dismissal in my mother's voice, "Aunt Amanda probably just couldn't find a husband."

At first, I was disappointed in my mother's response. Then I got upset by it. It had taken years for me to summon the courage to voice my thoughts. Hesitant to be the family's dissenting voice of conflict once again, I had been nurturing my Aunt Amanda thesis exclusively on the inside, creating a seamless, genius, feminist narrative. In mustering the courage to come out with my truth, I had cast my mother in a supportive role. And when she failed to play the part I had imagined for her, I was disappointed and, if I'm honest, also hurt.

In sifting through the muck of trauma, projections, emotions, and socializations, sometimes it feels impossible to find truth. These wicked webs have tricked me into thinking that there is only one unique objective truth that comes down from on high, which is established externally from a rigorous, objective, emotionless, bodiless, often academic, legal, or biblically written text.

Acknowledging and healing from Mistress Syndrome includes a paradigm shift toward holding multiple truths. And so I have to work to respect my mother's truths as she identified with the pain and isolation of what it meant for a woman to be single and childless but did not explicitly condemn the system that made that arrangement so. I have to work to build confidence in my own truths—in the agency of Aunt Amanda's decisions, in her queerness in bucking the status quo, in her subversion of the patriarchal family unit—while also acknowledging that those truths are partially based on my assumptions, hopes, and projections. My vulnerability comes in letting my truths be challenged and in trusting in my ability to discern when I need to change and when I need to let go. Just as my mother might have projected her own narrative onto Aunt Amanda, so might I have too.

Part of white women's inheritance from the witch hunt era includes these difficult and often disappointing conversations with our mothers. Our deep-seated fear of making waves comes from a time when making waves spelled fatal consequences. An emotional gulf between us and our mothers was established over time and by design. We have been taught to turn venom and envy toward each other, to socially gain from the suffering of those who look most like us. Historically speaking, the witch hunts helped us build this deep distrust of other women, of ourselves, of our bodies, and of our intuition (which is also a form of truth).

Witches played an ever-present and leading role in the Eurocentric canon of children's literature that populated library shelves and the big screen during my childhood, and I'm guessing yours too. The witches were usually villainized (also often portrayed with darker features) and the witch hunt justified. It wasn't until reading *The Crucible* in high school that I began to question the fairy-tale formula I had been spoon-fed. The stories we tell ourselves and the stories we tell each other hold particular weight. Within them we choose to maintain or disrupt these wicked webs, to help tighten or loosen their laces.

One such story is that the gains of white womanhood have made life better for us. And while there are material and psychological benefits, there are also profound losses. My mother's early return to the paid workforce was a decision influenced by the patriarchal work environment with its culture, norms, and expectations made explicitly for bodies that don't give birth. As the only high-income country that doesn't provide paid parental leave, the US is far behind. According to Jody Heymann of UCLA's World Policy Analysis Center, paid parental leave began during the Industrial Revolution in Europe, ironically in the same places that so effectively devalued reproductive labor during the witch hunts. "In the 1800s—as soon as women started moving from working at home to working in factories—countries realized they needed to do something to ensure that women could work and care," Heymann says, "so they started to provide across

Europe and across Latin America and elsewhere paid maternity leave—leave that would care for families, for kids and ensure that economies could succeed."[16]

Granted, this shift toward recognizing reproductive labor was to ensure continued profit rather than liberate humanity, but at this same time in the US, with our economic reliance on enslaved labor, and even after emancipation with the reliance on a racialized underclass, racist capitalism had no such need. Instead, the nineteenth-century gains of white womanhood made us more dependent on racist capitalism. We gained the privilege to outsource our own reproductive labor, and in ways that are clearly unsustainable. In 2023, the US Treasury reported that nearly sixty percent of families can't afford quality childcare. Some pay as much annually for day care as the cost of in-state college tuition.[17]

Of course, there are many more statistics I could quote. The books by my bedside table deftly quantify white womanhood's profits and loss. But what can we do with all that proof? How do we begin to feel it, sensitize, and get in touch with a deeper wisdom?

I sit quietly for a moment and invite the unpaid maternity leave, cost of day care, and abortion bans to land in my body. The rage begins to bubble. My shoulders respond by tensing again. I send the rage back down into my lower abdomen. I let it churn and gather heat. I try to listen to what it's generating. It confirms what I have known all along: my labor has been minimized, my sexuality ostracized, and I've been made afraid to speak my truth. I feel the deep psychological command of religious doctrine, the lies I've taken on and projected. I feel frustrated. Why are we so committed to this arrangement when it is in our power to change? I am disappointed and disgusted. We have built our identities and our livelihoods and our families on these lies. I feel ashamed. Why are we so cowardly in our resistance?

I begin to feel the storm in my gut moving upward. It shakes my whole body as grief overcomes me. I grieve the loss of our trust in each other, the toxic comparisons, the loss of wisdom that has been replaced by poison. I grieve the silence and the distance and the chasms of superficiality that keep us from knowing each other and really knowing ourselves, the fear that has us holding tight to our secrets, our money, our children, our little piece of the pie. I grieve the impact of our fear and stinginess on everyone else, especially on other people's children. I grieve the spiritual void and the loss of connection to the earth, which is us and is around us and is also divine.

I grieve our lack of will to say *enough!*, our lack of imagination for a better collective existence, and our lack of commitment to dismantling that which is causing so much harm. Because at the end of the day I still have the very high expectation that dismantle, we can.

I started writing this book years before the US Supreme Court overturned *Roe v. Wade*, which for the first time in nearly fifty years made legal state laws that ban and criminalize abortion. But even before that 2022 decision, states were already beginning to reinstitutionalize witch hunt era trends. One law passed in Texas in 2021 recalls those divide-and-conquer tactics by enabling citizens to report other citizens for having abortions after six weeks. People found "aiding and abetting" these abortions can be fined upwards of $10,000 for things as removed as giving car rides. Several states have likewise moved to ban abortion care and criminalize the medical staff who offer the care, even in some cases where the life of the person seeking abortion care is at stake.

I first heard the news on the car radio that federal abortion protections no longer exist. I was supposed to be on a relaxing vacation, but I started to scroll through my phone for more info. My shoulders began to tense. Their contractions most likely blocked my rage from spewing all over my friend driving the car. I asked him to pull into a grocery store parking lot. The brisk walk from the car to the entrance helped burn off enough of my anger so that when the automatic sliding doors opened for me, I did not flip over the gaudy July Fourth cookout display and smash the melons satisfactorily on the floor. Instead, I fast-tailed it to the back and successfully entered the restroom marked by a triangle-shaped humanoid.

I walked to the sink and ran cold water over my wrists as I stared blankly into the mirror. Then I focused downward. Oh! Some kind soul was thoughtful enough to introduce a pot of cheery yellow marigolds to the stale décor. I wondered if the men's room got such a consolation prize. But the flowers' generous cheer was hampered by the clash of shiny red, white, and blue foil wrapped around its base. Its patriotism taunted me. I stared at it angrily, then hostilely removed the foil. Crumpling it up with much exaggeration, I threw it in the trash. This helped for a moment, until the familiar pain in my upper trapezius returned, throbbing, reminding me that these ancestral traumas didn't only exist in the past.

Back in the car, I deepened my breathing. I reminded myself that I am not alone in my outrage, that this pain is not mine alone to carry, that I am not alone in my commitment to resist.

STAKES OF RESISTANCE

These wicked webs have something to teach us about our power, too. In Germany, after the Peasant War (1524–1525) resulted in widespread deaths of a generation of men, older women were the movement's advisors as keepers of the collective memory. The wise woman was both the icon of community guidance and aide at birth. Women often led revolts against food shortages and land enclosures because they were the most severely impacted by them. In these European systems built on patriarchy, Roper states, "Women's political action was virtually de rigueur because it supplied the conclusive demonstration that order was overturned."[18] We wouldn't have been massacred if we hadn't posed a threat.

The mythology of the witch was necessary for maintaining the political and economic power hierarchies, its symbolism so long-lasting we have shelves full of witch-themed Disney movies and adorn our baby girls' bedrooms with the same movies' matching prints. According to Federici, the witch's symbolic necessity was "the embodiment of a world of female subjects that capitalism had to destroy: the heretic, the healer, the disobedient wife, the woman who dared to live alone, the obeah woman who poisoned the master's food and inspired the slaves to revolt."[19] This debasement of women—a "necessary condition for the existence of capitalism in all times"[20]— was happening precisely because of our collective potency. And by collective, I mean everybody who's down. Which begs the question: What is the order that we are willing to overturn?

The stories we tell ourselves and each other are a source of our power. And so it is worthwhile to note the exceptions, to plant hope in resistance as we harvest our sorrows.

There was a stronghold in Europe where an indigenous identity still thrives today: Basque country. Located on the Iberian Peninsula, the Basque people are still engaged in independence movements. This was the only place where men collectively organized to stop the witch hunts. Federici quotes Mark Kurlansky's work when depicting this resistance in detail:

> [When the men] of the St.-Jean-de-Luz cod fleet, one of the largest [from Basque country] heard rumors of their wives, mothers, and daughters [being] stripped, stabbed, and many already executed, the 1609 cod campaign was ended two months early. The fishermen returned, clubs in hands, and liberated a convoy of witches being taken to the burning place. This one popular resistance was all it took to stop the trials…[21]

What if peasant men across Europe had stood against the cult of the witch hunt, rather than in it? What if they had seen how the persecution of witches was ultimately connected to the persecution of themselves and their communities? What if we understood this about racism today?

Healing from Mistress Syndrome means reclaiming the stake. Death by fire, burning at the stake, was the go-to fatal punishment for witches and heretics alike. This—our literal stake, the apparatus of patriarchal religious and state terrorism—is awaiting our reclamation. What is our *stake* in ending racism? Rather than a fluffy abstraction about the betterment of humankind, our stake as status quo and passing white ladies is the physical stake on which we were once burned. We do not have to look outside of our own communities, histories, or experiences to know our stake in uprooting the status quo. That stake is also our own.

Which brings us full circle to the Shoelace Metaphor.* If European patriarchy is the first knot in your tennis shoelace, proto-capitalist mercantilism, with its bottomless greed for free and cheap (able-bodied) labor, and colonization with its hunger to dominate Indigenous peoples and the earth, are the twin bunny ear loops that make up the second knot. And as any caregiver knows, a single knot can result in loose laces. You gotta tie those sneaker laces twice. The double-knot of modern capitalism and its co-conspirator racism make up the historical third knot that reinforces these overlapping systems of oppression.

As Felicia often pointed out to me, "In order to undo a knot, you must first go back through." Which is why white feminism has failed us and will continue to fail us. It is impossible to untie a double knot by pulling at its base. In fact, pulling at its base only tightens the knot. From suffragettes to the Women's March, white women have been vocal about ending patriarchy. And we should: patriarchy is foundational. But in order to undo that knot, as well as all the interconnected knots that keep this arrangement in place, our liberation depends on our ability to untie its more recent mutations.

---

*Shoelace Metaphor, a component of "The Wicked Webs of Patriarchy, Capitalism, & Racism," was created in collaboration with YogaRoots On Location. See the copyright page for the full attribution.

CHAPTER THREE

THE LABOR OF LABOR

And then they met—the offspring of Skywoman and the children of Eve—and the land around us bears the scars of that meeting, the echoes of our stories. They say that hell hath no fury like a woman scorned, and I can only imagine the conversation between Eve and Skywoman: "Sister, you got the short end of the stick."

—Robin Wall Kimmerer, *Braiding Sweetgrass*

When teaching kids to tie shoes, I tend to stick to the "Bunny Ears" method.* However, when left to my own devices, I prefer the more complex "Loop, Swoop, and Pull" knot.† As an adult, it's amazing how I do this without even thinking. I make that quick grab with one hand for a loop on the lace to my right. My left hand reaches for my right-lace loop at the same time the fingers on my right hand make contact with the left lace, guiding it through the gap. In one motion, both hands pull the two symmetrical loops taut.

As the initial knot of patriarchy was secured, the loop, swoop, and pull of mercantilism and colonization took hold.

A predecessor to contemporary capitalism, mercantilism developed alongside that of the male-headed nation-state as European governments promoted policies that would maximize

---

* In the "Bunny Ears" method, you create two loops, one in each hand, and then tie them together and pull tight.

† For more than you ever wanted to know about tying shoelaces, check out Ian's Shoelace Site: https://www.fieggen.com/shoelace/.

their accumulation (of wealth, of resources, of land, of control of people) while competing with other (European) state powers in a zero-sum quest for global rule. Mercantilism was marked by government actions such as high tariffs, subsidizing exports, and the charter of trade companies such as the British East India Company (in 1600) and the Dutch East India Company (in 1602), forerunners to today's multinational corporations. Before the modern-day stock exchange and globalization, before free trade and imperialism, before the Industrial Revolution and chattel slavery, mercantilism promoted the tenets of domination and exploitation that had previously been codified at home as European nation-states began to tyrannize the globe.

A few years into my first "real" job (the peace and justice nonprofit gig), I was interviewed by a filmmaker for a film about labor. He was focusing on the food service industry. "Funny about that word 'labor,'" I said, "how it is used for both childbirth and work that earns a wage. The first definition required for the latter." I could tell by the kind but slightly puzzled look on his face that the interview wasn't going as planned. My reflections on midwifery and childbirth at the advent of capitalism were not interfacing with his story arc of the lives of Pittsburgh's dishwashers and line cooks.

His film was grounded in the one-hundred-year-plus lineage of Pittsburgh's union base, but not necessarily in the several-hundred-year history of the devaluation and feminization of reproductive labor. I'm guessing he was knowledgeable about the steelworkers and the Homestead Strike,* but probably hadn't considered how the criminalization of sixteenth-century European women's reproductive control aligned with their exclusion from wage labor and craft guilds and what that had to do with twenty-first century labor organizing. I was newly learning this information, too.

---

*The Homestead Strike of 1892 occurred in the mill town of Homestead, which was outside of Pittsburgh, and was a labor dispute that turned violent (sixteen people were killed) after management locked out striking workers, eventually getting the state government to call in the National Guard (Library of Congress, "Homestead Strike: Topics in Chronicling America").

NOT "REAL" WORK

During early mercantilism, as land was privatized and the commons lost, working-class men gained increasingly "free access to women's bodies, their labor, and the bodies and labor of their children."[1] As Federici also notes, the devaluation of work done by women at this time was sanctioned by both guilds and the state. Local governments instructed craft guilds to "overlook the production that women (especially widows) did in their homes, because it was not real work."[2]

As a result, the at-home work that kept humans healthy and alive, the labor that brought humans into the world, nurtured and fed the bodies of laborers, supported mental and emotional well-being, and maintained relational and social ties, was both devalued and rendered invisible. This devaluation and feminization of reproductive labor also created a market for women to perform reproductive labor for the ruling class, albeit at the lowest rates. Outsourcing such reproductive work meant that most labor done by poor women was not for their own families, but for employers.

Of course, low pay would not be the case for millions of enslaved women for whom forced reproductive labor went hand in chain with enslavement. The extraction of reproductive labor in Europe set the tone for the horrific exploitation of reproductive labor under colonization and enslavement. Scholar Jennifer L. Morgan speaks specifically to the theft of African women's reproductive lives in *Laboring Women: Reproduction and Gender in New World Slavery*:

> The crucial matter of heredity and the permanent mark of racial inferiority situated enslaved women's reproductive identity at the heart of the matter in ways not always explicated by slaveowners and their visible archives. Women's lives under slavery in the Americas always included the possibilities of their wombs.[3]

In retrospect, we can see how one knot led to another, how the denigration of one's own mother and her labor readied the denigration of another's. Once the acts of reproduction had been deemed the segregated work of women, once the concept of (wage) labor had been separated from women's (reproductive) work and depreciated and invisibilized at home, how seamlessly the collective colonizer psyche shifted to the unpaid (reproductive) labor of peoples it judged inferior.

* * *

My mother was neither a stay-at-home mom nor a working mom—she was both, as are so many mothers in modern America. When I was six weeks old, before her uterus had fully shrunk back to size after thirty-plus hours of labor with me, she returned part-time to the labor that offered her a wage. The devaluation and feminization of reproductive labor that occurred at the dawn of capitalism in Europe helps explain why weeks after giving birth she would get paid to teach nursing in an academic setting rather than nurse me at home. This devaluation and feminization of reproductive labor likewise set the global scene for colonization and racialized enslavement, which helps explain why hundreds of years later, my mother would be able to earn her wage by employing Ms. Sylvia at a lower rate at home.

Ms. Sylvia came to work for my family when I was brand spankin' new. My mother asked around in her trusted social circles and Ms. Sylvia's name was mentioned as someone who was looking for work. My mother's usual worry was assuaged by the reassurance that my father would be working from home on the days this stranger was to be entrusted with keeping their new human alive. And so, way before I had any salient memories, Ms. Sylvia came into my life.

I have one distinct early memory though. It is the only one I have of the inside walls of a crib. In my memory, I am surrounded by a soft, pastel green-and-yellow knotted baby quilt as two rotund, melanated arms reach for me. I was at ease being scooped up in her arms; there was no fear. It is a memory filled with loving care.

I am aware of the dangers of romanticizing my relationship with Ms. Sylvia, as have so many other white people before me,* and I will further consider white sentimentalizing and the mammy stereotype in chapters five and eleven. But for this initial discussion of reproductive labor, I want to emphasize how reproductive, emotional, and productive forms of labor can't really be separated out. The emotional extension required for parenting and child-rearing can't really be removed from diaper changes, bottle-feeding, and appropriate hugs. I mean, despite patriarchy's gaslighting, those forms of emotional labor are always there, and they always have been.

Of course, I am not the first to recognize this. The concept of "emotional labor," first referenced in 1979 by Arlie Hochschild in *The Managed Heart: Commercialization of Human Feeling*, as a way to identify the invisibilized work of laborers in the service industry (such as smiling and catering to a customer's emotions) has become shorthand for a wide range of relational work. In activist circles, "emotional labor" is used to point to the many invisibilized ways someone with less systemic power does the work of educating and placating the emotions of someone with more systemic power. Like white women for white men and Black women for everyone, this type of unpaid, underpaid, and/or unrecognized labor is a necessary skill set in order to successfully do a job, maintain access to institutions and resources, and even keep oneself and others safe.

In an interview, Rose Hackman, author of the book *Emotional Labor*, notes that this "extractive coercive labor"[4] is a way men benefit from women's free (and unacknowledged) labor. Moreover, it hits those with the least access to systemic power especially hard. Hackman describes those who resonated with the concept the most:

---

* I recommend reading Lillian Smith's *Killers of the Dream*. First published in 1941, the book unpacks Southern white sentimentalization that, considering the popularity of *The Help*, is still very much present today. This BBC article provides a fascinating debunk of the stereotype as well as an analysis of it in media: https://www.bbc.com/culture/article/20190530-rom-mammy-to-ma-hollywoods-favourite-racist-stereotype.

The women who connected to this issue the most were actually working-class Black women, who were often carrying entire families along, not just financially, but emotionally.

They were expected to do an enormous amount of emotional labor that was extraordinarily invisible. They were maybe nursing assistants during the day, which is a huge amount of emotional labor that is not really properly paid for. And they were going home at night and doing an extra shift.[5]

As I sit here considering which story about emotional labor to share with you from my life, I am struck by how many there are to choose from. Do I share with you early memories of female family members sidestepping the wide range of my father's reactivity? Or about how the church mothers operationalized congregational life while the male pastors monologued for pay? Do I share about how I've left many a first date exhausted, realizing afterward that I had listened to him talk the entire time, inserting my voice only when it was time to ask a question? Do I share about how in one romantic relationship, those please-and-appease skills were what kept me safe, especially when I realized I needed to leave but didn't yet feel safe enough to do so? Do I share about how in almost every job I've worked, from childcare to education to community organizing, emotional labor really just *was* the job even though much of that wasn't written into its description?

I'm sure you have many stories, too.

I am thinking again about the 4Ds and deference as a survival strategy. Deference, as a form of emotional labor, is part of a vocabulary that we have had to learn to stay safe. Deference's please and appease can mean choosing silence in order to keep the peace or deflecting attention away from the ways we may be viewed as a threat. As author and editor adrienne maree brown writes in *Pleasure Activism*, "Our silence has protected us against potential violence, an unfortunately common response of patriarchy and/or other kinds of power when met with rejection."[6]

I am thinking about how the invisibilization of emotional labor may offer an added layer of protection. Or at least we've become skilled at leveraging it in that way. Perhaps the erasure of my emotional labor meant he didn't know that my please and appease was in fact a skilled exit strategy to get me safely out the door. Perhaps in the absence of an accurate job description, the institution becomes more dependent on me.

But like defensiveness, denial, and distancing, deference has its limits. These are survival strategies, not necessarily liberating ones. As brown notes, "Silence played some role in helping us survive to get to this moment. But silence will not get us to a place of power over our bodies."[7]

In Pittsburgh in the mid-2010s, as the concept of emotional labor was becoming popularized on social media and in pop culture, the people in my organizing communities were resonating with it too. Notably, the Black women around me seemed to find this term especially useful in describing the extra work they had been doing on behalf of men, but especially on behalf of white women. Done with overextending themselves, they sent many white women my way.

Often those conversations with fellow white women started with me asking why they thought their coworkers, colleagues, and friends may have set the boundary that led to our call. Often at some point, these white women would describe a parallel (though not equivalent) example of how they likewise felt pressured to overextend themselves (for family, partners, and bosses).

Naming the ways emotional labor serves power can be especially useful when a member of a marginalized group is expected to perform it unpaid or underpaid on behalf of a member of a relatively advantaged group. There is validation in reclaiming emotional labor as real work, in honoring the exhaustion and inequities and calling out the resulting imbalances.

Personally, becoming more connected to emotional labor as real work has helped me become more honest with myself about my capacity. It has helped me get clearer about how I've survived and how I've enabled. And, as we will continue to unpack in these pages, the emotional labor done both by and on behalf of white women certainly has something to say about Mistress Syndrome. That my one-on-ones with fellow white women revealed both their own emotional over-extension as well as an overdependence on the emotional labor of Black colleagues points to how our misuse has enabled us to misuse others. This dynamic is a tried-and-true strategy of the wicked webs and one that is in need of disrupting.

The era of mercantilism may have programmed us to think that reproductive labor does not constitute "real" work. But perhaps that programming is an indication of its deep worth. As Hackman points out:

> A huge way in which this extraction of labor is extraordinarily beneficial to men and how patriarchy, at large, is able to continue, is that we refuse to accept that emotional labor is real in spite of all the evidence that exists that shows that obviously it's extraordinarily valuable.[8]

Obviously.

Like much of our work in healing from Mistress Syndrome, noticing is a great first step. As status quo and passing white ladies, we can start by becoming more aware of when reproductive labor is happening. We can bring our attention to our deference, our silences, and the extensions of our emotional labor. This means becoming more honest about our relational dynamics, family systems, and workplace cultures. We can sensitize to when others are doing that work on behalf of us. We can notice who we (over)rely on and in what contexts. We can ask ourselves questions like: Do I feel entitled to feeling a certain way or having certain information right now? Is this something I could google? Could I perhaps vent or process with someone else instead?

As we become more sensitized to reproductive labor and its value, we have the opportunity to make external changes, too. These can be small shifts. Can I offer myself a deep breath in between tucking my kids into bed? Can I reschedule a phone call to a time when I have more energy or ask my partner to write the holiday cards this year? Could I share more of my opinions on a first date or try establishing a new boundary with work?

Depending on the moment, relationship, and your discernment, perhaps bigger moves are an option. Perhaps you begin a conversation with trusted coworkers or document unrecognized emotional labor to share with your supervisor. Perhaps you engage the people you live with in an at-home work assessment[*] and then shift tasks toward a more equitable arrangement. Perhaps you begin to demand compensation (as sex workers have been doing for millennia).

In her chapter "Fuck You, Pay Me: The Pleasures of Sex Work" in *Pleasure Activism*, author and activist Chanelle Gallant highlights how sex workers do the many things that "women and feminine people of all genders"[9] are supposed to do for free—but for compensation. Gallant expands the description of sex work beyond what I had previously understood (work like providing physical sexual acts or creating sexualized media and performances) to discuss a whole range of feminized labor. This scope of labor expected to be done by uncompensated women and femmes includes "be sexualized by cisgender men," "validate their masculinity," "make them feel important and wanted even if they're tedious," "create intimacy and hold vulnerability," and "pour time and money into white middle-class beauty standards."[10]

(Yes. I am over here nodding my head: "...even if they're tedious" especially resonates.)

As someone who passes for status quo, the time and money I have had to spend on white middle-class beauty standards is relatively low, as is the reality of "more intense control and violence" that "poor, working-class, trans feminine, fat, disabled, crazy, or racialized women"[11] are exposed to daily.

Pertinent to our focus on the labor of labor, Gallant observes that all women and femmes end up providing sexualized labor in one form or another. Whether it's putting on makeup, adding that exclamation mark to the end of a greeting, or listening with a smile, this sexualized work has been required for women and femmes to gain and maintain access to (white) men, their wages, and the institutions they control.

---

[*] Visit www.mistresssyndrome.com/resources to find out how to access this at-home work assessment, along with a discussion guide and workbook.

It's also worth noting, that the mercantilist devaluation and feminization of reproductive labor that caused working-class men to gain free access to women, their bodies, and their labor wasn't really all that great for the men who benefited from it. The separation of peasants from land that put the work of reproductive labor on family units also created a more mobile, more desperate, and more dependent workforce. Like the witch hunts, ultimately, this erasure was bad for the entire working class. The dissection and devaluation of at-home work, according to Federici, "inevitably devalued its product: labor-power."[12] Moreover, Gallant offers the reminder that, under capitalism, unless we come from the wealthiest classes, all of us humans end up selling our bodies and the work that they do in some form or another.

Mad respect to all the sex workers who are demanding fair compensation for their labor, to mothers and birthers who are claiming reproduction as work, and to all Pittsburgh's dishwashers, line cooks, and unions who are organizing for worker's rights.

PUTTING OUR EMOTIONS TO WORK (FOR US)

We need a diversity of tactics[*] if we are to seriously disrupt these wicked webs. Making emotional labor visible, establishing boundaries around the ways we extend ourselves relationally, and demanding just compensation are all important tactics. But I wonder if these tactics on their own might still have us arguing on patriarchy's terms. As in, are there limitations of talking about reproductive, emotional, and sexual labor solely in transactional terms? Can we understand emotional labor as more than something we've been forced to do, but as something we want, need, and deserve to thrive? Without erasing history and oppressive power dynamics, without ignoring people's constrained choices and very real disparities, could we also think of emotional labor as a form of coregulation, which professor of psychiatry Dr. Stephen Porges talks about as "a birthright"?[13]

---

[*] The phrase "diversity of tactics" is attributed to Malcolm X in his 1964 speech "The Black Revolution."

A key concept in trauma healing and somatic therapy, coregulation describes the various embodied ways that humans attune to and mirror each other's emotional and physiological states in order to manage distress, soothe, and ultimately signal safety. An important part of childhood and adolescence development, the need to coregulate continues throughout our lives as "a biological imperative meaning that we have to do it in order to survive."[14]

(Putting a pin here for us to later consider the harms of toxic (white) masculinity on those who have been conditioned away from this biological imperative.*)

With so much pop cultural focus on self-improvement and self-care, I appreciate Dr. Porges's attention to the relationship between the self- and the co-. "Coregulation," he says, "leads to emerging properties of being able to self-regulate; not the reverse." Or in other words, rather than asking if we've done enough self-care in order to show up for others, maybe we also need to be asking if we've had enough coregulation to regulate ourselves?

I mean, sure, there are many times when I just don't have it for other people. Let me be by myself, undisturbed, with a book, a cup of tea, and a piece of chocolate, says the childless adult who lives alone in a tiny house surrounded by trees and squirrels.

But rethinking coregulation, what Dr. Porges calls a human's "goal in life," puts a slightly different spin on it. While the solitude (and chocolate) may sometimes be what I need, it might also be reinforcing my burnout. Maybe extending emotional labor in the right context is not the energy drain that I've come to see it to be. Maybe within a more reciprocal dynamic, extending emotional labor can actually help us to recharge. As part of his work, Dr. Porges has become curious about the ways of "super co-regulators," or those who demonstrate such a range of coregulation that they don't reach burnout. What's interesting is that these folks don't burn out in the process of coregulating, probably because coregulation is in fact biologically rewarding.

---

* See chapter nine.

In the deficit mindset of these wicked webs, we are often left to see emotional labor as something that is coerced, something that has been misused and abused for the extractive purposes of those in power. And it has. But might it also be a source of our power? Might the survival skills we've had to develop within these wicked webs also help us to heal?

MYTHS OF OBJECTIVITY

I was taught the scientific method in elementary school beginning in grade four, along with myths of objectivity and control. One year, I spent several Sunday afternoons at the park recording temperature variations. Another year I used my good little white girl voice to gain access to an upscale jeweler who let me shine a laser pointer into some very expensive diamonds to determine the best angles for maximum refraction and reflection.

But my favorite science fair project happened the year that we did social science. I was much more interested in people than the refraction of light.

Sunday sermons had me convicted that no one should go hungry or without a place to live. Yet, growing up close to downtown, I had daily reminders that many of my neighbors didn't have a roof over their heads. At the highway exit, on trips to the library, in the park, and especially on our walks to and from the Atlanta baseball team's stadium, exhausted-looking people asked us for money. I remember a few times when strangers knocked on our front door. If my father was home, he would open the door and give people food, rides, and occasionally, money—despite my mother's objections that giving rides was dangerous. As a kid, I couldn't understand why homelessness was such a hard problem to solve. It didn't seem very hard. If the problem was that people didn't have a house, why couldn't we just house them?

When the social science project came around, my teacher told us to "choose something you care about." And homelessness was something I passionately wanted to end. My teacher pointed me to the library, where I found pages of numbers about humans. My mom mentioned that a friend's dad worked for a local café that served those looking for a meal, so I interviewed him about his work. My school's curriculum suggested I gather more info about the problem, observe it, find measures, and then make (rational) conclusions and award-winning trifold displays. So I did, all from the comfort of my family's kitchen table.

As you may have anticipated, I benefited much more from this middle school assignment than any of my unhoused neighbors. In addition to getting an A, I confirmed that homelessness was indeed a problem and memorized the numbers of people it affected.* I learned a little bit more about available services. But in other ways, this line of research took me further away from my original hypothesis—that to end homelessness, people just needed housing. The solutions that seemed so obvious based on my nascent understanding of bodies and shelter and basic needs became more complicated the more I worked on my social science project, all of which I did while my own body was warm, dry, fed, and adequately housed.

In addition to learning how to use the library card catalog (it was public school in the mid-1990s), I learned how to consider a more systemic picture. But that wider lens also meant that I had to distance myself from the empathy and passion that brought me to the problem—and the people—in the first place. The scientific method didn't really take into account the feelings that came up for me when I made eye contact with someone asking for spare change. Rather, it insisted that I become objective, take in the facts, listen to the experts (although not necessarily those with expertise based on lived experience), and draw a succinct conclusion. Maybe the reward of getting an A mitigated the bad feelings that came up every time I passed an unhoused neighbor on the street. Or maybe it didn't.

---

* Racial disparities exist in the unhoused population. African Americans, as well as American Indians/Alaska Natives, Native Hawaiians and Pacific Islanders, and people who identify as two or more races make up a disproportionate share of the unhoused population (National Alliance to End Homelessness, "Racial Inequalities in Homelessness, by the Numbers").

MECHANICAL PHILOSOPHY WASTES NOT ON WHITE WOMAN OVERWHELM

Mercantilism and colonization have something to do with why my school's curriculum included the scientific method. They had something to do with the invention of homelessness, too.

During that era, Europe began to shift its cultural relationship to the human body. Now that reproductive labor had been cut apart from wage labor, now that humanity had been further dissected for profit, humans and their bodies became viewed as raw material, disposable for the advancement of the emerging nation-state.[15] Mercantilism sought to equate the human body with the machine, and among other things, manufactured mass homelessness.

That more mobile, more desperate, and more dependent workforce? They were shipped to the European colonies as indentured laborers (who would soon be racialized as white). Those distant lands with abundant resources and diverse peoples? They were God's mandate to the nation-states, to be rationally used to fill up coffers at home. To quote Genevieve Vaughan from the essay "Patriarchal Capitalism vs. a Gift Economy," those "free gifts such as water, seeds, species, and traditional medicines [were taken] away from the people whose needs were unilaterally satisfied by them."[16] Just as European patriarchy had professed hierarchy and dominion, so too did the project of colonization extend Euro-centrism, as European men were christened to further the nation-state's reach of exploitation and control.

It was also during this era that any association between the body and the sacred—which might have morally compelled the City of Atlanta to end endemic homelessness—became greatly diminished. Seventeenth-century mechanical philosophy explained the natural world in terms of the mechanics of matter in motion. Using this lens, the body could be understood as a set of separate parts to be objectively studied, separated, measured, and dominated. As Federici points out, with mechanical philosophy:

One could investigate the vices and limits of imagination, the virtues of habit, the uses of fear, how certain passions can be avoided or neutralized, and how they can be more rationally utilized. In this sense, Mechanical Philosophy contributed to increasing the ruling-class control over the natural world, control over human nature being the first, most indispensable step.[17]

At public high school, as we read Hobbes and Descartes, I was taught rational philosophies and that the Age of Enlightenment was a triumph. Perhaps some of this philosophy was accurate, the repetitive science projects and disconnected musings of dead white men certainly neutralized my passions for studying them. But what wasn't in my school curriculum was how these remnants of mercantilism helped normalize the homelessness I felt so passionate about ending. As the prereq to capitalism, large-scale planned poverty was one of mercantilism's pillars.

In the article "The Reason You Answer Work Email on the Weekend Is Over 500 Years Old," Stephanie Buck writes about how mass poverty was part of mercantilism's design. Keeping people poor kept them busy and making people feel responsible for their poverty gave work ethic a holy meaning. It was at this point in history that idleness became a grave sin. Not working—even when there wasn't actual work to do—became wasting time. And wasting time was a sin that could lead to hell. To quote Buck:

> Now, not only were laborers contending with the demands of a relentless work week, they also experienced spiritual guilt and fear—would misusing time threaten their "fate in the afterlife"? What the church and the mercantilist economy could agree on was the destiny of the poor human's soul—or more specifically, how to profit off a collective fear of damnation.[18]

To paraphrase Buck, suffering from work, according to the British ruling class, was actually beneficial for poor people, who, if not preoccupied with back-breaking, endless labor, would be tempted toward laziness and free time. These cultural assumptions persist today: we shame the poor as lazy while idolizing the leisure of the wealthiest.

* * *

As a result of these wicked webs, and in the past couple generations, my family has had increased access to leisure time, educational pursuits, and the financial resources to travel for vacation. Yet
despite this generational class advancement, a mercantilist mindset
often pervades my thoughts, feelings, and actions. The Protestant
work ethic*, guilt, and scarcity mentality are somehow still constant
companions as I go about my privileged life, with intention.

I have always known the slightly musty smell of the thrift store,
the dedication of combing through hanger after hanger, rack after
rack, and the thrill of a great find. My mother exclusively bought my
childhood clothes from thrift stores or the department store sales rack.
When I was old enough to express preferences, I more often opted
for a thrift store excursion than roaming the mall.

I write this now as I would have written it then, with absolutely
no shame. Our white middle-class status afforded us the option to
thrift. And although shopping full price or designer would not have
been sustainable on my parent's fluctuating entrepreneurial incomes,
we did not have to thrift in order to make rent; we thrifted in order
to pay the mortgage and go on a summer vacation.

My mother's deft stewardship was often lauded as why we had
options, lovely Christmas gifts, and that one vacation to the Grand
Canyon. And I'm not saying this wasn't true. In fact, I'm sure it was.
But what gets overlooked in the celebration of her budgeting is that
our access to leisure while still having savings was not just because
of her financial eagle eye; it had to do with our positioning as white
and our generational and institutional access to wealth accumulation. This thrifty narrative also conversely implies that extravagance
in poverty is irresponsible and that extravagance in poverty is indeed
poverty's cause.

---

* The Protestant work ethic attaches religious importance to doing work. The
term "Protestant ethic" was coined by Max Weber to describe beliefs about work,
including "diligence, punctuality, deferment of gratification, and a primacy of work"
(Hill, "History of Work Ethic: 5.Two Perspectives of the Protestant Ethic").

For us, thrifting was not only *not* a source of shame, it was also a source of ~~pride~~ Mennonite Humble* since wasting food, time, and resources was sinful. Some of the cultural reinforcement for thrift probably came from previous generations who navigated the Great Depression and subsistence farming. But the call to godly austerity also stemmed from cultural interconnections with puritanism, the Protestant work ethic, and a slightly muddled interpretation of scripture. Jesus stood with the poor and condemned the wealthy. So, while not actually being poor, presenting as poor (or at least, not rich) is morally desirable.

These thrifty values played out in many ways over the course of my life. Wasting food by not cleaning my plate was stealing from impoverished children. Spending extra money on something fancy was bad stewardship of the resources God had entrusted to us. My Christian college promoted Micah 6:8—not doing justice, loving mercy, and walking humbly was an affront to one's Christian purpose. Every moment was to be lived with intentionality. And in the world of social justice activism, each choice—be it clothing or food, books or TV, paper or plastic, driving or biking—must conscientiously consider the environment, just labor practices, and one's potential imperialistic impact.

As someone who has struggled with workaholism, the constant moral anxiety of wasting time, resources, and energy creates an everyday battle. In this ongoing struggle, I can exhaust my emotional, mental, and physical reserves, yet the tasks still pile up. The residual guilt of not doing and not being enough is pervasive. It follows me around on my days off and my days on. There is always something I should be cleaning, something I should be doing, emails I should be writing, or someone I should be calling. A list cloud looms over my head.

Perhaps I come by it honestly: the women in my family are productive and hardworking multitaskers. My nonagenarian grandmother

---

* I use "Mennonite Humble" to describe how Mennonites may authentically feel a sense of pride about certain values (pacifism, thriftiness, etc.), but end up expressing it in indirect ways/performing humility because being prideful is condemned.

adamantly denies taking a nap even when caught in the act. Rest in the middle of the day is so reprehensible that it is unspeakable. Even though my family's economic circumstances have changed and my grandmother's daily needs are cared for, lingering guilt prevents full access to rest. Now that rest has become a real, sustained option, the guilt of having access to it (while so many others don't) prevents us from using the privileges we have to take better care of ourselves. My family and myself, like so many other middle-class white settlers, have deeply internalized that to be still is to be devious and thus we continue to uphold our own exhaustion even when we could do otherwise.

We may tell ourselves it's about being productive. But could a part of it also be about *looking* productive? And for whom? As Buck elaborates, "Simply *looking* busy is currency in itself, a way to sidestep the stigma that comes with idleness, especially for the poor and working class."[19] Is it even possible to truly be productive when your body needs rest?

* * *

As I ran the red light on my pink bicycle, my heartrate quickened. I was definitely going to be late.

"There's no late for yoga," was one of Felicia's mantras. I tried to remind myself of this as I swung my leg over the seat and locked my bike to the community center's bike rack.

There's no late for yoga, I thought, which helped me climb the stairs more slowly but didn't really quell my mounting anxiety. After pushing for months to shift the peace and justice nonprofit I worked for toward anti-racism, the pushback was pushing back. Felicia and I had strategized for hours, meeting before and after yoga classes. I felt supported and relieved by her advisement. Even though there had been many obstacles, at least she had my back. But that morning and despite all our strategizing, a committee member had resigned, dropping by the office to say they were no longer in support. Then I received a second resignation over email soon after. With months of overwork, this latest defeat had taken my body way out of her window of tolerance.*

The yoga class was nearing its end as I tried to quietly roll out my mat. Felicia moved throughout the room, offering students eye pillows and a hint of lavender essential oil. *At least I had made it for relaxation.*

I lay down on my back, heart and mind still racing, hands jittery. A wave of exhaustion hit me hard. Tears began to seep out the edges of my eyes.

"We need you." It was Felicia's low voice as she hovered over me, offering a facial tissue. "We need you," I remember her saying again after she placed the eye pillow gently over my eyes and moved to check on the next person.

I was too exhausted to let the small voice of guilt take much hold. It probably wanted me to feel bad about the emotional labor this brilliant Black woman was pouring into me, or how I should be at work fighting racism instead of lying down while the sun was up. But in that moment I didn't have the reserves to problematize it. Instead, I surrendered to my exhaustion and to Felicia's skilled extension of care.

That midday yoga break is not the only memory I have of pushing the limits of my health for work. It's not the only time I sacrificed myself on the altar of having taken on "too much." It's not the only time a Black woman has cared for my exhaustion.

I am reminded about how so often my conversations with other white women start with sharing about how busy we are and how overwhelmed we feel. I am reminded too about how the Protestant work ethic sets us up for shame and exhaustion on purpose, so that working people will be so exhausted that they won't have the time or energy to challenge the system. And working is ultimately

---

* According to the National Institute for the Clinical Application of Behavioral Medicine, "The window of tolerance is a concept originally developed by Dr. Dan Siegel, MD to describe the **optimal zone of 'arousal' for a person to function in everyday life.** When a person is operating within this zone or window, they can effectively manage and cope with their emotions" ("How to Help Your Clients Understand Their Window of Tolerance").

necessary for survival. I need to be able to feed myself and cover housing costs.

Yet, despite the structural limitations, I wonder if maybe I am opting into the stress. Who then suffers the consequences? As in, does my white-lady conditioning to not say "no" and my desire to want people to like me cause me to take on too many commitments? Does my wish to get it "right" drive me to exhaustion? Has the scarcity of not thinking I am enough propelled me to overcompensate? Has an awareness that I could opt out (because of my whiteness) guilted me into action? Other people don't have the privilege to choose not to fight.

These are questions worth asking ourselves: Who do I go to for care when I'm exhausted? Who's most impacted when I've become too exhausted to fight? Part of the paradox of white-woman overwhelm is that our commitment to overdoing it (often in service to others) can become an obstacle to sustaining those same commitments. We simultaneously don't value ourselves enough to rest and also don't fully grasp how rest impacts our collective ability to resist.

For status quo white ladies, these aspects of Mistress Syndrome hit us hard. With life's never-ending lists of tasks, we can buy into illusions about achievement, organization, and our ability to control time through our lists, schedules, and shared online calendars. With the mechanization of our work, bodies, and relationships, mechanical philosophy has tricked us into thinking it is possible to both plan and control outcomes. No matter that we have changeable human bodies with emotional unpredictability. Or perhaps precisely because we have changeable human bodies with emotional unpredictability.

Our religious approach to dieting is one specific way we've inherited this history. The French word for diet is "regime." The dieting industry makes bank off our belief that bodies can be regimented by counting calories, measuring quantities, and exercising them into submission. The guilt we feel when we don't live up to our internalized version of society's expectations of us—because the system sets us up so that we never will—keeps us stuck in the wicked webs rather than inciting us to disentangle from them. (I will say more about body ideals and disordered eating in the next chapter.)

The scarcity mindset has become deeply embedded in our cultural norms. It is the ghost of the very real experiences of poverty, war, and famine endured by our European ancestors. It is the impact of collective trauma unmetabolized that gets recycled and meted out on others.

I am thinking about how traumatic incidents can freeze us in the moment of their occurrence; childhood trauma may cause a return to the developmental age when they happened; what may have served us at one phase may not in another. In a conversation with Rev. Angel Kyodo Williams and Dr. Rae Johnson, psychotherapist Dr. Leticia Nieto talks about how it is developmentally appropriate for seven- or eight-year-olds to collect and hoard. "But," Nieto notes, "then we're meant to grow out of that....It's a step on the way to much wider and more complex functions."[20] Yet, here we have a generational culture of hoarding, even though materially we have enough. As one of the richest countries in the world, the US could adequately sustain all of its citizens.

SELF-HATE AND WHITE DEBT

The profiteering of mercantilism in Europe was made possible by the global exploitation of peoples across the globe in the name of Christ. While proselytizing a God-sanctioned work ethic for the poor at home, Catholic religious leaders began ordaining conquistadors to spread Christianity as part of a global campaign to subdue Indigenous peoples and bring them to "the faith." This religious cover for genocide via the Doctrine of Discovery fueled the growth of European economies as Europeans began to use horrendous force, cultural supremacy, and the divide-and-conquer strategies of the witch hunts to subjugate humans around the world and plunder their "natural resources."

Even the concept of "natural resources" that I tentatively refer to here stems from the mechanized mindset which separated interconnected aspects of life. Robin Wall Kimmerer, mother, scientist, professor, and enrolled member of the Citizen Potawatomi Nation, writes about the cosmological chasms between the Indigenous people of Turtle Island and invading Europeans. After telling the origin story of Skywoman Falling in *Braiding Sweetgrass*, Kimmerer points out the contrast of the different origin stories and the resulting consequences:

> On one side of the world were people whose relationship with the living world was shaped by Skywoman, who created a garden for the well-being of all. On the other side was another woman with a garden and a tree. But for tasting its fruit, she was banished from the garden and the gates clanged shut behind her. That mother of men was made to wander in the wilderness and earn her bread by the sweat of her brow, not by filling her mouth with the sweet juicy fruits that bend the branches low. In order to eat, she was instructed to subdue the wilderness into which she was cast....
>
> One story leads to the generous embrace of the living world, the other to banishment. One woman is our ancestral gardener, a cocreator of the good green world that would be the home of her descendants. The other was an exile, just passing through an alien world on a rough road to her real home in heaven.[21]

Just as they had first banished the daughters of Eve, European colonizers began to target the daughters of Skywoman.

Europe had already been practicing Christian dominance: persecuting Jews, Muslims, heretics, and witches in European homelands while trying to expel Muslims and other non-Christians from their own homelands (aka the Crusades*). But the religious justification for centuries of colonization was codified by Pope Alexander VI in

---

* Earlier edicts such as Nicholas V's papal bull in 1455 also had the impact of granting European Christians "divinely sanctioned" rights to "reduce [enemies of Christ] to perpetual slavery, and to apply and appropriate to himself and his successors the kingdoms, dukedoms, principalities, dominions, possessions, and goods, and to convert them to his use and profit" (The Coalition to Dismantle the Doctrine of Discovery, "Dismantling the Doctrine of Discovery").

1493, whose papal bull* backed Spain and Portugal's expansion and sanctified colonization.

Now through the Doctrine of Discovery, any land not already inhabited by Christians was proclaimed God-ordained for the taking. According to the Pope's Bull, it was now Christian obligation that "the Catholic faith and the Christian religion be exalted and be everywhere increased and spread, that the health of souls be cared for and that barbarous nations be overthrown and brought to the faith itself."[22]

I'd love to let the Catholics take this one, but this legacy of bloody colonization is, of course, also my own. My ancestors settled on Indigenous land, too, displacing the Lenape people and contributing to the violence of settler colonization. Its violence persists, as does ongoing resistance.†

As part of colonization, European invaders imposed patriarchal precedents. As gender scholar Oyèrónkẹ́ Oyěwùmí notes in *The Invention of Women*, "In Britain, access to power was gender-based; therefore, politics was largely men's job; and colonization, which is fundamentally a political affair, was no exception."[23] Oyěwùmí lays out how the category of "woman" (and "man") did not exist in precolonial Yorùbá society. Not only was gender not binaried or hierarchical as it was in Britain, but neither was the biological category of sex (female/male) fixed. Rather "social identity was relational and was not essentialized."[24]

In Britain, essentializing gender meant that qualities such as intellectual weakness, emotionality, and hysteria became synonymous with

---

* A papal bull refers to a public edict or document issued by the Pope of the Roman Catholic Church.

† Federici lays out some specific ways Indigenous women held power before widespread contact with Europeans and how they resisted the divide-and-conquer tactics of witch hunts and fought colonial hierarchy, highlighting examples from the Oaxaca region of Southern Mexico and in Peru. As in Europe, tactics of terror and torture were used. But unlike in Europe, in Peru witches were not shunned by their communities but instead became sought after. Likewise, in 1524 in Oaxaca, as the Spaniards waged war on the rebelling Chiapanecos, "it was a priestess who led the troops against them," turning the colonizers' ploy on its head, their witchcraft became the very resource of resistance (232).

female "nature." In *Good Wives, Nasty Wenches & Anxious Patriarchs*, historian Kathleen M. Brown describes how this gender essentialism and biological determinism embedded in the British psyche became projected onto the people groups they sought to colonize. Or, in other words, the British patriarchal order that saw gender hierarchy as the "natural" order of gender relationships was used to construct and justify a parallel claim to "natural" royal British authority over Indigenous and African peoples.

Not only did this transference happen by revamping the idea of women's "natural" inferiority into a justification of the "natural" inferiority of non-European (soon to be nonwhite) peoples, but also through a forced reorganization of societal relationships as gendered and hierarchical within non-European societies, which had not previously been the case. As Oyěwùmí documents, people who came to be called "female" and "male" in precolonial Yorùbáland navigated multiple identities not based on anatomy; thus "the creation of 'women' as a category was one of the very first accomplishments of the colonial state."[25]

* * *

When I first read Kimmerer's poetic passage of the fateful meeting between Skywoman and Eve, I felt a wistful envy reminiscent of my pre-patriarchal desires. When I read about the nonexistence of gender/sex hierarchy in Yorùbá society, I felt a similar tug. I so want to be a gardener for the well-being of all, to claim a pre-patriarchal place like Yorùbáland, where "power was not gender-determined."[26] I mean, who would want to be an exile, painfully passing through?

Along with my possible idealization of complex societies (that most likely had their own issues), I am also noticing an impulse to distance myself from the "daughters of Eve." I am trying to keep the feelings at arm's length. At this moment of the inception of colonization, as I let myself get closer, survivor's guilt begins to seep through.

Let's address that guilt for a moment. As white ladies on our journey to untie the wicked webs, guilt is bound to emerge. But that doesn't mean we need to invite it in and feed it supper. Maybe it's helpful to think of guilt sorta like the 4Ds. Guilt has been something we've learned to lean on as we try to make sense of having what others don't. Maybe, as with using the 4Ds, if we can accept the realities of our reactions and then get curious, we might be able to dig deeper.

On one hand, guilt might show up to get our attention (so we can make a change and no longer feel it). But guilt can also languish on the chaise lounge like a pouty diva (usually in cases when we invite it in and give it supper *and* dessert). Like how sometimes I feel good about feeling bad. Sometimes feeling guilty (at least I'm feeling something) proves I have a conscience. My guilt reminds me (and everyone else) that I am aware and informed. Yes, I know my home was purchased with gentrification, even though I wish it hadn't been. Yes, my career in anti-racism relies on the existence of racism, on the inequities I'm trying to end. I might not be able to end homelessness or transform the Nonprofit Industrial Complex,* but at the very least I can feel bad about their existence.

But typically, this type of guilt does not cause us to upset the collective tables of our lives. The guilt that languishes does not move us to sign over property deeds to the Indigenous peoples of the land we now own. It does not get us to send our children to the underperforming school. It does not have us volunteering to leave our positions of employment.

In those examples in which we know better but don't do better, this type of guilt might not actually motivate us to realign our lives with our values. Instead, such lingering guilt accommodates our suffering: if I'm not willing to make a change, at least I'm willing to make myself feel miserable about it. Mustn't that be worth something? (But who's keeping score?)

I don't think we need self-induced misery to prove that we care. And if you are still reading this book, I am fully convinced that you care.

To quote a white teenager I know who is wise beyond her years, "Guilt is just another form of self-hate." And I've come to agree.

---

* The phrase "Nonprofit Industrial Complex" points to the ways nonprofits are part of larger systems within capitalism that are likewise influenced by philanthropic interests and corporate business structures.

We've been taught to think that guilt helps keep us in touch with our wrongdoing. But maybe guilt is keeping us from our agency and keeping us from dealing with what we owe.

In her thought-provoking article "White Debt," writer Eula Biss unpacks the relationship between guilt and debt for white people, linking the historical root of the abstract concept of guilt to concrete material debt:

> The moral concept of *Schuld* ("guilt"), Nietzsche wrote, "descends from the very material concept of *Schulden* ('debts')." Material debt predates moral debt. The point he is making is that guilt has its source not in some innate sense of justice, not in God, but in something as base as commerce. Nietzsche has the kind of disdain for guilt that many people now reserve for "white guilt" in particular. We seem to believe that the crime is not investing in whiteness but feeling badly about it.[27]

And of course we feel guilty when we owe. But maybe our guilt has become so far removed from the work that would begin to repay our debts that we have lost touch with what we actually materially owe.* Or maybe in our overwhelming guilt we have given up on the possibility of repayment (and given up on the possibility of liberation). As Biss puts it:

> What is the condition of white life? We are moral debtors who act as material creditors. Our banks make bad loans. Our police, like Nietzsche's creditors, act out their power on black bodies. And, as I see in my own language, we confuse whiteness with ownership. For most of us, the police aren't "ours" any more than the banks are. When we buy into whiteness, we entertain the delusion that we're business partners with power, not its minions. And we forget our debt to ourselves.[28]

---

* There are many ways that white settlers can engage with repaying debts and learning about what is owed. One such way is to support HR40, which calls for reparations to Black citizens due to US slavery.

I agree with Biss that we confuse whiteness with ownership. We own. We save. We hoard. We accumulate zeros and stockpile things. We financially plan. We thrift. We are good stewards. We are fiscally responsible. We give and donate under the illusion that what we have belongs to us. We own the violence of transaction. We inherit the myth of white generosity.

What I want to say here is if it is possible to own—if we can own things, and parcels of the earth, and the earth's living beings—then we can convince ourselves it is possible to own people and their labor. It is the owning and controlling of wombs and the humans in whom they reside that allowed the privatization of land. It is the owning and controlling of human bodies and land that propelled colonization. It is the owning and controlling of private property that encouraged chattel slavery and free market capitalism and let the ideology of racism root in our psyches.

I'm guessing that few of us today would say that we believe in the Doctrine of Discovery, but maybe we kind of do. After all, the myth of ownership implies that we deserve it. We deserve to own what we have. If not gifted by divine mandate (as prosperity gospel* preaches), then we must have earned it (as bootstrap ideology has taught†). Leftover from mercantilism and colonization, both prosperity gospel and bootstrap ideology erase histories of exploitation, violence, and harm. At the risk of confounding metaphors, these modern-day takes convince us that the shoe is indeed ours. Not only do they have us thinking we are entitled to owning other people's labor, we have also become delusional about the worth of our own.

My editor asked me when reviewing this chapter: Is white guilt a form of labor? Well, it does take some effort to sustain, and it is easily monetized. Our philanthropic system has certainly modeled how to

---

* The prosperity gospel teaches that God promises prosperity (such as financial wealth and good health) to believers.

† Bootstrap ideology references the American Dream myth that one can get ahead in the US by pulling oneself up by one's own bootstraps and that success comes from hard work and individualism rather than from the biggest determinant of being born into wealth.

monetize white guilt for tax breaks and a return while keeping the wicked webs systemically entrenched.

But I think white guilt, like prosperity gospel and bootstrap ideology, is mostly a distraction. I mean, we could choose to indulge our inner white-guilt diva, just as we could choose to believe that owning nice clothes means we're godly and home ownership is something we've made happen all on our own.

Or we could get organized instead.

RECLAIMING OUR LABOR

In general, people want to live and prefer not to contract terrifying illnesses.

That either one or the other were made to be the exclusive options during a global pandemic is a testimony to the success of the shoe-lace's double knot, because work or death hadn't need be the only options available in a country with the vast wealth of the US. Instead of investing in the lives of workers, children, and the elderly, the US government opted to spend extraordinary amounts of money on backing and bailing out corporations.[*]

Though many politicians in the pandemic's early days used the language of sacrificing workers for the "health of the economy,"[†]

---

[*] Other countries decided to provide their citizens with enough income to ease the financial pressure of taking such unnecessary risks. This strategy of subsidizing corporate interests when their business models fail at the cost of providing preventive care to the citizenry is consistent with government strategies of the early 2000s. Today we are experiencing the echoes of bank bailouts and the refusal to adequately fund health care for all, to name only two instances of racist capitalism that have occurred in my lifetime.

[†] For example, Texas Lt. Governor Dan Patrick told Fox News that old people should volunteer to die to save the economy. In an interview, Indiana congressman Trey Hollingsworth said, regarding people dying as a result of reopening the economy ASAP: "It is policymakers' decision to put on our big boy and big girl pants and say, 'This is the lesser of these two evils'" (Levin, "Dr. Oz Is Sorry You Were Offended by His Comment That It's Fine for 2–3% of Schoolchildren to Die").

particularly disturbing was the rhetoric around sacrificing children.* The language about sacrificing some for the good of most also implied that there are humans both deserving and undeserving of sacrifice. Pitting groups of people against each other—vaccinated vs. unvaccinated, deserving vs. undeserving, children vs. teachers—is both a throwback to the divide-and-conquer of the witch hunts and a demonstration of callousness to the sanctity of human life, one we've been developing over hundreds of years.

Within a diversity of tactics, labor union organizing is a way that workers have come together to reclaim their labor and collective labor power. In the wake of the Covid-19 pandemic, labor organizing is one means of solidarity that's been making a comeback.

Beginning in 2021, headlines featuring the "Great Resignation," first coined by Texas A&M professor Anthony Klotz, quickly spread as news pundits puzzled over where it was coming from, how bad was it, and how employers could be bolstered to stem its tide. Some blamed recent stimulus and unemployment benefits for low-wage workers, who had become "so comfortable" that they would prefer "sitting at home" to being exploited at their service jobs. Others pointed to the stress of the pandemic, increased risk, and lack of health care as factors driving workers away from certain jobs. Some pushed for the Great Resignation to be thought of as job-switching and early retirement† rather than workers resigning en masse. No matter how pundits tried to explain it, it was clear that workers were increasingly willing to do something about their dissatisfaction.

And labor union organizing has emerged within well-known corporations in which such organizing has been unprecedented. Since

---

* In an interview, television personality Dr. Oz nonchalantly suggested sacrificing 2–3 percent of children: "First, we need our mojo back. Let's start with things that are really critical to the nation where we think we might be able to open without getting into a lot of trouble. I tell ya, schools are a very appetizing opportunity. I just saw a nice piece in *The Lancet* arguing the opening of schools may only cost us 2 to 3 percent, in terms of total mortality. Any, you know, any life is a life lost, but…that might be a trade-off some folks would consider" (Levin).

† See this December 2021 article in the *Atlantic*: https://www.theatlantic.com/ ideas/archive/2021/12/great-resignation-myths-quitting-jobs/620927/.

the pandemic began, workers have been engaging in their right to organize—and winning. According to investigative journalist J. Dale Shoemaker, "October 2021 came to be known as 'striketober' because tens of thousands of hospital and industrial workers walked off the job."[29] With a surge in union petitions,[30] the past three years have seen big victories for Starbucks, Amazon, and Apple employees. As Shoemaker notes, "With regard to race, Black and Brown people are leading the union wave." An Economic Policy Institute report documented that new members have almost exclusively been Black.[31] Those most impacted are leading the charge.

Despite the hardships of recent years (and decades, centuries, and millennia) I feel buoyed by these recent wins. It reinforces how critical it is to know our history so that we don't repeat it. Mercantilism and colonization may have readied the working poor for exploitation and expanded the ruling class's access to labor beyond the geographical confines of Europe, but that second bunny-eared knot of capitalism and racism is what has successfully sustained the worship of profit, the callousness for human life, and the blame on individual and cultural idleness, which our earlier knots began. It is that second knot of capitalism and racism we must learn to untie if we are not to repeat and further reinforce these histories.

There is much more I could say about how the wicked webs have been revealed in the era of Covid-19. There is much more to say about how profit continues to override the sanctity of human life, how a few very wealthy benefit from the violence done to many, and about the suffering of those who are most harmed.

In the early days of the Covid-19 pandemic, the rich in Paris and New York City fled to their summer homes while the poor, institutionalized, and incarcerated were (sometimes literally) entombed in cities, nursing homes, and prisons. Like the deep-seated racism revealed by 45's election, these disparities have existed since before this country's founding. However, moments like elections and the global pandemic expose to the rest of us that which many already know—that is, if we're willing to take a look.

As I reflect on the early days of Covid, I remember a moment at the very beginning, a portal so to speak, as the first few fatalities were named. It was a moment in which I noticed, and maybe you did too, how we were able to see the death of a body as belonging to a fellow human, before the numbers got so large we ceased to empathize and before the narratives and misinformation poured in to fill the gap. And even though in that early moment we were afraid and uncertain, there was a feeling that the person contracting the ambiguous disease could be you or me or my parents or friends. Before the mechanisms of profit rationalized human sacrifice, before my dad began to scoff at mask-wearing and refused to get vaccinated, there was a moment when he, too, prioritized the health of his employees, family, and friends. There was a moment, however brief, when the pandemic had the full attention of our humanity.

As we move between the metaphors of trauma here, as we note the devaluation of life and of reproductive labor, the disconnect of body from mind and the white-woman overwhelm of never being enough, as we question the myth of ownership and control and the guilt that comes with knowing we have what others don't, as we move toward the invention of white womanhood and all the harms that came from it, can we recall the full attention of our humanity?

CHAPTER FOUR

WHITEWASHING BODIES

Perfectionism is the voice of the oppressor, the enemy of the people.
—Anne Lamott

W hen I was fifteen, I spent a semester starving myself in France. Highly influenced by white feminine beauty standards but also driven by an adolescent religious zeal to be perfect in the eyes of God, I was at the height of my overachievement. While the stress of being an exchange student propelled my symptoms, I had learned to hate myself and my body long before I left home.

I remember one particular moment in second grade. It happened during my last year at that school before I transferred to the "more challenging" one across the train tracks. The class lined up against the painted concrete walls as we did every day. A classmate kicked at the wall while trying to climb it. One of my two white girl friends giggled and pointed his way. I remember having to look down to see her expression. When had she become so small? We used to see eye to eye. Then I looked down at my belly, critical of its curve for the first time. When I looked up again, I noticed how my friends' scrawny legs barely took up any space inside their shorts. I looked down at my thighs, which touched the edges. A wave of shame rolled over and through my prepubescent body.

This was the first of many moments that compiled as time advanced: the curiosity of hair under my arms and between my legs, the rolls of pudge beneath my soccer uniform, the month I experienced my first migraine and my first menstrual flow. Instead of a constant build, these moments of bodily shame came interspersed between perfecting my good little white girl act and the reckless abandon of just being me.

My friends began noticing body things too, and since I was without the guidance of an older sibling, I relied on them and their older siblings to teach me cool and beautiful. By seventh grade, I had finally arrived. My friend circle was secure and so was the body-hating.

I remember one time at the mall when we were trying on bathing suits—two-piece suits, to be precise. My friend commented disparagingly that her stomach wasn't flat. She wished it was more like mine. I was unable to receive her self-effacing compliment. My thoughts were occupied by disdain for my thighs. Even if I had appreciated my curves, I knew better than to take the compliment given the unspoken rules of the dressing room. To make her feel better, I had to join in the game of reassurance to confirm to her as well as to myself that we were peers in our insecurities. I responded with one of my stock retorts, "Sure my waist is small, but I've got to do something about these thighs!"

It was a competition of sorts—beauty followed self-loathing and its performance. In addition to my friend groups, there were the magazines and TV shows of the '90s, pop stars, and fashion models to confirm the skinny white ideal. The fashion billboard I saw daily from the back of the minivan on the way to school featured a menu of new advertisements, all depicting models who were equally emaciated. I knew I had a lot of work to do. Suddenly attraction had mutated into a thing with social currency, and I felt as though I had nothing but lack.

But while the tools of attraction were new to me in their social currency, the narratives had been carved into my psyche since my day of birth. The '80s and early '90s anthems of commercialized racist patriarchy commodified my white-girl existence and infiltrated my mind. *The Little Mermaid, Cinderella, Snow White,* and *Beauty and the Beast* were the teachers in my white-girl schooling. Thin, pretty, and pale. Pure, peppy, and righteous. Smart enough to know when to let a (white) man take charge. Pretty enough to command his attention. Savvy enough to sway his devotion. Beauty, brains, and charm constructed the holy trinity of white woman winning. The implicit goal was to attract, catch, and keep a (white) man, preferably one with money, preferably one with style, preferably one with good looks.

This calculated US marketing of courtship rituals to white women has a history that predates Disney princesses and romantic comedy. Its formula was baked into the plantation era. As Kathleen M. Brown observes, courtship was an unusual opportunity for elite young women to flip the power relationship present in white family dynamics:

> Courtship's liminality offered an unparalleled chance to intervene in the course of her own life and influence the men in it. A woman could reject a suitor, shattering fragile egos and blasting family pretentions. She might also influence her father to accept a man he would otherwise consider unworthy.[1]

This time in a white woman's life marked a singular culturally approved moment to dissent from the white men in her world. Her liminal power was derived from her ability to attract, reject, and ultimately accept the best white man suitor/provider/savior—a message we continue to teach our daughters two hundred years later. Let the Disney choir and rom-com crowd testify that good little white girl dreams are made from the illusion that we just want to be saved.

Of course, the savior effect reaches deeper into the mindset of those of us raised in this Christian nation. Prince Charming is not just the answer to fairy-tale happiness; in the warped patriarchal violence of white supremacy, he is God.

MY BODY BROKEN FOR YOU

In my generation of growing materialism—the disconnect of object from maker, consumer from consumed, owner from owned—the modern revival tent wooed the souls of Christian kids like me. By

revival tent, I mean the arenas, convention centers, and nondenom-
inational megachurches whose Jesus-themed rock concerts, highly
produced light shows, and (always) attractive worship teams led our
small band of visiting youth through a phenomenal circus of sensuous
attraction, suspense, doubt, guilt, fear, altar call and response, release,
and soothing lullaby of assured rightness. *Whew!* An emotional, spir-
it-full answer to the emptiness of white, middle-class (sub)urban life
that plagued our souls.

While many of my classmates looked to drugs, sex, and alcohol
to combat the loneliness, I hid in church. Church felt safer and was
more convenient. It also offered something I did not readily encounter
in the frenetic halls of high school or the fast-moving currents of
Atlanta highway: belonging.

While it is easy to see more clearly in retrospect, my church experience is and was nuanced and full of contradictions. In church I found
both the spaciousness of expression and the denial of self. I felt intense
belonging and severe rejection. I knew freedom and oppression. It
was in my small home congregation that I was encouraged to lead.
I led at the piano. I led worship. I led singing. I performed. I read. I
played. I knew everyone. I wore bright dresses and an array of fancy
hats. My eccentricity was nurtured, my brightness loved. Growing
up, I was as loud and assertive as I wanted to be.

And throughout those same years, I learned to repress and deny.
I learned to intentionally and then later less intentionally ignore
the small voice of wisdom within. I learned to accept the dismissal
of my boundaries. I learned to self-censor, compartmentalize,
and hide.

Also during second grade, we learned the story of Esther in Sunday
school. Finally, a female biblical character with agency! Finally, a
protagonist with whom I could identify! In my loudly relational way,
I let every adult in sight know how thrilled I was that there was
a book in the bible written by a woman. Turns out not. An elder
in the church, also my friend's grandpa, was quick to correct my
nonsense. The story of Esther was not written by a woman, he said

matter-of-factly; in fact, there were *no* books in the bible written by women. And why would I expect such a thing?

Not all bible stories are created equal. Devastation. Ultimate betrayal. How could a community that nurtured my gifts undermine me so severely? I know I am not the only one with this story.

My therapist and I (well, mainly just I) have been considering what makes me feel safe in relationships. The quick answer is that I feel safe when there is space in the relationship for me to be fully myself. At church, I learned that this is always a compromise, that there were things to be loud and things to be silent about. At church I learned to settle. I learned my place as a girl and as a woman. I learned that God does not reflect me and so it is impossible for me to be a full reflection of this God.

Yet despite this betrayal on the precipice of the age of reason, I doubled down on devotion. I committed to a religious zeal to please this God through perfection and the perfection of intention. I committed to loving this God by being the best, kindest, purest, smartest, holiest, most self-disciplined, fittest, most flawless young (white) woman possible. Maybe I could make up for my deficits through zealous devotion. This commitment consumed my mind, resulting in continuous obsessive thoughts and compulsive behaviors as I attempted to starve myself into holy perfection and into those size 4 jeans that would help me attract the ideal hybrid of Prince Charming and Jesus.

Perfectionism is a hallmark of white culture. It is also both a manifestation and a root of eating disorders. My racial socialization into whiteness declared perfection (in the form of a white, middle-class, able-bodied beauty ideal) the desired end goal with inhumane levels of self-control as the desired means to achieve it. However, my predilection toward self-harm through anorexia, bulimia, and the abuse of diet pills and exercise came from an internalization of patriarchy and misogyny that taught me to objectify, assess, and hate bodies deemed similar to mine. In other words, I acted out the violent tools of white supremacy on my own gendered body.

Eating disorders are endemic to white womanhood.* But that collective nature wasn't something I was thinking about as I suffered in silence,
wandering the halls of adolescence feeling awkwardly inadequate and
trying to make myself small. In my daily obsession of counting calories
and avoiding social eating, I was convinced that this struggle was mine
alone. I self-isolated. I guarded my secret with lies. Although in retrospect, I mostly was lying to myself about its secrecy. (Those around me
who cared suspected something was up.) I found both comfort and
contempt in the way the eating disorder made me special.

Then one evening, my mother, brother, father, and I found ourselves
sitting around a small, dimly lit therapy room. A few months before, I
had worked up the courage to ask for help. The eating disorder that had
once made me feel so in control was beginning to control me, and I was
scared. I walked into the family room where my mother was reading
the paper, and told her everything. As one of those who had suspected
something was up, she heard me and immediately mobilized.

My parents were able to get me a spot in an area outpatient
program. After school, my days filled up with appointments. I saw
an individual therapist and a nutritionist, attended meal groups, and
got to choose from other therapy groups—art therapy was my favorite.
The program required all patients still living with their family of
origin to attend family therapy sessions, too, which is how the four
of us ended up in this small, dimly lit room with its neutral colors
and an abundance of throw pillows.

I remember this particular session because of what the therapist said.
I've filed this memory away in a very special folder labeled "Moments
That Turned My Horizon Upside Down." I don't remember
if it was the first or the last of our sessions. I don't remember the

---

* While eating disorders may be endemic to white womanhood, "skinny white
affluent girls" are not the only people to have them. In fact, People of Color are
half as likely to be diagnosed or receive treatment as their white counterparts
(Sonneville and Lipson, "Disparities in Eating Disorder Diagnosis and Treatment
according to Weight Status, Race/Ethnicity, Socioeconomic Background, and Sex
among College Students"). Nonwhite groups are also underrepresented in eating
disorder research (Burke, Egbert, Hunt, Mathis, and Williams, "Reporting Racial
and Ethnic Diversity in Eating Disorder Research over the Past 20 Years").

context of the conversation. I don't remember much at all about that evening (except that my thirteen-year-old brother clearly wanted to be someplace else). But at some point, our therapist paused the conversation to share a bit of extraordinary information. "You know," she said, "the person who has the eating disorder is carrying a symptom of a problem that belongs to the whole family. There is a greater family issue that's happening here. Amanda just happens to be sensitive to it."

I don't remember if her words impacted anyone else in our small circle, but as I let her words sink in, I felt some relief. It wasn't all my fault. Her words, at this pivotal moment in my life, began to break open my perspective: This eating disorder was not the result of my individual failure or even a unique affliction; it was a symptom of the greater dis-ease of my family, community, and culture. Now I see it as a normal, human response to the toxicity of the wicked webs, a result of the trauma of Mistress Syndrome. I share my story because it is my experience, but also because it highlights these patterns. Having an eating disorder was one socially reinforced way that I coped with what I'd inherited.

Patriarchy's objectification, sexualization, and control of gendered bodies, coupled with Christianity's limiting role for women as chaste (yet still perfectly attractive) mothers, wives, and daughters, contributed to my negative self/body image and unrealistic cookie-cutter anatomical goals that pitted me against other women and against my body. Anxiety led me to starve, stuff, and purge my body, to self-police my white-womanness. I regret all the mental and emotional energy I put into my self-destruction. And yet my body resisted. I am still learning resistance. Turns out these hips are here to stay.

FROM WITCHES TO WHITENESS

Long before Disney princesses and the modern epidemic of eating disorders, white feminine beauty was being fashioned through the institution of slavery. In *The History of White People*, author and historian Nell Irvin Painter traces the history of enslavement before it became synonymous with Blackness. While the extreme multigenerational brutality of chattel slavery is a uniquely American invention,[2] its institutional foundation was laid in the eras of Greek and Roman rule throughout Europe and the Mediterranean, which helped normalize the politics of domination.

Emerging in prominence after the fall of the Roman Empire, the Viking system of slavery had two distinct forms, which Painter identifies as either associated with brute physical labor or "valued for sex and gendered as female."[3] Throughout Europe, sex slavery became a profitable business.* To be closer to female—or at least further removed from an embodied masculinity—was also to be ownable. As Painter describes it, "Eunuchs were also a facet of the business."[4]

The ideals around sex slavery that linked forced sex, youth, gender, and Europeanness took hold in fifteenth-century Europe, and, as Painter notes, "This union of servitude and beauty would endure in the European imagination."[5]

And endure it did. The association of physical attractiveness with submission and sexual availability crept into the prevailing sciences of the time through that historically dominant instrument of academic rigor: a European man's preferences. From 1600 to 1900, several race "scientists" constructed racial stratifications from their own evaluation of desire in order to rank and control gendered bodies. Painter describes how "scientist" after "scientist" relied on a beauty ideal that had been established in the fetishization of sex slaves. The terms Georgian, Circassian, and Caucasian, all names at the time for people groups from the Caucasus Mountain region,[†] became interchangeable references for the young, enslaved white women of the idealized harem.[‡]

---

* Sex slavery even set the standard for money, as in Ireland where "a female slave represented a unit of currency, like a dollar or a euro" (Painter, *The History of White People*, 36).

† Notably from those same geographic regions as Gimbutas's Kurgans.

‡ As in this 1810 account in *Travels in Various Countries of Europe, Asia, and Africa* by Edward Daniel Clarke: "[Circassian] women are the most beautiful perhaps in the world; of enchanting perfection of features, and very delicate complexions. The females that we saw were all of them the accidental captives of war, who had been carried off together with their families; they were, however, remarkably handsome" (Clarke quoted in Painter, *The History of White People*, 50).

Johann Friedrich Blumenbach, the European responsible for naming white people as "Caucasian," candidly linked Caucasian to beauty. In the late 1700s, Blumenbach used these mythologized beauty standards, along with a creepy obsession with collecting and measuring skulls, to justify a racial hierarchy that placed (spoiler alert!) Caucasian at the top.[*]

But even skull measuring—the supposedly scientific part of his methodology—couldn't escape a direct connection to sex slavery. As Painter writes, the notorious skull that Blumenbach used to name the entire "Caucasian Race"

> came from a Georgian woman the Russian forces had taken captive, precisely the kind of situation figuring in so many descriptions of beautiful Caucasian and Circassian women: as an archetype, she is a pitiful captive lovely in her subjection.... *Ironically, perhaps, the woman whose skull gave white people a name had been a sex slave* in Moscow, like thousands of her compatriots in Russia and the Ottoman empire.[6] (emphasis added)

The skull used to justify whiteness as superior and thus associated with freedom was that of an enslaved adolescent European woman. Embedded in the earliest schema for race was a patriarchal economy determining value and controlling access to human bodies based on sexualized beauty standards.

Which leads us into our shoelace double-knot: the institutionalization of racism and its partner in crime, capitalism. The fetishization of sex slaves—which originated as a commodification of European women—was relocated in the enslavement of women of African descent. Brown points out that during the eighteenth century, words

---

[*] Alongside Blumenbach, the field of racial pseudoscience is crowded with European men arranging and rearranging humanity. Collectively, they came up with a wide array of often contradictory schema for human taxonomy, with two, three, four, five, six, and at times, seven racial varieties of humans. The number of categories and the geographic regions associated with those categories would be drawn and redrawn over time based on European colonialist politics and the requirements of white supremacy.

previously reserved for lower-class English women, such as "wenches," became associated with enslaved women of African descent as they "began gradually to shoulder the economic and symbolic burden formerly carried by English servant women."[7]

While eighteenth-century "scientists" developed theories of race to justify historic and ongoing European racism, the emergence of whiteness a century before had granted even the poorest of European women a track toward "good wife" status. Notably, good (white) wife status existed in codependency with its contrast. The pedestal carved uniquely for white women upheld an idealized standard of beauty while disembodying them from sexuality. Like the Madonna, white women gained status from the contradictory requirements of chaste virgin/attractive ideal/fertile bearer of (white) progeny. The closer Black womanhood became associated with wickedness, lasciviousness, and immorality, the closer white womanhood came to holiness, chastity, and purity. These fundamental ideals became culturally embedded in American aesthetics *and* in its institutional foundation. At the end of the day, these cultural beauty standards were about control. They still are.

Almost two centuries before Blumenbach theorized race in Germany, the British founded the colony of Virginia during a time of intense allegiance to patriarchy—and as Brown observes, anxious ones at that. Possibly, the need to reinforce this narrative of British male superiority was heightened by the reality: finding a European woman to subordinate in early seventeenth-century Virginia proved difficult.

While large numbers of European men had been brought as laborers to the early British colonies, markedly fewer European servant women had made the trek. In the book *Birth of a White Nation*, scholar Jacqueline Battalora notes that for every seven adult men, there was only one woman in the Virginian colony.[8] Due to this dynamic, "a woman could likely have her pick."[9] And many did. Frequently, European servant women chose African men; in 1660, one county reported that one-quarter of all children born to English servant women had joint African and European ancestry.[10] Unlike the antimiscegenation sentiments later imposed by the British elite, these marriages between similarly classed people were widely accepted and commonplace.

But this was not to last; after all, women having their pick flies in the face of whiteness and the European patriarchy that preceded it. Beginning in 1640, a series of laws were constructed to differentiate Europeans from their African and Indigenous counterparts. Many of these laws specifically targeted reproductive labor and other forms of labor in gendered ways, ultimately carving out separate legal, economic, political, and social spheres for women based on their race.

The ways that race and racism became institutionalized in what would become the United States of America was not a gender-neutral endeavor. Instead, similar to European colonization in West Africa, US concepts of race and racism also carried a gendered dynamic. If we are seeking to end oppression as white women, then it is important that we interconnectedly seek this.

As we work our way through history toward legal whiteness, we can see how the colonial government began to codify race on gendered terms. The colony of Virginia created a separate, gendered tax category reserved exclusively for women who would soon become white. In 1643, and further legislated in the decades that followed, the Virginia Assembly required a tax on African women that was consistent with the tax on English men ages sixteen to sixty and on all African men.[11] With this new law, English women became the only category of women who were tax-exempt and, rather than being taxed for their labor, they were instead classified as dependents (both servants and free) along with (English) children and old men. As Brown puts it, "The distinction between English and African women created a legal fiction about their different capacities for performing agricultural labor."[12]

The consequences were immediate. Rather than advantage individual English women with economic independence, the tax exemption privileged English women above their non-English counterparts in exchange for their dependence on (racist) patriarchy. In the eyes of the law, English women (soon to be labeled white) became considered "physically weak and economically dependent."[13] Like in earlier efforts to devalue and invisibilize women's reproductive labor, this new good-wife status came with conditions. As Brown describes:

> Few English women actually benefited from their own tax exemptions. Even when single, they often lived in households of masters and fathers who owned their labor and paid their taxes. English women's privileges usually translated into gains for [mostly white] men who benefited from female labor.[14]

This economic bias for English women had other consequences too. It incentivized free African men to marry tax-exempt English women rather than African women, creating a major obstacle for African women to achieve good-wife status since, according to Brown:

> The tax on the labor of African and Afro-Virginian women was one of the first obstacles black people faced if they wished to achieve the patriarchal family forms that conferred social standing upon white people. These taxes similarly made the large family lineages of West Africa more costly and difficult to attain.[15]

Then, in 1662—turning back centuries of British common law in the service of racism—Virginia made the status of a child (whether enslaved or free) inheritable based on that of their mother. Under British common law, land, child custody, and inheritance had all flowed through lines of paternity; now, horridly, slaveholders became financially incentivized to systematically rape enslaved African women. The children begot through such rape would no longer follow their British paternal line as a responsibility of and inheritor to their father's name, property, and status (as free). Instead, these children would become his property.

   In addition to the traumatic legacy of institutionalizing the rape of Black women, this law delegitimized Black parenthood by simultaneously relocating parental authority of Black children to enslavers while erasing evidence of their white paternity. Enslaved women found their children, along with their productive and reproductive labor, legally entitled to their slaveholder in perpetuity.

It was on Black women's bodies that racism was thoroughly codified. Clearly, I am not the first to name this. Black women and femmes have been pointing this out since racism's inception and have been resisting every step of the way. Created by Black women and femmes, the Reproductive Justice Movement* is one recent manifestation of centuries of organizing by those who know the embodied horror of racism most intimately.

This gruesome history has something to teach us about the sexualized and gendered violence of racism and about our positioning within it. What did incentivizing and legitimizing the systemic rape of African women mean for European women and their reproductive labor? How did it carve out a pedestal for white womanhood built from the dehumanization of Black womanhood?

As with all things racialized, there is a flip side to the coin. Battalora describes how these laws desexualized British (soon to be white) women, making them "the only possible production site of 'pure' British (eventually white) children,"[16] while at the same time repositioning African women as both hypersexualized and masculinized laborers.

Perhaps it is helpful for us to reconceptualize Federici's "devaluation and feminization of reproductive labor" at this point in history as the devaluation and *racialization* of reproductive labor. This devaluation of motherhood in Black women glorified an idealized virgin

---

* According to the National Black Women's Reproductive Justice Agenda, "Reproductive Justice means the human right to control our sexuality, our gender, our work, and our reproduction. That right can only be achieved when all women and girls have the complete economic, social, and political power and resources to make healthy decisions about our bodies, our families, and our communities in all areas of our lives" ("Reproductive Justice").

As a reminder, this book is not a substitute for accounts and analyses that center the perspectives of Black women; it is a complement. There is a tremendous wealth of resources, work, and wisdom that has been created from centuries of intellectual, emotional, spiritual, and embodied labor by Black women, often unpaid and underrecognized. Please, seek out their work with compensation.

motherhood in white women, ultimately creating very specific, very different, yet entirely interdependent functions for the wombs of Black and white people based on race.

Another major legal development happened as both Virginia and Maryland turned their focus to the sexuality of English or freeborn women by passing laws in the late seventeenth century that targeted these marriageable women, who were still in short supply. After enslavement was made inheritable through the bodies of African women and after Bacon's Rebellion,* which challenged the ruling class's rule, in 1681 the word "white" was first used to describe a distinct legal category of humans. As Battalora points out, legal whiteness was wielded to regulate the sexuality of "Freeborn English and other whites,"[17] notably legislating who so-called white women could marry (i.e., have sex with, have children with, be family to): not African or Native men. At its very inception, the legal category of white was invented as a means of patriarchal control. Battalora identifies this 1681 law as the legal invention of "white" people: "This moment in history does not reflect a genetic mutation that is linked to a race called 'whites'; it represents the need of elites within the colonies to control large masses of laborers, and their desire to have greater access to women."[18]

Eventually antimiscegenation laws† would later prohibit *both* white men and women from marrying nonwhite people. However,

---

* During Bacon's Rebellion, an armed coalition made up of Europeans and Africans challenged the English ruling class. I will go into more detail about Bacon's Rebellion when I talk about toxic (white) masculinity in chapter nine.

† It was at a PISAB workshop where I first heard historian and core trainer Dr. Michael Washington journey through A. Leon Higginbotham Jr.'s book *In the Matter of Color*. In an hour, Dr. Washington painted a bone-chilling picture of the road to the invention of race, how European indentured servants and enslaved Africans had at one point lived, married, raised families, and resisted the oppressive class hierarchy side by side. But what stood out for me long after the cloud of the training passed was Dr. Washington's description of the introduction of antimiscegenation laws soon after Bacon's Rebellion sparked the fear of lower-class revolt. These scholars showed me something that white feminism has failed to highlight for hundreds of years: baked into the very construction of race is a Euro-centric gender hierarchy that was leveraged to keep the European class arrangement in place.

as Battalora points out, these laws were, with very few exceptions, only enforced for white women, rendering white women exclusively available to white men and subsequently *all* women available to white men. At that same time, patriarchal privileges (like carrying firearms) were stripped from men of African descent and members of Native tribes, centering patriarchal power solely within white men.

It is here that we begin to see the effectiveness of the double-knotted shoelace strategy.

In those early years of shoe tying, in haste or laziness, I might have made the first looped knot before running off to play with friends, anxious about being left behind. But as I got wiser, I learned that a single knot inevitably cut into my play time. Similarly, while one knot might have eventually come untied, it was the invention of race and the institutionalization of racist economics through a capitalist system that made the wicked webs so wicked strong. As a control mechanism, this double knot has served the elite of this country incredibly well.

Approximately one hundred years after the word "white" first appeared in Virginia colonial law, the United States of America was founded on the premise of inherent white superiority. While on paper, the Constitution professed "liberty and justice for all," the intention of this country at its onset was not for those ideals to be realized. While elements of the colonial divide-and-conquer strategy that invented "white" people and institutionalized racism have morphed and become more sophisticated over time, the cocktail of shiny rewards and looming threats is still in this country's original recipe.

As key ingredients in Mistress Syndrome, the devaluation and racialization of reproductive labor morphed our social positioning in some pretty gnarly ways. The mistresses of the plantation, the elevated mothers of racist wealth's inheritors, would not have been needed without those subjugated to be inherited. As Battalora writes, "black women's reproduction advanced the property value of the plantation while English women's reproduction ensured 'pure' inheritors of this property."[19] Just as today, the purity of the wealthy (white) Christian suburban soccer mom would not exist without the promiscuity of the (Black) poor welfare queen.

THE FORGETTING OF FEMINISM

The history of race is certainly about the control of bodies, but it is also about the control of minds. Much more successful than childhood corporal punishment were purple princess tutus, Sunday school promises of heaven, chore sticker charts, and A-pluses.

Throughout the course of my lifetime, these wicked webs did not need witch hunts or enslavement or antimiscegenation laws; all they needed was for me and my Mistress Syndrome to perform as (pre)programmed. That's not to say that violence hasn't been used at times to keep me in line. It has.* But in the aftermath of my few and relatively limited encounters with physical and sexualized violence, I was not incited to overthrow the tables of whiteness. If anything, I doubled down on good little white girl/nice white lady in order to try to keep myself safe.

When #MeToo began to appear in the social media spaces I frequented, it took me a couple days to post anything even though I had long accepted that I, too, had had some of those experiences. As I read the wave of #MeToo posts pouring into my feeds, I felt a sense of power, and then overwhelm and confusion. I both wanted and didn't want to be a part of the collective experience. I wondered if my experiences were serious enough to merit a public post, and if, as a white woman, I would be appropriating #MeToo's intent.

#MeToo is a social movement that was started in 2006 by Tarana Burke to create solidarity and empathy among young Black women and girls as survivors of sexual assault. Originally intended by Burke as a way to build "empowerment through empathy"[20] among some of the most marginalized, #MeToo went viral as well-known celebrities went public to call out sexual violence, beginning with Alyssa Milano in 2017.

---

* In addition to the ways white women are vulnerable to gendered and sexualized violence, white women are also not exempt from state violence when challenging the wicked webs. Heather Heyer and Rachel Corrie are two such white women who lost their lives for participating in nonviolent resistance movements alongside countless numbers of nonwhite victims of state violence.

While not diminishing the very real impact of those celebrities' #MeToo experiences—or mine—it's worth considering how race, class, and gender can shape our experiences of sexual violence and our capacity to respond to it. It's worth considering how (white) feminist movements have missed these intersections and thus been ineffective at untying the double knot.* In general, white feminist strategies have tragically misunderstood how sexism is impacted by whiteness (and transphobia, classism, etc.). As I will continue to discuss, white feminism has historically tried to mitigate the impacts of sexism by leveraging racism. Ironically, tightening the wicked webs' racist double knot makes it more difficult for us to untie its initial one. Our historical ignorance has us reinforcing the sexism we say we are against.

At the very least, foregoing intersectional sexism has made us exclusionary and thus ineffective (in excluding those closest to the problems, we are also excluding those closest to the solutions†). One recent memorable example of white feminist exclusion was how, in the wake of 45's election, white women all over the US zealously began crocheting pink pussy hats without considering that not all people with pussies have pink ones.

These criticisms of feminism may be difficult to hear. They might initiate feelings of the 4Ds. While I had early exposure to Black feminist and womanist thinkers, I also found deep resonance with writings I read after college by white feminists of the '80s and '90s. The words of Sue Monk Kidd and Riane Eisler gave me the courage and information to begin challenging the patriarchal Christian traditions in which I was raised. They described feelings I had felt deep in my body and spirit but had not known how to name.

My intention is to move into these discussions of white feminism holding the both/and: we can both respect those who have come

---

* See resources like Rafia Zakariah's *Against White Feminism* and others in Resources for Further Support.

† The phrase "Those closest to the problems are also closest to the solutions" is often referenced in activist spaces. It is derived from a similarly worded quote by Glenn E. Martin: "People closest to the problem are closest to the solution but furthest from power and resources" (@glennEmartin).

before us and be critical of them. We can recognize the efforts of our movement elders while also acknowledging the ways the wicked webs limited their perspectives, strategies, and lives. We can work to get more and more specific about how these wicked webs function and stay in place and we can get specific about our roles in it.

In not being nuanced about race, one thing white feminism has missed is how the existence of modern white womanhood relies on a careful psychological cocktail of shiny rewards and looming threats. White womanhood grants us an elusive promise of safety, of progress, of ultimate and indefinite security. And while there are real, tangible advantages (economic, physical, psychological, emotional) to white womanhood, those are only advantages in comparison to the fatal disadvantages of nonwhite womanhood. Without the threat of nonwhite womanhood, would we be so committed to its costs?

The somber reality is that white women have sold out our bodies, minds, and souls in order to play the game of imperialist white-supremacist capitalist patriarchy. Our legitimacy depends on delegitimizing others. Just as beauty, brains, and charm constitute the holy trinity of white-woman winning, so too must ugliness, stupidity, and immorality prop up its contrast. The sleeping princess needs a wicked witch, the innocent daughter an evil stepmother. These white feminine ideals exist only because of the dehumanization and violence done to Black, Indigenous, and other women of color and their bodies and that is something to mourn.

Modern gynecology and white feminism's pro-choice arm are elbow-deep in Black women's blood. I have a personal connection to professional obstetrics—my grandfather left his Amish Mennonite agricultural inheritance to practice medicine in Appalachia, and several in my mother's generation followed in practicing medicine. So, I come to this history having generationally profited from the profession, a legacy with secrets and practitioners about which and whom I am just beginning to learn.

Perhaps most notorious in this bloody history is James Marion Sims, the "father of modern gynecology," who performed torturous procedures and surgeries throughout the 1800s on enslaved Black women without anesthesia and operated under the racist notion that Black people did not feel pain. Many patients died as a result. We only know the names of three of his patients: Lucy, Anarcha, and Betsey.* Lucy, Anarcha, and Betsey, among many unnamed others, are the reasons we have gynecology today.

This grotesque history didn't end with slavery. Margaret Sanger, the founder of Planned Parenthood and early twentieth-century champion of birth control, had deep roots in the eugenics movement, which supported the forced sterilization of people the movement deemed "unfit" to reproduce, including people with disabilities and People of Color.

Sometimes, we white women forget this history. We forget that the construction of our womanhood and motherhood has been, from its foundation, a racialized arrangement. We forget there is no universal womanhood, and yet we try to organize our movements in ways that erase the distinct and critical differences in our relationships to gender due to race.

Sometimes, we white women forget how our racialized history has harmed us. We forget that a pedestal restricts our expression and movement. We forget that a pedestal is not really a safe or a liberatory place to be. We forget that we have been put there as a rallying cry for systems of oppression. We forget—or maybe we've never actually understood—that the pedestal is the problem and that in dismantling it, we will at times feel like we're falling, even though as humans we have the capacity to survive such falls, and to collectively thrive.

RECOVERING FROM PRIVILEGE

The problem with privilege being bestowed is that it can also be withdrawn. I believe that deep down or at least at a subconscious level, we white people know this: the privileges that whiteness and its subsidiary white womanhood bestow are ultimately unearned. It is worth asking: What has this done to our human psyches? For

---

* The *Mothers of Gynecology* monument in Montgomery, Alabama as part of the More Up Campus "honors the sacrifice of Anarcha, Lucy, and Betsey" (More Up Campus, "Anarcha, Lucy, and Betsey | The Mothers of Gynecology").

one thing, the acceptance of unearned privilege comes with an ever-present fear that those advantages could be taken away at any time. (This is so anxiety producing.) Moreover, to receive unearned benefits at the cost of others' disadvantage puts us in the position of having to constantly prove and defend the disparities that we keep, particularly if we believe racial disparities are inherently wrong.

I think the perfectionism, competition, and performative nature of dominant white culture is likewise driven by these feelings of self-doubt and unworthiness. As humans, we want to make sense of our place in the world. We want to know we are worthy. In a consumerist culture that constantly tells us we are not enough, of course we try to find ways to feel like we are.

This way of thinking about psychological distress has something to say about why I used my eating disorder to prove my value to myself and to whiteness. You see, I've always had a hunch I wasn't truly a Disney princess on the inside.

For my fifth birthday, my aunt took me to the Nutcracker Ballet. I picked out a black velvet dress for this very special occasion. It had a fancy collar with white lace and a little pink rosette in the center. I was giddy with excitement. As I got ready, my mother helped me into a pair of white tights and shiny black patent leather shoes. When my aunt and I stepped into the Fabulous Fox Theater, there were bright lights, plush carpets, and children twirling all over the lobby. My aunt bought me a pewter necklace from one of the vendors in the atrium. It came in a precious little round box with a lid and ballet slippers stamped on top. Standing at the vendor's table, I held it close to my chest. I still have it to this day.

At the time, I was taking my first (and last) ballet class. I watched our fuzzy VHS recording of the TV-aired Nutcracker over and over again. I loved the shimmer. I loved the twirling. I spent months spinning around the house mimicking the dancers. After that magical event, imbued with grace and lace, I came back home and ran down our long hallway, aggressively shoving my kid brother into a wall as I rushed to tell my mother how pretty and refined Princess Clara was.

The suspicion that I wasn't really a Disney princess began to seed that same year, when I entered the public school system. The more I conformed to the expectations of the classroom (being quiet unless asked to speak, having the "right" answer, listening to the adult in charge), the more my good little white girl was reaffirmed at school. But six and a half hours of playing good little white girl at school meant a lot of suppression. Sitting still and only speaking at the right time with the right answers was exhausting. I released my loud self-expression the moment I came home.

There were still inopportune times when the pent-up aggression I reserved for home and family broke through. Once on a playdate with a friend, I got angry and threw a chair. The next day she told another friend what had happened. Mortified that my home persona had come out, I didn't know what to do. I have a vague memory of denying it. I certainly wasn't ready to take responsibility for a trait I associated both with my father's masculinity and the sin of violence. Mostly, I was afraid that if my friends discovered this side of me, they would kick me out like those playground witch hunt excommunications.

As I entered middle school, hiding my loud, assertive, and aggressive sides took even more effort. Making myself small by suppressing what I really thought and suppressing my caloric intake helped me contain the growing fury that might erupt in the wrong place at the wrong time. I prayed to God that deep down I would become kind and loving. Perhaps if I could atone for my shortcomings through rigorous self-discipline, then I might be enough—then I just might be worthy of friend circles and Prince Charming Jesus's love.

Harriet Rossetto, founder of the Beit T'Shuvah, a residential treatment center, describes the damage of perfectionism, either/or thinking, and entitlement on children of privilege as a result of "over-parenting, helicopting, [and] indulging our offspring."[21] Rossetto writes about how a culture of privilege has led to a generation who is acting on self-destructive behaviors. Perfectionism is a driving force:

The parents need to produce a "perfect" child, wherein the child's successes are a reflection of the parents' worth. This creates in the child a sense of being a commodity — "valuable but not valued." They alternate between grandiosity and self-loathing or depression, unable to integrate *self* and *self-image*. They live in a paradigm of Either/Or: *I am either No. 1 or a total loser*. Their "self" is fragmented, divided, at war. They keep asking themselves the wrong question: Which is the real me?[22]

I am reflecting on the expectation of performance in an era of social media as I scroll through photos and videos of my adorable nephew that get uploaded weekly to our family's shared drive. Sometimes he plays unaware of the camera's eye, but more often than not, even as an infant, there's something in his gaze that hints at his knowing that he is on stage. His every life phase has been documented by his parents, caregivers, and other family members. And I appreciate the documentation. Did I mention he's adorable? The incessant images have allowed me, his long-distance aunt, to feel connected to his rapid development.

My nephew and I share the experience of double oldest (eldest child to parents and eldest grandchild) so I hope the relentless messages I internalized around the need for external approval won't overrun his psyche the way they did mine. Part of that twisted history we have inherited as white children communicates that we are only valuable in performing perfection. Our merit is conditional and open to judgment by those in power at any time. And those in power are often those closest to us: our parents and family, the people who are supposed to love us unconditionally.

Though Rossetto singles out parents for their responsibility in child development, neither my siblings nor my parents have ever explicitly expressed an expectation that their children live up to a perfect standard. They also never had to; it is implied. Perfectionism is embedded in our education system (it's possible and highly celebrated to get perfect and sometimes more-than-perfect scores), in our sports and reality TV shows (competitions require clearly defined winners and losers), and in our religious doctrines (imperfection = sin = distance from God). If you or me or any of us fall short in these systems, then we are to blame for our failings. If we do not live up to the productive and aesthetic ideal ascribed for us by ableist racist capitalism, then we are assigned little to no value.

I see now how, wrapped up in both good little white girl and eating disorder, I was trying to prove myself to the wicked webs. If I could achieve the perfect archetype of embodied white womanhood, then perhaps I could be released from it. Rising above it by playing by its rules, I could beat the wicked webs at its own game.

Rossetto's phrasing of "valuable but not valued" resonates deeply. The more I fit into the good little white girl/nice white lady archetypes, the more valuable I became to the wicked webs. And the more I am valued for my performance, the less I am valued as the real human who is me.

BECOMING ENOUGH

My hunch was spot on (as I'm learning it often is). I'm not truly a Disney princess on the inside. Besides, could those princesses ever be the real *anyone*? These archetypes distort our sense of ourselves and can so thoroughly occupy our focus that they distract us from paths toward healing and liberation.

On the individual level, my perfectionism has resulted in self-isolation, secrecy, workaholism, exhaustion, overwhelm, an eating disorder, obsessing, and constant low-level anxiety, shame, and fear of abandonment, because I can never do enough to meet these unrealistic expectations. I spent the majority of my adolescence wrapped in a constant (often subconscious) anxiety of self-checking and self-regulating:

Am I attractive/smart/competent/appropriate/friendly/nice/good/wealthy/humble ENOUGH?

If we, as status quo and passing white ladies, are so wrapped up in justifying our value to a system that was not set up to value us, then how could we possibly find the time, space, and energy to come together and pull the web apart?

This book is devoted to the question of how we will come together and pull the web apart. But before we continue, it is worth pausing to practice finding some compassion for your unique self and for our collective predicament. What would it mean to offer yourself some self-compassion? Can you offer yourself some love for what you have been through and what you have done to survive? Can you give your past, present, and future self a big hug? No, really—this is an invitation to give yourself a big hug.

The practice of self-compassion is one way to work with the shame that emerges from Mistress Syndrome. Dr Patrick Carnes references the work of family therapists Merle Fossum and Marilyn Mason in describing the "shame cycle" in family systems: "People who grow up in such families experience a loss of self in their unending effort to meet the unreachable standards."[23] In these systems, family members cycle between "acting in" and "acting out" behaviors. When trying to reach such impossible standards, they use "control behaviors" such as compulsive saving, hoarding, cleaning, exercising, and restrictive eating. Eventually, those same people will need a release from the severity resulting in "out-of-control" behaviors such as compulsive violence, substance abuse, and workaholism.

While there are many ways to act in/act out, the wicked webs have helped shape which behaviors are accessible and acceptable to whom, with whom, and in what contexts. Many acting out behaviors have not been available to white women within the context of white patriarchal family structures. Acting in behaviors have been much more accessible and acceptable within family systems, while at the same time acting out behaviors may be available to white women within the context of relationships with Black, Indigenous, and other People of Color, due to power dynamics. Even within those relationships, white womanhood still prefers that acts of domination appear as acting in behaviors. As in, white women's violence ought to seem effortless, innocent, perhaps a little self-sacrificial. (We will unpack themes of white women's violence in section II of this book). The acting in/acting out framework offers an explanation for the recklessness of extremely entitled white folks and how competition, blame, and projection have become hallmarks of white supremacy.

Deep down remains the question about where our value lies. The competition and comparison we internalized during our early shoelace knots have taught us that value is relative and finite. Meaning, we have value when others don't, and precisely because others don't. The false categorization of people into a hierarchy of races was invented to attribute value to some by lowering the value of others. According to Battalora, the system of relative advantage on which race was constructed "did little to raise Whites from their standing prior to Bacon's Rebellion."[24] However, what legislating whiteness did do was "dramatically lower the social bottom through worse conditions and treatment of non-Whites."[25] And so today we have inherited a legacy in which our cultural scale for value is based on unhuman and inhumane extremes.

One of the problems with being categorized as a white person in this unhuman system of value is that being more than human is impossible. To be human is to be *im*perfect. So of course we carry a constant fear of not being enough. Of course our teenagers have anxiety disorders. Of course we use extreme sports, extreme work, extreme achievement, and extreme diets to try to justify our merit to a system that doesn't give a damn about our humanity. The pervasive fear of not being enough that we hold is legit. Because as long as our value lies in the extrinsic measurement of an inhumane system, we can and will never ever be enough.

The constant anxiety and ever-present fear that comes with striving for perfection grates on our souls. Like rushing water, it needs somewhere to go. Part of what whiteness does is encourage us collectively as white people to externalize and project fears about not being enough onto others: "the other." We are afraid of ourselves, of our shortcomings and our failures, and we don't want to be. So instead, we are afraid of *them*, the person praying to Allah on our flight, the person asking for bus fare at our car window, the person selling DVDs or cigarettes, the person hanging out at the construction site in our neighborhood. There is shame in being afraid when we have been taught through our systems and cultures that we as white people are supposed to be superior. Because we are ashamed of being afraid, our fear must be controlled, dominated, brought to its knees—so we destroy it by destroying, blaming, and scapegoating "the others."

After all, whiteness was founded on fear.

DANCING WHILE WHITE

We know that on the individual level, fear can induce a traumatic response in the human brain; according to psychiatrist Bessel van der Kolk, "traumatized people cut off their relationship to their bodies."[26] When I was eighteen, alongside my eating disorder, I destroyed my anterior cruciate ligament (ACL) while trying to prove my value at a pickup soccer game at the park.

Like overachieving and workaholism, both my experiences of an eating disorder and an ACL tear received positive reinforcement by a culture that gave me sympathy points for extreme self-sacrifice. The extremity of my injury was evidence of the extremity of my commitment to the competitive cause. It was harder to feel the emotional wounds of losing a soccer match through the throbbing pain of my ripped-up knee. From my new vantage point on the couch, I could safely nurse my knee and my ego back to health while garnering sympathy points in the process. And as someone who's been conditioned to perform Damsel in Distress, both my eating disorder and my sports injury provided paths toward racking up those much-coveted sympathy points.

This disembodied approach to looking for external validation through extremes is incredibly harmful. Within the eating disorder and sports injury lies my loss of the ability to self-regulate. Over time, in practicing self-inflicted starvation, I taught myself to ignore and numb sensations of hunger and fullness. Likewise, in my athletic discipline, I became desensitized to pain, exhaustion, and my physical limits.

Without moderation, limits became the responsibility of external forces—the therapists who weighed me and threatened hospitalization if I didn't eat, the sports physician who monitored my physical therapy and determined when I could walk again. In short, an ideology of all or nothing meant I didn't have to take responsibility for knowing when enough was enough. It absolved me of having to be accountable to listening to my intuition, of checking in with what I wanted and needed, and of having to trust myself. In all-or-nothing thinking, I had value—and I *only* had value—in being either all or nothing.

If whiteness was founded on fear—fear of "the other," fear of not being (white/wealthy/masculine) enough, fear of abandonment, fear of loss of control, fear of scarcity, fear of the poor masses rising up against the rich—then, what does that mean for the bodies of those of us navigating this culture today? How does the numbing of our bodies—through eating disorders, extreme sports, substance abuse, compulsive violence, and workaholism—perpetuate cycles of harm?

The work of somatics practitioner Tada Hozumi * scales up this individualized, embodied dissociation to the cultural level in describing cultural somatic context, or "how bodies move, breathe, think, feel, and know themselves within a culture."[27]

Several years ago, I was at a training that was all about being in body. I still love to dance (my ballerina dreams resurface every few years); I was at a training about trauma healing, where we were being taught samba and house steps. I was loving it, building confidence and fully participating with great joy.

At the end of the day, we formed a circle. Each person was invited to dance in the middle of it, something done in slightly different ways in many cultures. It was a freestyle moment—to share and celebrate each of our human individualities as part of the collective, with everyone watching and cheering on. Needless to say, it was a very supportive environment.

When it was my turn, I froze. Panic set in. When the facilitator gently glanced my way, I shook my head abruptly like a stubborn four-year-old. *No.* Our cipher continued, moving on to the next person, and the next. Then it came back around to me. I forced myself to move my body to the middle of the circle and just did whatever came

---

* I came across Tada Hozumi's *Selfish Activist* blog in 2017, and it became a key resource and was where I was first exposed to these ideas. Most of the early articles have been removed from the internet and I haven't been able to track down current reference points, but I still wanted to attribute their work as an important early influence for me in cultural somatics.

to me. It was not elegant. It was not graceful. But there was instant release. After I offered my awkward flail to the group, I burst into tears and fled the space.

As I was outside in the courtyard bawling tears of humiliation and release, I thought about dancing in my tradition, or rather, the absence of it. The trainer* shared about how the Black Panthers would celebrate after an intense day of organizing by dancing together. I was furious and incredibly sad that there was no such tradition of dancing for me to draw on. In fact, Mennonites of Swiss German ancestry often forbade dancing. For generations, we have lost a profoundly human way of knowing—and healing. In my Mennonite subculture, celebration and pleasure is mostly seen as evil or at least less valuable. Sex, play, really anything "unproductive" was sinful or a waste of time (which is also sinful). Our bodies had long been reduced to being valued in terms of work—reproduction, physical labor, competitive sports, pragmatic nurture. Our bodies, like our psyches, were forced to prove their worth.

The dance circle moment was both terrifying and liberating for me, and there were many witnesses. And some of us wonder why white people can't dance.

This is not to say that individual white people can't dance—there are many exceptions.† I, myself have decent rhythm and enjoy dancing, even though my ancestors swore it off and there is no cultural tradition in my family. I attribute my dance affinity to those early tutu dreams alongside my childhood exposure to multiculturalist and Afro-centric arts movements (thanks Atlanta Public Schools!). Yet, even with multiculturalism and that one Nutcracker Ballet VHS, the confidence and ability to freestyle (especially with witnesses) generates in me initial alarm and lingering dread.

Collectively speaking, there is a way white people's inability to dance and dance without inhibition (yet still in rhythm with the

---

* My former colleague, Nia Eubanks-Dixon, is also the founder of Creative Praxis. Learn more at https://www.creativepraxis.org/about.

† While Hozumi acknowledges the various traditions of dance in European cultures, they also note that many European dance traditions involve keeping the hips and spine rigid.

music) connects to an embodied racism. Menakem makes a similar connection when describing how white-bodied people disassociate from the body as a cultural pattern of white-body supremacy. This embodied dissociation is part of secondary trauma. He notes, "Often, the perpetrator tries to avoid this trauma [the trauma of inflicting harm on others] by dissociating (a form of flight) during the event, and then, immediately afterward, overriding any impulse to process the trauma or discharge its energy from his or her body."[28]

For a long time, I have told myself that self-hate of my body and of myself for not being enough was what propelled my eating disorder and severe athleticism. But given what I know now about trauma and my historical relationship to whiteness, I am realizing that it might have more to do with fear. That fear—of not being enough, of losing external validation or status, of loss of identity or control, of abandonment, of eternal damnation—has been the traumatic motivation of white womanhood.

The deeper I dig, the more I feel that white womanhood, as a microcosm of whiteness, is dissociation from the body. Uncomfortably for me, healing might mean getting out of the comfort zone of my intellect and into the awkwardness of my body—less reading and more public hip-wriggling. Uncomfortably for us, it might mean fewer white-lady dos and white-lady don'ts. It might mean more layers of messy stories with no one right, clear, easy takeaway.

What I get most from both Menakem's and Hozumi's work is not the naming of cultural aspects of embodied trauma (although that is certainly helpful), but rather the invitation to embodied discomfort as a means of healing.

This call to discomfort flips our white-centric understanding of healing on its head (like a breakdance move or a headstand). The vulnerability of appearing unskilled and out of control, the awkwardness of getting it wrong, the discomfort in not being dominant or centered in the ways we have been taught to expect, and the call to notice, feel, and be fully in the icky newness that comes with dancing while white will not be found in most glitzy yoga periodicals or surefire self-improvement programs pitched at looking good and feeling great. Our collective liberation is not in the polished advertisements of white culture's waiting rooms, but instead is linked to the embarrassing, unpleasant, uncoordinated movements of white people learning to dance.

IS IT TIME FOR A BREAK?

This book is a lot—a lot of words, a lot of history, a lot of memory, a lot of trauma.

Remember: You are more than just a mind pursuing information. You have a body with a heart that feels things and also stores trauma.

It is okay to take a break.

It is okay to make space to rest and digest.

Dance awkwardly. Sing loudly. Go take a hot shower. Dig your toes in the dirt.

Whatever it is that you decide to do, please put this book down for a moment and take a break.

(You can do this whenever you need to.)

This book, along with oppression, will still be here when you return. Just like your body, mind, and heart will always be your resources in the midst of hard things.

PART II

NAMING OURSELVES

CHAPTER FIVE

ON BEING THE MISTRESS

Obviously, the very idea of a violent white womanhood
was antithetical to the reigning ideology and to the gender
ideals that equated power over slaves with white men.

—Thavolia Glymph, *Out of the House of Bondage*

I have three kids and I work from home, so people
always ask me how I stay so calm and organized…

—Chatbooks commercial

here is a myth in white America that white Southerners are solely responsible for the racism in this country. Despite being raised in the South, I grew up with some of this messaging too. After all, I wasn't really *from* Atlanta, and neither were a lot of the white people around me. My mama grew up deep in the mountains of Appalachia, but she wasn't really *from* from there either. One generation back, her parents were solidly from Amish Mennonite* Pennsylvania. My dad came directly from north of Philly, so there was no question on his

---

* The use of Amish Mennonite in this case denotes a specific branch of Anabaptism whose adherents once belonged to the Amish Church and then made a shift to worship with Mennonites in eastern Pennsylvania. Emerging as a decentralized movement in Europe with a congregationalist approach to church structure, Anabaptists have become adept at dividing and subdividing with even the slightest pressure of conflict. As a sectarian faith tradition, there are many Mennonite and Amish denominations and varieties.

side. And with both lines being *from* from Swiss German Anabaptist pacifist roots, we were in the clear when it came to being on the side of racism = bad and having no history of slaveholding (*whew!*).*
So when my childhood caretaker Ms. Sylvia told me stories of mean white boys at the bus stop and taught me to be a different kind of white person, I knew there was some connection between them and me. I knew I was white. But I also knew I wasn't Southern in *that* way.

Cue Scarlett O'Hara.

THE LEGACY OF *GONE WITH THE WIND*

Despite "not being Southern in *that* way," upon reflection a number of curious circumstances stand out to me. On one hand, I was given all sorts of concrete examples of how not to be like the mean, angry lynch mobs and slaveholders of Southern history. I was steeped in Rev. Dr. Martin Luther King Jr.'s legacy. In my eighth-grade Georgia history class, the first semester covered the evils of slavery and the wickedness of the Confederacy and the second semester focused on the Civil Rights Movement. Black History Month lasted the entire school year, and in high school we read nearly as many books by Black authors as we did by white ones.

Yet on the other hand, *Gone with the Wind* made a very short list of parentally approved films for my childhood viewing. This encouragement included tours of the Margaret Mitchell home and a general sense of ~~pride~~ Mennonite Humble that Mitchell was from Atlanta—a white woman role model and artist/writer who succeeded in her field

---

* While the Mennonite church forbade its members to enslave people, given the sectarian nature of the church and opportunities for immigrants to assimilate into whiteness, many Mennonites today have ancestors from their family tree who were in and out of Mennonite church denominations throughout its history. This trajectory includes some of my Mast ancestors who moved to North Carolina in the 1700s and fully assimilated into Southern whiteness, including enslaving people for several generations. The Mast family history of slaveholding is outlined in *Kinship Concealed: Amish-Mennonite & African-American Family Connections* by Sharon Cranford and Dwight Roth.

despite the sexism of the day. When I watched the film for the third time (I loved the dresses), maybe Ms. Sylvia silently shook her head in disapproval while doing dishes, but not one adult indicated to me that it contained a problematic narrative. When I was confused that things didn't match up, there wasn't any critical discussion to address my questions and help me process it: Why were the white men all eager to go off to war when white men in my church said war was bad? Why was Prissy screaming hysterically in the midst of crisis when the Black women I knew were composed and knowledgeable? Why did enslaved people stick around when in all the other stories I read they were trying to get the hell out?

When my precocious second-grade self read the book and then wanted a *Gone with the Wind*–themed birthday party (complete with hoop skirts), not only was this idea supported by my parents, but other people sent their children (mostly white). Of the birthday party goers, maybe only one of my peers was *from* from the South.

Cue seven mini-Scarletts and one Rhett Butler.

Many other Southern cultural things slipped in uncomplexified. These included visits to the Cyclorama[*] (which was practically in my backyard), many picnics at Stone Mountain Park[†] with its highly patriotic yet oddly Confederate-leaning laser show, and that one-time trip to a plantation outside of Charleston, South Carolina. Somehow Southern white overt racist culture ended up being kitschified by our Atlanta Yankee parents—not totally taken seriously yet not totally dismissed. Like your cute kid brother on a good day: harmlessly annoying, but you're feeling generous and proud of yourself for your generosity, because *whew!* at least you didn't make *those* mistakes.

---

[*] The Cyclorama housed the wraparound immersive painting *The Battle of Atlanta*, which depicts the Civil War. It has faced criticisms about its use in uplifting Lost Cause narratives of the Confederacy and was rehoused in 2019 to the Atlanta History Center.

[†] Along with being the birthplace of the modern Ku Klux Klan, Stone Mountain Park features a relief carving of three Confederate figures. It is the largest such relief sculpture in the world, so they are unnervingly huge.

But tempting as it may be, we must not be swayed by a theism of *whew!* This work is a practice of self-discipline to repeatedly and honestly revisit our life histories. It takes effort to delve deeper into the truths that have been covered up for us and by us. This work asks for courage to break through self-pity and self-loathing, to use this honest look to inform how we can change. Healing from Mistress Syndrome means acknowledging our *Gone with the Wind* birthday parties so that we might enter into hard, challenging, life-long dialogues about racism and our connection to it. Which repressed stories do we need to surface? Which truths from our own histories do we need to resurrect and exhume so that we can know, learn, and do different? Let us make space to examine our internalized Scarlett O'Hara.

Scarlett O'Hara is not just a literary racist emblem of the Confederate South of yesteryear; she is alive and well inside white womanhood today no matter our regional birthplace. Scarlett O'Hara epitomizes someone suffering from Mistress Syndrome. She is both the mistress of the actual plantation, groomed her entire life in Southern socialite circles to elegantly administer the violence of enslavement's domestic arm, and also an aspirational adulterous mistress throughout two marriages of her own. She has been positioned in the Southern plantation system to play a leading, yet supportive, role. Embracing her corseted destiny, Scarlett deftly understands the limitations and the power of white womanhood and uses her gendered femininity to manipulate and survive the white men in authority while leveraging her whiteness and class to exploit, command, and violate the Black people around her. These characteristics of white womanhood are intricately intertwined and are especially potent during her moments of desperation. Like her male counterparts who rally enthusiastically for the Confederacy, Scarlett makes decisions that further entrench and entangle her in Mistress Syndrome.

The lens of the novel and film center, glorify, and pity her white womanhood as Vixen Mistress and Damsel in Distress while minimizing the violence of structural and historical power that erases the principality of those who were most impacted by it. Both novel and film paint the enslaved characters as equally dedicated to upholding the plantation system out of dependency, ignorance, and childlike naivety, often doing so happily. As a foil to Scarlett's flamboyant white womanhood, supporting character Melanie plays the part of the Good Plantation Wife, a silent martyr who eventually goes full-on martyr and dies. These Mistress Syndrome archetypes of Vixen Mistress, Good Plantation Wife, and Damsel in Distress (more about her in the next chapter) merit further exploration, as they still are with us today.

VIXEN MISTRESS AND GOOD PLANTATION WIFE

Being the Vixen Mistress is a source of specious power, one that gets funneled into our white-lady pipes with every romantic comedy we've ever inhaled. Scarlett O'Hara grew up no differently. In *Gone with the Wind* there is an aura of fated love around Scarlett's affair with Rhett Butler. He is the alluring unknown, the titillating draw, the adventurous contrast to her first love's blond-haired, blue-eyed, and Confederacy-approved—yet also untouchable—Ashley Wilkes. Butler's dark features indicate a sinister danger, one that Scarlett ultimately can't resist. Scarlett is bored to tears with the life she's inherited and dismissive of her privilege. She is aware of the confines of white womanhood within plantation society and as she approaches adulthood becomes desperate to loosen its grip. At the same time, the plantation infrastructure is beginning to crumble around her. The white supremacy that she depends on to uphold her womanhood is eroding. But as there is for the Good Plantation Wife, for the Vixen Mistress there is an illusion of liberatory power. The Vixen Mistress is just another bed in the house of these wicked webs. And just as Rhett up and leaves when Scarlett is most in need, so too will the wicked webs betray us. They are not made to support our best interest. They never were.

Having spent most of my childhood identifying with Scarlett, I now have been considering how I've internalized meek Melanie's archetype as well. As Ashley's wife and mother to his children, she is depicted as the weaker, kinder, and more helpless of the Scarlett/

Melanie pair. Melanie has clearly chosen the role of Good Plantation Wife (both to her husband and to the Confederacy) and oozes purity, faithfulness, kindness, humility, and goodness out of her racist pores. Melanie symbolizes the white woman ideal that justifies the violence of racism. As the committed, self-sacrificing daughter/wife/mother, she is what the South is fighting for.

Scarlett is begrudgingly tied to Melanie just as Melanie's goodness depends on its contrast to Scarlett's vixen ways. However, rather than building together over their shared situation, keeping up appearances, blatant lies, and manipulative deceit divide Scarlett and Melanie, playing out the age-old conflict of the witch hunts. *Gone with the Wind* author and white lady suffering from early twentieth-century Mistress Syndrome Margaret Mitchell ultimately positions both Melanie and Scarlett as tragic victims, but we know better. Plantation mistresses have always been just as complicit in humanity's demise.

Professor Thavolia Glymph has much to say about the complicity of plantation mistresses in humanity's demise. In the book *Out of the House of Bondage*, Glymph lays bare the mistresses' brutality by combing through their own words, WPA interviews* with those who were formerly enslaved, and other historical evidence.

In contrast to *Gone with the Wind*'s sentimentalized portrayal of the plantation as a quaint home that centered power dynamics between Southern white men and women, Glymph describes the plantation house as "a workplace,"[1] and one in which mistresses commanded labor and deference. She goes on to describe how white male dominance—unlike what our conditioning has led us to believe—"was not the controlling force within the plantation household"[2] but rather, "white women wielded the power of slave ownership. They owned slaves and managed households in which they held the power of life and death,

---

* The Works Progress Administration was a federal program beginning in 1935 to stem unemployment. While much of the public works focused on infrastructure projects, programs like the Federal Writers Project via the Slave Narrative Collection documented oral histories, "letting ordinary people tell their own life stories" (Library of Congress, "The WPA and the Slave Narrative Collection").

and the importance of those facts for Southern women's identity—black and white—were enormous."[3]

While Southern white men wielded tremendous power through owning property, voting, and legally subordinating everyone else, white women held considerable power too. This power has often been overlooked by historians focusing on white women's patriarchal subjugation, as if that power dynamic existed in a bubble, removed from its race-based context. To paraphrase Glymph, white women's power to uphold the racist order was reinforced by both state institutions and dominant culture in ways that were obvious to the humans they enslaved, even as white women's violence poked holes in notions of their genteel "nature."

Plantation mistresses exercised violence against those they enslaved frequently and with intention. Their ability to do harm was amplified by their proximity to the humans they were bent on controlling. While plantation masters administered most violent punishments by proxy of overseers, plantation mistresses were the direct line of command in the house. This level of intimacy rendered Black women and children particularly vulnerable to daily psychological torture and physical abuse. Glymph acknowledges the violent reach of plantation mistresses:

> Mistresses's [sic] violence against slave women in the plantation household ran along a continuum: Bible-thumping threats of hell for disobedience, verbal abuse, pinches and slaps, severe beatings, burnings, and murder....The weapons mistresses took up against slaves ran the gamut from brooms, tongs, irons, shovels, and their hands to whatever was most readily available....[The cowhide whip] sat beside mistresses as they read to their children, knitted, or as they sat and rocked in their chairs.[4]

Interviews with formerly enslaved people reveal testimony after testimony describing tales of brutality at the hands of plantation mistresses. But perhaps the most significant evidence of white womanhood's violent power was communicated through resistance by enslaved Black women. As Glymph points out, "When black women resisted the plantation household, they resisted the authority that mistresses exercised."[5] The fact that "domestic workers were often the first to flee slavery,"[6] and many times chose field labor over domestic work after emancipation, challenges the idea that fieldwork was the main site of white violence.

THE ALLURE OF SCARLETT O'HARA

Unlike the frilly dresses, this history is not pretty to look at—just as Glymph's book was not an easy one to read. I don't want to be associated with the "sadistic behavior"[7] Glymph outlines so meticulously. I don't want to be implicated in the crimes of elite Southern plantation mistresses of 1844. Feelings of defensiveness are definitely making an appearance. So, I have taken the time to create this handy checklist of why their legacy doesn't belong to me:

1. I'm not elite: I'm working- to middle-class, depending on which side of the family you look at, how far back you go, and my personal marital status at the time.

2. I'm not Southern: At least not in *that* way, as previously described. My direct ancestors stayed put above the Mason-Dixon Line until 1956, and then moved to Appalachia.

3. I'm not "plantation": My ancestors worked their own farms and birthed plenty of their own children to help with the work.

4. I'm not violent: Historically, what with the pacifist lineage and also according to my current beliefs.

5. I was not alive in 1844: Yep, definitely born in 1983, which both my mother and birth certificate confirm.

Now that I've acknowledged my defensiveness, validated my values, and affirmed non-Scarlett aspects of my identity, can I go a bit deeper? Despite my checklist, there was something undeniably attractive in Scarlett's story that drew my seven-year-old self to *Gone with the Wind* and resonated beyond the pretty dresses. Glymph calls the plantation mistress "one of the most powerful and influential icons of womanhood in American history....There have been other powerful and influential ideals of American womanhood but, arguably, none as coveted and admired."[8]

And in all honesty, I did admire Scarlett. I admired her ease of access to wealth (as symbolized by the pretty dresses and humans attending to her every need). I admired her idealized beauty, her power to attract suitors, sway her father, and get what she needed from white men (at least most of the time). I identified with her rebellious spirit, resourcefulness, and wit that made the expected life of Good Plantation Wife unappealing to her, just as I felt unimpressed with the gendered roles presented to me of good Christian wife and mother. I gravitated toward her dramatic expression, which set her apart from all the other (boring) white girls.

The iconic plantation mistress images that were planted in my imagination helped construct my own identity into white womanhood. Scarlett's tragic victimhood in the face of (white) patriarchy suggested that I too could hide both my agency and complicity beneath a mantle of gendered victimhood, a key strategy for staying in relationship with white masculinity.

Scarlett's melodramatic martyrdom also points to a narrative that has played out in contemporary (white) feminism encouraging white women to overidentify with the experiences of women of color because we have all been gendered women. Or, as Glymph puts it when challenging historians' standard view of the plantation mistress:

> Here were hardworking women so handicapped by patriarchy and paternalism that their lives more closely resembled those of enslaved women than the white men who were their fathers, husbands, and brothers; here were women who found in their own subjugation the basis for an alliance with enslaved women. Slaves rarely thought this.[9]

Just as Black women today rarely see our experiences as equivalent.*

White women's overidentification with women of color happens because we underidentify with whiteness. As per my checklist, we can defend ourselves as not-Scarlett, not-Southern, and not-racist. Yet, the legacy of the plantation mistress doesn't only belong to elite Southern white women; it belongs to all of us who can access whiteness. Whether or not we are Southern in *that* way, we can inflict a lot of harm when we don't realize how our identity is connected to the legacy of the plantation mistress.

THE VIOLENCE OF MICROAGGRESSIONS

While we may no longer occupy the same position of power as the plantation mistress, white women continue to have disproportionate access to and impact on the lives of women and children of color since we are overrepresented as frontline workers in education, health care, social work, and nonprofits. In the next chapter we will get into the history that bridges plantation mistress and social worker, but for now I want to emphasize how our disproportionate proximity means we have disproportionate opportunities to cause harm.

One way that harm happens is through everyday microaggressions. I am thinking of the many stories women of color have shared with me about the microaggressions they experience in the workplace from white women. Things that we may consider benign, well-intended, or reflecting our individual character and expression are often experienced by our nonwhite peers as disrespect and aggression. According to Derald W. Sue, author of "Microaggressions in Everyday Life,"

---

* Historically, we know that the Southern white women of the plantation South did not align with the people they enslaved. With very few exceptions, some of those women may have complained about the limiting path for upper-class women, but they did not collectively, or even individually, work to undermine the cultural and economic foundations of enslavement on the which their lives were built. Perhaps the only examples we have out of the hundreds of thousands of Southern white women from slaveholding families is that of the abolitionist Grimké sisters, who I profile in chapter twelve.

microaggressions are "the everyday slights, indignities, put downs and insults that people of color, women, LGBT populations or those who are marginalized experiences [sic] in their day-to-day interactions with people."[10]

I'm using "microaggressions" in this book because even though these insults happen in casual and daily ways, there's nothing small about their aggressiveness or impact. Because these microaggressions call upon patterns of multigenerational oppression, they serve to compound trauma, trigger feelings of not being safe or belonging, and can reinforce oppressive power dynamics.

We can cause these harms out of ignorance, fear, spite, or the shame of our own insecurities, such as projecting our discomfort in moments when we are receiving correction. Racialized microaggressions can come from our language, such as indicating surprise at one Person of Color's skill or intelligence, i.e., "She's so smart/articulate/intelligent…(for a Black person)." Whether we finish the sentence or not, the exceptionality is implied and is historically linked to how racism has stratified intelligence. Microaggressions can come from our cultural ineptitude, such as incessant questions and curiosity about family dynamics, hair, food, music, language patterns, dance, etc. in which our questions—though innocent to us—can reinforce exclusion, emphasize the otherness of nonwhite cultures, and fetishize for a white audience. They can also come from our physical bodies and learned white-body supremacy—such as touching Black women's hair, inserting ourselves uninvited into Black and Brown spaces, or in placing our hands on the arms of a coworker, as in the story I'm about to share.

While I've known about some of these microaggressions from growing up in proximity to Black cultures, I did not become aware of many others until my adulthood. The hardest lessons have been in instances when I've microaggressed and been corrected (though I wonder how many times I've committed a microaggression and not been corrected). These moments are hard on the ego and often take me a long time to process and learn from. Much easier on my ego has been witnessing other white people's microaggressions and learning from their mistakes.

Having worked closely in relationship with Black women in organizing spaces has meant that I have heard many stories of proximate
white women causing harm. One friend and colleague has had weekly,
if not daily, experiences with these types of microaggressions, especially in her workplace. With her blessing and collaboration, I am
sharing one of these instances. We've decided to share it with you
in order to honor and acknowledge the harm she's experienced and
also in the hopes that by sharing her experience, others will not
have to experience the same. It's important to acknowledge the risk
she is taking by sharing this story, even though it happened a while
ago. Because institutional power dynamics are still at play, there are
potential repercussions in publishing this.

The story begins when my friend and colleague, who has chosen
to go by the pseudonym Empress, was attending a Professional
Development day. At some point, an older white woman began
talking about the children of East Indian families, claiming that
Indian parents allow their children to run wild until the age of
twelve, when they start to focus on their education. In hearing this,
Empress had a strong reaction and looked around the room to see if
anyone else was responding in the same way. Empress's supervisor,
also a white woman, stayed silent, as did other supervisors in the
room. Empress began to feel increasingly disturbed at this white
woman's overgeneralization about a culture to which she does not
belong. It became apparent to Empress that no one in the room
was going to address it.

Thankfully, the meeting paused for a break. As Empress was on her
way back, the coworker who had made the offensive remark was also
returning from her supervisor's office. It seemed that this coworker's
supervisor had communicated something about the remark, although
Empress was not sure what had been said.

Across the hall, there was a Black student sitting behind a desk
who would witness the coming encounter. The coworker approached
and placed both of her hands on Empress's forearms, and holding
tight, said, "I have an Indian relative who says that's right. I'm just
speaking the truth of their culture."

Empress looked around the space and when she noticed the student, asked if she and the coworker could take this conversation elsewhere. But the coworker ignored the request and continued to stand there with her hands violating Empress's bodily autonomy. The coworker began talking about her Irish heritage and said that she's not offended when people stereotype Irish people.

Empress had to physically remove the white woman's hands from her body and push her away. Empress responded, "You're also white even though you're Irish, and as a white woman you get to say what you said in the meeting even though it's inappropriate."

Empress comes from a background in which there are many people of the Indian diaspora and had never experienced the culture her coworker described. But even if it were the case, Empress realized how inappropriate it had been to label a whole culture based on one individual's perspective, especially to a room of people also not from that culture. In reflecting on the dynamics, Empress noted, "Hovering over me, this white woman said super-racist shit, and now she's coming to me to justify why it's okay for her to say these things because she has one family member [who's Indian]. That doesn't have to do with a whole nation."

After the moment was over, a wave of intense feelings came up for Empress. She had been physically violated. She had been forced to have a conversation she didn't want to have in front of a student. She had been put in a position where she could potentially be stereotyped as an angry, overly sensitive Black woman who told a white woman about her whiteness without any context in front of others. Fear began to creep up as she considered how her job might be jeopardized.

Empress decided to confide in her supervisor and seek support. Her supervisor was seated with a Black colleague when Empress walked in. Empress was visibly upset. Instead of finding institutional support and emotional refuge, her colleague made light of the situation and her supervisor talked about how their department was building a relationship with that of her aggressor. Empress's supervisor offered sympathy but was not willing to take on the responsibility of addressing what had happened.

Empress left the meeting feeling even more vulnerable. Her white supervisor had basically told her to put down her feelings for the institution, and her Black colleague had cosigned it. She was disgusted, disappointed, ashamed, and afraid that if she said anything further, she might risk her job.

The impact on Empress was severe. Leaving her supervisor's office, she felt defeated. She wanted to leave, to go home, to go to other Black folks for support—none of which she could access in that moment. She lost her ability to concentrate but still had to collect her emotions in order to perform and not give the institution a reason to terminate her.

Empress reflected on that moment:

> I was mad. All the history was in my head and thoughts of how she would be communicating with Black students. I felt so sad for the students that would have to deal with her. How do I show up [in these spaces and moments] and not lose aspects of myself? This is the battle I've confronted because it's not just her. I had no support in my office space to deal with it. It was left up to me to reconcile the situation. My supervisor feels bad, but her feeling bad doesn't equate my safety. There was sympathy and acknowledgment, but no follow-up and comfort for me.

> I wanted to take it to HR, but I knew that would make my experience harder for me because I'd be going behind my supervisor's back. It affirmed that the institution doesn't give an F for me. All my health problems at work, stress…they're [the institution is] not about work/life balance. It's about how well you survive this situation so you can get up and do it again. When I say that it is uncomfortable, yes it truly is. It affirmed that it was institutionally problematic, statistically and historically affirmed: Pittsburgh's poor outcomes for Black women.

As Empress has courageously and generously shared with us, these daily microaggressions take their toll on Black women's health. A

2018 Duke University study on infant mortality confirmed the impact of daily stress and aggressions on Black women. Whereas higher levels of education and income correlate to decreased infant mortality rates for white women, the same cannot be said for Black women who "experience the highest infant mortality rates among any racial or ethnic group in the United States."[11] Although infant mortality rates decrease for Black women as they rise in level of education up to a bachelor's degree, the infant mortality rate is actually highest for Black women who hold master's and doctorate/professional degrees.[*] Black women's gain of socioeconomic status and education, which serve as protective factors for white women, further exposes Black women to the impact of structural racism and the daily racialized stress of navigating white neighborhoods, professional workplaces, and academia.

Black women with higher levels of education and socioeconomic status also experience an increase in daily interactions with white people's biases, particularly those of white women.

THE DOUBLE LIVES OF WHITE WOMEN

I am thinking of the violence that workplace hierarchies create and that managing other people necessitates. I am thinking of the masks of effortless perfection those of us socialized into white womanhood have become used to wearing. The iconic plantation mistress taught me to emanate effortless control. Historically, the plantation mistress was expected to play the part of both lady and household manager, to be perceived by white masculinity as helplessly in need of patriarchal

---

[*] When controlling for factors like age, "risky behaviors," and obesity, the disparity between Black and white infant mortality rates persists. From the March 2018 report "Fighting at Birth: Eradicating the Black-White Infant Mortality Gap": "There is a strong tendency to attribute racial disparities in infant mortality to the prevalence of obesity in black women and engagement in risky behaviors during pregnancy such as drinking alcohol, using illicit drugs, and smoking cigarettes. Indeed, these risky behaviors are associated with an increased incidence of infant mortality and morbidity. However, it is crucial to recognize that the greater vulnerability of black infants cannot be explained by these factors" (Smith, Bentley-Edwards, El-Amin, and Darity, 4).

protection while at the same time commanding a household of forced laborers. The plantation mistress was to be "both submissive and dominant,"[12] as Glymph notes, leaning more to one side or the other depending on the audience.

My father loves to tell the story of how he was taken aback by my kindergarten teacher's opinion of my classroom demeanor. Early on in elementary school, he went to school for Parents' Day. I imagine that he walked up the concrete steps of my inner-city elementary school ready for anything. I had not been the easiest or the quietest of children in the five or six years he had known me. Surrounded by macaroni art and alphabet posters, he was caught off guard by my teacher, as he tells the tale. She lauded me as a quiet, polite, and well-behaved student, such a joy to have in class. My teacher's praise contrasted with his experience of my larger-than-life personality at home. At home I was not well-behaved; I loudly spoke my mind and used force to dominate my little brother. My father usually tells this story with a mixture of pride and disbelief—pride that I was performing so well at school, and disbelief because my teacher's experience of me was so different than his own.

What is interesting to me in this story is how early I had begun to internalize the performative nature of white womanhood—that as young as five, the Good Plantation Wife in me was already navigating the split personality that white womanhood demands. At five, I was becoming proficient in the discourse of public and private personas. I knew that the effortless shine of my public-facing school behavior was to be safeguarded from the effortful and unladylike exertion and expression of self at home. I learned to be nice and compliant in public and especially to those in power and to be naughty and commanding only with those closest to me, especially with those I could dominate.

These expressions of violence and control at home evolved as I matured. To go back to the acting in/acting out and victim/aggressor cycles from chapter four, as I aged into white womanhood, I began to take out these expressions less frequently on my brother and more frequently on myself. Like the plantation mistress's performance of elegant violence, my high school years were a fastidiously performed act of effortless perfection. And when I began to live with people outside my family of origin, my living spaces thus became public facing as well. Faced with the choices of revealing my honest ugliness or keeping up my perfect public façade, I opted for the latter, raking in a couple housemate-of-the-year awards and a trail of goodwill from those with whom I'd lived.

That began to change as my former partner and I bought and began to renovate a home and invited housemates to live with us. Now we had sweat equity. With ownership, material things began to matter more. Those kitchen counters our housemate just scratched equaled hours of painstaking sanding and staining. The accidental hole my brother put in the wall was something we'd now have to patch and paint. With ownership came responsibility and bills and maintenance and a challenge to my nice white-lady façade. Now I wanted to have clear boundaries and expectations. Now I needed to express my feelings. Now I knew conflict had to be aired. Now that I was no longer the guest, it was time for my "real" self to come through.

* * *

It had been a casual invitation at first. I remember Felicia mentioning during one of our tête-à-têtes that she might not be renewing her lease in the new year and might be soon on the lookout for a two-bedroom. "You could come live with us," I remember saying. My invitation was sincere, though perhaps a little impulsive. After extending it, I realized I needed to check in with my partner.

By this time, Felicia and I were in constant communication. We had almost two years of work collaborations behind us. The white liberal resistance to deeper levels of anti-racism work on my committee had meant hours of debrief and strategy. I had also been supporting her yoga business whenever I could. She had been spending quite a bit of time at our place anyway. I had been getting to know her daughter better, too. The three of us were considering taking a trip together, somewhere with sunshine and sandy beaches. So, when she again brought up my invitation to cohabitate, it felt like an organic next step. I was thrilled, if not a little anxious to get things right.

By the time Felicia and her adult daughter Kayla moved in, I was well aware of the power dynamics at play. Hypersensitive to what two Black women moving into a white cis heterosexual couple's home might mean, I was determined not to play out the racial dynamics of yesteryear. We set expectations up front with a community conversation. We set the rent at a rate with economic justice in mind. My partner and I took on the responsibility of cleaning shared spaces.

I could pull out my emotional files from this era, but I don't need to. My social media says it all. Photos of us bundled around the kitchen table with huge mugs of tea (due to winter winds and a house built in 1889), hugs at the kitchen sink, sharing home-cooked meals surrounded by healthy houseplants and fresh-cut flowers: these moments were marked by laughter and smiles.

I remember us getting ready for some event, not a super-fancy one, but one that merited a little freshening up. This type of cleanup usually took me twenty minutes, max. I showered, dressed, applied a quick lip, and headed downstairs to see if we would be leaving soon. I could hear laughter as I descended.

As I approached their floor, the laughter became louder. Still in her bathrobe, Kayla offered me a glass of wine. Then Felicia waltzed by with a stack of clothes to choose from. "Come on in, Amanda," she said. I plopped myself down on the corner of the bed as we swapped stories and opinions on which outfit to wear. I don't remember if we even made it to the event or not. The getting ready together had become the event.

There had been a few logistical challenges to figure out, a major shift to my marital partnership that happened weeks before their move-in date, a lesson I needed to learn about being a responsible landlord and the timely deposit of rent checks, but it wasn't navigating the material aspects of our interracial cohabitation that challenged me the most. For me, it was the emotional labor of honestly naming what I wanted and needed and vulnerably talking about how living together was impacting me in the moment. That honest expression that had become easier for me within the power dynamic of home-ownership with white renters became a block now that there were Black people renting and living in my home.

I still sometimes struggle to be honest about how I am thinking and feeling in the context of these relationships, themes I will return to in the following chapters. But one important lesson this era offered me was about my fears around conflict. Looking back, I can see how open conflict with these Black women terrified me. I was afraid that the private self that had been allowed in my childhood home and my "real" self, with her conscious and unconscious racism would do harm to those who had agreed to live in vulnerable proximity with me. I was terrified to be fully seen. I was terrified I would act out my inner Scarlett and, inevitably, I did just that.

REVEALING MY INNER SCARLETT

Ugh. New York City is exhausting, I thought to myself as I dragged my bag down the Manhattan sidewalk. *It's so dirty.* I averted my eyes, trying not to identify the ambiguous pile of gunk I almost stepped in while looking for the subway entrance. *Why would anybody want to live here?*

It had been a while since I last visited the Big Apple—twenty-seven and a half years, to be exact. That last time was when I was five and had contracted Lyme's disease in my Pennsylvania grandparents' backwoods just before traveling with my mother to visit my aunt. I had memories of being tired and also of giant stuffed animals, my favorite jean jacket, and a park where I leafed through a new picture book.

This time I was visiting family too—sort of. Several months before, Kayla had moved out of our shared living arrangement to find out what a non-Pittsburgh (read: real) city was like.

It was a quick visit. We were catching a flight early the next morning to be at my parents' for Thanksgiving, so any New York (pre-Covid) partying that may have happened was tempered by our travel plans and also because—although it's taken me a long time to admit it—partying really isn't my thing. Despite some anxiety, we made it to the terminal with little traffic. We plopped down in empty chairs to await our boarding call.

"Ms. Kayla?" a voice asked. It was one of Kayla's students; their family was also waiting for the same flight. "Oh, hello," she greeted them warmly, yet formally. They introduced her to their family and then there was a slight pause. "This is my sister," Kayla said, introducing me. A brief flash of confusion moved across their faces. One of the adults recovered enough to say "Nice to meet you," and we parted ways with mutual wishes of safe travels.

Another filing cabinet moment emerged as I pretended to flow with it in real life. This particular memory has changed over time. Originally, I put it in a deep-blue folder, but in lifting it out of the filing drawer now, I see that it's a faded gray, cloudy in the corners as if I had spilled hot tea on it, causing the dye to bleed off of the edges.

That moment is also more complex because of what came after— our trip to Atlanta, pet-sitting for my aunt's geriatric cat, a fight I had with my father at lunch over his business associations, and Kayla's visit to my childhood home and observations of my Atlanta life, though much of it had changed since I lived there a decade and a half before.

Both leading up to the trip and also during, I had been concerned about how my father might trigger her. I already knew he would trigger me. I was relieved we were able to stay at my aunt's. We had an alternative place to be if and when things got heated. I hadn't exactly been on the best of terms with my parents since going public with my blog earlier that year. Even if Kayla hadn't been with me, I would have chosen not to stay with them.

Overall, I thought the visit had been going well despite a couple of tense moments. In the heat of the lunch argument—hot because of the energy in the room, not because of the November weather— after something particularly offensive my father said, Kayla excused herself to go outside. The only other indication something might be wrong was when my mother was showing photographs of my artwork from my senior art show.

In describing the show to Kayla, I mentioned I had also made a quilt out of money. I was proud of that work. It was the culmination of my undergraduate artwork and later inspired several iterations of work. I was using the metaphor of quilting—something women traditionally did collectively to reuse things no longer deemed valuable for their original purposes (like worn out clothes), transforming them into practical objects of beauty, comfort, and warmth. If feminine ways of knowing and co-creating could do this with rags, then what incredible transformative actions could be done with the symbols of US racist imperialism and economic exploitation (i.e., US currency)?

Kayla was not impressed.

When I carefully retrieve this file from the very back of the cabinet, I see that it's a bit dusty. I haven't thought about this moment in several years. But as soon as I begin reading the words on the page, anger, defensiveness, and feelings of betrayal rush toward me. In my parents' family room, in the house in Atlanta where I grew up, seated on their cozy couch and antique rockers, she said, in front of my parents (I paraphrase because my disbelief has impacted my memory) that making that artwork was irresponsible and wasteful. This person who had just called me sister was judging me in front of my parents. She knew my relationship with them was tenuous, including our intense political disagreements.

Perhaps this moment should have gotten my attention, yet all other indications were that the visit was going smoothly—even pleasantly. Everything else seemed "sisterly," as she had described our relationship at the airport. We went on an enjoyable fall stroll through the neighborhood. We tried on clothes at the place where my mother had an antique booth, finding the jacket she'd been looking for. We indulged at the international farmers market and café. We went out one evening to (lightly) dabble in the Atlanta night scene. We even giggled and had semi-slumber party pillow talk over a glass of wine on my cousin's bed.

It was then that I confided in her about a brand-new romantic relationship. She asked me if I was going to tell my parents about him (he was Black) and then later advised me not to. The relationship was pretty new, and I usually didn't tell my family about my dating until relationships got serious. Moreover, I was still technically married (though separated) and opening up to them about the truth of my intimate relationships so far had only caused further distance and judgment.

My experience with the trip was that things felt fine. The night we arrived, emboldened by her calling me sister in New York, I shared with my parents that Kayla was the sister I'd always wished I had. At any rate, I returned to Pittsburgh, satisfied with our visit, excited to see my new beau, and grateful to be in my own space again.

But four days later I received an email from Kayla titled "Frustration and Disappointment." Among other things, she shared how she felt "very used" in going to Atlanta, that she felt like I used her as a crutch, a Black person I paraded out in front of my family. Her email stated that I "emit a homily persona" but in actuality "have traveled the globe, a privilege [she had] not been able to have and [that I] almost act like the rebellious teenager who is mad at her parents for not showing her the real world." She told me how much "work" I had to do ("A LOT") before entering into a relationship with a Black man. She said that she could find another place to stay when she came home to visit Pittsburgh at the end of the month and concluded with: "All I can say is I will not be the black friend who is showboated around when convenient but is in the closet when it isn't."

Taking out this file now, I feel sick to my stomach. In rereading her email, all the old feelings come roaring back: confusion and anxiety, anger and grief.

This was not the first, last, nor only time when I would have an interaction with her or her mother, or both of them together, and in the moment feel like everything had been fine, but only later—the next morning, that night lying in bed, or in this case, four days later—receive an email or text outlining feelings of hurt, anger, disappointment, and frustration and feedback about the things I had done to cause it.

That's not to say that the feedback wasn't ever helpful, justified, or true. Often this feedback pointed out aspects of my whiteness and my unawareness of it. Often it was the first time I learned about how I had caused racialized harm and which of my actions called on long-standing racialized dynamics.

My purpose in telling this story is to emphasize how complex and messy unpacking these dynamics is. These relationships don't only exist within the context of race. Clearly, we are all imperfect humans navigating our triggers and traumas and mental health and unhealed family stuff, and we are doing this as we bump up against each other. And also, as someone who's been racialized as white, there is racialized harm I will never experience or know. There are dimensions of racialized harm I will continue to have to learn to even perceive. As I am specifically unpacking in this book, the way I navigate these lessons and relationships—or choose not to—has very much been shaped by my inheritance into Mistress Syndrome.

It got to the point when I would see I had a text from Felicia or Kayla and my hands would shake and my heart rate would spike. Even though mostly they were positive or neutral, any text or email from these women—who were becoming chosen family, whom I so deeply loved, admired, and respected, and whom I knew cared for me—would incite panic. It took me five years to be able to work up the courage to name to Felicia that receiving those texts induced panic in me.

But back to the Atlanta Thanksgiving Disaster file: receiving Kayla's email felt devastating—which is not to discount or minimize her experiences or truths. She was clearly triggered by aspects of our trip and our relationship dynamics. In my calmer moments, knowing what I do know about historical trauma, I can imagine why she didn't tell me in the moment. I can see how the approach might be connected to a historical survival strategy of her own—that in the Mistress's house, with her family and dependent (or at least a perceived dependency) on her hospitality, it would not have been safe to speak her full truth. Intellectually, historically, and analytically, I know that written communication allows the safety of distance, the agency to frame one's own truth. I know cognitively that I have the racial advantage and that that is not an abstraction. In both the visit to Atlanta and in having her and her mother live in my home, I had the material access to real, lived security. That power dynamic was not hypothetical, at the end of the day; my name was on the mortgage.

But and also those moments were incredibly intense for me as well. I cautiously pull out the file: Atlanta Thanksgiving Disaster, Part One: She Sent Me That Email. Feelings in the file: confusion, fear, anger, hurt, more confusion. Fear that I did something to jeopardize the relationship. Confusion that I really didn't understand what she was naming. Frustration that I disagreed with how she perceived and interpreted what happened. Anger that she preempted dialogue. Frustration that there was no opportunity to ask follow-up questions, clarify, or come to a mutual understanding. Hurt that she would make an accusation that I was using her or misrepresenting myself. Activated that she claimed a single definite, permanent narrative. Rage at feeling silenced (perhaps my biggest trigger of all).

It is a painful file to read. When I read it again, my chest hurts, my shoulders hunch, my heart rate soars. I check out for a moment and think about what I'll eat for lunch instead.

The pain of the file had made it look succinct. But then, I realize there is in fact a lot more information here. Along with her email, the folder also contains my response.

In reading her email, I relived my pain, hurt, fear, and anger. But in rereading my response, I feel a wave of shame. I feel queasy. My email lands in my stomach, swirling around unevenly. Unsettled, my body refuses its digestion. I am disgusted at myself.

The folder has a second tab: Part Two: My Panicked Response. My panic is dripping all over my email. *Oh*, I think, *this is what's causing the blue dye to run.*

Like a puppy rolling over to submit, I apologize in each paragraph. I fully agree with her evaluation of me and am careful to be honest in my appeasement. I say I was raised to emit a homily persona (which is true). I say that I feel sick to my stomach that she felt used (also true) and that I genuinely wanted her to come to Atlanta because I thought she would enjoy it and I wanted her in my life in that way (true again). I tell her she was absolutely right that I have a lot of work to do when it comes to being in healthy relationships with Black folks (lifelong work for any white person). I write how I hate that either her or her mother would not feel like they could stay in my home (also true). I go on and on about how grateful I am for her and her mother and how much I've been learning (which, again, is and was true), followed by this self-depreciating ending: "I am upset at myself for the role I played in you both feeling these crappy ways and for the ways I have impacted you and made you feel terrible and have frustrated and disappointed you" (this one is only a partial truth). And then, in a grand finale of dramatic appeasement, I throw myself at her feet, even offering to stay somewhere else while she visits and to talk about splitting home ownership, ending with, "I also recognize that material things matter but are no substitute for trust and honesty and respect and the immaterial things I'm responsible for in relation-ships." This last line especially feels hypocritical.

I've said before that Mistress Syndrome is about the inheritance of lies and self-lies. What I've learned from being a white woman is to appease the person in power. Sure, the roots of deference come from the legacy of survival in close proximity with white men, but when directly transferred onto other relational dynamics, it shows up in other ways. In the world of anti-racist organizing, in which white folks are instructed to follow the leadership of People of Color, I have taken it upon myself to reindoctrinate my mind to positively bias the experiences, wisdom, and leadership of Black women.

Yet, I am beginning to understand how I have interpreted the directive of following Black leadership as an all or nothing. I have replaced the actors but kept the white patriarchal ideal of hierarchy intact. When in conflict with Black women, it has been easier for me to defer without question than to engage my agency. It also has felt familiar to do this; it draws upon my internalized self-depreciation, martyrdom, and self-doubt.

In looking back at these emails many years later, I can more clearly see what was probably her stuff and what was mine, when at the time it was so confusing. I can see, too, how the filing cabinet strategy prevented me from being fully honest and authentic with her in the moment. I see how holding onto my emotional filing cabinet system—as opposed to more fully showing up in the actual moment—has been facilitated by my access to white womanhood. I see how it has allowed me to divide and hide, keeping what I truly thought and felt withheld privately compartmentalized from that of my public persona.

Just like my public-facing persona, the niceness of the plantation mistress was always a falsehood. Falsehoods, even when they're dressed up in lace, impair the building of trust. And trust is the cornerstone of any authentic relationship, especially one that attempts to untie hundreds of years of history. I see how this form of protective dishonesty has caused distrust in my relationships, especially with Black women.

My well-intentioned white-lady goal of emotionally shielding my housemates and chosen family from my whiteness hasn't made any of us safer in the long run. Just like the nineteenth-century plantation mistress, I might have been only deceiving me.

This self-deception has been part of what propelled me toward the writing of this book. Now that I am practicing more authenticity, there are many files to sort through and much to unlearn, just as those of us status quo and passing white ladies have many files to sort through and much to unlearn. I am realizing, with increased compassion for myself, how the filing cabinet strategy has protected me in moments when I felt like I had few options. Perhaps I've often had more options than I thought.

I am thinking of the other times I have microaggressed and disrespected the women of color closest to me within the context of antiracist organizing, collaborations, and friendships. This even happens in my seemingly insignificant use of language. My use of the word "my," for example, to claim ownership of collective space, collective work, and stolen land that never belonged to me reveals the ease of violence in my speech. The danger to the lives of People of Color is that my unexamined use of "my" is an assertion of ownership sanctioned by the state. In claiming "my home" to housemates who are renting from me when my name is on the mortgage, in claiming "my work" to the people I'm organizing with who were sometimes unpaid while I had a salaried position, in claiming "my book" to those who have done the labor of helping me to learn the things I am writing about, my casual and careless use of "my" can alienate those with whom I'm organizing through the assertion of my ownership (of land, labor, and intellectual and creative property) based on systems that have historically validated white people as the rightful owners—and taught me the same.

The reality is that despite my professed commitment to anti-racism, I could at any moment access the racist power of the state. I could legally evict my housemates. I could move up in the organization while documenting the work as solely mine. I could profit from the publishing of this book without reciprocity.

And even in this argument, my perfectionism is seeping in. I am afraid of enacting the power I do have in violent ways. I am afraid of living out the plantation mistress. I am afraid of not being the "anti-racist organizer" that has become central to my identity. So, in response, I swing the other way. I avoid any use of "my," running away from the responsibility of ownership and access.

On one hand, this is in alignment with the ideals of communalism and alternatives to the individualism of white culture. But, on the other hand, my intentional nonuse of "my" is just as much about me not wanting to be responsible. It is just as much about me disliking the power I have, or perhaps being afraid of it. Denying I have power and responsibility does little to change the reality of it. Denying my feelings and real opinions when in conflict with Black women does little to build a solid foundation of mutual trust. I see how I am trying to get out of my Mistress Syndrome, even as I continue to play the part.

MARKETING THE MODERN PLANTATION MISTRESS

These stories of realizing and navigating my internal plantation mistress are particular to me, but they also exist because of the societal air we breathe. We are all navigating these cultural waters. You don't have to have had *Gone with the Wind*–themed birthday parties or developed a split kindergarten personality to have been impacted by these long-present messages. You don't have to have acquired an emotional filing cabinet system to have relied on the notions of public and private personas that whiteness has enabled. Glymph speaks to how the plantation mistress ideal has been planted in our collective psyche:

> Birthed in proslavery ideology and elaborated in prescrip-
> tive literature, southern white women's educational models,
> memoirs, and diaries of the Old South, the iconic image of the
> southern lady became a fixture of post-Reconstruction white
> supremacist campaigns.…This message was conveyed in film,
> commercial product advertisements, federal programs, popular
> fiction, white women's social club agendas, and every sort of
> domestic efficiency and home alliance organization, whether
> targeted to black or white women.[13]

While *Gone with the Wind* is one such remnant of white supremacist propaganda that effectively shaped my socialization into white
womanhood, another and even more ubiquitous remnant of this
historic propaganda for whiteness flashes across our TVs, laptops,
and phones in the form of marketing campaigns.

In product ad after product ad, advertisers sell us the upcycled
ideal of plantation mistress. In commercials for cleaning products,
bargain shopping sites, online banking, easy dinner options, and even
lingerie, we are served a particular white woman to relate to. Dressed
in J.Crew casuals, she is thinnish with middle-aged, mom-appropriate
mid-length brown or blonde hair. She is married, presumably to a
white man who occasionally makes a brief appearance in the background. Her home is immaculate, stylish, and proclaims upwardly
mobile middle-class appeal. As the camera zooms in closer, she lets
us in on a little secret. Despite the perfection of her home, there
is one stubborn imperfection: a grease-stained dish that just won't
get clean, a messy closet, or errant, dirty little hands aiming for the

spotless upholstery. Usually her dilemma is time. Both moms that go to work and moms that stay at home are constantly shown as pressed for the time and patience that would put the finishing touches on their American Dream.

These ads tell us that this idealized white woman is solely responsible for the management of her household, as was the plantation mistress of not too long ago. Self-sufficiency is the name of the American game. Erased from the screen are babysitters, nannies, and relatives who help out with childcare. Gone from the set are house cleaners, lawn care services, and maintenance workers who keep her environs sparkling. Wiped out along with the spots and stains is the labor of underpaid retail workers who sold her the immaculate household items and the exploited factory workers who made her outfit and had their hands in making the products being advertised. Also invisible is the work her off-screen husband does for a living. We seldom get a peek at who he oversees in his field(s) of work. Like the plantation mistress ideal, these advertisers paint a picture of beautiful, good, patient household managers while simultaneously pointing out a key yet surmountable weakness.

Their strategy plays on our insecurities: even though we might appear to have it all together, a part of us knows that we are imposters. Just as the gentle façade of Southern white womanhood was at odds with the reality of white women's dominance in the plantation home, these advertisers are telling us that they know we are lying. These advertisers tell us that with the help of their one little product, we can hide the stress, struggle, and violence of managing white supremacy, all while keeping its material advantages in place. They normalize an affluent, heteronormative, white, feminine ideal left over from our plantation era foremothers.

But what if the good housekeeper didn't need the help of the helpful product? What if we weren't trying to hide the scuffs and get rid of the grease and prevent the errant hands? What if our goal wasn't to tame the disorderly and manage our households? What if advertisers couldn't use our shame at the messiness of our lives in order to sell their brand?

Moreover, what if we weren't trying to cover anything up? What if our households did not depend on cheaply made products and underpaid labor? What if we had nothing to be ashamed of because we had refused to be part of the exploitation that creates the material substance behind our closed doors? What if we refused to accept that exploitation in the first place?

Why then, the advertisers would have nothing to sell. The factories would have no need to exploit. The husbands would have no fields to oversee. The corporations would have no profit. The savior would have no one to save.

Without the one little flaw, without the fear of imperfection, without the projected shame, white patriarchy would have no damsel to rescue. And without the Damsel in Distress, the wicked webs would have no one to lynch and no excuse to do so.

CHAPTER SIX

DAMSEL IN DISTRESS AND OTHER WHITE LIES

If Southern white men are not careful, they will over-reach themselves and public sentiment will have a reaction; a conclusion will then be reached which will be very damaging to the moral reputation of their women.

—Ida B. Wells

Nothing in the world is easier in the United States than to accuse a black man of crime.

—W. E. B. Du Bois

I have always liked boys. In my earliest recollection of this awareness, I am lying on the top bunk bed I shared with my younger sibling, Rainbow Brite sheets pulled up snugly under my chin, the roar of the slightly off-balance ceiling fan overhead. As I begin to drift off to sleep, I sweetly visualize a certain preschool classmate veering through the playground mulch on his Big Wheel. This sandy-haired, blue-eyed white boy was my first crush. Many followed.

In kindergarten I expressed my affection in a variety of ways. During recess when the boys declared their intent to chase after and capture the girls, I rejected their "boys rule!" propaganda and organized the girls to chase after them instead. During naptime I would frequently edge up to one of my many love interests and, once the lights were dim, spend the half hour whispering and planting kisses behind their ears. I'm pretty sure I got this notion from an ad I saw on TV.

Both my playground and naptime shenanigans, along with my long list of childhood crushes, included both Black and white boys. And later in elementary school, when I had a classmate of Mexican descent, it included him too.

In some ways the multiculturalists got this one right. As someone who grew up surrounded with many examples of interracial families, my early love of boys did not necessarily racially discriminate. In fact, I was far more likely to discriminate along class lines, feeling much less attracted to the white boys who lived in subsidized housing than my scholastically achieving Black classmates.

Of course, there was still a racial component to my class bias, since the ideal of whiteness has been defined in terms of upper-middle-class-ness; poor whites have historically had their whiteness policed by elites. In nineteenth- and early twentieth-century relationships with Black men, poor white women could figuratively lose their whiteness "because such relationships placed white women outside white space,"[1] according to historian Lisa Lindquist Dorr. The poorer the white woman, the more likely she was to be viewed as morally depraved and thus outside the full scope of white patriarchal protection.

That I was comfortably allowed to be unaware of my white(girl)ness within the context of these infatuations, playground chases, and naptime kisses can also be attributed to my race and class privilege, which shielded me from the knowledge of potential consequences. The most punishment I ever received from my grade-school teacher was an indication that I should stop the naptime kisses, offered as she suppressed a smile. More importantly, I was not privy to if, when, or at what age my Black classmates were warned of the historic and lasting dangers of pursuing and/or rejecting the advances of white girls and women.

That history is a gruesome one, which I have struggled to fully expose myself to and implicate myself in. I avoided preparing for this chapter for months, moving stacks of books on the subject from one side of the room to another, shelving and reshelving titles like Dorr's *White Women, Rape, and the Power of Race in Virginia: 1900–1960* in hopes that the harsh titles might disappear, or, better yet, transmit only the most critical information into the recesses of my mind from the safety of their shelves so I could avoid the emotional pain of reading and, especially, feeling this horrible history.

Yet, moving with and through feeling is paramount to our work with Mistress Syndrome, and—after being gently called in by Felicia on this topic—I eventually found myself under a comforting blanket with pen and notebook in hand, ready to open the pages, read, and process this repulsive section of our history.

PURITY AND PATERNALISM

The violence done to Black men and their communities based on white women and their families' accusations of rape and/or other "offenses" was a form of brutal terrorism. While extreme and ongoing violence happened both to enslaved and free people of African descent during Southern slavery, as historian Martha Hodes documents in the book *White Women, Black Men: Illicit Sex in the 19th-Century South*, this particular era of brutal torture, extrajudicial killing, and state-sanctioned murder burgeoned during and after the Civil War as a reassertion of white supremacy. Hodes describes the ways the rape of white women became a rallying cry for white violence:

> The ramifications of the sexualization of Reconstruction politics would be fully realized toward the end of the [nineteenth] century when the conflation of politics and sex transformed into the conflation of politics and rape. When lynching reached its height in the 1890s, white apologists invariably invoked the rape of white women as justification for extralegal execution.[2]

One third of all lynchings were in response to alleged sexual crimes against white women. And even if the person accused was to escape death at the hands of a lynch mob or the death penalty during court sentencing, the accused Black man would almost certainly be convicted by the white (male) judge and jury and injustice would be served.

While I'm not going to describe graphic details of the violence here, I do want to acknowledge the immense physical pain and psychological terror Black men and their communities experienced. Far from randomized acts of violence, mob lynching was an organized, highly coordinated, strategic terror campaign that received support from everyday white folks and the institutions they ran. To paraphrase Hodes's work, victims of lynchings were often pulled out of jail while awaiting trial, with no interference by law enforcement. Detailed descriptions of the violence as well as notices for upcoming public killings were printed in local newspapers. Stores sold souvenirs including photographs, postcards, and most disgustingly, body parts of the humans who had been mutilated. Trains added extra cars to transport an uptick in white families traveling to view the murders, and children were officially excused from school in order to attend.

This history is far from in the past. As I was originally writing this chapter, footage was released of two white men, a former police officer and his son, taking the life of Ahmaud Arbery, a Black man who was out on a run in Brunswick, Georgia. A neighbor didn't intervene, but instead participated by documenting the murder on his phone, which is why we know what happened and why, eventually, charges were brought. "Protecting" the neighborhood from Arbery's vaguely alluded criminality was his murderers' defense. Arbery's death via lynching is one of many in the past years, deaths that have increased, if not in number, in their visibility to white society.

As accusers of rape, white women played instrumental roles in this violence. Whether directly or by proxy of male family members, white women's accusations of rape or attempted rape required white men and their institutions to come to their rescue. By saying they had been assaulted by Black men, white women could invoke power as fearful, innocent, upstanding ladies in need of protection. While there were a very few white women who joined Black-led antilynching campaigns, the vast majority complied with this racist victim narrative, leaving a lasting legacy. Decades and even centuries later, those of us socialized as white women are still being acculturated to the idea that we are damsels in distress in need of paternal and state protection.

* * *

Despite my grade-school precociousness, my preteen and teen years were tragically uneventful in the love department. At home and at church, I received very clear messages about guarding my (white) female purity. Racial whiteness in regard to sexual purity was never explicitly named, but there were plenty of associations in hymns and during sermons equating whiteness with cleanliness, purity, and—oddly for such a southerly climate—with the moral spotlessness of being white as snow (an unhelpful reference given that I rarely got to play in the wonderfulness of this alleged snow).

My church youth group and the Christian-themed books my father sent my way positioned me in and out of an abstinence-only pop culture that equated true Christianity with sexual purity and a long list of (white) middle-class values. Classically, on my sixteenth birthday, he gifted me a book titled *I Kissed Dating Goodbye* that encouraged, along with abstinence, a type of courtship reminiscent of the plantation in which physical affection including kissing was admonished until the precise moment of matrimony.* The messages I received from this purity culture script were twofold:

1. I should be fearful and suspicious of boys' intentions due to their uncontrollable and constant sexual urges. My father and other older men signaled with their jokes and exaggerated performances of protective fatherhood that boys were not to be trusted and I would be kept safe only by playing by their paternal rules.

2. I should be fearful of myself and my own sexual urges, which were sinful and sneaky and could emerge without warning anytime. Kissing was a slippery slope, which, like dancing,

---

* Contemporary purity culture is linked to evangelical Christianity and includes things like strict binaried gendered norms, abstinence only, and modesty (Turner, "Purity Culture: Repercussions and How to Heal"). #ChurchToo came out of the #MeToo movement to expose how purity culture leads to rampant sexual abuse (Allison, *#ChurchToo*).

could lead to the sin of sex. And sexual desire was a switch I was supposed to keep officially off until my one-time marriage to one "right" Christian male mate.

As with other manifestations of Mistress Syndrome, this internalization of Damsel in Distress is a reaction to the violence of patriarchy. The Damsel in Distress invents agency for white women even as our systems and cultures disempower us. This Damsel in Distress trope warps the real historical gendered violence that white women continue to experience by exploiting the idea that we are in perilous, often sexualized, danger, don't have agency to do anything about it, and the wicked webs are our saving grace. We are positioned as beautiful, weak, delicate, pure, good, helpless, and in need of a strong, capable white man/savior/father/police officer to handle our problems. When we call on this narrative, we are positioning ourselves as blameless victims and centering ourselves with dramatic flair, and to our detriment.

Playing the Damsel in Distress has been anything but harmless. Even before Reconstruction-era lynch mobs, the idea of elite white women as damsels in distress was being fashioned on the plantation. In "Sexual Relations Between Elite White Women and Enslaved Men in the Antebellum South: A Socio-Historical Analysis," J. M. Allain describes the dual role of plantation mistresses as both sexually virtuous and sexually vulnerable in upholding white supremacy in the antebellum South. Allain writes, "Coupled with the notion of elite white female sexual virtue was that of white female vulnerability—the idea that plantation wives and daughters needed to be protected, defended, and sheltered."[3] Allain goes on to note how this served as a means of control citing political scientist Iris Young, "the role of the masculine protector puts those protected, paradigmatically women and children, in a subordinate position of dependence and obedience."[4]

Plantation mistresses used this notion of virtue to protect themselves from accusations of wrongdoing. If an elite white woman's sexual virtue was ever called into account, she could use an accusation of rape by a Black man to divert attention from any perceived sexual misconduct on her part. As Allain explains, "Because black men (like black women) were seen as inherently lustful and prone to sexual vice, for an elite woman to have illicit sex with a black rather than a white man might have been a slightly safer bet; it was easier to blame a black man of rape than a white man."[5] Both during and after the time of enslavement, elite white men were rarely tried for rape and even more rarely convicted.

Aligning ourselves historically with this victim narrative has come with many costs, for embracing the victim role perpetuates white supremacy *and* feeds into the scheme of patriarchy. Or in other words, this racist power dynamic was enabled precisely because of the patriarchal dynamic (white women were rendered sexually vulnerable with limited choices) and also despite it (Black men were excluded from the seat of patriarchal power). Allain points out how white women of the time used the tools of their own repression, mainly rape and the threat of its accusation, to abuse people they enslaved, ultimately reinforcing both patriarchal and racist oppression:

> In doing this, elite white women used one of the primary instruments of patriarchal repression—the idea that that they were weak and in need of white male protection, and by extension, in need of control and domination by white men—to exercise racial control over slaves. Instead of attempting to dismantle the white patriarchal hegemony that oppressed both slaves and (to a lesser extent) white women, predatory white women who coerced slaves into sex through threat of rape opted to perpetuate both white supremacy and patriarchy, by reinforcing paternalistic notions of female sexuality.[6]

After emancipation, white women continued to use claims of rape by Black men to cover up sexual indiscretions and reclaim a narrative of purity and innocence. As historian Dorr writes, "Accusing black lovers of rape renarrated a white woman's sexual indiscretion in a way that protected her respectability."[7] Through this uncomfortable and gruesome history, we white women learned that claiming victimhood works to deflect negative (and often unjust) consequences away from ourselves and toward another marginalized group of people. Thus, projecting a victim identity is a deeply embedded and sneaky dynamic with which we twenty-first century white women must contend.

DON'T WAKE THE DAMSEL

Once learned, it can be difficult to let go of a victim identity. When I feel hurt, it can be hard for me to see myself as having also caused harm. In those instances when I have felt the most wronged, it has been difficult not to grasp for a moral high ground—out of desperation, a sense of entitlement, or revenge. I see this in Mennonite communities—how our collective self-story has been so tied to righteous martyrdom that we are unable to see ourselves as complicit in the violence of the state. I see this in my relationship with my father, where my unhealed hurt has created a fixed narrative with him as the bad guy and myself as a victim, powerless to shift the dynamic. I see this with white women who are comfortable blaming white men for the ills of the world but refuse to see ourselves as oppressor. I see it in our equating catcalls with sexual assault or our impulse to call the police about a showing of disrespect by teenage boys.

It is very unpleasant to be enjoying the sunshine and blue sky on a walk to the park for a moment of respite and emotional fresh air and then be wrenched back to reality by lewd observations critiquing my body and unsolicited sexual invitations, like that one time I was a few blocks from home and walked past a group of preteen boys who decided to exercise their newly developing catcalling muscles. They were all Black children in a neighborhood being rapidly gentrified by white bodies like mine. And as they squeaked out a few choice phrases, carefully calculated at the moment I had just passed their group, a small flame of rage lit up in my insides.

As quickly as their phrases were uttered, my internal calculus was put into motion as I assessed their number, their ages, the proximity of other humans, the damage to my dignity, the potential damage to theirs, and if further confrontation would be dangerous and/or unhelpful to me, them, their families, the neighborhood, the City of Pittsburgh, and the universe. A slew of verbal responses flashed through my mind, mostly comebacks about their age (to minimize their manhood) or a reference to me being their grandmothers' peer (to pull rank based on age and to minimize their manhood). None of my draft responses seemed sufficient to address the complex age, race, and gender dynamic. Ultimately, I kept on walking. But half a block later, I felt frustrated with my lack of response. There was a residual ickiness because I had defaulted to inaction. I promised myself that next time I would engage in sincere, vulnerable, meaningful dialogue while communicating firm boundaries. Why had I been so afraid to engage with them? They were children.

On my best days, catcalling irritates me. It is a psychological reminder of how feminized bodies including mine are still vulnerable to the whims of men in power. And, while those preteen catcalls triggered a deep psychological nerve, those same preteens were far from the actual men in power. The truth is, I could walk away from them confident that my safety was not in jeopardy and also confident that any move I might have made in that moment would draw on the power vested in me by white supremacy. A scream, a text to a concerned friend, a post on Nextdoor, a photo on social media, a call to the police—evoking my white-lady Damsel in Distress in any way could have had serious, life-determining, and even potentially life-ending consequences for the catcallers. The gentrifying neighborhood, with its attentive police zone and concerned citizens, was ready and waiting for my Damsel in Distress to be activated at any time.[*]

On one dreary Pittsburgh evening, I found myself in the local grocery store shopping for beer. This was in part an effort to improve

---

[*] This readiness of response toward white women victims is not an abstract conjecture. In my neighborhood of over thirteen years, there was a clear disparity in police response based on the race and gender of the victims. When two white women were murdered in 2014 several blocks away from where I lived, there were helicopters and mass media coverage and street closures and an all-hands-on-deck search, which resulted in the apprehension of a suspect within weeks as a result of much acclaimed detective work. Around the same time and within a block radius of my home, four young Black men were murdered—one at the hands of police. The officer was exonerated. The three other cases received minimal news coverage and as far as I know, no one was ever arrested.

my relationship with my father by getting him a Christmas present I knew he'd enjoy rather than something sneakily pointed at helping him become the parent I wanted him to be. The ambience in the grocery store that night was festively fluorescent. The Salvation Army volunteer rang their bell and gave me a practiced stare meant to inspire the guiltiest of giving. I located the cardboard empties and proceeded to peruse the beer section.

Within moments a man appeared from behind the oranges to advise my selection. (Can't a girl read beer labels in peace?) This middle-aged white man got a little too close to my personal space bubble. I sent him away with a death stare, only to turn around and have another man approach me, this time someone who was younger and Black. Within seconds there was a white security guard at this Black man's back who—judging from the guard's eager expression—was looking for a reason to kick my unwanted admirer out of the store. Thus proceeded a delicate dance of letting my (it turned out, very persistent) admirer (who was still unaware of the presence of the security guard) down in a way that was clear, firm, polite, and did not arouse any emotion that would signal necessary intervention by the security guard. As with the catcall situation, I went into advanced calculus mode. I watched myself interact with him as warmly as possible while simultaneously processing a confusing mix of emotions that began with concern for my well-being, moved to anger and aggravation, and then, after realizing the reality of the situation, transformed into fear for his safety and my complicity in his danger. Ultimately, the interaction ended peacefully. When the admirer moved on, the security guard drifted on to another aisle, presumably to racially profile other customers.

All of this happened in under two minutes and was intellectually and emotionally draining. And while I was able to improvise this time, there were many more times when I have missed the subtleties or have become paralyzed by not knowing how to respond. Afterward, I began to reflect on the intensity of the moment and the options that had been available to me. In retrospect, I see how it would have been easy, even effortless, to let whiteness take care of the situation. I could have made a concerned sound, or been quietly irritated, or simply made eye contact with the security guard, and white patriarchy would have valiantly come to my aid. In fact, if the white security guard had not been directly in my line of sight, I might not have been so calculated in my response. Had the enforcement arm of white capitalism not been so visible, I might just as easily responded out of hurt and irritation, like I have done so often in the past. I might have reflexively reacted out of my own sense of injustice, seeking to flip the scales and dispel my feelings of disempowerment by telling him off or feigning distress without caring that it was whiteness doing the job. However, on this particular day at this store, the visibility of the security guard served as a clear reminder that my access to white power is predicated on my victimhood.

This is of course not to discount the many and real dangers of sexualized and gendered violence. As I have and will continue to emphasize, these wicked webs are set up so those dangers persist. Indeed, it is precisely because of our trauma responses to very real lived (historical, collective, and ongoing) experiences that such immediate fight mechanisms come through.

At the same time, I am curious about the specific contexts in which our defensiveness arises and those in which we feel comfortable enough to let it out. How might we have more options than past traumas would have us believe? When might we be safer than European patriarchy has taught us to think? Moreover, how do the rules about which men are dangerous activate our fear responses, meanwhile lulling us into a false sense of security about which men will keep us safe?

* * *

With the increased ability to document and share the ways Black and Brown communities are violently policed—via cell phones, the internet, and social media—now white people who care have been given an opportunity to learn what BIPOC communities have known for decades. The emergence of the "Karen" meme, for example, highlights a modern-day Damsel in Distress. These memes document how white women frequently call the cops on Black and Brown people who are going about their business in order to remove those same people from public (and also private) spaces. As political science and sociology professor Vesla Mae Weaver writes, the white people—and I would add, especially white women—who do this are not unaware of the racialized power they are invoking in this act. This perspective helps deconstruct a narrative of white-lady innocence that the Damsel in Distress trope would have us believe. Weaver writes:

> Most white Americans have little doubt about the distorted responsiveness likely to occur when they call the police on black people. They know, without having read the scores of **studies** on the subject, that whites are seen as more law-abiding by officers of the state, and that blackness itself is construed as suspicious and threatening....The odds are not in black people's favor if they contest police requests for ID or submission, as the examples of Philando Castile, Eric Garner, Sandra Bland, and too many other Americans attest.
>
> The breezy deployment of police by whites at Yale, at Starbucks, Walmart, and in other social spaces vividly reveals how white people use law enforcement to exert control over their fellow black Americans.[8]

By contrast, Weaver's research also documents the dangers of calling police for Black people: "Black Americans are more likely to be seen as defiant if they ask questions of the police, are reluctant to furnish their identification, or ask the police to leave."[9] Specifically, Weaver describes the structural barriers for Black women who call for help, including how Black women who report domestic violence often:

> **face eviction by landlords based on "nuisance" ordinance.** Such ordinances were designed, in theory, so that landlords can weed out people who call the police too often for frivolous reasons. In practice, they often penalize black women for seeking protection

from abusers if they have the misfortune of needing to call more than once or twice.[10]

Similar to my fellow white Americans, I was not unaware of this racialized dynamic as I worked on this manuscript for this book one hot and muggy July day. The windows were open and the box fan was buzzing. Unlike most of those white Americans Weaver references, however, I *had* read the studies on the subject (or at least some of them), so when the yelling outside began, I tried to block it out and stay focused on the pages of scrawled notes spread across the dining room table.

I must have read the line "At the advent of capitalism..." seven or eight times before standing up and moving to shut the front window to block out the neighborhood argument. As I was reaching up to grab the window's bottom edge, my eyes followed the voices. A young Black man was standing on one side of a car, while a young Black woman was shouting at him from the other side. Both were neighbors I'd seen before, coming and going. But other than the occasional brief wave, I had not built a relationship with either of them.

Seeing who was arguing (whom I perceived as a heterosexual couple), my immediate response was concern for her. I felt a wave of anxiety rush over my body. *Was she in trouble? If so, was there something I could or should do?* Stories of domestic partner abuse flashed across my mind. Yet, doubting both my ability to helpfully intervene and the appropriateness of a white lady stranger/neighbor doing so, I decided to stay put but keep watching in case the situation escalated or in the rare case a streak of anti-racist brilliance came to me about how to intervene without causing more harm.

I watched as my neighbor began furiously going in and out of the apartment's front door. She was shouting obscenities and throwing things, though I couldn't entirely tell what she was throwing without my glasses on—something lightweight? It floated before landing. But then a hard object hit the pavement and shattered into pieces. That one was definitely glass.

Well, it seems like she's more in control of the situation than I originally perceived, I thought. The man ducked behind the vehicle as another object flew his way. He wasn't responding aggressively. If anything, he was trying to de-escalate and avoid contact.

My shoulders relaxed a bit. There was some relief even as the distressed energy continued just feet from the table where I had more or less comfortably been writing about the discomfort of racism. Maybe I didn't need to feel such responsibility after all. I tended to my feelings of helplessness by reminding myself that my presence was neither going to rectify the immediate situation nor the five hundred years of what had enabled it. What I could do in the moment was keep furthering the anti-racist efforts of my book. I sent them positive energy, said a little prayer, and moved to sit back down.

As I was turning back to my pages, I noticed the young woman opening the back passenger-side door. She pulled out a baby. The yelling intensified and then the situation got physical as the young couple began to yank the child back and forth. She was throwing punches, even as the baby was right there between them.

I share these details not to voyeuristically pathologize this young Black family (and I hope you don't either), but to share with you how intense it became and how I responded.

Once the child emerged, my body went cold. My hands began to shake. Fear traveled up and down my spine. My auntie energy came out in full force. I felt a wave of concern for the child. In rushed protectiveness, my adrenaline spiked, and in a matter of seconds, without engaging the frontal cortex of my brain, I grabbed my phone, went outside, sat down on the front stoop, and dialed 911.

And then immediately hung up.

And then went inside and cried.

Had I avoided being a Karen? I'm still not sure.

I don't know if the couple took much note of my presence on the front stoop. Soon after my tears subsided, I heard a door slam and a car drive off. I felt relief and also regret and some shame. I regretted having used my body in that way. I regretted inserting myself and my whiteness because ultimately I needed to expel the discomfort of being in proximity to the symptoms of much bigger structural issues. And it wasn't that I had only cared about my own comfort—I was genuinely concerned for the well-being of my neighbors. And also, in this moment, my body revealed her white-body supremacy. Rather than draw on the hours and hours of my regular meditation practice, rather than ground down in faith traditions of prayer, rather than pause to notice the 4Ds, my body instinctively moved to remedy the situation and coerce—even if out of genuine concern—the Black bodies of my neighbors into stopping their fight or, at the very least, taking their argument far away from my concerned white-lady eyes and ears.

I write this last line with some level of hyperbole because I hold multiple truths here. It is both true that by calling the cops I would have been leveraging whiteness to quite literally police Black bodies in a public space (the street) as an extension of a private one (my home). And it is also true that all human bodies, including that child's, deserve access to safety. The problem was not that I wanted that situation to be different—we should have humane solutions and appropriate interventions to violence and harm, especially when there are children involved. That couple should not have had to navigate the myriad of unjust and inhumane things that were being thrown at them (poverty, structural racism, crappy housing, potentially inadequately supported young parenthood, etc.). The problem is and was that in that moment, the options available to us, and specifically to me, a status quo and passing white lady, are and were woefully inadequate, and having gone through with a phone call to the police would probably have exacerbated the harm (the parents might have been arrested, the child might have been put in state custody, etc.).

Perhaps, then, the gift from that experience came from being able to feel in my body—in my nervous system—the stress of one isolated moment. Perhaps it offered me the smallest of windows into an important reminder: that transforming violence and repairing harm without relying on the structures of whiteness is not something my white body, or any one person, could accomplish on their own.

That muggy July day sobered me to how the Damsel in Distress still could have dire consequences. This moment was not unconnected to white lady Amy Cooper calling the police on a Black birdwatcher for asking her to leash her dog, nor was it disconnected from the spine-chilling pursuit of a white neighborhood patrol hunting down Ahmaud Arbery. Like with the preteen catcallers and my persistent admirer in the beer section, such moments of blatant disrespect may trigger my own deep and insidious wounds. Like with my concerned auntie energy, our reactions aren't always coming from places of ill intent. However, in each of these instances there is context beyond the interpersonal interactions. That most white women aren't skilled in the advanced calculus of computing race and gender, that we aren't aware this advanced, emotionally draining calculus even exists, or (like me, on that July day) that we don't always slow down enough to do the math, is both a product of and function of our Mistress Syndrome. That we opt to leverage our Damsel in Distress, no matter our intent, is a decision we make with agency, a framework that, as Allain reminds us, has ultimately "served as a means of patriarchal control."[11]

DATING AND NOT DATING

At the same time I received those messages about dating and my Christian virtue, I received somewhat contradictory signals about dating from my peers at school. By middle school, most of my friends were beginning to date. As far as I could tell, "dating" meant passing notes that confirmed mutual admiration and sitting together on the bus while the singles fawned and talked about the couples. As a single who still fostered many crushes, I was deeply disappointed that these relationships weren't happening for me. I too wished to receive the romantic attention that seemed to flow abundantly toward many of my friends.

Alongside my wistfulness for middle school romance was confusion. Hadn't I been warned that I would need to fend off advances? Hadn't I been assured public displays of interest? Wasn't I supposed to be on guard for the throngs of boys so eager to test my boundaries? Where, then, were all the promised advances?

What began to emerge for me was a feeling of inadequacy. Over the course of my brief dozen years on the planet, I had received constant messaging about my (white) feminine desirability. Sitting on the school bus, watching my friends receive cleverly folded notes proclaiming affection, I began to equate the lack of public declarations as a failure of my own. Sandwiched between the fear of male advances and the thrilling expectation of them, I began to believe there was something wrong with me. In the face of my inadequacies, I began to feel a sense of shame.

Just as it had for early twentieth-century white women, victimhood came to my aid. I began to hide behind my religious upbringing and blame my lack of a dating life on my father's strict and weird conservative views. When friends giggled about passing notes in class and the upcoming school dance, I made sure to remind them that my dad had declared dating was off the table until I was at least thirty. Technically, this was true. My dad had said that. But also true was that I wielded much more power within my family system than I was willing to reveal. Rather than rebel or take my dad's platitudes in stride while continuing to flirt with the possibility of dating, I opted to hide under the mantle of white patriarchal protection. I sought to cover up what I perceived as my intrinsic faults in a (dis)guise of enforced Christian purity.

I recognize that using my religious father as a cop-out to avoid the stress and anxiety of the dating world is not exactly equivalent to white women's accusations of rape in the segregated South. For one thing, scapegoating a white man for acting in ways consistent with white patriarchal power has extremely different consequences than for Black people accused of subverting race hierarchy. Yet despite this vast difference, I am curious how my invoking the protection of white patriarchal power has resulted in its reinforcement. Perhaps its reinforcement happened in my internalization of it: that good girls are responsible for keeping their sexual purity intact and that only good girls deserve this protection. Privilege, after all, has its conditions.

As Dorr points out, calling on white supremacy, as in the planta-tion-era South, "did not guarantee a woman's place in the sheltered arena of white womanhood."[12] Instead:

> Considerations about women's class and willingness to uphold gender norms determined the power of their whiteness. Only when paired with respectability did whiteness grant women true social power and earn them the full measure of white men's protection.[13]

In almost all of the cases of rape allegations in Virginia between 1900 and 1960, as Dorr documents, Black men were convicted, but that didn't necessarily mean the white women were believed.

Even beyond perceived respectability, this conditional protection did not extend to protect white women from the very white men who were so publicly concerned about their vulnerability. As Hodes points out, in instances when white fathers and husbands coerced white women to testify against Black men, physical force was often used. The bruises and other markings of violence which came at the hands of white family members could then be used in court "as evidence of rape by a black man."[14] Hodes quotes activist Nannie Buroughs on her observations of the limits of white patriarchal protection, "The same man who will join a [lynch] mob…will outrage a black or white woman any time he makes up his mind so to do."[15]

I found out about the limits of Damsel in Distress firsthand when finally sharing with my father about my childhood abuse by a peer at church, to which he responded with an air of dismissiveness. I will share more of that painful story later, but what is important for this moment is to note how early the paradoxes of white-girl purity and victimization had already settled into my psyche. As young as eight or nine, I somehow already knew it was my responsibility to both fend off male advances and also to keep them secret and thus keep my respectability intact. Despite the rhetoric of paternal protection, my nine-year-old self did not have enough confidence in its existence to seek it. And when I eventually did call upon that white patriarchal protection (twenty-five years later) and expected that at the very least it would muster some rage on my behalf...*poof!* It was gone. It turns out it was not available to me if it meant holding another white man (or boy) accountable, or perhaps if it meant white patriarchal protection had retroactively failed.

INTERSECTIONAL HARMS

Racial justice was the theme of Felicia's wedding. It was integrated into the vows, the music, the organic farm on which they were married, and the organic food that we ate. The guest list was a testimony to the diversity of their friends and family as well as to the work they have been part of cultivating in the world. Among many guests I was eager to meet were folks who had been anti-racist organizers long before I knew the term existed.

I found myself alone with one of these anti-racist exemplars, a man of color much older than me. I was eager to connect with him around our work and mutual network, so it caught me off guard when one of the first things he did was tell me what a beautiful woman I was.

We had been the first to arrive at the designated meetup and it was just the two of us when he led with the compliment. Immediately, I felt uncomfortable and confused. *Had I heard him right?* The only time men I didn't know commented on my appearance like this was when I was being hit on. Aware of our differences in age and career status, I felt vulnerable to the layers of power dynamics at play. It brought up a mixture of shame and anger, the familiar feelings of being objectified.

Many of the above reflections were things I was able to name later. Because at that moment, I froze. In my confusion and discomfort, I managed a thin and awkward "thank you" as other guests began to roll in.

A second interaction happened during the wedding.

Getting the bridal party to the wedding site had been an ordeal. There had been wardrobe problem-solving, last-minute makeup tweaks, and some tense family dynamics, but eventually Felicia, Kayla, and I made it just as the first wedding guests were beginning to arrive. Almost a year after the Thanksgiving Disaster file and with my apology email long in the past, the three of us had gone on an epic vacation. Besides, the flurry of wedding planning had given Kayla and I much to bond over.

All this is to say that my brow was probably wrinkled and my lips terse as we arrived at the wedding site. I headed over to the area where we were supposed to line up when a second uncomfortable incident occurred.

"Smile," he told me, which was the precise moment I began to feel rage.

And then it was time for the festivities. Not wanting to cause a scene (and not sure how to succinctly address his comments), I ignored them, took a deep breath, and prepared to walk down the aisle. But the rage was still boiling inside. I thought about the history of men telling women to present happily in the face of violence done against them. I ruminated on how feminized bodies have been judged and valued based on white patriarchal standards of beauty. I contemplated consent. Who gave this man the right to comment on my appearance or tell me how to express my emotions? I certainly had not agreed to be in that type of relationship with him.

I was not naïve to the intersectional dynamics at play. While feeling rage, I was also aware of the long history of white women accusing men of color of sexual inappropriateness and of the consequences. I was aware that outside of our little anti-racist organizing bubble, and even perhaps in some nooks and crannies within it, I held significant power despite our differences in age and status. I was aware of what alerting external institutions to my Damsel in Distress might bring.

I knew I didn't want to cause unnecessary harm, and I also knew I shouldn't have been put in that position. I certainly didn't want to be part of an anti-racist culture that wasn't intersectional. So, what could I do?

Thankfully, I am not the first to have asked this question. There is a long history of communities most marginalized by the state—sex workers, communities of color, people with mental illness and other disabilities—coming together to address harm, co-create community accountability, and work toward repair in ways that don't rely on external systems. Similar to restorative justice approaches, which seek to address harm in nonpunitive and relational ways, transformative justice goes even further in its assessment of harmful systems and seeks to transform systemic violence while building toward mechanisms of accountability.* Notably, as Prison Industrial Complex (PIC) abolitionist Mariame Kaba points out, the origins of transformative justice and movements to end the PIC come out of work "by anti-violence activists of color, in particular, who wanted to create responses to violence that do what criminal punishment systems fail to do."[16]

The anti-racist work Felicia and I had been organizing around sought this too, and our relationships became a space of practice. Perhaps even this super-uncomfortable moment was an opportunity for such practice? But I still wasn't sure. Doubt crept in. Was such a small exchange worth bothering Felicia on her day of celebration?

I also wanted to be sure my white-ladyness wasn't blowing the incidents out of proportion. I found a moment to mention to Kayla what he had said. She concurred that it was creepy. *Okay*, I thought, reassured. *I don't need to doubt that there had been some inappropriateness.*

I waited until the day after the festivities to bring it up with Felicia, although I was still hesitant. She could tell something was up. I confessed I didn't want to take away from her celebration. "What is it, Amanda?" she pressed me to share anyway. I told her how he and I had been alone, what he had said, and how I had felt. I remember her pausing thoughtfully, her brow gently furrowed. She thanked me for letting her know. "We'll address it," she said and then we resumed the busyness of post-wedding cleanup.

---

* I find Anthony Nocella's distinction between restorative justice and transformative justice helpful: "Restorative justice stresses that the system is flawed, overworked, and retributive, but does not address why it exists, how it is racist, sexist, ableist, and classist, whom it benefits, and how it was developed. Transformative justice…is about looking for the good within others while also being aware of complex systems of domination. If the world is to transform, we need everyone to transform and everyone to be voluntarily involved in critical dialogue together" ("An Overview of the History and Theory of Transformative Justice," 4.).

An extended time later, she convened the three of us for a phone call. I anticipated an uncomfortable conversation but was optimistic for some level of resolution; after all, this was the type of movement work I wanted to be a part of. I was new at naming this level of discomfort directly to the person who had caused it, especially in navigating such a complex web of identities and power dynamics and especially in sharing feelings of discomfort or harm with a person of color. *Okay Amanda, you can do this.* I prepared to challenge myself by being vulnerable and speaking courageously. And during that conversation I did feel proud about having honestly shared my experience and feelings around it.

What I was not prepared for, however, was his response. He apologized for making me feel uncomfortable and in the same breath denied any sexism. His view was that in naming my discomfort, I was calling upon the trauma of men of color having to police themselves around white women.

I left that conversation with more questions than answers, feeling lifetimes away from any resolution. I felt newly enraged from having my experiences qualified. Sure, I could hold the both/and that naming my discomfort summoned his own trauma, but shouldn't my discomfort have some weight? Did it not matter that I was bringing it up within the safety of an anti-racist community who highly regarded him? Didn't it matter that I was quite aware of the racialized dynamic and had chosen my confidants carefully? I had hoped at the least that he would have considered how his words were sexist and inappropriate instead of dismissing them because of my whiteness.

I'm sure he would reflect on the above experience very differently.

* * *

As with the other archetypes of white womanhood, the power of the Damsel in Distress lies in its conditions—conditions that have caused immense suffering. If the Damsel in Distress is not the power we want to yield, then what is the power that we do?

The healing work for us Damsels in recovery is both a self-reflective path and one that happens within community. When I reflect back on that makeshift attempt at community accountability, it's easy for me to feel dissatisfied and perhaps a little bitter. I wish I could tell you that his flaws humanized him for me, but I'm not so sure that's true. I'm not so sure he didn't go from anti-racist exemplar to disappointing sexist villain in my mind. I wish I had a neater intersectional anti-racist epiphany to share with you, one that illustrates how an accountability process led us to organize better together. But this one wasn't that. Perhaps this epiphany was more about starting to externalize the internal work, about me beginning to practice, and about the spaces, and moreover, the relationships in which I felt safe enough to try to not go at it alone.

This discernment is part of the process, and as I reflect on the feelings that still linger, I wonder if my bitterness also points to some important information. My bitterness points to some level of expectation of better and different. It points to my capacity to dream. I want to have meaningful courageous relationships. I want to be a part of co-creating something new.

And even as I reclaim these desires, the unfortunate truth of section II is we are only halfway through. Good Plantation Wife. Vixen Mistress. Damsel in Distress. We still have more patterns to acknowledge and mourn. Great White Mother. White Savior. There is still work to do in order to revolutionize.

Today, even in a city as white as Pittsburgh, public displays of interracial affection have become a familiar sight. Since 1967, the interracial marriage rate has steadily risen in the US, and Black men are twice as likely as Black women to marry someone outside their race.[17] Likewise, the rate of nonwhite children born to white parents has increased, along with rates of transracial adoption. Which brings us to a complex and tender area of consideration: What does it mean for white women to raise nonwhite children?

CHAPTER SEVEN

(THE GREAT WHITE) MOTHER KNOWS BEST

These women guaranteed that racial segregation seeped into the nooks and crannies of public life and private matters, of congressional campaigns and PTA meetings, of cotton policy and household economies, and of textbook debates and day care decisions. White women were the mass in massive resistance.

—Elizabeth Gillespie McRae

These mothers, victims themselves, have unwittingly become wounded wounders.

—Sue Monk Kidd

At the time of writing this book, I do not have children. Nor do I plan to.

While some of my classmates drafted long lists of baby names, I found parenting play odd. I did not have a list of potential names amongst the pages of my diary, nor had I fantasized about having children of my own. In fact, except for a three-year window in my early thirties, this disinterest in parenting continued into my adulthood.

Don't let my desire for childlessness fool you; I love kids. I am proud to be an aunt in keeping with my namesake and have been helping to raise children younger than myself since I was one, back in my Atlanta church nursery.

Still, being an aunt—through my family of origin and chosen community—is very different than being a parent, which is why I have hesitated to write about Mistress Syndrome and parenting. I planned on avoiding the topic altogether until Felicia (a parent of two and community mother to many) pressed me to reconsider. "I see white women raising Black children everywhere," she said to me, her pain becoming clearer as she mentioned the young white couple who had recently moved in next door, appearing one spring day with their deeply melanated infant. As they paraded around the gentrifying neighborhood, their child tucked securely in the posh stroller, they seemed unaware of what they were bringing up for their Black neighbors. They seemed equally unaware of the racialized harms they might end up causing their child in their own home.

In my organizing with other white ladies, parenting is one of the most volatile topics we discuss. Parents are often emotionally tired and physically sleep deprived from the daily and lifelong grind of being responsible for another human's well-being. In our individualistic society, we have few parental supports, yet very high demands. Parents, especially mothers, receive unsolicited pressure and advice about their parenting from a wide spectrum of advisers, from close confidants to strangers on the street.

That mothers specifically have been told, both implicitly and explicitly, that their children's behavior directly reflects their moral competence is one part of our Mistress Syndrome inheritance. Historically, this moral competence was measured by the plantation mistress's ability to elegantly control her household—children included, just as today's mothers are expected to effortlessly keep everyone happy, healthy, and well-behaved. Add in the devaluation of reproductive labor and I get why conversations about parenting incite defensiveness.

I also don't know the details of your unique story. If you are a parent, I don't know how you became one and why, or the details about with whom you may or may not parent and how that relationship impacts your parenting. What I do know is that in the past few decades, a lot of white people, and white women in particular, have become parents to children of color. I know, too, that many of these parents are new to thinking deeply about their children's race and, moreover, new to thinking deeply about their own. I also know from my experience organizing with young people that many youth who realize the painful realities of racism in adolescence have been ill-prepared for these realizations and often have little to no support to talk honestly and deeply about race with white parents at home, especially when this means confronting the racism in how they were raised.

With celebrities making transracial international adoption trendy, with the rise of fetishizing People of the Global Majority and appropriating their cultures, with saving the children becoming a way to virtue signal generosity, clarifying the connection between Mistress Syndrome and parenting is unfortunately unavoidable. Since the invention of race, the reality of white women raising children of color has not been warm and fuzzy. It is a history that impacts the way we parent today and one that I have rarely heard white parents consider.

Before the Civil War, there was sometimes a small degree of tolerance for illicit liaisons between white women and Black men. But that tolerance ended the moment children came into the picture. Children from these liaisons formed a direct threat to race-based slavery, especially when born to a white mother. According to Hodes, "It was the presence of free children that precipitated a local crisis."[1] Hodes further explains, "The children of white women and black men were of partial African ancestry but also free, thereby violating the equation of blackness and slavery."[2] For the children who grew up free and Black, their very existence challenged white patriarchal norms.

Within this fraught context, white women responded to getting pregnant by Black men in a variety of ways. In many of the cases Hodes highlights, they responded in ways that protected their whiteness first and their children second, frequently accusing the father of rape. A horrendous, little-discussed part of our history is that when faced with bearing a nonwhite child, white women were known to leave newborns at church doorsteps, commit infanticide, and sell their own children into slavery. We have yet to acknowledge these painful parts of our legacies; we have yet to even begin to grieve them.

In cases when white women kept and raised their children of mixed African and European ancestry, their families were pushed to the far margins of white society and endured a distinctive set of economic and social hardships.

* * *

There is a symbolic nature to interracial families that we've been taught flies in the face of racism. Indeed, these interracial love children challenge the purported logic of racism in many ways. However, throughout history and especially now, the isolated act of having children of mixed-race ancestry has not succeeded in bringing racism to its knees. Decades after the end of legal segregation, having an interracial family does not necessarily challenge the intransigence of racism, nor does it end it. The symbolism of interracial families can be so loud in its calling upon courageous love across forbidden racial boundaries that it can silence the ways these familial arrangements continue to uphold racism, especially the impact on the children raised within them.

I'm thinking especially of white women who have defied their openly bigoted white families in order to be in relationships with People of Color. One of my colleagues comes to mind. She married a Black man and had given birth to and raised children with him. Her sorrow was evident as she told me about the lengths to which they had gone to create their family and the painful loss of relationship with her family of origin because of it. It must have been a harrowing feat to defy her family and her socialization so thoroughly. As she put it, she gave up all she had known for love.

She was in tune with the discrimination her children, husband, and family faced. She was sensitive to the ways her kids were treated differently at school and how she was often not read in public as their parent. In the same way she fought against the racism within her birth family, she fought racism on behalf of her kids, which is awesome and important. But this sense of herself as victim and protector was, in many ways, where her narrative stopped.

Then she traveled with a Black colleague to attend a comprehensive anti-racist workshop. Despite her intimate family relationships and thus cultural familiarity with Black people, her colleagues at work complained about her ongoing ~~micro~~aggressions in her interactions with them. One of the things they observed was how her interracial family relationships gave her a sense of overfamiliarity with Black people and cultures. She extended this overfamiliarity to the Black women with whom she worked, perhaps assuming that because of her proximity to Blackness as a wife, mother, daughter-in-law, etc., they would be comfortable with her being so comfortable with them.

Unfortunately, she returned from the anti-racist workshop feeling she'd been attacked. The analysis shared at the workshop contradicted her self-story, one in which she saw herself as the victim of her family's bigotry and as a fighter and protector in the face of such hardship. How could anyone accuse *her* of perpetuating racism when she had restructured her life so completely to defy it?

I share parts of my colleague's experience here, because hers is not a rare contradiction. How heart-wrenching to have been rejected by her family in those ways. Her pain is deep and legitimate, her sacrifices real. I want her to be able to name the injustices of her situation and feel safe to express her pain. Those are some deep wounds to tend to.

And also, her story has me wondering about when and how our hurt gets misplaced. What are the ways we white women misdirect and project the wounds of Mistress Syndrome? The perpetrator of my colleague's pain is not the anti-racist analysis delivered at the workshop or the feedback given by her colleagues. The culprit of racism is much bigger and more insidious. It persists despite her individual courageous actions and their hurtful and disappointing consequences.

This contradiction can be a hard one. Being victimized in one extremely painful dynamic does not make us a victim in other situations. Standing up courageously against racism in one context does not mean we will automatically make anti-racist choices in future scenarios. How might an identity of victim/protector hide other aspects of parenting while white? How might it cause us to then misunderstand our agency to protect (our) children both inside and outside of our home space?

Among other things, it's hard to prepare children to navigate the world in their racialized bodies if we don't know how we navigate the world through our own. Many white parents (and people) have not deeply investigated their own whiteness, including how their family of origin was racialized and how race shaped them, what that means when it comes to parenting, and how they can disinvest from parenting out of whiteness. These are all important things to consider and fortunately there are a growing number of resources out there and communities coming together to do this work.*

I bring this up not as critique, but as encouragement. For the many white parents out there raising children of color, there is so much important, difficult, and wonderful work to be done. Whether you are in an interracial relationship, whether you are the primary parent or caregiver, whether you and a white partner(s) have adopted children of a different racial, cultural, and ethnic background regardless of your specific interracial family configuration, there are so many things within your power to change. A great place to start is beginning to learn more about how you've been racialized as white and what that means culturally for you, your parenting, your extended family dynamics, and your child.

In my experience of organizing with youth, some of the young people who struggled the most with the anti-racist analysis were youth of color who had been raised primarily by white parents. At home, many of them had been raised within white culture and had been taught to navigate the world through the lens of whiteness. Yet when they moved out into the world, and increasingly so in adolescence, without the racial advantage of having a white parent nearby, they began to be treated outside of the bounds of whiteness as a racialized other. There was so much their parents had missed in preparing them to navigate the world in their Black, Brown, and Asian bodies. Strategies of multicultural celebration and individual exceptionality had not offered them the deeper tools of psychological resilience that communities of color have been cultivating for centuries.

---

* See Resources for Further Support and Bibliography.

I name these dynamics not to blame or shame parents. I offer it as an invitation for all of us to learn and unlearn and to grow. I offer it as an invitation of interdependence because, as a nonparenting person, these are crucial contributions I can't make, and they are contributions that are so needed.

I have seen adoptive white parents embrace multiculturalism and celebrate their child's ethnic origin and identity, supplementing their parenting with cultural exposure like cultural and religious school, language learning and retention, visits to birth communities, and celebrating cultural holidays. I've witnessed white parents building community with other adoptive families and connecting to local communities that align with their child's culture of birth. All of this is significant and important. Supporting a child in knowing where they come from and who they are is critical identity work.

And also, there is a nuanced aspect to this identity work that usually gets missed because whiteness restricts identity as individual rather than collective. Given the way race functions today, white parents, no matter how racially aware, will not be able to adequately prepare their children of color to navigate racism. Even if they have spent decades of life in anti-racist practice, white parents can never be fully equipped because they will never know what it's like to be in the world racialized as nonwhite and through their child's specific racialized identity.

I get that no parent is ever truly able to entirely prepare their child for anything, but there are things white parents can do especially when it comes to prioritizing reciprocal relationships within the communities from which children of color belong. Are white parents engaging in long-term, accountable peer and mentee relationships with adults and elders of their children's racialized and ethnic communities? Are there peer relationships in which there can be both loving support and honest challenge? Our children need these deep, authentic, and ongoing relationships, too. That most white parents exploring adoption or who are in transracial partnerships have not prioritized these community relationships is of real concern. From my vantage point, many white parents don't have these preexisting relationships, haven't considered how they will support their children in growing up within a different cultural context, and don't know how to identify what their own culture is, including the presence of white culture in the home.

ADOPTING ETHICS

During my three-year baby-temptation window there were a few possible scenarios that would have had me raising a child of color. My former partner and I had decided against bringing biological children into the world. Our options for parenting then were limited to adoption, fostering, and being named guardians in an aunt and uncle's will.

My short and shallow dip into the adoption and fostering innerwebs was sobering. I found out that adoption rates are higher for white babies and that white babies cost more. For one thing, the fact that babies *cost*—that people are paying for children, that white people can and do pay for Black and Brown babies—deeply disturbed me. I felt the nausea of the slave auction block, that troubled feeling in my gut when I first heard about the graves of Native children found behind boarding schools. I remembered how poor European children were sent into servitude an ocean away.* Certainly, adoption agencies are not the first to have commodified children.

I understand intellectually that adoption agencies have staff, legal, and childcare costs, and that is what adoptive parents are paying for, but there is still something gut-turning about the industry's proximity to buying and selling children, the dis-ease of racist capitalism's supply and demand. Many of these children may be in impoverished and sometimes desperate situations, often without family support. Yet adopting one child does little to address the causes of racist imperialism and economic injustice that likely created the need for adoption in the first place. Adopting does not fix the reasons why children enter

---

* Boats of European children were shipped as indentured colonial servants to families who paid for them.

adoption and foster systems. It won't address the economic realities of their birth families, the disempowerment of their birth parents' reproductive choices, the depletion of mental health resources, or the internalized racism of the teacher or social worker who handed over the child to the state. It certainly doesn't address how an international industry has been established to cater to wealthy white North Americans.

Like any decision made within these wicked webs, there are fraught ethical dilemmas within fraught systems, but that doesn't mean we shouldn't try. One of the many things we can do is to educate ourselves about adoption agencies and their contexts. As I began research for this chapter, what I found was sobering.

Frequently—and this was news to me—many children made available for international adoption actually do have family in their lives who have been misled by the adoption agency, never consenting to give up parental rights. As in the story of one white woman, Jessica Davis, who adopted a child from Uganda and later realized the orphaned child she and her family were trying to "save" already had a family. In her article "The 'Orphan' I Adopted from Uganda Already Had a Family," Davis identifies her family's motivations for adopting:

> We were already parents to four biological children, so this was not about "having another child" or simply "growing our family." For us, adopting was about sharing our abundance—our family, love and home with a child who lacked these basic necessities.[3]

Davis also points to Catholic Relief Services statistics that reveal that the "vast majority of children in orphanages, and countless children adopted internationally, are not orphans at all."[4] In this case, Davis's good intentions—her recognition of her family's privileges, having the desire to share, the welcoming of a child into her family with open arms and love—ultimately helped reunite this stolen child with their family, but it also was what motivated the separation in the first place.

THE GREAT WHITE MOTHER

I am thinking about the messages that lead up to such problematic situations, how white motherhood has been signaled as blanketly benevolent, the model for what all children need. Those of us with younger siblings or who grew up in homes with strictly defined gender roles learned from an early age that helping take care of others earned us the praise of "mother's little helper." From baby dolls to kitchen sets, there are many ways we signal to white children gendered girls that they should become white mothers.

Personally, I started taking care of babies at the church nursery when I was practically still one myself. Not only was it fun to play with the younger kids and their toys and help my parents on nursery duty, but I also got to skip sitting through the sermon and lengthy prayers. By middle school, childcare had turned into a lucrative business, one that helped pay for my first car, college living expenses, and travel. As an added bonus, the positive reinforcement was amazing. It turned out (mostly white) mothers all over the country needed me! And so did their kids. I was paid and praised to help. My helping skills put me high in demand.

As I will continue to go into in the next chapter on white saviorism, today's positive maternal reinforcements come from centuries of messaging about our role in helping, fixing, and saving others. Likewise, we have received very specific messaging about our entitlement to parent poor and nonwhite children. Today's messages go back to a history that positioned white women as benevolent bearers of (white) civilization.

On the antebellum plantation, enslavement had been justified through a paternalistic narrative in which elite white women were responsible for the order of the household. Such "order" was maintained through the relentless use of psychological and physical violence for the purpose of "civilizing" those they enslaved, including children. As we touched on in chapter four, US chattel slavery stripped the paternal and maternal authority of enslaved parents, relocating it to the master and mistress of the plantation. The characterization of people of African descent as childlike and in need of protection on one hand and as dangerous, primitive, and hypersexual on the other imbued the white plantation owner and his mistress with an inflated sense of self-worth based on their (God-ordained) role as parent, protector, disciplinarian, and enforcer. Glymph describes the civilizing role for white women:

> This civilizing mission cast enslaved women as the antithesis of civilization, as a standard against which white women and their progress on the road to civilization would be measured. In the U.S. South, as elsewhere in western bourgeois culture by the mid-nineteenth century, order, management, and discipline became important touchstones of the meaning of civilization.[5]

This contrived role as civilizer, domestic manager, and tough love disciplinarian set a maternalistic precedent for helping, fixing, and saving in the name of racism. As the US Civil War ended and enslaved people were no longer available to "manage" (as in the case of elite Southern white women) or "save" from slavery (for those in the north), white women were promoted out of the home and into a more public "civilizing" role.

The post–Civil War Reconstruction era* was a harsh wake-up call for plantation mistresses who had built not only their material lives upon enslaving humans, but also a sense of self as "honorable, just, and loved by their slaves."[6] In the waning months of 1865 and throughout 1866, people who had been domestic slaves defected in droves, undermining this narrative of dependence and loyalty. Now without humans to enslave and without people who required management, discipline, and Christian direction, what foundational identity did white women have to call upon? Glymph chronicles one such former mistress, Mrs. Thomas, who

> despite emancipation and trying financial times…still defined herself as a mistress. That was her identity, and when the basis

---

* The period of time after slavery was abolished (except in cases of incarceration), called Reconstruction, was short-lived (twelve-ish years) and ultimately inadequate to repair two hundred years of chattel slavery and brutal structural racism.

for its creation and existence was destroyed, maternalism was all she had left.[7]

At the same time as Reconstruction, the suffragist movement gained momentum from white women's newfound access to public spheres and was strengthened by appropriating Abraham Lincoln's white male liberator into one of the white female civilizer.[*] This included white women's role in the forced education of Indigenous children through boarding schools and through a descent in droves by Northern white women to educate Black children in the South.

This shift in relocating the role of civilizer to upper-class white women meant a reclamation of the emotional and sexual traits—i.e., reproductive labor—that had been so devalued by white men in the past (see chapter three). As historian Louise Michele Newman notes, "Instead of denying that 'female instincts' were inherent to white women," as other suffragists had argued against gender essentialism before, "[Ora] Brashere [a white woman suffragist] and others responded that feminine qualities ought to be more highly valued for their centrality to the white race and to US society as a whole in its competition for international status and power."[8]

During this era, the term "Great Mother" (referencing Queen Victoria) was invoked within the parlance of treaty negotiations

---

* According to Newman: "Social-Darwinian theories encouraged and enabled the development of ideologies concerning white middle-class women's emancipation that emphasized (white) women's specific role as the 'conservators of race traits' and the 'civilizers' of racial and class inferiors. The Anglo-Saxon Protestant woman's self-proclaimed burden at the turn of the century was to help her nation in rescuing these so-called primitive and working-class peoples from stagnation and decay, to protect them from the violent abuses of the U.S. government (and primitive and working-class women from the supposed abuses of their men), and to assimilate evolutionary inferiors into a more advanced Christian civilization. White women who participated in domestic and foreign missionary societies, in the local, national, and world temperance movements, in the settlement house movement, in the international peace movement—in any of the organized white woman's movements at the turn of the century—built their institutions on the premise that they, as Anglo-Saxon Protestant women, were the best conveyors of advanced civilization" (*White Women's Rights*, 23).

between Great Britain and First Nations people in current-day Canada. Similar to "Great White Father" references stateside, this relational styling signaled to Indigenous people that there had been "created an irrevocable, perpetual familial relationship with the British Crown, based on concepts, principles and laws defined in Cree as *wahkohtowin* (good relationships)."[9] As the Manitoba Historical Society Archives goes on to note, the mother/child relationship within Cree culture "is characterized by mutual respect and reciprocal duties of nurturing, caring, loyalty and fidelity."[10] Needless to say, mutual respect and reciprocity was not what Western consciousness had in mind in its maternalistic/paternalistic conceptualizations of the terms.*

Elevating female power without disrupting the racial hierarchy was tricky business for suffragist strategists of the time. Late-nineteenth century concepts of white superiority relied on the hierarchy of sexual difference as modeled by the more "civilized" white race. Thus, developing this maternalistic niche was key to white women's reassurance "that increasing the similarity of activities performed by themselves and (white) men would not bring about racial degeneration or undermine their own racialized conceptions of themselves as belonging to a superior race and civilization."[11]

FRAUGHT SYSTEMS, FRAUGHT CHOICES

When my aunt and uncle decided to adopt internationally, they recommended a resource for the rest of us to read. Adoption was new to our (very white) family. I wanted to be supportive and figured I could learn something too. I promptly put the book on hold at my neighborhood library branch.

---

* Such "Great Mother" invocations may not have always had their desired effects: As one August 1874 record notes: "During the Pow Wow Col. French, in order to impress them with the wide power of Queen Victoria said 'The Great White Mother has Red Children, white children and black children.' Whereupon one of the back row braves remarked in a loud stage aside 'Well, it seems to me that the Great White Mother must be a woman of very easy virtue'—or words to that effect" (Carter, "Manitoba History: 'Your Great Mother Across the Salt Sea'").

I remember it being a quick read. I flipped through the pages while propped up in bed, reading for new information and also searching for subtext. What was it that my family members wanted me to know, or, more importantly, to do? The book's title seemed an accurate summary. *In On It: What Adoptive Parents Would Like You to Know About Adoption. A Guide for Relatives & Friends* tried to clue in the clueless and educate the extended communities of adoptive families on the background information, motivations, and details of adoption so that adoptive parents wouldn't have to. And I sincerely appreciated the author's perspective, especially the explanation of the adoption process and examples of hardships adoptive parents face and how adoptive families are often othered, even by well-meaning family and friends.[*]

At the time, there were few resources about international/transracial adoption, very few written from the perspective of international/transracial adoptees, and fewer still that integrated an analysis of anti-racism and examined whiteness within transracial adoption. While thankfully today there are more of those types of resources, narratives that center the experience of white adoptive parents, and without an examination of whiteness, persist.

Years later, having tangentially experienced the intense ups and downs of their international adoption process, I have forgotten most of the book's advice, though something about its title has stuck with me. "In On It" implies that there is indeed something to be *in on*.

Considering the title now, new questions come up for me. What exactly is *it*? And what does it mean to be *in on it*? Given the history I was learning about whiteness and imperialism, did I even want to be? I knew even then, as is still true for me today, I wanted to be supportive of diversity within our family. I knew I valued expanding our understanding of "family." I knew I loved my family members and deeply cared about our relationships. I knew I wanted to welcome any and all new family members with unconditional love, especially

---

[*] Though written from the perspective of an international and transracial adoptive parent, *In On It* did not really address racism, imperialism, or whiteness, although it did list a few transracial adoption resources.

children. But what was it exactly that I was invited to get *in on*? And moreover, what is it we are getting in on when white people become adoptive and foster families?

* * *

It had been five days since the extended family email thread exploded after my mom's cousin's email alerting the family to racist, misogynist, and transphobic social media posts by another family member. In her email, she shared about how harm had been directed at Black, Brown, and LGBTQ family members—her children included—and the decision that she, along with two of her siblings and their families, would not be attending this summer's reunion.

At first there was silence, perhaps expected from a family conditioned into European Mennonite conflict avoidance. But then my aunt, mother of my Latina cousin, replied with support. Soon other supportive voices popped up in my inbox. As if permission had suddenly been granted to speak, the moderates began to chime in, too. They asked for peace and reconciliation and shared sermon notes on forgiveness. *Couldn't we all just get along?*

The email floodgates had been released.

The responses from the young people of my generation were quick and biting, their analyses precise. *There was no place for hate and bigotry in our family.* They were exhausted from suffering the continued aggressions. They were tired of fighting the hypocrisy of white Christian peacemakers. Eventually there was a proposal for a family values statement against racism and homophobia. If family members didn't sign on, they would be expelled from the family table. A second cousin accused all the white people of being complicit: the white family masses had insufficiently addressed the harm. I sensed fear in people's refusal to further engage, along with some indignation. Some who had started off being more supportive could not stomach such expressions of anger. Those who had long ago committed to silence doubled down. Those who were committed to fighting kept emoting into the void. Several people asked to be removed from the email thread. Notably, the original social media offenders never bothered to engage.

The multigenerational assimilation into whiteness we talked about in chapter one is worth revisiting here, as my family struggled with addressing racialized, misogynist, and transphobic harms: How did we get to this point? How might we have indeed become *in on it*?

When my ancestors immigrated to settler Pennsylvania in the early 1700s, were they aware they were getting *in on* the colonization of Turtle Island and the violent displacement of Lenape people? When my grandma unpinned her head covering and retired her cape dress to the cedar trunk, did she know she was getting further *in on* her access to whiteness? Was my parents' generation conscious of the racism, maternalism/paternalism, and imperialism they were going to be getting *in on* with transracial and international adoption?

Furthermore, how did getting *in on it* entrench the patterns we now want to change and heal? How did experiences of oppression further my Swiss German ancestors' denial? How did the sexism of a patriarchal culture trigger my grandma's deference into whiter ones? How did our chosen trauma/chosen glory stories incite my family members to respond defensively to accusations of harm, distance themselves when the conflict intensified, and deny and erase the pain other family members had experienced and were bravely naming for us all?

When it comes to our Mistress Syndrome, what is it that we white women are getting *in on* within our increasingly racially diverse family systems? What are the cultural roles white women have historically had with children of color? What are the legacies of maternalism and saviorism that were constructed long before our children were born?

And can we bring curiosity and compassion to our inquiries? What is it that we have perhaps not known and not anticipated? What is our work to do now? How has our own racism been shielded from us? How has Mistress Syndrome taught us to justify unintended harm?

I know the questions I'm posing are difficult ones. Venturing into conversations about our children can incite that Mama Bear (or Papa or Auntie or Uncle Bear) energy. Even though the questions aren't meant to hurt, they can be painful. These types of questions don't have easy answers. Some might not have answers at all.

But I believe these questions can coexist alongside the joy and the love we have for our families, and they need to if we are going to do anything differently. The problem is not that we seek to create families of love and care; the problem is that our families and their creation don't exist in a vacuum of love and care. Like my earlier attempts at community accountability and not calling the police, we find ourselves with fraught choices because we exist within fraught systems.

The scripts we've been given within these systems are important to scrutinize. What will we choose to do with the scripts that tell us we exist to help; we exist to fix; we exist to save?

CHAPTER EIGHT

WHITE SAVIOR ON THE PROWL: THE VIOLENCE OF HELPING, FIXING, AND SAVING

26 In the sixth month of Elizabeth's pregnancy, God sent the angel Gabriel to Nazareth, a town in Galilee, 27 to a virgin pledged to be married to a man named Joseph, a descendant of David. The virgin's name was Mary. 28 The angel went to her and said, "Greetings, you who are highly favored! The Lord is with you."

29 Mary was greatly troubled at his words and wondered what kind of greeting this might be. 30 But the angel said to her, "Do not be afraid, Mary; you have found favor with God. 31 You will conceive and give birth to a son, and you are to call him Jesus. 32 He will be great and will be called the Son of the Most High. The Lord God will give him the throne of his father David, 33 and he will reign over Jacob's descendants forever; his kingdom will never end."

34 "How will this be," Mary asked the angel, "since I am a virgin?"

35 The angel answered, "The Holy Spirit will come on you, and the power of the Most High will overshadow you. So the holy one to be born will be called the Son of God."

—Luke 1:26-38 NIV

Being needed is not the same as being loved.

—Bekezela Mguni

A s I sit down to begin this chapter on the white savior complex, it is Christmas morning and my body is being ravaged by Category 5 menstrual cramps, an appropriate physiological state on a day many celebrate Jesus's birth.

I gave up painkillers three years before to work on how I distanced from my body. Rather than numbing to sensations of pain, I was curious what it would be like to feel it. And lo and behold, I have experienced it in an embodied way. Once a month, for three to five days, I have received waves of mind-numbing pain with valleys of continuous ache. I wonder if the intensity even comes close to contractions in labor.

My sister-in-law recently had given birth to a baby, and this also being my brother's child put me genetically closer to the miracle of birth than ever before in my adult life. It was awe-inspiring to be in tangential proximity to her pregnancy and birth experience as each seemingly minute physiological development grew a whole human. The baby's uterine positioning as breech signaled a potentially dangerous labor and also a potential disappointment regarding the birth they had so carefully researched and planned for.

Mostly in the history of my conscious life, the "miracle of birth" has rung cliché. The overused phrase has numbed me to the Christmas story and, although I love babies and children, for me, the miracle of their birth has largely been detached from their existence. My dad still talks about the story of my mother's labor and my birth with tears in his eyes, which feels tender and reminds me he still loves me despite our disagreements (and there are many). But I hadn't felt personally connected to birthing until my nibling* was about to be born. It was through that nearness that I began to see the power of pregnancy and birth as at the core of the Christmas story, even though most traditions rarely focus on the details of Mary's labor.

In the days leading up to my nibling's birth, I began to notice in a way I hadn't before how those around my sister-in-law dealt with

---

* "Nibling" is a gender-neutral term for the children of your sibling. I've seen it both with one "b" and two, but am choosing to spell it "nibling" because it reflects "sibling." It is thought to have been coined in the 1950s and is making a comeback.

dependency, helplessness, distance, well-wishes, encouragement, and support. No matter our hopes and bedside presence, ultimately she alone would be the one to push this child outside of her body and into breathable air, and I was powerless to do anything but wait for the news of birth.

* * *

How has the reproductive takeover that removed European midwives from labor rooms and enslaved the wombs of people of African descent (as we learned about in chapters two through four) appropriated the Christmas story? And what are the implications when the story focuses on the arrival of a savior rather than the pregnancy and labor of the one who brought him into life?

In some traditions, Mary, the mother of Jesus, is more prominently revered, but in the way I was raised, Mary has a limited supportive role. She gets an occasional reference during advent, a mention in a song that was written to her but not about her, and a cliché casting appearance in the nativity scene. She kicks off advent season when the angel appears to tell her—not ask her consent—that she's getting impregnated by God.

But on the day of her labor, it is not her reproductive work we celebrate but its severed results, as if once out of her womb Baby Jesus was independently walking around performing miracles. We hastily move through the stigma and shunning she would have experienced in patriarchal Jewish society as an unwed pregnant teen and her courage in the face of it. We decenter Mary's labor, how the Roman occupiers required her to walk seventy miles while pregnant and possibly while experiencing the beginning stages of labor when traveling to Bethlehem. We don't center the physical pain she navigated without painkillers.* We neglect that she gave birth to her first child while unhoused. We trade quaint manger scenes for the reality of animal feces. We have learned to gloss over the reproductive labor it takes to bring children into this world and keep them alive.

---

* Though possibly there were herbal supports.

I am still working through my own bitterness around the rape connotations of Mary's reluctant impregnation and the way Jesus's paternity relegates Mary to a vessel for male holiness, will, and power. But my religious trauma aside, I have become keenly aware of the way this symbolism provides an ideological foundation for the white savior complex so prevalent in our mainstream media, politics, and theologies today.

HOLY CONQUEST AND THE BIRTH OF THE WHITE SAVIOR

There are many threads leading to the "white savior complex," a term epitomized by a white person who wholeheartedly believes that they are, have, or know what other people absolutely need to survive, thrive, and prosper. Someone navigating white saviorism has so deeply internalized the necessity of their saving that they feel obligated, often divinely appointed, and driven by a sense of urgency to help, fix, and save others. When the white savior complex is invoked, one's sense of self becomes (co)dependent upon others needing to be saved. Or in other words, the white savior complex depends on projected dependency, and it depends on physical, structural, and cultural violence in order to render people groups dependent on their saviors.

Just as all of us socialized as white women and girls are connected to Mistress Syndrome, all white people interface with the white savior complex in some form or another. We learn these messages growing up white and contend with them every day. And in a culture so replete with Christian hegemony, we don't have to have grown up on Jesus to have gotten this messaging too. In this chapter, I focus on Christian narratives because Christianity is so intertwined with white saviorism's origin story, and of course, my own.

As I talked about in chapter three, while the entitlement culture of the Crusades, inquisitions, and class wars certainly prepared Europe for the white savior complex, the 1493 papal bull officially tied European Christian identity to global saviorism and unleashed a fervor of violence in the name of Christ.

Contemporary archetypes of the modern superhero, the savior Christ, and the celebrity politician all have origins in the "holy" conquest that propelled Europeans to systematically kill, plunder, rape, and enslave the non-Christian (and later also nonwhite Christian) other. The white savior complex rationalized this history as God's work and will: not only were Europeans in the right, but they were fulfilling their Christian obligation by saving those non-European non-Christians from their brutally savage, ignorant, and disobedient ways. The irony of course is that Europeans operated in brutally savage, ignorant, and (biblically) disobedient ways.

This violent hypocrisy repeated throughout history adapted and mutated based on the needs of those in power. Where those being colonized and enslaved were cast as barbaric, childlike, sexually predatory, uncivilized, animalistic, or heathen, the colonizer and enslaver were ever cast in the white savior light. Whether conquistador, soldier, or priest; whether planter, missionary, or governor; whether general, president, or academic; whether educator, nurse, or charity founder; whether social worker, volunteer, or service provider—the alchemy of the white savior complex turned blood into holy vinegar. Corrupting the Jesus story, it recast the role of savior not to those who suffered as Jesus had, but to those who inflicted the suffering on others.

Under the magnolia trees of the antebellum South, white saviorism became especially serviceable in justifying slavery. This was preached from the pulpit and from the courthouse: slavery was a necessary system to promote the will of God in saving those "poor" Africans from their own self-imposed demise. Christian denominations invoked scripture and were proud purveyors of enslavement's biblical justification.* Both before and after emancipation, white families would dress in their Sunday best, sit in the church pews and praise God, and then take their picnic lunches for church fellowship hour under the lynching trees to witness the gruesome murders of other human beings.

---

* Antebellum Christianity used the story of Noah cursing his son Ham's descendants to be slaves as biblical justification for racialized chattel slavery (Goldenberg, *The Curse of Ham*). The "Curse of Ham" was also touted by Christian leaders as recently as 2012 in a video featuring pastor John MacArthur ("Slavery and Liberty").

Today the white savior complex has found a home within the culture of youth mission trips,[*] motivated by an evangelical zest to go forth and convert (or to serve) others. The complex may have begun by colonizing people dismissed as "savages" in order to "free them of their sins" (and their gold); but these days it shows up as the US invading other countries to "liberate" (Muslim) people from their government leaders (and their religions and their oil). It used to look like civilizing; now it looks like Teach(ing) for America.[†] In these modern examples as missionary, liberator, and teacher, we have internalized that those people must need what we have. They need our God, our help, our resources, our military might, our political systems, our ways of knowing. The white savior complex justifies intervening in other people's lives as holy and good. It lets us believe that we are not driven by our own volition, but instead by the God-given bequest to show others ~~THE~~ *our* way. Despite our good intentions to build an orphanage on that youth mission trip or bring (our) services to those underresourced schools, the impact of our actions can result in more harm than help while making us feel good about what we have contributed.

Our religious communities uphold this white savior standard in a myriad of ways. Youth mission trips and charity drives are built on an assumption that there are people poorer and less fortunate than us (often whom the event organizers have identified as such) who need what we want to give. In these religious settings and in mainstream culture, we especially celebrate certain types of giving: heroic acts of self-sacrifice, donations of large sums of money from those who have

---

[*] While not a one-for-one, short-term mission trips are similarly motivated by an evangelical go-forth-and-conquer mentality, which characterized the Crusades. It is worth questioning the underlying Crusader-like assumptions of evangelizing, including the idea that "we" have what "they" need, that we are doing "God's work." Despite our intent, the impact of our actions might result in harm.

[†] As noted in NPR's Code Switch podcast, "Teach for America gets young people to teach at some of the nation's poorest, brownest schools." Teach for America has faced criticism for bringing in white, affluent, and unqualified volunteers to teach at schools where students are most in need of skilled, culturally sensitive educators (Donnella, "2 Teach for America Alums Say TFA Has Big Problems When It Comes to Race").

plenty to give, and volunteering of time from those who don't need those hours to work to survive.

The white savior complex makes us the protagonists in the story of fixing a world, as if we are somehow innocent and separate and arrive heroically on the scene just at the time of need. But how did we end up in these positions of power? And why do we feel so compelled to help other communities while often neglecting our own?

ON HELPING AND DYING ABROAD

In March of 2017, they found my college classmate MJ's body in a grave in the Democratic Republic of Congo (DRC) alongside his Congolese and Swedish comrades. He was part of a UN team investigating human rights abuses and the targeting of civilians by armed groups in the Kasaï-Central province, during the course of which he and his team were abducted. When I first heard he was missing, I feared for his life. I also held out hope because maybe as a white American he would be more valuable alive than dead. But at the end of the day, neither white privilege nor his US citizenship saved him.

I had held out hope because I knew that in a global context of international violence, white lives matter more. Given our history of white supremacy, colonization, and Eurocentrism, we can trace the threads that explain how white lives have come to matter more. We know that people of European descent have had direct access to the DRC since King Leopold II's ruthless rule of Belgium. We know there are entire industries—international development and peace-building among them—that channel well-educated white people into contexts that aren't their own in order to "fix" things. But we seldom examine what drives white people to do this. Why would a young white Christian from the Midwest—who could have lived a life of material comfort and physical safety—risk all of that and place himself in the middle of some of the most dangerous conflicts in the world, places where the locals are desperately trying to leave?

We do talk about this drive to leave home on some level, though. We glorify it: The Martyr. The Deliverer. The Hero who risks all to save others. MJ's name will be written alongside others who died in the name of peace: Gandhi, Rev. Dr. Martin Luther King, Jr., Jesus. Now MJ's name is spoken in pulpits on Sundays alongside Matthew 5:9: "Blessed are the peacemakers for they will be called children of God."

Some who hear his name will grieve because they knew and loved him. Some will grieve because now there is an irreplaceable MJ-shaped hole on this planet. Some will be proud because he was "one of ours." Some will revere his name and work because his sacrifice means their children won't have to, they won't have to live out the Martyr's Call.

But I believe there are deeper reasons young white expats risk their lives in the name of peace and international development. MJ's story has helped me dig deeper into my own layers of the white savior complex and ask new questions of white culture and of myself. Something else is going on that propels the relatively affluent to helicopter into conflict zones and study other people's wars. While MJ and others (me included) have been shaped by martyr messaging and our embedded spiritual socialization of service, there are fundamental motivations that a lens of white savior glorification would have us ignore. This is not to take away from the intrinsic value and awesomeness of MJ's life and work.* It is to complexify and complicate our one-note melodies and turn them into narratives of harmonious dissonance so we can practice holding multiple truths at once, even as we are working to challenge some of our own.

When I told Kayla that my college classmate had been kidnapped in the Congo she said (and I paraphrase), "Well, what do you expect, getting involved in other people's wars? That white man had no business over there." And she's right. And she's wrong.

She's wrong because the wars in the DRC do not purely belong to its people. Those wars belong to us all. I don't mean in an esoteric kum-ba-ya all-wars-are-our-wars-and-all-people-are-our-people kind of way, but in the specific way that white people in the United States of America are intricately connected to the geopolitical sources of

---

* To read more about MJ's life and work, check out his biography, *Disarmed: The Radical Life and Legacy of Michael "MJ" Sharp*, which was written by Marshall King.

Congolese conflict. This includes the history of colonization in Africa, in which European nation-states carved up and occupied vast areas of the continent. This includes the historic and continued economic, cultural, and religious colonization by Europeans and North Americans (including Mennonites and other religious entities), which has sponsored missionary and service workers to aid in Africa's colonization, sometimes referred to as "international development." This also includes today's international corporate exploitation of the DRC for its natural resources, reinforced by the militarized influences of white Westerners and market capitalist–driven consumerism. We directly participate in these wars as consumers of the latest technologies, such as cell phones and batteries for electric vehicles built with conflict minerals.*

She's right too, because that *is* what one gets for interfering in other people's wars. Her comment made me reflect on why I would ever deign otherwise. Why would I expect someone who consciously and willingly planted himself in the middle of violent conflict to survive it? To have a right to survive? To have the right to survive while at the same time expect all those people born and raised in the context of that war to most likely not survive? What part of me could exceptionalize MJ's survival while normalizing others' deaths in their own contexts?

There is another layer to the "call" that drives white expats to peacebuild in war zones, takes white missionaries to Kenya, propels white college students into the field of international development, and gives hundreds of thousands (maybe millions) of white folks employment doing "good work" in cities through the Nonprofit Industrial Complex (which I too have done).

Perhaps we rush headfirst into other people's wars because we are escaping our own.

---

* Conflict minerals are thus called due to their origin in places like the DRC, in which "approximately six million people have been killed since 1996 and more than six million people remain internally displaced" (Lawal, "A guide to the decades-Long Conflict in DR Congo"). Minerals such as tin, tantalum, and cobalt used in our day-to-day electronics are mined in very dangerous conditions and often use child labor and extreme forms of exploitation (Brigham, "How Conflict Minerals Make It into Our Phones").

Somehow it is easier to helicopter into a foreign conflict zone where we know no one than face the conflict zones of our homes. It is more alluring to negotiate the violent disputes elsewhere than navigate the personal trauma of our hometowns. It is better to run and deal with other people's messes, no matter how dangerous they may be, than hold up a mirror and confront the ugliness of our own. There is more hope in convincing Congolese rebels to put down their guns than convincing our conservative fathers to give up their allegiance to whiteness. And while I am not privy to the particular dynamics of MJ's family of origin, there is a pattern of fleeing home directly reflected in this pattern of helping. It is easier to imagine peace elsewhere than work toward peace in our own families, in our own churches, and in our own bedrooms.

I say this not to blame MJ's life and work, but to identify with it. The root causes of Congolese violence are intimately close to home, and staying engaged in either context—home or away—risks our emotional, spiritual, mental, and physical health. Rather than see MJ's journey as exceptional, as something that could only happen in the dangerous jungles of Africa, what if MJ's journey was in fact a mirror of our own? What if we engaged in our own context with our whiteness, our relationship to our families, and the roots of this interconnected mess with the same purpose and courage that will be ascribed to MJ's life?

And to take it one step further, what if we left martyrdom and white savior complexes behind? What would that mean for those of us who are still in the land of the living?

For one thing, it will mean getting in touch with our own messes first.

THE HIDDEN POWER OF WHITE-LADY EGO

When I think of egotistical foolishness, the first images that pop into my head are white businessmen in power suits, then corporate lawyers and real estate developers, followed by televangelists, Ivy League frat boys, and last but not least, politicians. Definitely politicians. Ego in these archetypes gets built on ultramacho hypermasculinity, entitled white privilege, inherited wealth, and those dollar signs in the eyeballs. The ego is clear, bold, arrogant, assured.

It is that inflated ego that allowed an elite white athlete at an elite white school to commit sexual assault with the confidence of minimal repercussions, that same athlete's father to plead for leniency positioning his son as the real victim,* and a Superior Court judge to basically agree as in the story of former Stanford University student Brock Allen Turner, who raped Chanel Miller while she was unconscious.† Turner received only six months' time—of which he served half—and was cast by his attorneys, father, and elements of the media as a shining star athlete.

But unlike white male entitlement, white-lady ego is usually less blatant, much more refined, couched, and stealthy. It sits quietly in the corner, legs crossed and looking perfect but effortlessly so, as in I-woke-up-just-like-this-with-hair-and-makeup-and-a-cleanly-pressed-dress-and-matching-bag. White-lady ego is meant to attract but give off the appearance of not wanting to, meant to impress but with a helpless performative humility, meant to dominate without you ever realizing that you are under its spell.

White-lady ego is sneaky.

Or maybe not as sneaky as we'd like to think. Black women pick up on it. So do many other People of Color. All. The. Time. Mostly though, we are just fooling ourselves (and other white people…perhaps).

White-lady ego is wrapped up in the message we've received about our role in helping, fixing, and saving others as one that justifies our worth. In these wicked webs, such (co)dependence continues to propel us into roles in which we do for and on behalf of others as the value of white womanhood gets reinforced.

---

* Dan Turner, Brock's father, wrote a letter asking for leniency for his son, arguing that punishment was a "steep price to pay for 20 minutes of action out of his 20 plus years of life" (Koren, "Telling the Story of the Stanford Rape Case").

† You can read Miller's story told in her own words, *Know My Name: A Memoir*, by Chanel Miller.

* * *

Testing out of fifth-grade math and reading, I had nowhere else to go in a K–5 building. What started out as an independent study of sorts quickly turned into a tutoring gig. I still remember the muggy Atlanta day when Mrs. Jones put me in charge of my classmate's education. She stood at the front of the room in her sensible heels and schoolmarm glasses. "Amanda," she said, singling me out, "you can take Chris out in the hall and work on chapter four with him." She singled him out, too. We both walked slowly to the door, somewhat unsure of what this new setup would entail.

At the age of eleven, it didn't surprise me that I would be called upon to help my classmates with their assignments. I already did that in group work or when studying with a friend. I was practiced at being in charge, too. From kindergarten to fifth grade, when teachers occasionally had left the room, they assigned me the responsibility of snitching on my classmates or collecting class work. But this peer-tutoring gig was next-level helping. On one hand, it felt uncomfortable. I felt pressured to know what to do, and I most certainly hadn't been prepared to be in charge of anyone's education. On the other, it felt like the natural flow of six years of daily messaging about how responsible and smart I was. I understood and did not question why Mrs. Jones had chosen me for this task.

Of course, Chris knew the game was rigged. He spent our tutoring hours defying the arrangement with the tools of resistance he had at hand, taking frequent bathroom breaks, deflecting the shame of not knowing an answer by making jokes, and flipping the power dynamics by trying to grab my butt. When I got annoyed (especially about the butt grabbing) and asserted my authority, he increased his resistance. *If only he would focus*, I remember thinking, oblivious to the blow to his ego, oblivious to the boost in my own. At eleven, I learned that I could know what was best for others, especially for Black children, even when I was still a child myself.

Fast forward to fourteen years later. At a school with a 99 percent Black student body, I was offered a high school teaching position despite having no previous experience teaching those grade levels and no experience being Black. There was never a formal interview. I showed up looking capable and white and had been introduced by the right white person. I took the position and a year or two later was featured on a popular blog that interviewed young and exciting people in Pittsburgh. The photo that accompanied the interview was me seated on a stool. My students, all of whom were Black, stood around me, framing me as the poster lady of the white savior complex. The message was clear: How wonderful that I was educating and inspiring these young (disadvantaged) students! How wonderful was I to pour my generosity into their (empty) cups!

When I think back on that teaching gig, I don't remember how proud I was to be in that role. What I do remember, though, is fear, and specifically, my fear of inadequacy. Yes, I was thrilled to find paid work somewhat related to my previous experience. Yes, I was excited for the challenge of learning new things. But also, a part of me knew I was not qualified. A part of me was deeply insecure about my ability to perform the job.

White saviorism is one of the ways the wicked webs are a setup. It puts us into positions we are underqualified for, yet demands we effortlessly and perfectly play the role. In both my short stint as a peer tutor and the above teaching gig, a part of me felt inadequate. But a part of me was also eager to do the job well, to get my classmate to focus, to teach those children what I knew, to justify my value and worth to a system for compensation, to prove my value to myself.

* * *

The suffragist era, often mythologized as the start of feminism, offers us further historical context for the rise of the white-lady savior. During the late nineteenth and early twentieth centuries, the suffragist movement advocated for the rights of women to vote and hold elected office. Newman's work provides an in-depth study of the ways in which the movement for the "universal" suffrage of women was in fact a quest on behalf of white women, more often than not at the direct expense of nonwhite people and nonwhite women in particular.

This trend in white supremacy was consistent with its predecessor, the abolitionist movement of the early 1800s. Even while working toward the abolition of slavery, most white abolitionists did not necessarily believe in the full and equal humanity of those who were enslaved. This became especially obvious when suffrage for Black men became a real possibility, prompting several prominent white abolitionist women to threaten to go against the cause unless they were also granted the vote.

Still others rejected suffrage for Black men outright based on perceptions of Black inferiority.* By contrast, as Newman notes, Black women, who still advocated for women's suffrage, did not view Black men's suffrage as a threat to their own status, but rather a clear gain for their families and communities and a clear gain for them.

As noted in the previous chapter, by the late 1800s white women were repeatedly leveraging their role as white supremacy's cultural keepers, an abundant affirmative action for the white ladies. This was not just a solitary feat with individuals gaining status; white women organized with each other to increase collective power within a racialized hierarchy. At this time, as Newman writes:

> Extensive women's organizations developed through which white women could derive enhanced status and power by serving as exponents of civilization, in carrying the ideals of Christianity to "primitive" peoples, whether they lived within or outside the borders of the United States.[1]

Along with their organizations, Newman profiles several self-proclaimed white-lady saviors including Alice Fletcher, who fled the confines of patriarchal constructed white womanhood in order to mess with the lives of people on the Omaha reservation. I paraphrase Newman's work in the telling of her story below.

---

* Key leaders of women's suffrage such as Susan B. Anthony and Cady Elizabeth Stanton took active stances against suffrage for Black men.

Connected to the Women's National Indian Association, Fletcher became a rare female appointment to the US Department of the Interior as a special agent and "scientific expert" on the Omaha and Nez Percé people. In 1883, Fletcher advocated for giving out individual allotments to members of the Omaha Nation rather than keeping the land held collectively as the Omaha had done. Convinced that this strategy would "civilize" the Omaha and instill in them a monogamous patriarchal nuclear family structure, Fletcher tried to sell it to the tribe. When it became clear she didn't have their support, Fletcher reached for white supremacy's reinforcement arm, having the "reservation police round up the resistors, force them to appear before her, and compel them 'to make their mark in the presence of witnesses indicating that they accepted a designated piece of land.'"[2] Unfortunately, Fletcher was only one of many such white ladies at this time who used the savior mindset to influence US Native American policy.

In a span of two hundred years, organized women had transitioned from being European patriarchy's public enemy number one to its most sophisticated savior. Rather than fighting the paternalistic control that kept white women restricted and identifying with the history of land enclosures in Europe that persecuted her ancestors (as discussed in chapter two), Fletcher used those same wicked webs to maternalistically oppress the Omaha people, among others. After being excluded from the European power structures of church and state for thousands of years, white women in the US suddenly had been granted a seat at the table of patriarchal power.

Something happened between the peak of the witch hunts and the debut of white-lady saviors. Something changed for the European women who arrived in the thirteen colonies that shifted their position of lowly laborer, harlot, and witch into the model of womanhood and mother of civilization. Essential for Fletcher's access to law enforcement, this transition from victim to savior lay in the (d)evolution of whiteness.

CONFRONTING THE WHITE SAVIOR COMPLEX IN OURSELVES

Over the course of the twentieth century, the influence white women had in "the body politic" only continued to grow. According to author Elizabeth Gillespie McRae, in the 1920s:

> White supremacy became bureaucratized in a new social welfare infrastructure, and white women regulated intimate matters with the legitimacy of state sanction. In doing so, this new cadre of female workers translated their gender-specific authority as white mothers into public authority as workers for the state.[3]

The fields of education, social work, and health and human services are now dominated by white women.

Like in the plantation system, women and children of color are highly susceptible to the daily racism of white women precisely because of our overrepresentation in the institutions of their lives.* We are the frontline offenders at the beginning of the phenomenon known as the "school-to-prison pipeline,"† a phrase that illustrates how students of color are disproportionately and intentionally funneled out of the education system and into the criminal justice system. As classroom teachers, caseworkers, counselors, and health workers, we statistically disproportionately suspend and expel students of color while disproportionately advantaging white students through academic tracking, magnet, and gifted programs.

---

* From 2017 to 2018, 79 percent of public school teachers were white (National Center for Education Statistics, "Race and Ethnicity of Public School Teachers and Their Students"). In Pennsylvania, from 2019 to 2020, half of public schools only employed white teachers (Rayworth, "This Innovative Program Is Bringing Tomorrow's Teachers of Color to Pittsburgh Today").

† Marian Wright Edelman, founder of the Children's Defense Fund, expanded on the concept of the school-to-prison pipeline, coining the term "Cradle to Prison Pipeline" as a way to identify the ways Black children, babies, and infants are funneled into the Prison Industrial Complex even before their entry into the education system.

And it's not just the ways we may single out Black and Brown children for punishment; it's also the ways we may criminalize their families, too. A decision to call Child Protective Services because of perceived abuse and neglect can alter the course of a family's trajectory for generations while harming the child we are supposed to be protecting. Although we don't intend to harm—in fact, our intention is to help—we make this call based on our own biases and cultural perceptions.

Our biases assume that state-sanctioned intervention will be healthier, safer, and better than the self-determination and interdependence of this child's family and community. We assume that whiteness—both our own and that of the state—will ultimately help, despite a historic precedent that most state intervention has caused harm and disenfranchised communities of color.

The disproportionate funneling of Black and Brown youth out of schools and into the juvenile system; the removal of Indigenous children from their communities and forced placement in boarding schools and foster homes; the separation and detention of immigrant children from their families—these are all recent policies with histories embedded in the belief that whiteness knows best. Because of our institutional proximity and this history of racism, when we are following our job descriptions as competent managers, we are usually upholding a racist status quo.

An example of this taken to the most tragic extreme is that of white woman Renee Bach, whose calling to "help" was sparked as a teenager on a youth mission trip to Jinja, Uganda, in 2007, where, according to NPR, "U.S. missionaries had set up a host of charities."[4] Three years later, inspired by her experience and what Bach described as "a calling from God," with a high school diploma and no formal medical training, Bach established a charity, which came to provide quasi-medical care for severely malnourished children, many of whom had advanced and complicated conditions and should have been treated in certified Ugandan facilities by trained medical practitioners. At least 105 children died at Bach's center or in their homes soon after their treatment, including Twalali

Kifabi (age three) and Elijah Kabagambe (age one) whose mothers sued Bach for medical malpractice, eventually settling without admission of liability.[5]

What's notable in reading the many news articles on Bach is the mixture of ignorance and arrogance. Bach seems to truly believe that God was calling her to help these children. Despite the reality that there were competent Ugandan medical facilities available (NPR reporting notes that "Jinja's regional referral hospital had a well-established malnutrition unit to care for complicated cases of severe acute malnutrition"[6]), despite that she had no idea what she was doing (Bach used Google searches and books to perform blood transfusions), despite that she witnessed many children die under her care (an estimated 20 percent of children who entered the facility died), and despite that she was breaking the law ("under both international health guidelines and Ugandan law, if a severely malnourished child has the kind of extra complications Bach's center was taking on... this child must be treated in an advanced medical facility"[7]), Bach persisted in claiming she was doing God's work.

As easy as it may be to dismiss Bach as an individual bad actor, she was raised and supported by a culture, community, and system that enabled her with resources, reinforced her disillusionment of "a calling from God,"[8] and celebrated her for acting on it.

How can we white (Christian) folks grapple with our role in the harm of the white savior complex? How do we white ladies unlearn our (co)dependency on helping? And where can we start?

Perhaps we can start by looking at our need to be needed, which is a very limiting relational path.

* * *

In between the Thanksgiving day disaster and her mom's magical wedding, Kayla had reached out to me, asking for help. "Absolutely," I imitated her mom's modeling. "Of course, what do you need?"

This was not the first time Kayla had asked me for writing and editing support, nor was it the first time I had gone above and beyond to provide this type of support to others. As a white neurotypical person—or at least, neuroconforming*—who had received the benefits of a formally educated family, I viewed my writing skills as something that didn't really belong to me. In many ways, they had been bought and valued through whiteness. Sharing them was a strategic way I could leverage my resources to support others in navigating one barrier of white middle-class institutions. It was an obvious way I could contribute to the cause.

When she texted me to ask, I was away at a work training and was beyond exhausted. Our local youth organizing had just imploded in a big way. I was trying to keep tabs on its unraveling from afar, while still coming through with the daily requirements of my job and while spending all day at this obligatory training. Needless to say, my capacity for taking on more commitments was low.

Besides, this was our first real interaction since the Thanksgiving blowup, so it was not with the most genuine of intentions that I took the project on. *Maybe this will help smooth things over.* I may or may not have noticed my sneaky white-lady ego. *At least this was something I had to offer.* Perhaps I overextended myself so she wouldn't abandon me. On some level, I must have realized how the skill sets I gained through my access to whiteness had created a need for me.

Kayla was on a deadline, so I made her request a priority. I pushed through my exhaustion and stayed up late so she would have something to turn in the next day. I justified my decision as what an anti-racist white woman was supposed to do. *Making (self-)sacrifices to help Black folks was part of the job.* I reassured myself that I was living

---

* According to Disabled World, "neurotypical" is used to describe those who are not neurodivergent, whereas neurodivergent "is defined as divergence in mental or neurological function from what is considered typical or normal (frequently used concerning autistic spectrum disorders)" ("What Is: Neurodiversity, Neurodivergent, Neurotypical"). Though many question if it's truly possible to be neurotypical because we have no set standard for a "typical" human brain. I was introduced to the term "neuroconforming" by Expressive Arts Therapist and educator Conly Basham and prefer its use here as someone who usually has the capacity to conform to academic norms such as strong standard English written communication skills.

into my purpose. *Even if the organizing is shit at home, at least this was one win.* Though resentment had already started to seep in.

There are layers to our internalized saviors.

As good white people, and good white women, we have been taught that we are so good at helping and that helping is so good. This teaches us that we have the right to help whomever, whenever, and however we choose. Because we have been given such far-reaching access to Black and Brown communities by the institutions where we work, volunteer, and advise, we rarely need to consult with those we serve about how (or even if) our help should be offered.

For most of my life, my white savior complex went uninterrogated by me. Helping, fixing, and saving others was a virtuous no-brainer. Of course God wanted me to help save the world. I cringe now. But I remember in college speaking those exact words when asked what I wanted to do with my life. And even after I became aware of the White Savior and moved into a paradigm of collective organizing and power shift, in my own drive for purpose, I can view my anti-racist organizing through a lens that centers the world's need for me. In moments of insecurity, when I am most vulnerable to wanting external validation and a sense of belonging, my white-lady ego sneaks through. Mostly, she's needed to be needed too.

What's wrong with wanting to help? you may ask. *Is wanting to help always wrong?*

When those questions come up for me, they usually surface because my white-ladyness desperately wants to sidestep deeper reflection. Those questions usually have a quality of defensiveness because I want wanting to help to be righteous, at least some of the time. Those questions can provide a distraction because they tempt me to avoid taking responsibility. I defend my motives so I don't have to feel uncomfortable or make a change.

Instead of getting stuck in that hamster wheel, I am trying to refocus on questions that lead me deeper into knowledge of my Self and my motivations:

How was I acculturated into wanting to help, fix, and save?

And why?

What is my relationship with those I want to help, fix, or save?

What are the histories that established those relationship dynamics?

Is there an invitation to help? How may I be imposing my ideas of what someone else wants?

Perhaps the most revelatory questions for me have been:

How do I feel when those I want to help, fix, and save aren't interested in my helping, fixing, and saving? What is my immediate, honest reaction?

When do I overextend in my helping? When does it cause resentment? What can that resentment teach me?

How do I sit and reflect in that moment and sort out where those thoughts and feelings originate?

This last set of questions is powerful because even in my most seemingly inconsequential moments of helping, they reveal my true intentions. Imagine I offer you a second helping of food I made, you refuse it, and I am taken aback by your refusal. In which case, my helping is not about a genuine offering of sharing what's available, but rather about propping up some sort of insecurity on my part. Maybe I'm unsure about my cooking. Maybe I'm worried about our relationship. Maybe I'm insecure about the choices I made regarding the ingredients or whether I accidentally poisoned you because of an unknown food allergy. Maybe I'm feeling guilty about something I said to you last week/year/decade/lifetime and am projecting my concern of your resentment onto every crevice of your body language, because why else would you refuse this plate of my love? Whatever the reason, our interaction just downward-spiraled from a simple offer of more food to a moment about my insecurities, self-worth, and communication skills. I have transferred my insecurities onto you, as I wait to see whether or not you will accept that second plate of food.

Not only is this magnified insecurity psychologically draining, but it also impedes relationships, taking the focus off the needs, wants, and agency of the other person—to whom I was offering help (or in this case seconds)—ultimately undermining their self-determination. Rather than honoring the agency of the person I'm trying to support, rather than centering consent and mutual respect, I have shifted that focus right back onto me and my insecurities and feelings.

White-lady ego can be sneaky, but it also can be exhausting. Perhaps I stayed up all night to prepare the above-referenced meal, whether or not you requested it. Or maybe, as in my dynamic with Kayla, you did request it. Either way, I suppressed my exhaustion, jumping at the opportunity to prioritize your request for a meal in order to reassure myself about my purpose and worth.

Those insecurities come from somewhere.

Baked into the trauma of Mistress Syndrome is an internalized gendered inferiority that has taught us to doubt, loathe, control, and constantly second-guess and fear our Selves. Rather than channel our internalized gendered inferiority into our collective liberation, we find our energy diverted into helping, fixing, and saving others so we *feel* powerful and justified. The white savior complex allows us to redirect our own guilt, shame, unworthiness, and helplessness rather than working with it, taking responsibility for it, and organizing to build collective power that might move us toward actual liberation.

Healing from Mistress Syndrome means locating the sources of our insecurities, addressing our fragile egos by loving and nurturing our Selves, and working through our urge to put on capes of white saviorism. In our run to help others, we are neglecting this Self work and neglecting the way our well-being is interconnected to the well-being of others.

We white women absolutely have a role in making change happen, but to be effective, that role won't come from the glamour of individual celebrity or from approaches meant to shore up our egos. It won't come from white saviorism. It will come from attuning to the vast networks of communities already organizing. It will emerge when we begin to tend to the part of the web that is ours to tend. It will come from organizing our own. And, as the above history shows, we white women have historically been pretty good at doing that.

* * *

These days, I am feeling more open to the symbolism of birth as redemption for humanity. Perhaps in some way, I can embrace how our children are our saviors. They are our collective chance at redemption. With each generational cycle, we get a chance at a do-over, a repeat, an opportunity to evolve in our parenting choices and community child-rearing. Our children link us to the future, miraculously taking us beyond our lifespans. Their births signify that our community's DNA will live on even after we are composting in the earth (or, more than likely, pumped with chemicals in boxes).

Holding my nibling as a newborn was indeed a holy experience that traversed the confines of time and space. It was a moment of perspective and prioritizing and recentering and commitment and recommitment. The labor of their mother, the commitment of their parents to bringing them into this world, and their birth story inspired feelings of connection to the Christmas narrative for me for the first time in a long while.

What I learned from Jesus and Black women is that change comes from working together with all our children in mind. If we can organize to uphold these wicked webs, then we can surely organize against them. Cooperative ways of being in relationship with each other require the subversive leadership of many, rather than the saviorism of an exalted few. The generosity of experience requires humility, because the next time around it might be you. This type of collective liberation manifests in reciprocal relationships that help our spiritual Selves, not our sneaky egos.

TIME FOR ANOTHER BREAK

In the past chapters, we've unpacked five white-lady archetypes:

- Vixen Mistress
- Good Plantation Wife
- Damsel in Distress
- The Great White Mother
- White Savior

We've covered a lot of gruesome history, and uncomfortable feelings may be coming up. Take a moment to notice what's true for you here and now.

Get curious. You might ask yourself:

Where did I learn these?
How did I learn these?
How do they show up for me today?

You might sit still for thirty minutes and reflect. You might take out a pen and paper and journal. You might talk it out with a friend (preferably another white person).

As you're reflecting on the questions, you might begin to notice your responses on many levels. Become curious about the following:

What does it feel like to be asked these questions?
How does it feel to respond to them?
What is happening for you in your body?
How might the 4Ds be showing up?
How might you go a little deeper?
How might you support your body in feeling hard things?
How might you give yourself a loving break? And then how might you return, again?

PART III

UP CLOSE AND PERSONAL

CHAPTER NINE

FOR FATHER AND FOR MOTHER...

Just because a woman is silent does not mean she agrees...
—Clarissa Pinkola Estes

We can learn to work and speak when we are afraid in the same way we have learned to work and speak when we are tired. For we have been socialized to respect fear more than our own needs for language and definitions, and while we wait in silence for that final luxury of fearlessness, the weight of that silence will choke us.
—Audre Lorde

My brother's birth rocked my world. Whether it is an actual memory or an internalized scene shaped by decades of family lore, I threw a tantrum on the hallway runner upon first hearing the news of his birth. I was two and a half years old and convinced I was supposed to have a sister. At this young age, I was already distrustful of men, a contempt I spent the next twelve years taking out on my brother.

My brother was younger and smaller than me and scrawny up until his preteen years, making him an excellent target for my pent-up aggression. Besides, he was accessible, usually an arm's reach across the backseat, on the bottom bunk, or around the dining room table. And I took full advantage of my heavier body weight and further-developed brain.

I was born not only the eldest child, but also the eldest grandchild on my mother's side. This status ensured two and a half years of sole stardom as the chief focus and main concern of a small community of doting adults. This has got to be why I'm so fabulous. It is also why I spent much of my childhood in competition with my sibling for attention and praise. It wasn't so much the sharing, caring, or cooperative play that proved challenging for me; it was more the expectation of having input into who comes in and out of my life, the need to have control, and fear of abandonment. Clearly my parents had neglected to consult me in their decision to expand our family. And on top of that, he was a boy. How rude. I resented being excluded from this life-altering decision-making process and took it out on the easiest most available target.

I understand now that my brother, or rather the dynamic of our relationship, schooled me in the ways of white supremacist cultural values: competition and comparison, hierarchy, command and control. It was either him or me. When in direct competition, my triumph came in his failure. When performing as a good little white girl, my reward came in getting credit for my role in his achievement. I saw scarcity in my parents' love and favoritism because I suspected that as the baby and as the storied easier child and easiest labor, he was my mother's favorite. By two and a half, I had already internalized the message that there wasn't enough love to go around. I had internalized that my family's love was conditional and scarce.

This deep-seated fear of abandonment cannot be entirely blamed on my parents' choice to have a second child. It has roots in puritanism, the witch hunts, Mennonite sectarianism, and weekly sermon messaging that says if you aren't a believer, God will abandon you... for eternity. My fear of abandonment also has roots in the dynamics of the antebellum plantation household, in which the fear of parental childhood abandonment often proved true.

SLAVERY AND ABANDONMENT

On the plantation, children Black and white alike were exposed to the daily violence of slavery.* As members of households in which the ideology and practice of slavery was intimate and pervasive, white children were witnesses, perpetrators, and recipients of an environment that normalized daily violence and abuse in the home. In the book *Southern History across the Color Line*, Nell Irvin Painter writes about how "owning as well as owned families paid a high psychological and physical cost for the child and sexual abuse that was so integral to slavery."[1] Painter observes that despite contemporary assumptions about strict divides based on one's racialization, the human psychology of attachment and loss flowed across these superimposed barriers, psychically impacting not only those who were enslaved but also those witnessing abuses, especially children, who were ultimately forced "to identify with the victim or the perpetrator."[2]

White parent-child relationships developed within this violent milieu. In writing about the violence of the plantation mistress, Glymph explains that mistresses took out their "anger and rage against slaves (and sometimes against their own children)."[3] Likewise, Painter describes how violence that enforced the peculiar institution's values of obedience and submission "prevailed within white families as well."[4] Culturally, obedience and submission were likewise reinforced by Southern religion and also by legal structures. Perhaps unsurprisingly, Southern states were especially lax around prosecuting cases of sexual abuse, child abuse, and incest.

In addition to the direct abuse suffered by white children at the hands of white family members was their acculturation into the praxis of slavery. Alongside the psychological abuse experienced by Black children, the contradictory messaging of entitlement and (co)dependence, emotional distance and nurture, and care and disdain must have done a job on white children's psyches, too. Drawing from the work of

---

* While beyond the scope of this work, the psychological violence and consequences for enslaved children is very important to acknowledge. Please see the Bibliography and Resources for Further Support for more such resources.

many psychologists, Painter notes that children as observers of abusive acts are pulled to identify with either the victim or the perpetrator, often eventually playing out those roles, "either by becoming victims themselves or by abusing others, especially younger siblings or children in positions of relative weakness."[5] In cases where white children—and especially white boys—chose to side with the enslaved victims of abuse, they were rebuked, forced to witness further and repeated tortures, and sometimes met with violence themselves. Painter notes how fathers were usually responsible for "inculcating manhood, which included snuffing out white children's identification with the enslaved."[6]

The repercussions of resisting white supremacist abuse intersected with misogyny, sometimes with profound consequences. In the case of one slaveholding white woman, the mistress of Peter (Sojourner Truth's son) was murdered by her husband after displaying visible grief for Peter's abuse and extending medical care to him. Violence was the price for compassion.

However, many plantation mistresses conformed to their expected role as compliant wives, competent household supervisors, and doting—if distant—mothers. Unlike their great-great-great-grand-mothers, now as managers of the plantation household, white plantation mistresses often performed less of the day-to-day reproductive labor. Instead, white children were ferreted away to Black nursemaids and raised by caregivers they saw suffer brutal treatment at the hands of their own birth mothers.[*]

Plantation mistresses emotionally and physically abandoned their children, imposing the most intimate of tasks, such as breastfeeding

---

[*] Glymph chronicles some of the attitudes plantation mistresses held toward their own children: in desperation, plantation mistress Tryphena Fox expressed a willingness to bring back Susan (a woman she had previously enslaved) despite all her complaints in order to rid herself of "the burden of her own children" (68). As soon-to-be-outgoing plantation mistress Gertrude Thomas took solace in 1865 while searching for childcare, at the age of four "the child was growing 'so fast I will almost be able to attend to her myself'" (143). And historian Elizabeth Fox-Genovese notes that while the diaries of plantation mistress Sarah Gayle often allude to her caring for her children herself, upon closer examination Gayle's reproductive labor was always supported by the women she enslaved (*Within the Plantation Household*).

and caring for injuries, on the people whom they enslaved. What psychological imprint must this have left on white children to have their parents violently outsource their care? What emotional underdevelopment occurred as a result? What pain and confusion for mothers to have been so unavailable yet still nearby? What disassociation was required to rationalize the violence done to those who mothered us? What wounds were left open to later project onto those who did the labor of raising white children?

Talk about abandonment issues.

This relationship with abandonment, an integral part of the history of white childhood, has been etched into the psychology of whiteness. For white children, proving one's allegiance to whiteness was synonymous with proving one's allegiance to parents, family, religion, culture, and the state. And proving this allegiance necessitated curbing empathy for the victims of abuse. Allegiance to whiteness necessitated allegiance to violence and allegiance to psychological self-harm.

It still does.

BELONGING TO NO WHITE COMMUNITY

Like the conditional love lorded over victims in dynamics of abuse, whiteness as a biological category is fictitious.[7] Whiteness is an illusion, a false security blanket, a chase that will never end. Established as a way to keep the European masses distracted by striving for proximity to the ruling class, part of the psychological distress built into whiteness is a constant worry of belonging, a never-ending pursuit of being white (enough) both within our families and dominant culture.

Professionalism in the workplace? Credentials by your name? Do you have the right gear? Listen to the right music? Drive the right car? These are all measures of white (enough).

Within the wicked webs, advertisers play off our insecurities and the mythical measurement that to be white (enough) is to be happy. Satisfied. Complete. To have status. To have arrived.

To belong.

Unfortunately for those of us worrying about being white (enough), there is no actual static measurement of whiteness (hence the constant striving). Along with its biological speciousness, whiteness has proven historically malleable, expanding over time to include people of ethnic and national backgrounds not previously deemed white (enough), such as the Irish, Italians, and most recently, light-skinned Latine people, and occasionally excluding people previously deemed white (enough) as in the case of people of Arab descent in the aftermath of 9/11.

If the privilege of being white (enough) can be granted, then it can also be revoked. Which means the validation of white society is entirely and foundationally conditional. The fear of its membership being revoked is fundamental to white culture, and by extension, to white family systems.

Did I mention we have abandonment issues?

Biss takes this analysis one step further, questioning the existence of white community all together:

> Whiteness is not a kinship or a culture. White people are no more closely related to one another, genetically, than we are to black people. American definitions of race allow for a white woman to give birth to black children, which should serve as a reminder that white people are not a family. What binds us is that we share a system of social advantages that can be traced back to the advent of slavery in the colonies that became the United States. "There is, in fact, no white community," as [James] Baldwin writes.

These shifts in belonging, away from our ancestral cultures and close communities into striving for the conditions of whiteness, have deeply disturbed our sense of safety, security, and belonging. If there is no white community, if there is no white family, then what is left to build our family cultures around?

* * *

While I have many joyous memories throughout my childhood, including with family, neighbors, church community, and friends, I also have this pervasive memory of loneliness, especially as I reached my preteen years. When I call on one such memory that describes that feeling, I am standing by myself in the dimly-lit, long carpeted hallway of my childhood home. I am just outside my bedroom door and the house is still and eerily quiet. Perhaps in this moment I was home alone, something I often chose as a retreat from my social anxiety and the overstimulation I so often felt at school. But just as likely, I was not the only one sharing the space. Despite the quiet atmosphere, my brother might have been at one end of the house, in his room, door closed, absorbed in the adventures of his computer screen. Just as likely, my dad might have been at the other end of the house, among his religious books, weights, and conservative media. If it was as still and quiet as I recall, my mom would have most certainly been out, occupied with one of her many hobbies, business ventures, or volunteer gigs.

No matter the exact scenario, I can still feel that unmistakable aura of loneliness like a dense fog, permeating the carefully curated antiques, family photos, and walls of my artwork on display. In my unhealthier moments, I assuaged the lonely feeling with food. Sometimes I was able to access other resources, granting myself a moment of reprieve by walking down the long hall and out the front door. I'd find myself swaying gently on the porch swing while listening to the birds harmonizing with interstate traffic.

Like whiteness, the ideal of the contemporary nuclear family unit was also made up, another result of the witch hunts. Before the witch hunt era, European family structures were localized communally and more collective in their arrangements (see chapter two). The nuclear family unit, arriving in sixteenth-century Europe alongside mercantilism and cottage industries, became part of the propaganda machine for whiteness on the antebellum plantation. Inside the walls of the plantation households, our racial ancestors were taught to suppress empathy and deny human connection. We were taught that our nuclear family unit, too, was about coercion and control.

Those nuclear family ideals get reconstituted every couple of generations. In recent decades, conservatives have used the rallying call of family values to harken back to an idealized time—notably before racial desegregation. Slogans like "Make America Great Again" yearn for this fictitious white community, sometimes represented through a 1950s ideal of the (government-subsidized white) suburbs and other outcomes from centuries of white affirmative action. Growing up in the 1980s and '90s, the expectations imbued into the white Christian nuclear family seeped through the walls of church, television, and my father's attempts at dinner table family devotions. My actual experience felt far from the idealized Christian love, safety, and belonging that these family values professed.

As I sift through my emotional filing cabinet for these memories of loneliness, my coping mechanisms jump out. My eating disorder, my workaholism, my escapism into a compelling book, my communing with the old oak trees, my obsession with making art. I am noticing how they are mostly solitary activities perhaps facilitated by my family's climbing class status, which ensured each family member had their own space, downtime, and separate spheres for existing. But unlike many people who have come to be called white and despite centuries on Turtle Island, I come from a culture that knows communal ways of being. In the Mennonite subculture in which I was raised, family extends beyond the walls of one's childhood home. Family is your community, your work, your friends, your church, your home. For better or for worse, in all its enmeshment, family, community, and faith are an all-encompassing conglomeration.

Yet my parents put a long day's travel between themselves and their families of birth. The small Mennonite communities in which I was raised were geographically diffused across the metro area's 8,376 square miles. So, I am particularly interested in how patterns of flight and distance—whether physical or emotional—make up part of our racialized inheritance, a coping strategy facilitated by access to white—and class—mobility.

There is a story my mother sometimes tells about me running away from home. It was warm enough to sit outside on the front porch of my parents' home, yet not so warm that swarms of mosquitoes appeared the moment my chubby bare feet touched the porch floor. I was probably swinging on the wide porch swing, something I loved to do while singing to myself or daydreaming.

As my mom tells it, this time out on the porch, I was upset. Who knows about what; before I became adept at playing the good little white girl, I unleashed my fiery temper with much more frequency and ease. In the midst of my fury, I threatened to run away from home, something she evidently hadn't taken seriously. The moment my mom went inside the house, I took my bare feet to the brick sidewalk and stormed up the street without looking back. I made it just past the Methodist church, an approximate two-block walk, when my mother pulled up in our family's sand-beige Volvo station wagon. I don't remember the specific consequence I received, but I do remember that she was pissed as she told me to get into the car and buckled me in. I also remember the freedom and power I felt as I rounded the corner toward the church. That was a feeling I would go after again. This instance marked the first of many times I would run away.

The second time I ran away from home, I was fifteen. A semester of study in the Midi-Pyrénées might not have seemed like running away at the time—after all, it was school-sanctioned and looked fabulous on my résumé. But after leaving for France at fifteen, and then again for Germany at eighteen, then directly from there to college in a different state, and traveling for a year, eventually settling seven hundred miles away from my childhood home for a year of voluntary service, I began to notice a pattern.

DISTANCING AND DISPLACING

My parents moved to Southeast Atlanta at the tail end of white flight, bought and put countless hours of sweat equity into their home, and raised two children in it. They, along with many others, were part of a wave of white Mennonites who headed South to take part in the Civil Rights Movement and who later began to work in the growing nonprofit sector.

The recent decades of gentrification have done a number on my parents' part of town, displacing many longtime residents and causing property values to soar. Over the past fifteen years, parts of the neighborhood where I grew up and the adjoining area have become practically unrecognizable to me.

It was disorienting to visit my parents during their last years in my childhood home. Landmarks that had been central reference points in my childhood had disappeared, entombed by oversized new developments and fancy open-air hipster shopping centers. In the blocks where hundreds of families used to live in subsidized housing remained an eerily vacant stretch of grassy lots running toward the gilded dome of the Georgia State Capitol. Occasionally, a lonely tree still stood as witness to the children and families who once called this place home.

I have heard friends and neighbors in Pittsburgh describe the disorientation they feel when visiting the neighborhood where I lived in the same way. Having already borne witness to the rapid gentrification of Atlanta and D.C., I moved to Pittsburgh somewhat educated about gentrification's signs. But when I moved to the Steel City in the late aughts, Pittsburgh didn't appear to be gentrifying, or at least not at anywhere near the rate of cities like Atlanta and D.C. With its smaller scale and reputation for being behind the curve, I felt hopeful, optimistic even, that Pittsburgh could be different; that 15206 would not have to go the way of 30312 and that I could be a part of that change.

My former partner and I bought a house that was blocks away from the voluntary service program I did. Because we were aware of gentrification, there were things we paid attention to. The block we were considering didn't look anywhere close to flipping. Several brand-new speculative homes sat empty, overpriced, and unsold for over a year. There was a balanced mix of renters and homeowners and a mix of white and Black neighbors who fell into both renter and owner categories. What ultimately cleared my conscience to move forward with the purchase was that the home we would buy had sat empty for several years prior. We would not be displacing people through our act of buying, living in, and fixing up the place.

I was never so wrong.

And it's not for lack of trying. I am genuinely proud of the intentional and respectful ways we entered the neighborhood, centered humanistic relationship with our neighbors, and tried to organize against displacement.

Upon one visit to the house we would buy with its adjacent lot, a small-scale yet serious football game was in motion. Halfway into the game, some older teenagers shuffled through the lot, taking its convenient cut through to the next street over. The group let a giddy younger sibling take a turn with the ball before resuming their game. It was full of jeers and laughter as the football players demonstrated their skills, dodging each other and deftly sidestepping the dog poop at the back end of the lot. It didn't take long for me to realize that this vacant lot was not vacant at all but was a resource well-used by many in the community, these children included.

When the community development corporation (CDC) shared their plans to fence it in as part of our house remodel, we asked them to put those dollars elsewhere. When spring came around and it was time to put in a garden, we planned the raised beds with the football field in mind. And when one neighborhood elder gifted us children's play equipment and preemptively recruited a local youth to install it on the lot, we opted to lean into relationships with the children and their families rather than capitulate to the fear of potential litigation.

This relational commitment meant hours of relationship building, work, and unanticipated childcare. It meant not calling the cops even when the threat of violence was present. It meant making our white bodies visible and voices heard in ways that let the police know we didn't condone their presence. It meant challenging Nextdoor neighbor posts, tearing down "suspicious person" signs from the telephone pole up the street, and writing letters to the editor about the CDC-sponsored crime reports targeting our block. It meant getting involved in local activism, attending community meetings that the CDC organized (sometimes we were the only actual residents at these "community" meetings), connecting neighbors to resources, and trying to mobilize with other white folks to fight against pending evictions.

And lest you read the above paragraph as idyllic, these everyday choices to disrupt gentrification were not without discomfort. For one thing, the stark contrast of our neighbors' experience with racist poverty was a constant, uncomfortable reminder of our privilege and whiteness. Living in ongoing proximity to the structural violence of poverty and racism—a dynamic we freely chose and which many of our neighbors hadn't—added stress that would not have been there had we lived in an affluent white community in the suburbs. It was stressful to be woken up at five a.m. by militarized SWAT vehicles who trained guns on the house next door as the four-year-old and his family came out with their hands in the air. There is no doubt that I experienced a level of secondary trauma from witnessing the violence done to fellow humans, feet away from our windows. In these moments of potential and realized physical violence, I often felt helpless. Instead of calling the cops, I debated with my internal white saviorism. Sitting on the stairs feeling helpless in my immobility, I became more in touch with the inescapable pain. Some days I was able to use that stress and discomfort as a motivation to keep fighting and as an inspiration to get creative about how my household could subvert oppression.

But in the end, the neighborhood gentrified just the same. Of all the renters that were there when we moved in, I know of only two households that remained. In retrospect, the CDC needed our young, white middle-classness and Urban Redevelopment Authority grant to flip the street, and we needed the CDC and URA grant in order to afford the home. The shiny new houses up the street eventually sold. Since then, many others that were shinier and newer were built and sold for much more money.

People settle in and around their family and community networks. But for those of us who have come to be called white, our racialized impact has very specific consequences, whether intended or not. Just like how Black families desegregating white neighborhoods in the 1970s caused real estate values in those neighborhoods to drop, white homeowners buying up properties in low-income communities of color cause displacement and housing instability for community members.

Perhaps our presence, as opposed to that of other young middle-class white folks the CDC would have eventually sold the house to, did slow down gentrification's course. Perhaps our small acts of resisting gentrification rather than encouraging it were partly why our block was deemed the criminal holdout of the neighborhood long after other blocks were cleared for new buyers. But ultimately, our neighbors were evicted and the dozens of children who had flooded the street during the summer months most likely struggled to find safe play space elsewhere. At the end of the day, our hard work, resistance, and relationships were no match for the way gentrification leveraged our whiteness. And that is a maddening outcome.

What I am saying is that despite good intentions and strategic awareness, my presence still helped tip the scales of whiteness. It is not because of some personal individual shortcoming on my behalf or evil intent. In many ways, I was replicating my upbringing in finding a neighborhood similar to the one in which I grew up. Unlike the flux of white peers who grew up in the 'burbs and the country, I was not a first-generation city dweller. Besides, there were many human-centric decisions that went into the purchase of this home: affordability, its proximity to our social networks, an accessible location, room to host family and housemates, the potential to grow some of our own food, and space for a weaving studio.

Having sought to satisfy the wants and needs of cultivating our quality of life was not wrong. Yet racism as a system has been set up so my life decisions will negatively affect others and so the choices I have depend on the suffering of others. This is another way whiteness denies the humanity of white folks while at the same time does violence to those who have not been racialized as white. We have been conditioned to benefit from a system that clearly harms our neighbors. Knowing that gets me closer to rage.

Personally, I must constantly work to hold the both/and of having invested the best of my Self in a community I loved and also in which my very presence assisted in its harm. I have to work to hold this both/

and with grace and compassion, rather than surrendering to a guilt-laden self-hate. I have to work to refuse that there is something inherently wrong about me, even as I work to accept the violent impact of my whiteness. I have to work to get in touch with my rage and grief and identify its origins.

From here, the only way to go is down: to the root. Gentrification helps describe the fruits, the symptoms of the problems, but I am interested in root causes. How do versions of this pattern keep replicating? And moreover, why do we keep running away?

BOYS WILL BE BOYS

Moments after writing the above question, I had the lapse in judgment to hop over to social media for a break. Thanks to the highly sophisticated artificial intelligence of algorithms, I have spent most of my social media existence blissfully unaware of my father's posts. Mostly, he has chosen to email me with articles he wants me to read or thinks I can connect to. I don't doubt his good intentions, but since he is someone who believes in a biblically endorsed patriarchy, what he sends me is inevitably triggering.

My inbox has served as the frontline of our boundary wars. Over the years, I have asked him repeatedly not to send me articles even if he thinks they might be well received. To give him credit, he has (slowly) worked to send me fewer links and has also exercised restraint with some of his more recent shares (articles about the enneagram has become a safe zone). To my credit, I have worked on healing my victim mentality, giving less power to the triggers, and allowing myself the time and space to read his DMs only if and when I choose, and then deciding if and how I want to respond (with the support of a very skilled therapist).

The enneagram safe zone seemed to be working, but then I made the mistake of liking one of his more neutral social media posts and, soon after, clicking on a more inflammatory one that the site artificially thought I'd like, or hate, or at least have a strong reaction to (which I did).

That was several weeks before I typed the question, "Why do we keep running away?" and then took a break to pull up my feed. The first thing that popped up on my homepage was an article my father had posted titled "Hard Men in a World of Softness: Because Soft Is Not What God Called Men to Be." (I give this post a five-star trigger-warning due to rampant homophobia, misogyny, and harmful—very weird—theology and highly discourage your googling of it.) I took the bait and clicked on the article and was rewarded by the mix of disturbed, concerned, enraged, and sick-to-my-stomach feelings that usually happen when I read what my dad has been reading.

However, this post was right on time. Reading it gave me a visceral answer to my question of why we run. The article demonstrated almost verbatim patriarchy's first act of violence (as quoted by bell hooks in chapter two). In it was a rant against any form of masculine softness—described through examples of church leaders who didn't hunt, men who cared about shirt thread count and the theater, and pastors who were interested in theological precision—along with a warning as to the ways Christian institutions are attracting "effeminate" leadership (particularly focused on condemning intellectualism, potters, beards, skinny jeans, and—no surprise here—being gay). The article reads as a contemporary litany of the ways men should "engage in acts of psychic self-mutilation...kill[ing] off the emotional parts of themselves,"[8] and of other men. Biblical masculinity, according to the blogger and a person he interviewed, is about unsentimentally facing and causing violence, including both literally and metaphorically pulling the trigger. Biblical men repent of any softness and "pursue their own godliness with a holy violence," including replacing those men in church leadership who show effeminate traits (I'm assuming traits like empathy, compassion, and pastoral care) or those who are repulsed at the violence of the manly men who embrace it.

These casual references to masculine violence as God-ordained are terrifying, the homophobia and misogyny enraging. To understand that this was just one 1,200-word piece among thousands that my dad has read and agreed with continues to feel devastating. That these are sentiments he's expressed in many ways throughout my life has festered a deep soul wound. Clearly the (self)hateful opinions promoted in the post are harmful and not something I particularly want to be around. Why would I want to be in a relationship with someone who thinks God has made them superior to me? Being in relationship with "hard men" is, well, hard.

Which brings me back to my question: Why do we keep running away?

I run because of the pain.

After years of working up the courage to tell my father that a peer of mine at church and close family friend molested me by touching me inappropriately and making me feel creepily uncomfortable over several years as a child and preteen, my father dismissed it.

We were talking on the phone. Me in Pittsburgh. Him in Atlanta. But the distance was much farther than the miles between us.

"That's just normal behavior for boys," he said.

I wasn't necessarily surprised by his words, but they were still painful to hear and are even now painful to remember. When I hung up the phone, I wondered if there was still a part of me that was holding out hope for his validation of my pain. I guess hard men don't acknowledge their children's pain when it challenges the hardness of other men (or boys). Or perhaps the acknowledgment I've been seeking might mean he'd have to acknowledge his failures to protect his daughter, putting into question his own interpretation of his masculinity.

This wasn't the first time I shared with my dad about how I've experienced harm. Just as the article promises (and celebrates), his masculinized toughness has been successful at killing off many things, including, among other things, my trust, and the possibilities of us having a deep authentic relationship.

Almost always when one person reports abuse, there are many others in that community who have experienced it, including the person responsible for the abuse. And here I want to make a specific connection to the ways whiteness and patriarchy have impacted our family structures. White communities aren't the only ones who harbor deep cycles of child sexual abuse, but white people have been able to pathologize abuse in other racial communities while professing the innocence and exception of it when it happens in our own. There is a particular racialized way that toxic masculinity has been constructed and propagated and a particular racialized way that we white women have fortified it. But, first let's start with the advent of homegrown hardmen.

BACON'S REBELLION AND ANXIOUS PATRIARCHS

In my search to understand how my father could have reacted the way he did, I again mine the books of history. Maybe contextualizing his choices will offer some explanation that helps me feel a little better, or at least supports me in taking his reaction less personally.

We need not look further back than seventeenth-century Bacon's Rebellion to uncover a key point in the development of toxic white masculinity. Led by Nathaniel Bacon against Governor William Berkeley, Bacon's Rebellion was an armed attempt to overthrow the Virginia colony due to grievances against government land treaties with Native Americans. Along with being the first in the thirteen colonies, the rebellion seized Jamestown, prompting the British government to send in military reinforcements in order to regain control.

In the anti-racism workshops where I first learned about this 1676 event, Bacon's Rebellion was pointed to as the pivotal moment when the ruling elite realized that European indentured servants coming together with free, indentured, and enslaved Africans had the potential to overthrow their class hegemony. After all, it was shortly after Bacon's Rebellion that the category of "white" people was legally created in order to rearrange the class structure to one based on race. But a critical aspect of this history that wasn't talked about was how, beginning with Bacon's Rebellion and leading up to the Revolutionary War, European patriarchy was renegotiated and refashioned into something that would become solidly red, white, and blue.

Brown spotlights the anxious patriarch aspect of the book's title in examining Bacon's Rebellion, noting that despite attracting a wide range of supporters, Bacon's Rebellion was really a power struggle over discourses of "honor, manhood, and authority"[9] between Virginia's elite and "largely disenfranchised but armed and politically sensitive white male householders."[10]

Among other factors, Brown points to the expansion of gun culture in the colonies. Unlike in Britain where only men of a certain class were allowed arms, in the colonies, European indentured servants were intentionally armed at the end of their indenture as part of the war on Indigenous peoples and to help keep people of African descent enslaved. In the pre-Bacon climate, tobacco prices were plummeting,[11] upward mobility was becoming more challenging for European men,[12] and, as Brown writes, there was a "rising male ethic of armed resistance to perceived political and economic injustices."[13] Even though both Nathaniel Bacon and his archnemesis Governor Berkeley both agreed that it was the birthright of elite European men to rule, Bacon was willing to leverage lower-class European dissatisfaction to further his cause.

Sound familiar?

Bacon was hundreds of years ahead of his time. In his precociousness, he employed several racist strategies that are part and parcel of toxic white masculinity's playbook today. To paraphrase Brown's research, Bacon's references to the injustices of slavery resonated with his African supporters but moreover with larger numbers of European men newly freed from their terms of servitude and upset about economic factors and peace treaties with Native tribes, which reduced their access to Native land. Talking of "slavery" and "liberty" allowed European men to project their feelings of powerlessness about "the condition of their own status and honor"[14] onto discourses of slavery. And at the end of the day, what really united his supporters was Bacon's rallying cry against the racialized Indigenous "other."[15]

Bacon's emerging discourse in masculinity was built on a trifecta of populism, militarism, and racism that intentionally excluded women. While early on he had drawn popular support from women, Brown notes that soon Bacon decentralized women's role in his rebellion.[16] When brought to trial in the aftermath of the rebellion, many rebels ended up blaming their wives and children for their involvement.[17]

The hundred years between Bacon's Rebellion and the Revolutionary War proved to be plenty of time for a toxic white masculinity to cement itself into colonial culture. New laws were passed to ensure the "legal denial of African and Indian masculinity"[18] and to exclude white women from male privileges and legal access. Brown writes about how during this era there was a "renewed legal commitment to patriarchal social forms, particularly those constituting the domestic authority of ordinary men."[19]

The rhetoric of slavery and liberty was once again taken up by Virginia patriots protesting the "tyrannical" rule of Great Britain. In fact, this new patriarchal populism founded on gun culture and racism not only paved the way to the Revolutionary War, it also poured the very foundation of the United States. As Brown puts it:

> The political subject recognized by the Constitution was defined in contrast to seemingly natural dependents: he was not a slave, and he was not a woman. So complete was the separation between domestic relationships, defined by the laws of nature, and political relationships, recognized and defined by the state, moreover, that his own privileged position appeared to have no connection to the diminished status of these dependents. The political man was not, therefore, the architect of his own political authority, but the recipient of natural rights. He participated freely in political life, not as a consequence of his ability to coerce or dominate dependents, but because he was the rightful heir to such a political legacy.[20]

Thus the "natural order"—embedded in the constitutional law of the US—both necessitated and blessed the domination of a natural, God-given white patriarchal authority. Or in other words, "soft is not what God called men to be." The effects linger today.

VIOLENCE INTERNALIZED

There are more connections than room in this book to link the particular US history of toxic white masculinity to its present-day iterations (the Christian Right, anti-immigration, libertarianism, the meat industry, the anti-choice movement, professional sports, gun culture, etc.). Although it is not mine to write, I look forward to reading about these many important connections in a future book about Post-Traumatic *Master* Syndrome.

I will say one thing about gun culture, though. For all our debates on gun control and gun rights,* mental illness and toxic masculinity, (school) safety and (homeland) security, we seem to have glaringly omitted a conversation that includes white supremacy. And the denial runs deep. Having been historically dismissed as exceptional incidents, or as happening elsewhere—as in regarding gun violence as exceptionally endemic within Black and Brown communities—even the suggestion that the Sandy Hook school shooting, in which twenty elementary schoolchildren and six adults were killed, didn't happen,† demonstrates this deeply rooted denial.

Narratives of patriarchal protection especially ring dissonant with 2022's tragedy in Uvalde, Texas, at Robb Elementary in which nineteen children and two adults lost their lives. Particularly disturbing was the armed law enforcement whose well-funded show of force proved incompetent. A Texas House committee reported that although 376 law enforcement officers (including school, local, state, and federal officers) arrived at the scene, it took over an hour for the attack to be ended.[21] Hundreds of officers stood around the scene while an active shooter had eighty-one minutes to murder children and their teachers.‡

Recommendations to further fund law enforcement or to arm civilians and teachers(!) will do little to prevent future gun violence. According to several studies, arming civilians does not help stop

* I strongly support gun control laws. However, if not paired with undoing racism, these laws will reinforce white supremacy by further restricting access of firearms to People of Color without actually addressing how guns have historically, and still today, upheld whiteness.

† Conspiracy theorists like Alex Jones who've denied that the shooting at Sandy Hook even happened were taken to court and lost their cases (Bond, "How Alex Jones Helped Mainstream Conspiracy Theories Become Part of American Life").

‡ Eighty-one minutes is the time that passed between the first 911 call alerting authorities to the shooter's presence and officers finally gaining access to the shooter and reporting that the shooter had been subdued.

incidents of gun violence either. In fact, in the 2011 shooting of Congresswoman Gabby Giffords, an armed civilian almost shot the wrong person while trying to help to subdue the shooter.[22] Similar to having guns in the home—especially when not properly secured—having guns in the classroom actually increases the chances of someone being shot outside of an active shooter incident.[23]

As the news in Uvalde trickled out, one of the stories that hit me the hardest was how parents and family members stood outside, blocked from entering the school. They pled with officers to enter the building and even started to organize amongst themselves to charge into the school when law enforcement inaction became clear. I cannot imagine the frustration and pain and feelings beyond words of what it must have been like for those parents and family members to be forced to stand by and to be prevented from protecting their children. Angela Villescaz, the founder of Fierce Madres, shared with the school board that she "can't help but wonder if they just didn't find our children worthy of being saved."[24]

This traumatic dynamic is something communities of color have been forced to navigate since the advent of white supremacy. With patriarchal power being deliberately removed from communities of color and placed in the hands of white patriarchy, we have many traumatic, ongoing, and historical examples of communities of color being forced to surrender their abilities to protect their children to the state and from the state.

While those of us familiar with how racism functions might agree with Villescaz's suspicions, what might come as a surprise is how these white advantages built into white supremacy ultimately don't protect white children either. That an elementary school such as Sandy Hook in a small US town with a 90+ percent white population could experience such a tragedy and not be met with widespread, systems-overturning (white) outrage exposes the myth of white patriarchal protection. It is incredibly painful, though not surprising, that those invested in the wicked webs choose to deny reality even as their own children are put in harm's way.

Talk about abandonment issues.

As Bacon's Rebellion reminds us, guns and whiteness are high school sweethearts. The hardness of white masculinity has been derived from an entitlement to Indigenous land, the exploitation of Black, poor people, and People of Color's labor (including women of color's reproductive labor), along with white women's submission and an erasure of the existence of those who don't fit neatly into its "natural order." Until we get clear about the connections between gun culture and white supremacy, gun violence is going nowhere (or more likely, wherever it wants).

* * *

Particularly poignant in Brown's analysis of Bacon's Rebellion is the description of the emotional self-harm required to maintain control of others for these anxious patriarchs. Brown chronicles how the narrative for the white man was that his power over others originated not from systemic violence but from "his ability to subdue within himself those qualities he attributed to subordinates: passion, weakness, and dependence."[25] It was up to his individual will to conquer his own failings, to suffocate his vulnerability, to push down his emotionality and be the "hard man" God intended.

In the face of his own failures, this has also meant the ultimate self-harm of taking his own life. According to the Center for Disease Control, of the 45,222 people who died from gun-related injuries in 2020, more than half (approximately 54 percent) of those deaths were suicide.[26] Unfortunately, rates of suicide have been growing for everyone—in particular, non-Hispanic American Indian or Alaskan Native people, and tragically, amongst the youngest,[27] which many scholars point to as a direct and lasting effect of ongoing colonization.[28]

After non-Hispanic American Indian or Alaskan Native males, white males have the second highest rates of suicide for ages fifteen to forty-four and the highest for ages forty-five and older. Not unrelatedly, white men are more likely than other racialized/gendered groups to own guns.[29] And studies show that attempts at suicide are more often completed when guns are involved.[30]

While it is not always easy to extend compassion to those society has most advantaged, it is worth considering how the group who has accessed the most systemic advantages has become so likely to not see their own lives as worth preserving.

To flip the consideration, it is also worth wondering how almost all other groups, who experience much more systemic violence and disadvantage, are less likely to complete suicide. A 2020 *New York Times* article compiles several studies that seek to better understand some of the protective factors from suicide completion, including a sense of belonging, collectivist cultures, and caretaking responsibilities.[31]

I can't help but think about how the acculturation into white childhood—white boyhood in particular—and how the denial of empathy, the repression of emotions deemed inconvenient or associated with the feminine, and the hardness to human connection has led white men to disregard the lives of others and also their own. The wicked webs have taught white men to be separate, that they *should* be separate, and also above. But it is devastatingly lonely at the top. Human beings were not meant to live in such isolation.

I can't help but think about how *we* have taught them that they should be separate.

Despite our prayer vigils and our mourning, the fact is that the (white) gunmen are doing exactly what they were raised to do. Or, more accurately, exactly what *we* raised them to do.

We white women are the mothers and aunts who bought them toy weapons as children, bought them violent video games, and took them to see action films. We are the parents and grandparents who told them to toughen up and take it like men and be competitors. We are the friends, bullies, and siblings who beat them up for not being (strong, brave, smart, big, fearless) enough and made fun of them for their tears. Those are our babies with the guns and the gun wounds. Their state of mind reflects our own: a violence of white masculinity and white culture that proclaims value and worth and material reward and holiness and heaven for a select few at the cost of us all.

My mother taught me that people who bully have been bullied, which offers an explanation, although not an excuse, as to why we white women take patriarchy out on others and out on ourselves. It helps explain why we raise sons to abuse us and daughters to be abused. It helps clarify the pathways to white feminism and why we've adopted white masculine ways of being to gain access to patriarchal power. It provides context when thinking about the recent history of US presidential elections and why the majority of white women voted for our own harm.

The ugly truth is that we white women have been as dedicated to the violence of toxic white masculinity as any white man. As a collective, we have been socializing our sons, brothers, and nephews to hate women, queer folx, and People of Color, and we have prepared them to shoot up schools, killing plenty of children, white kids included. This is also part of our inheritance of the multigenerational trauma of Mistress Syndrome.

In the years following Reconstruction, white women made deliberate collective efforts to continue the white supremacist patriarchal order of the antebellum South. McRae chronicles some of the lesser known twenty-first century history of the grassroots activism of white women, especially white mothers who "shaped and sustained white supremacist politics."[32] Noting the particular role these white women and mothers played in maintaining both public policy and private at-home culture for white supremacist goals, McRae writes:

> White segregationist women capitalized on their roles in social welfare institutions, public education, partisan politics, and popular culture to shape the Jim Crow order. From there they provided a political education that mobilized generations and trained activists for white supremacist politics.[33]

The conclusion of McRae's research carries this history up to my lifetime with the fight to stop school busing in Boston in the 1980s. Even as late as the early 1990s I remember hearing about parental fights in Atlantan suburban districts to end school busing policies. Debates on "school choice" have continued in Georgia throughout the past decades, once again coding racial segregation in the language of liberty and freedom.

White women also organized to install those many Confederate statues people have been working so hard to take down. The Daughters of the Confederacy, initially established in 1894 to celebrate the Confederacy and reinterpret motivations for the Civil War through the Lost Cause narrative—emphasizing states' rights over slavery and racism—were responsible for erecting anywhere from 450 to 700 monuments. They even founded chapters for children, which shaped how generations of white people learned their history, some of whom are still alive and voting today.

While these examples may seem blatant, my point is that we white women have incredible influence in both subtle and overt ways as to how whole generations of white people come to understand themselves in the context of the wicked webs. It is especially in our familial, social, and faith-based networks that status quo and passing white ladies have the potential to shift this legacy for future generations.

MEDITATING ON SILENCE

Over the course of my life, it has felt effortless to blame my father. But it is only in the last few years that I have begun to look at my mother's role in upholding these systems as well. For decades, I have been highly sensitive to the ways the church fathers have kept patriarchy in place. I have had much less practice at identifying how the church mothers have been just as committed.

In my home congregation, our mothers were strong. They were steadfast. They were the ones who consistently came to church even as their husbands' attendance fluctuated. Despite always having a male pastor on church payroll, the church mothers and grandmothers were the ones who made the logistics of church happen. Everyone knew (although no one would say it) that they ran the church.

And they ran it on silence.

There are ways our church mothers' silences were inherited from the plantation. In examining how obedience and deference prevailed within nineteenth-century white family structures, Painter shows how these values were embedded within both evangelical piety and white womanhood. Painter profiles one such plantation mistress who advised white women to "'[r]everence' her husband's wishes," by counseling other white women toward "not only 'submission,' but also silence when self-defense was called for."[34] These plantation mistresses should smile, whatever the circumstances. Concurrently, in southern states like South Carolina, the authorities regularly advised women "to remain in abusive unions and to bear abuse in a spirit of submission."[35]

Among reasons to adhere to submissive silence was the way victims of abuse, and especially, incest, were put on trial—rather than their perpetrators—and often ultimately "seen as accomplices in their own ravishment"[36] in very public ways. (We still see this dynamic play out in very public ways as in how Christine Blasey Ford and Amber Heard were publicly humiliated and their credibility attacked when testifying to their experiences of (alleged) rape and sexual abuse by Supreme Court Justice Brett Kavanaugh and actor Johnny Depp, respectively.) Silence has been a strategy white women have used to protect ourselves and our children while allowing us proximity to white patriarchal power.

The first time I shared with my mother about my childhood molestation, she was supportive. She listened. She asked questions. She took me seriously. She expressed sadness and grief and questioned her part in it. We were sitting around my aunt and uncle's table, one that had held so many warm family gatherings. I was at the end of the table in one of the tall backed wooden chairs that had arm rests. She was to my left, in one of the chairs that didn't.

When I take this memory file out of my cabinet, the folder shape-shifts, depending on whose memory I wish to describe. In my version, I am nervous. It had taken me years to come to terms with what had happened to me and to legitimize it as abuse.

The peer and childhood family friend had been a consistent presence in my life. His unwanted touching ceased when I entered middle school, but that hadn't meant that I was free of the constant reminder of it. Between church, youth group gatherings, and our families' friendship, I would see him almost weekly and sometimes even more frequently. Of all things, I responded to his frequent (and often confusing and uncomfortable) presence in my life by moving closer to him, performing to our families and community that we were the closest of friends in what I now understand was a fawn response to the trauma. My silence around what had happened, along with my performance of our friendship, lasted as we got older and ended up in overlapping friend circles. He eventually became one of my partner's friends, too. It wasn't until after my marriage dissolved and #MeToo became popularized that I began to get clarity and become honest with myself about the relationship.

Honestly, in the years since his actions ceased, I had felt uncertain if I could (or should) name my experience as abuse. Compared to the haunting stories the #MeToo movement was exposing around workplace rape and extortion, compared to the grizzly stories of spiritual terror and childhood sexual abuse by clergy, compared to the extreme rates of missing and murdered Indigenous women (ten times the national average),[37] and the ongoing and historical systematic sexual abuse and exploitation of Black women and femmes, a few years of dodging a peer's devious hands seemed relatively innocuous.

But once I gave myself permission to more thoroughly remember and legitimize my memories as a form of sexual abuse, many other informative memories followed. I began remembering the icky feeling that came up for me around him and how I also had that feeling around certain friends' fathers, including his. I remembered how I already had a sense—at the young age of eight—that I was supposed to navigate those icky feelings in silence. I already knew, for example, that I was supposed to dodge his advances without anyone knowing and especially without anyone finding out he was the one causing me strife. I already knew I was supposed to suppress my intuition. I already knew my silence in the face of discomfort was the expectation.

I remembered, too, how my parents sat me down at our kitchen table one time when I was around eleven or twelve. They told me that I shouldn't be alone with his father. If his father ever did anything to me, I should tell them. It was a one-off conversation, an exception to the silence that shrouded talk of sex and sexualized bodies—that is, unless the sex was deemed immoral. There were plenty of loud and clear messages about the types of sex we weren't supposed to engage with (basically, any outside of heterosexual marriage). I began to remember how the warning about his father clicked for me. It offered some comfort by way of explanation: perhaps that explained my peer's behavior.

Then, I remembered a conversation I had with a church friend as a teenager several years after his unwanted touching stopped. At a church event, while hanging out in one of our families' minivans, I confided in her that he used to make me feel uncomfortable, or something to that effect. She shared in return that he had also inappropriately touched her sibling, though she thought the incident was being addressed.

The first time I shared with my mother about my childhood molestation, I felt relieved and believed. But then, months later we were on one of our semiweekly phone calls. She told me that she and my father had visited these close family friends (the family of the person who had molested me) over the holidays. Her friend had baked a delicious pie! It was great catching up with the family. All of their kids were there. She launched into a detailed update on my peers, including the person who had molested me.

As she went on sharing about their lives, I began to doubt my memory. Had I actually shared my story with her? Had I perhaps dreamt it? I was pretty sure it had happened. As my mother continued with her updates, I reassured myself that it had. We had been at my aunt and uncle's dining room table while my aunt and uncle had been away. We were sitting in their chairs. Mine had the armrests, I remembered; hers didn't.

"Mom," I interrupted her. "Why are you telling me about him? I'm not sure I want to hear about their family at all. You're acting like we never talked about what he did to me."

Silence.

The next time I shared with my mother about my childhood molestation, she remembered.

Since these initial confrontations with my parents, I have been seeking out more information about how environments become rife for abuse. Not surprisingly, silence and shame, especially around bodies and sex, are cultural dynamics that enable abuse. Experts on childhood sexual abuse prevention widely advocate that children learn the anatomically correct names for body parts, including sex organs, in ways that normalize and do not shame their bodies. Normalizing fluency around body parts, bodily autonomy, and appropriate boundaries (such as about appropriate touch, in which specific contexts, and with whom) supports children—and really, everyone—in having language to protect themselves. Normalizing conversations around consent and practicing saying no (like actually practicing it with children, out loud) are also important, as is normalizing the practice of consent and bodily autonomy around everyone, close family and friends included, because the "stranger danger" lessons I learned dangerously left out the likelihood that people who abuse are most likely to be someone the victim already knows.[38]

I wonder what might have happened if the instances of child sexual abuse in my home congregation had been handled differently. I wonder how things might have turned out if the church had reported his father to authorities when the first adult found out. I wonder how things might have turned out if his father had had actual comprehensive skilled support and accountability instead of a well-meaning yet unqualified pastoral team and a counselor who was rumored to have said that he was cured. I wonder what could have been prevented if a known child abuser hadn't been allowed to continue as congregant, father, and husband and help raise his children, often unsupervised, protected by the silences of his family, church family, and friends. I wonder what might have been if I had been encouraged to trust my gut and if I had been prepared to shout "No!" at my friend the first time he had made me feel that way. I wonder how I might have felt empowered to do so if I had known about his dad's history at a younger age. I wonder if I might have told my parents the first time it happened if celebrating bodily autonomy and saying no had been a part of our weekly family devotions instead of the lessons on purity, obedience, and devotion.

In describing the psychological enmeshment of enslavement, Painter remarks on how the attachment and resentment that enslaved women often felt toward their mistresses for the abuses of their mistresses' husbands mirrors the bitterness and betrayal many sexually abused children feel toward their mothers and mother figures who were unable to and/or didn't protect them from the abuse. Noting psychiatrist Judith Herman's work, Painter writes, "Victims who do not display anger at their abusers may displace their rage on to nonabusing but impotent parental figures: mothers."[39]

I have only recently been able to feel that sense of betrayal, to access anger toward the church mothers who were supposed to protect us. My anger toward our mothers feels complicated. The church fathers' abandonment has always been clear to me; the church mothers' abandonment less certain. Behind their silences they were trying to protect us the best way they knew how. Perhaps I am more easily able to access compassion for our mothers because I know what was done to me was also done to them.

Identifying with my father's hardness is much more difficult. I am reluctant to see the many difficult parts of him as also parts of me.

Within this fraught inquiry, I seem to keep returning to my fear. I keep coming back to how it is fear buttressed by shame, and not some evildoer's hate, that fuels these harmful dynamics. My father's fear of being soft, my mother's fear of being exposed, my fear of abandonment results in his hardness, her silence, my urge to flee. Perhaps I have been projecting my coping mechanism onto others. Perhaps we all have.

In its relative advantage, my whiteness has granted me the access to come and go as I please. I can run from the traumas, but I can't hide from their impact.

Before I landed in Pittsburgh, I was tiring of running. The summer before, I spent four consecutive months traveling, averaging three nights to a bed. When I was deciding on my next move, I knew I wanted to make a commitment to a place and a community. I knew I wanted to be more still. I knew the type of work I wanted to do necessitated strong relationships and those would take time and commitment.

Part of my healing from the multigenerational effects of Mistress Syndrome has meant disrupting my family's track record of running (if only for a season). Over the past decade, my commitment to putting down roots and staying even when things got tough gave me the opportunity to face myself and my lineage in incredible and scary ways.

Since my first experience with yoga, I began practicing some type of seated meditation. Usually meditation happened during group classes or occasionally on my own when I was especially in need of a moment of calm. But in deepening my meditation practice, I have been challenged to make a more consistent commitment.

Which has me wondering what a practice of sitting still could offer those of us who have become racialized as white. How might it help us to disrupt our flight patterns? How might it support white settlers to interrupt the temptation of what Linda Tuhiwai Smith calls the "imperial imagination"?[40]

Could it help us learn to be with our pain, our discomfort, our hurt feelings, and our fears? Could a practice of silence help us become less so? Could a practice of stillness better mobilize us toward justice?

Moreover, could a practice of better seeing and being with myself help me better see and be with those I haven't chosen and with those whom I have? Could it help me feel and metabolize the pain? Could it help me access compassion for those who have hurt me? Could it help me move toward solidarity and not away? Could it help us to do the same?

CHAPTER TEN

LOVE AND MARRIAGE

By marriage, the husband and wife are one person in law:
that is, the very being or legal existence of the woman
is suspended during the marriage, or at least is incorpo-
rated and consolidated into that of the husband: under whose
wing, protection, and cover, she performs every thing.

—Sir William Blackstone

We do not have to love. We choose to love.

—bell hooks

Once upon a time, I tried being married. And it was surprisingly hard.

Relationships in general are hard, and long-term, committed ones are next-level difficult. That part I had expected. No, the unexpectedly hard part of the marriage was not working out our differences, not communicating complex feelings, nor even navigating conflict (although all of these were hard, and I can't say we ever really figured them out). The hard part I had not anticipated was the relentless pressure to conform to a white heteronormative family ideal and the expectation that no matter what, you stay married.

If you had a childhood devoid of purity culture or conservative Anabaptism, try to stay with me here. The pressures and privileges of (white) heteronormativity still have likely influenced your perspectives on family, but possibly not the same way. While it is said that half of all marriages in the US end in divorce, this had only been the case for one marriage in both of my extended families. Staying married was not some fairy tale; it was the only option on the menu.

I married one of my best friends soon after college. A few years younger than 2009 US standards,[1] we were plenty mature by Mennonite ones. Many of our peers had followed the ways of our parents by finding that one right Mennonite lifemate at a Mennonite college. Even before we graduated, we had already received dozens of wedding invitations from classmates and cousins.

Our engagement was practical and mutual, the way I imagine my parents' and grandparents' must have been. My year of voluntary service was going to end, and it didn't make financial sense for us to pay twice the rent to live separately when we could pay once. Even though we had already lived together as platonic housemates, once we started dating, the option of living together was not something we considered. Living together while dating implied sex before marriage—our families would never approve. Instead of joining many of our nonreligious peers in moving in together, we did what my parents had done and their parents before: we got married. Years later, I would wonder: if we hadn't felt so much pressure to not look like we were having extra-/premarital sex, would we have still chosen this moment to get engaged? If the financial incentive hadn't existed, would we have even wanted to cohabitate?

The marriage talk happened one evening when we were hanging out in my room. "Do you want to talk about getting engaged?" I asked matter-of-factly. "Sure," was his response. We planned a nice dinner to mark the occasion and decided to exchange gifts instead of rings.

Like many betrothed people, I entered marriage with enthusiasm and optimism that we could make our relationship work for the particulars of us. I had always liked boys, and I knew I really liked this one. I had always craved attention, connection, and collaboration, and a lifelong partnership seemed to offer an excellent container for that. Besides, I had always liked a challenge, and defying cultural norms from within was the kind of subversion I was into.

At the moment all this made excellent sense to me.

Our wedding ceremony was in several ways nontraditional. We had everyone sit in a circle outside on a communal farm. Instead of a groom waiting at the altar for his bride's father to "give her away," we both entered the circle at the same time with our parents. Instead of exchanging rings, we wove ribbons into a weaving, and so did our guests. My dress was turquoise and cream. While we both had vows, our family and community members did too.

And we were publicly explicit about many other things. We used the gender-neutral term "partner" instead of referring to each other as "husband" or "wife." We planned on living communally with other people. We both kept our last names and even entertained taking my mother's family name. We were 99 percent certain that we didn't want to have/raise children.

Even though I knew about and disagreed with the sexism, classism, and racism built into the legal and religious construct of marriage, I was not prepared for the constant marriage-specific ways patriarchy had us in its scope. One early affront came at our wedding. Minutes after the ceremony, in our receiving line a family friend gave me a warm hug of congratulations and expressed their excitement for us to have kids. I was too surprised to respond. *We hadn't mentioned anything about wanting children in the ceremony. Strange. Why would they make that assumption?* But they were older and my parents' friend. Lots of our peers had had weddings recently. Maybe they were confusing us with another couple? I wrote it off as a mistake and kept it moving. There were other guests to greet.

But then, right there in the receiving line, it happened again. A dozen or so guests later, this time someone much closer to my age alluded to us becoming parents. Then a family member did the same and so did a childhood friend. By the third or fourth future parenting/ child reference, my confusion shifted to irritation. I began to respond with a stifled politeness: "Thank you, but we probably won't have kids."

That night in our hotel room, exhausted from months of wedding buildup and celebration, I remember mentioning to my partner how annoying it was that everyone was talking to us about being parents. "Oh?" he responded, "No one said anything about kids to me." This was the first of many times I would receive a specific (racialized) gender reinforcement around being married and he would not. The wicked webs were reminding me that (white) women were supposed to have (white) babies and our marriage signaled it was now time for me to do my part.

And while these parent/child references may seem insignificant and well-intentioned, they built up, in the same way that the smallest adaptations in footwear have a big impact on one's gait over time. The wicked webs have become so efficient, all they need are these slightest of constant corrections to ensure conformity and exhaust resistance. By the ninth future-children reference in the wedding receiving line, I smiled silently back, too tired to expend the energy. I have been very critical of our mothers' complicity in patriarchy's arrangement, but in looking back, I realize how it only took one night for me to run on silence, too.

(WHITE) WIFELY PRIVILEGE

I have been working on bringing love to the spaces in which I tend to blame, which has allowed me to access a new level of compassion for our mothers and for myself. Through my own ten-year journey of engagement, marriage, separation, and divorce, I got to experience a fraction of the specific pressures put on married and mothering (white) women. I am grateful for these experiences, because it has helped me bring a level of humility and understanding as to why our mothers have so often chosen silence and deferred to the status quo.

It has also made me question my own arrogance in thinking I could pick and choose the aspects of marriage that worked for me, that I could be exempt from the ways it didn't. Even with my aversion to the patriarchal structure of marriage, a part of me still thought that with hard work and good intentions, we could be the exception. As much as it hurts to admit, my internalized Mistress/Damsel/Mother/Savior had me out here thinking I could absorb the benefits of whiteness and none of its costs.

And let's be honest, there were many benefits to being married to a white man.

Our first year of marriage had its emotional ebbs and flows, but unlike many young newlyweds, finances were not a main stressor for us.

A few months before the wedding, my partner found a full-time nonprofit tech job with benefits and opportunity for advancement. I had also found paid work via that (very part-time) gig as a teaching artist. While we spent most of our marriage dependent on his earnings, neither one of us alone would have been able to live off mine. His access to a livable wage as a cis white man in tech was why we were able to get a loan and buy a house during our first year of marriage. His paid work paid off my student loans and allowed me to secure new ones. His stable and rising income meant I could make art every day, access birth control, attend graduate school, and take on one very large-scale community organizing public art project, which ultimately facilitated me in getting my first full-time livable wage job.

I had never cared about earning money, but I also hadn't really had to. There is a both/and here that feels important because on one hand, I feel quite Mennonite Humble about my anticapitalist values. I am proud of the ways I have chosen work and life paths that align with those values. When faced with the financial insecurity of the unknown—in leaving my job, in leaving my marriage—I have opted to take the risks that felt right in my soul rather than hold onto a fear of scarcity and material benefits. With the whole Mennonite being-in-the-world-but-not-of-it indoctrination, I've been suspicious of private property for a long time. When gaining access to property and a large sum of money, I opted to share it. On my best days, I know my worth could never come from the underrated price that gets put on my labor. My labor, I've told myself, is for things beyond the status quo.

And at the same time, it's worth considering how I so easily, and preemptively, opted out of the money game. As an artist and organizer whose work is critical of systems and institutions, sure, I never expected those same systems to legitimize my work. I've had little to no expectation that someone would purchase my hand-embroidered money pillows criticizing US foreign policy, especially at the actual cost of hours upon hours of skilled handiwork.

And also, much more obvious to me now, having a white middle-class family and a white college-educated cis man husband who were invested in (or at least willing to play) the money game meant that I didn't have to do so in order to survive. Other than the year after I graduated from college, when I scraped through on odd jobs and a cheap roommate situation, I had always been propped up by family, Mennonite institutions, and him. As became clearer to me throughout our marriage, my access was predicated on his. There is a long history of this being so.

Within European patriarchy, marriage and divorce mostly fell under the jurisdiction of the church (and before that to the family's discretion). It wasn't until the Protestant Reformation of the 1500s that marriage became seen as a type of contract and divorce became a civil matter. In seventeenth-century Britain, where the law of coverture reigned, it literally took an Act of Parliament to secure a divorce. The law of coverture merged a married woman's legal existence and financial resources with that of her husband, after which all legal and financial matters (owning property, making contracts, child custody, engaging in court proceedings, etc.) fell under her husband's purview.

Initially, marriages in the American colonies followed British precedent. Yet as Battalora notes, while American "colonists brought with them the patriarchal order of the household that existed in premodern England,"[2] they also began to invent a "new body of crime"[3] in the legislation of antimiscegenation. Such aforementioned laws and others, such as a 1664 law that punished "English or freeborn"[4] women who married an enslaved man of African descent with her husband's terms of enslavement, impeded relationships that "took an intimate and consensual form from being legitimized by the community."[5]

As mentioned in chapter four, built into the invention of legal—and fictional—white womanhood was a financial incentive for the (white) men who'd marry them. White women of the seventeenth and eighteenth centuries might not have independently owned their own labor, but in exchange for their patriarchal loyalty to white fathers, husbands, and brothers they at least had the promise of indirect access to legal, state, and financial power, from which their racialized counterparts were excluded.

In the eighteenth century throughout the South, elite families used marriage to further entrench the racist classist status quo. Strategic marriages kept land, enslaved people, and political power within elite control, which, according to Brown, ensured their daughters' "economic security and a release from some of the manual labor that characterized the lives of less wealthy and enslaved women."[6] Or in other words, upper-class married women forfeited their rights for all the material and psychological advantages that white womanhood could afford.

Many of the marital truths and consequences of white womanhood are not that far behind us. Along with winning the right to vote, (white) women's legal rights increased in the early twentieth century. Now (white) married women could have property in their name and have citizenship independent of their husbands. But it wasn't until the 1960s that the Supreme Court ensured the marital rights of interracial heterosexual couples. It wasn't until the 1970s that married women could hold credit in their name (nonmarried women weren't eligible). It wasn't until the 1990s that marital rape was illegal in all fifty states,[7] the 2000s that all states had removed antimiscegenation from their constitutions, the 2010s that no-fault divorce was possible in all fifty states, and 2015 that same-sex marriage became legal nationwide.

Today, as in centuries past, there are still legal and economic privileges that come with marriage including tax deductions, inheritance benefits, and increased access to health insurance.[8] Since white people in the US marry at 1.7 times the rate of their Black counterparts, those advantages continue disproportionately for those who have been racialized as white.[9]

What might I have unknowingly forfeited for the promise of indirect access to legal, state, and financial power that came with institutional marriage? And, relatedly, for what was I not prepared? It turns out I am not alone in having felt unprepared. In a 2024 article, personal finance and legal writer Christy Bieber reports that "a lack of knowledge about what marriage entails is one of the leading contributing factors to divorce."[10] Factors couples cited include not fully understanding the commitment involved and not being able to cope with new problems such as changes in their partner.

I am thinking about how tax deductions and health insurance aren't usually the main plot lines for rom-coms and TV. (Now that I think of it, staying married isn't typically the subject matter, either.) Plenty of people get married for legal, state, and financial reasons, yet our popular discourse revolves around falling in love.

I am thinking again about those colonial laws in 1600 that blocked marriages built on intimacy, mutual consent, and community support when such marriages threatened the people making the rules. Across media platforms, we are fed stories of intimacy, mutual consent, and community support, yet the institutional structure, and its ramifications, are rendered invisible and assumed normal. Kind of like white middle-class patriarchy.

In Mennonite contexts, as and in many evangelical and other religious settings where purity culture has been in vogue, the protection of heterosexual marriage came with many benefits. Once married, my shoulders could relax; I would not be constantly judged by my community for my sexuality with the threat of excommunication. If anything happened within the confines of our marriage, we would be covered—or it would be covered up by the church's exhale of relief; two fewer souls to fret over. Unlike so many of my queer friends, my married soul could relax now that the threat of hell had been exorcized.

Yet, if Evangelical Protestants have a higher divorce rate than any other group and 69 percent of heterosexual divorces are initiated by women,[11] it's worth questioning the integrity of that protection.

MONEY, MONOGAMY, AND OTHER UNMENTIONABLES

I had planned on staying married for the length of my life—or at least of the length of his.

Correlation is not causation. But the cracks in our marriage became more obvious after I took my first big-girl job. The conservatives' fears are perhaps valid: women leaving the home is bad business for the patriarchal enterprise of marriage. Once I took a full-time job earning a livable wage with benefits, it meant, among other things, that I could access loans on my own, including the one that would eventually buy him out of his share of the house.

Correlation is not causation. But in our dynamic, a gendered role reversal shook up our partnership's foundation. After half a decade of relying on his income, I hoped my new job would help balance the undercurrent of resentment that had begun to permeate our asymmetries of time, money, and joy. But ultimately, the increase of my out-of-the-home responsibilities coupled with the increase in his unstructured time did not strengthen our dynamic. Instead, it exposed the places where our foundation was weakest.

Correlation is not causation. Yet my frequent work-related travel allowed me to expand my world beyond the one we were co-creating in Pittsburgh. It brought new and energizing relationships into my life. It facilitated my heart in expanding beyond the commitment of our partnership.

It was not the first time I had developed strong feelings for someone else, nor would it be the last. Mostly we had worked this out between us, behind the sturdy façade of our heteronormative monogamy so as not to create anxiety for our families, church, and community. The first time I developed serious feelings for someone else, I confided in him. The feelings had surprised me, but I hadn't needed to act on them. It helped to process them with him, and with my therapist. It was good to be self-aware, I told myself. It felt good and right to trust him first and foremost with this information. It just provided information for us to take in and navigate together.

But the next time it happened we were in a much rockier place.

Though an interest in racial justice was not new for me, the resources and analyses I was connecting to rattled my sense of identity and belonging in some deep, devastating, and incredible ways. For one, I was realizing the extent to which whiteness had infiltrated my mind and my body. I was also gaining language to tear injustice apart, sharpen my analysis, and stoke my passion. Being a part of a movement felt powerful and like something my soul had been yearning for for a long time.

But at home, that fire wasn't shared. Or at least, not in the ways I wanted it to be. As I further internalized the words of anti-racism, the chasm between our languages and commitments widened. Differences that had seemed less relevant while in college now glared at me from the past, widening the gap between where we were and where I wanted him to be. I judged him especially harshly when he wasn't willing (or ready) to learn from me.

* * *

We were sitting around the wobbly kitchen table, in the vintage yellow chairs that fit me perfectly but were probably uncomfortable for his tall frame. I remember pleading with him to do "this work." Maybe he knew what I was asking for, but most likely I was asking for things he didn't fully understand and I couldn't fully articulate. We were unpacking an incident that happened earlier that evening at a community meeting about the gentrification in our neighborhood. I had engaged publicly with the director of the local CDC, a Black woman who the organization hid behind every time they evicted people. Well, actually after I stood to comment, she had engaged with me. She cut me off a couple of times when he abruptly yelled at her to stop interrupting me.

"That was unhelpful," I told him afterward. "I don't need you to come to my rescue. I was handling it," I said. "I know you had good intentions, but you just played into their hands, becoming this angry white man rescuing his ill-informed white woman."

He got defensive. We had a fight. I closed future folders when I filed that memory away, doubtful we would be able to grow in these ways together, aware that the chasm was expanding with every move I made.

The couples counseling wasn't really doing much. Our therapist somehow wasn't grasping that there were deeper issues at play. She wanted to problem solve around the dishes while I was questioning our shared values and if monogamy was my thing. I mean, I hoped it was, but I kept feeling attracted to other people.

After a particularly unhelpful session, I texted a friend for book recommendations about polyamory.* I read each diligently, like any educated white lady trying to figure out her stuff without yet being ready to make a change. As I read about the history of monogamy and how many humans are wired for promiscuity, the silent expectations of generations began to feel suffocating. I felt angry. And indignant. If our families and communities wanted us to stay together so strongly, then why weren't they offering us adequate support?

When I take out my emotional files from that time, the pages are rigid and weighted down by the disapproval of generations of church and state. A fear of excommunication from beyond my lifetime had left an imprint on the page. "Whatever you do, stay," Ms. Sylvia had told me on the phone after I shared with her that I was engaged. *What would I tell her? What would I tell my dad?* It seemed almost impossible that there might be another way. Almost.

In retrospect, I most likely had unrealistic expectations of family support. Perhaps, I always have. Our parents stayed together even when things weren't good. They had been taught that too. I wondered how my aunts and uncles had maintained their unions. Occasionally, I had worked up the courage to ask. But mostly there was silence, or me talking into it. When, at the long, crowded dining room table, I finally shared with my extended family that my partner and I were separating, no one said a word. Then my cousin cracked a joke. (I feel so grateful to her for that.)

EXCHANGING ONE RULEBOOK FOR ANOTHER

Correlation is not causation. Leaving a white heterosexual monoga-mous marriage is not necessarily leaving white patriarchy, but for me in my Mennonite subculture, just considering divorce was momentous.

---

* Polyamory is a relationship practice in which people have multiple consensual intimate relationships (romantic and/or sexual).

On the morning when I realized my marriage was over, I drove to the top of a mountain. I had woken up with a sudden urge for perspective. There was a heaviness in my chest. I needed to get up high. I needed to breathe better, to get my body above the pressure of heavy uncertainty.

I made it through the morning's rush-hour traffic to the little city park overlooking the place where the Monongalia and the Allegheny rivers converge. The water rushed at a chilly pace on either side of the fort that marked the settler violence of the past 250 years. From the park, I could see a thick layer of smog lodge in between the concrete and the steel. The tallest of the colonial monuments to racist capitalism still poked through the clouds. Yet the seven-hundred-foot drop down to the winter rivers' flow didn't satisfy my urge. I needed more altitude. I needed more space to feel, enough to believe there was possibility on the other side of venturing beyond what my ancestors had dreamt for me.

After my partner temporarily moved out and Felicia and Kayla had moved in, Felicia and I were sitting around that wobbly kitchen table when I told her how over it I was. I was beyond ready to divvy up our assets and move forward with the divorce. "I think you should give him time," she surprised me by saying, since ending it felt like the most revolutionary thing to do. "I think you need to honor the process, otherwise you might regret it." I took her gentle advice to heart. No one in my family had experienced divorce, but she had.

And I'm so glad I did. While our separation process was far from perfect, over the following months, moving more slowly allowed space for humanizing each other, which my anti-racist rulebook had failed to do. It supported me in accessing more care.

Moving more slowly through our separation and divorce process also meant I had the opportunity to process my grief, too. While I had been already mourning my marriage's ending as I was coming to terms with ending it, during our separation process I found there were other things to grieve. I especially grieved the failure of not being able to make our relationship work for the particulars of us. It felt like the wicked webs had won. We had not been able to infiltrate white heteronormativity and flip institutional marriage on its head. Instead, it had dragged us around, exhausted our creativity, and gave us the middle finger on the way out.

I am finding that it is within these intimate partnerships and marriages where white women often struggle the most. I have worked with white women who have been eager to look at their own whiteness. They are ready to dig deep. They want to make changes. But then there's a moment where they realize that the work we are doing together might challenge their relationships. Her boyfriend isn't interested in examining his racism. Her husband resists any critique of the ways they've been doing things. Her partner refuses to look at his parenting or consider the sexism embedded in their relationship. Often this realization has been the point where the white women I'm working with send me a polite email. She still finds this work incredibly valuable, but she needs to do it elsewhere.

I am slowly learning to push and judge less. On my most skeptical days, I can become overwhelmed by the doubt that the collective of us white women will have the courage to truly divest from this arrangement. On those days I fear that our attachment to silent loneliness, the familiar discomfort of sexism, the benefits of a gilded cage, and the protective façades will continue to be more attractive than the messy, scary unknown of whatever else could be.

Swapping out one rulebook for another can be more attractive than the messy, scary unknown of whatever else could be. Leaving a white heterosexual monogamous marriage does not mean other options will automatically exist. And maybe it wasn't as much about the options as how I approached them. Racist or anti-racist, married or divorced, monogamy or polyamory, when read a certain way, the books of polyamory offered me rigid rules too. Rather than reacting with an "opposite," how might we find a different way?

I am inspired by polyamory's invitation to imagine alternative relationship structures. I am here for the values of mutual consent and clear communication. I am all about relationship anarchy's goal of subverting connotations of ownership and power imbalances that are embedded in how we've been taught to do romantic relationships. I especially appreciate the permission to become more and more honest (and courageous) about our desires, needs, realities, and capacities.

It reminds me of the harm reduction model,[12] which strives to lessen the harmful impact of behaviors (like substance use) while also acknowledging greater structural, cultural, and generational factors. Given that our intimate partnerships are fraught by the systems we live under, how might we—married to white men or not—navigate intimacy, consent, and community support while reducing harm?

These are not new questions, though they might be for some of us. These are questions many communities have been asking for a long time.

THE LAWS OF EXOTIFICATION

On my high school campus at the turn of the twenty-first century—three decades after the 1967 landmark case *Loving vs. Virginia* banned antimiscegenation laws and fifteen years before *Obergefell vs. Hodges* extended state-sanctioned marriage to same-sex couples—interracial and pansexual flirtation was commonplace. This spring, amidst the seasonally limiting packed lunch offerings of Passover and Lent, there was a generous dose of flirting and much talk of prom dates. My school's namesake, Henry W. Grady,* an avowed white supremacist, was surely turning up dirt along with his peers in their graves. Yet, in spite of an abundance of multicultural flirtation, the same racial legacies that criminalized cross-race relationships were still around us—particularly those governing relationships between white women and men of color.

In *White Women Race Matters*, Ruth Frankenberg conducts a series of interviews with white women in late twentieth-century California to research white women's "daily experience of racial structuring and the ways race privilege might be crosscut by class, culture, ethnicity, gender, and sexuality."[13] In these conversations with white women

---

* In 2020, the Atlanta Board of Education voted to change the name of my alma mater to Midtown High School due to the white supremacist views of the school's namesake.

a generation or so older than me, Frankenberg documents aspects of taboo and rebellion in dating men of color. Whether explicitly stated or implied, interviewees indicate an awareness of whom not to bring home.

While some of Frankenberg's white women and many of my Atlanta peers similarly rebelled by bringing home men of color and other people on the margins of middle-class white masculinity, I skipped town—actually the entire country—and found a lover in France. I use the term "lover" here loosely to mean my-first-recip-rocated-love-interest-who-declared-his-attraction-to-me-after-I-was-back-home-and-whose-affections-were-only-ever-expressed-in-written-communication-an-ocean-apart.

After living in France, I no longer found crude Americans of any race appealing. Instead, I sought out more "interesting" love interests, and spent the next four years exclusively dating people who had not been made in the USA. I collected my list of love interests like one might mark off countries visited on a map: France, Brazil, Canada, the Congo, Brazil again, and a white Mennonite who had been born in Bolivia (by this point I was stretching it).

While pursuing young men of a wide spectrum of racial identities might not on its surface seem connected to contemporary racism, the exotification and fetishization of People of the Global Majority is one of the ways modern racism gets expressed. That I was drawn exclusively to people and cultures outside of the US, though in superficially positive ways, highlights another way racism dehumanizes. Through my fascination with non-US-born men, I was likewise denying their full humanity. After all, my international lovers were just as flawed as those born in the US and had the potential to be just as uninteresting. Then what had me so attracted to their foreignness and what exactly was I so eager to reject about the boys at home?

There's a piece here for me about notions of consumption and ownership that feels icky to name, as if collecting a history of "exotic" relationships made me more "interesting" by proxy. The idea that relationships can be a thing one "collects" puts me uncomfortably close to the notion of ownership that justified both slavery and male-headed households. Plus, this overreliance on relationships with others in order to define my own status seems connected to how people socialized as women have been taught to assess our value based on the value of others with whom we are in relationship.

The "exotic" allure of these non-US-born young men had been shaped by my internalization of white womanhood, but it also had been shaped by years of US foreign policy that defined who could be a citizen and who could not. Historically one's eligibility lined up with one's access to whiteness.

Pretty much as soon as the US declared its independence from England, Congress went about determining who could be American. In 1790, this was free whites of "good moral character" who had lived in the US for at least two years (later changed to five). While the long-time Indigenous residents of Turtle Island were excluded from citizenship (until 1924), enslaved Africans were counted as three-fifths of a person for the purposes of determining congressional representation. This Three-Fifths Compromise lasted until 1870, when people of African descent gained full citizenship. Up until the 1950s, the US used a quota system that severely restricted immigration from Asian countries and privileged those from European ones. Although people from Latin America had long been able to cross the US southern border with fluidity, the 1965 Immigration and Nationality Act abolished the national-origins quotas and formalized paths for citizenship for people born in Latin America and Asia. As Pew Research Center editor D'vera Cohn writes, "Since enactment of the 1965 Immigration and Nationality Act, immigration has been dominated by people born in Asia and Latin America, rather than Europe."[14] And racist othering continues to be part of public discourse on immigration and "Americanness."

In addition to antimiscegenation laws, white women's relationships to non-US-born men were shaped through policy on nationality and immigration. Even though there were many patriarchal restrictions on white women at the founding of the United States, they were still considered citizens. However, a married woman's citizenship was determined by her husband's. Further clarified by laws such as the

1907 Expatriation Act, (white) women could lose their citizenship when marrying a foreign husband. Hence, white women marrying nonwhite, non-Americans was legislated to be rare.

In the ten years that I was partnered and married, cultural exotification/fetishization seemed to have intensified. Listening to young people share how their white sorority sisters saw hooking up with Black guys as a rite of passage and seeing how white female celebrities use proximity to Black men to build their brands, these centuries-old stereotypes about the criminality, foreignness, and hypersexuality of men of color combined with a temptation to violate social norms (and piss off fathers) have evolved, but nevertheless continue to serve racism. And because these modern-day expressions of racism have been so thoroughly glamorized, we may fail to recognize them as such.

These contemporary dynamics help mitigate any real threat to our racialized status quo. That increasingly higher numbers of white sorority sisters actively pursue Black men for hookups does not mean that higher numbers of these young white women are committing to long-term relationships, planning to integrate these new partners into their elite white lives, or preparing for the harsh reality of what proximity to racial marginalization carries.

CULTURAL DIFFERENCES AND MISOGYNOIR

As my partner and I were working out the details of our divorce, I started to think about dating again.

I didn't know exactly what I was looking for, but I knew I wanted to date someone who shared my passion for anti-racism. Not yet brave enough to try out the apps, I began to notice who was single in my organizing networks. I also began to notice the not-so-subtle disapproval Black women had for white women dating Black men. While this initially surprised me—I assumed anti-racist organizers in multiracial spaces would be supportive of interracial relationships—the criticisms got louder the more I tuned in.

Sometimes it was a disparaging comment about Black men's preference for white women. Sometimes it was a shake of the head about white women pursuing Black men like an accessory. Sometimes it was an empathetic sigh for a child of color being raised exclusively by their white mother. Sometimes it was frustration about yet another organizing coalition formed by Black men and white women, yet again neglecting to center the intersectional experiences of Black women and other Black folks at the margins.

I let their concerns simmer in the background as I started to date a fellow activist. Over the course of our short-lived relationship, there were many ways I experienced his sexism: the ways he casually objectified women, the ways he favored the anti-racist philosophies of Black men to the ones of intersectional feminists, the ways he concealed that he was in other relationships, the ways he took advantage of reproductive labor. When I would bring these concerns up to him, he responded by saying they were simply cultural differences.

As a white person committed to digging up my internalized white supremacy, hearing that a Black organizer saw my concerns as cultural differences, I began to doubt myself. My whiteness, as I was realizing, was something I had been taught explicitly *not* to see. So, when the intuitive small voice inside me called out in alarm, I shushed her because I thought being an accountable white person meant deferring to his assessment of my racism.

In retrospect, of course there were cultural differences. How could we be in a multicultural relationship without constant cultural differences? That cultural differences could coexist with sexism, however, had not occurred to me. Even now, I am still unpacking why I let myself be shut down so easily. In this brief relationship I tolerated a level of deceit and narcissism I never would have tolerated from a white man.

I was afraid to "get it wrong," so I deferred out of fear. Yet, by shutting myself down, I reinforced the pattern: I would bring up my initial concern. He would say it was a "cultural difference." I would doubt my perspective and decide it wasn't worth the emotional energy an argumentative stalemate might bring. Then I would retract my concern and his behavior would continue.

I believe he used this tactic to confuse and gaslight me, deflecting attention away from his actions and avoiding having to make a change. I can also recognize his stuff and claim the ways I opted out of holding him accountable. Particularly how, as a white woman, I did not depend on his allyship for my survival. At the time I was willfully unaware of how my choice to opt out of holding him accountable also continued his misogynoir.* I failed to consider how Black women and femmes would ultimately be most impacted by my yielding to his sexism.

Later I learned how Black women have repeatedly asked white women to hold Black men (and all men) accountable to misogynoir, how allegiances between Black men and white women have historically excluded Black women and their perspectives. I have learned more about white feminist history and the way it has pushed Black women's concerns to the margins. No wonder so many Black women voiced their concerns.

Historically, Black women's voices were notably missing from records regarding liaisons between Black men and white women. Hodes documents that the most audible voices on record were those of white men as judges, journalists, and courtroom witnesses, followed by those of white women whose testimonies as accusers, accused, and, infrequently, witnesses were invited into court proceedings. Very occasionally, Black men's voices were written down or (more often) summarized and translated indirectly through the words of white male attorneys and witnesses. The least recorded voices were those of Black women. Little is known from Black men's communities about what they thought of these relationships. As Hodes writes, "black women's voices are the faintest in the antebellum historical record."[15]

I am remembering Kayla's comments after our trip to Atlanta, how she told me I needed to do so much more work before dating a Black man. Maybe she had a point, I thought, beginning to understand for myself some of the intersectional difficulties of being in such a romantic relationship. I certainly had not figured out how to name the complexities of "-isms" within this earlier dating dynamic.

---

* "Misogynoir" is a term coined by Black feminist writer Moya Bailey in 2008 to describe the specific misogyny that Black women face.

Maybe being a "good" anti-racist meant not even considering whole racial demographics of the dating pool? That felt particularly ironic, though maybe it would be easier if I just opted out...

And then Karriem came along.

* * *

Karriem came to yoga class a couple of times before I began teaching. I remember a conversation in the hall by the elevator as we waited for the studio to be unlocked. There was warmth, perhaps a slight spark? But mostly I was too preoccupied by my own thoughts to pay much attention. After my separation and that last dating disaster, I had given myself time off from men specifically and dating in general.

All that to say, I was not necessarily looking when Karriem began frequenting classes, or when Felicia invited him to go with us to a line-dance event, or (at least at first) when we lingered after class in the parking lot, standing and talking as the temperature dropped and the rain began to fall. It became hard to pull away. On one of those nights after yoga, he asked me out. By this point, I was ready.

After months of not dating, I was giddy for a first date. Since line dancing had already been a theme for us, I suggested we go around the corner to the class at the senior center where Felicia occasionally went. I had changed my outfit a few times already and was putting on my shoes when Felicia rushed down the stairs. "I don't think you should go line dancing," she said. I paused and frowned at the idea of sudden change. "Why not?" I asked. "It's just that not everyone there will approve of your bringing a Black man. I don't want your relationship to start off with that energy. Maybe try somewhere else for your first date instead?"

Okay, then we would do something else. These potential ramifications had not even occurred to me. I had missed the subtleties of what bringing Karriem to a Black community space on a first date might mean. I felt grateful for the guidance; Karriem less so. When I shared with him Felicia's concern, he was annoyed. "I don't care what they think," he said. "But I do," I responded. "I don't want to offend people, especially elders."

It turned out to be a lovely date. We spent some quality time with plants at the local botanical gardens, ate ice cream, and discussed current events and my blog. Afterward though, Felicia's heeding stuck with me and my sense of self-doubt grew. If I hadn't known about the cultural landmines of going with Karriem to line dance, what other offenses might I miss? Moreover, could I ever be prepared enough to navigate an interracial romantic relationship respectfully? What if things got serious? What if—gulp—we ended up having children together? The feelings of self-doubt rushed toward me. I was beginning to really like Karriem. The thought of my ignorance causing him harm landed solidly in my gut.

The line between denial and deference here is a fine one. In over-correcting for the ways racism claims to "not see color," I leaned into the analysis of our identities. I wish I could tell you that I began our relationship totally focused on Karriem's individuality, and in a way that also didn't erase his lived experience. I wish I could tell you that I was fully able to honor my own individuality as well. But while there were many moments of appreciating him for who he was as a person, there were also others in which I was so focused on "the rules" of anti-racism.

I aspired for an anti-racist relationship in which we would be able to talk about race as it connected to our day-to-day, to name for each other when racialized dynamics were at play (which they certainly would be), and do all the anti-racist things I saw Felicia and her husband modeling. Karriem listened when I shared these things and he engaged to an extent, but he was not as enthusiastic as I had hoped. He had his own history with community development and organizing. I interpreted his lack of enthusiasm as a sign that this could never be the ideal anti-racist relationship I had constructed alone in my head.

In pulling out the many file folders of this period, I can see how my perfectionism obstructed intimacy. In my anti-racist fantasy, in my quest to live out the anti-racist identity I had become so attached to, I was missing all the ways he *was* holding me accountable, even though he hadn't used the "official" anti-racist terminology. Along with files that attest to his lack of enthusiasm for the anti-racist analysis, there are ones in which he pushed me to go deeper in naming my feelings and challenged me to be more emotionally vulnerable, ones where he called me out when I was not being completely honest with him, another where he named my perfectionism and control issues without ever uttering those words. In my striving to get the relationship "right" (whatever that meant), I was missing that I'd gotten much of what I'd been asking for. And what I'd asked for pressed up against my comfort zone just as much if not more than checking off a list of anti-racist terms.

The "problem" that activated my 4Ds had to do with one of them: denial—how white folks claim not to see race, which ultimately denies the full human experiences of those with whom we're in relationship. I definitely did not want to do that. But acknowledging race, racism, and power brought up a lot of self-doubt. How could I trust a self who'd been steeped in whiteness and so unaware? In my fear of enacting racism, I deferred. Yet, deferring to the Black man I dated was often in conflict with what I was hearing from his community. Who was I supposed to follow? Whose perspective was the anti-racist one? With Karriem, I had my rulebook ready. I defended it and when I was disappointed by his response, I began to distance myself from him, from the relationship, and from my dreams of intimacy and connection with another human being.

But what would it mean to go deeper than the surface of the 4Ds? What are the fears and insecurities that the 4Ds have been protecting me from? How has my overreliance on them perhaps caused harm? In my attempt at self-protection, how have they prevented me from humanizing him? From humanizing others? From humanizing myself? What might it mean to go beyond the 4Ds and humanize ourselves and each other within intimate partnerships? What might it look like, feel like, be like to do so?

LOVE (AND NO MARRIAGE)

Karriem and I ended up out on a date one evening at a local vegan-friendly Tex-Mex spot. He and I were sitting across from each other at a booth tucked in by the kitchen entrance. It had been a while since we had been out together. Our work schedules were both pretty intense, so finding daytime hours when we both synched up was a rarity. This was an occasion I was expecting to enjoy.

It wasn't long after we had been seated that we began to disagree. I can't tell you what about, nor did I file away a memory about what brought on the tears, but I felt their swift approach, swelling up from my gut toward my throat. I didn't have time to feel inconvenienced like I might have in the past, because, along with the anger/frustration/sadness about whatever had brought on the tears, was concern.

A part of me wanted to lash out and argue back at Karriem. Whatever he had said had ignited a spark. Oh, I'm remembering a little more now: I think I might have been pissed. A part of me wanted to let myself fully feel, to not stuff it down, to be present with what was happening in the moment in my body and with my heart as I had been trying to practice in life. A part of me wanted to just be honest, to just let it out, to just have a lover's quarrel in the neighborhood eatery.

In that split second as my tears welled up, we made eye contact. Feelings: rage, frustration, disappointment, compassion, love, care, concern.

I took a deep breath in and excused myself. Sliding past the waitstaff, I walked to the restroom and released my tears in the privacy of the bathroom stall. Afterward, standing in front of the mirror, I cleaned up my face as best I could and returned with more composure. When I sat back down, he asked a question with his eyes. I nodded in acknowledgment, and we moved the conversation on to things that were more publicly safe.

Not crying on a date in public was not something I'd ever had to think about during my marriage to a white man.

Mistress Syndrome is so much about trying to keep us from the pain. On one hand, there is an allure, an attraction to being in relationship with People of the Global Majority. For white folks who grew up in very white spaces, there might be elements of exotification. Perhaps being around People of the Global Majority feels shiny and new or a little risky, a way to rebel against externally imposed restrictions. I hear white folks in anti-racist spaces express an attraction too. I hear us yearn for deeper community, for life-giving cultures, for ways to become whole. Yes, we want to be in multiracial, multicultural community. Yes, we want to humanize our friends, family, and partners of color. Yes, we want to have better relationships with and be in solidarity with those whom racism most harms.

But what happens for us when the pain of racism gets too real and too close? What happens after we realize the 4Ds won't facilitate intimacy or sustain (chosen) family? How do we know when we've reached the limits of the 4Ds and how else might we respond?

CHAPTER ELEVEN

CHOSEN FAMILY: TAKE ONE

Relationships create resilience; transactions don't.

—Edgar Villanueva

The person who loves their dream of community will destroy community, but the person who loves those around them will create community.

—Dietrich Bonhoeffer

"She chose them," I told my friend, anger coursing through my body. "Felicia chose her daughter and her husband over me. She said she wouldn't choose. That there was enough room in her family for us all." It was after all of us had left Pittsburgh, and the reality was beginning to sink in. She had told me an untruth, or perhaps it had been a wishful inkling, ungrounded in reality. At any rate, she had given her word and then went back on it. The bliss of my chosen family narrative was crumbling to pieces, and I was just beginning to pick through the rubble.

"Of course she did," my friend said with a matter-of-factness that I was struggling to appreciate. "She should have."

Righteous rage, Felicia would call what I was feeling. The Enneagram Type 8 in me whose indignation boils up at the slightest of slights. The injustice of it all. There was a looming feeling of betrayal. When I dwelled on it too long, a deep sadness clouded my lungs.

I deserve to be chosen, I told myself.

"You deserve to be chosen," Felicia also once said to me. It was about a man, who was lying by omission until a social media platform played crystal ball and revealed what I was actively trying to deny. He had in fact not chosen me, nor had he ever intended to.

"Although I'm not sure it's an exact parallel," I explained to my new therapist on the phone. I was trying to remember correctly as I explained why I was seeking out help. "I mean, she had chosen me for years and our relationship had been beautiful and real, hadn't it?" My grief was coming in waves. This loss of an important relationship on the heels of several other painful relational endings: a marriage partner, a best friend, a fated affair, mentees and colleagues, and now, the one person who stood by me through all the drama and attacks on my character and work.

A few years before, my therapist (a different one) gently mentioned enmeshment as something to consider in my relationship with my yoga teacher and mentor. I placed too much trust in the relationship to follow the therapist's suggestion at the time. But then Felicia herself, with the therapist that I had connected her to, brought it up. By that point she was willing to examine what I had been too afraid to let go of.

For a while now, I had been looking for ways to blame myself. Or extend an anti-racist analysis. Or both. Sometimes it was hard to tell them apart. Maybe I couldn't show up fully in the relationship because I'd been so afraid of my own feelings and truth? But also, hadn't I been trying so hard to do and get it right—to process emotions and share my thoughts in a way that was true, accurate, and acceptable to the many cultural norms that our organizing community had established as humanizing and anti-racist? That I struggled to do this, that my trauma response of freeze kept appearing, had been an incredible source of frustration. I was so tired of my immobilization, so frustrated with the feelings that took over my body and mouth as I tried to fit myself into an ideal shape of honest, vulnerable, courageous anti-racist practitioner. I don't know if it's that there wasn't room for my actual shape or if I never gave myself the chance to find out. I'm guessing it was a combination of both.

She left Pittsburgh without even saying goodbye.

Whenever I search through my emotional files, this same sentence leaps to the forefront and hovers in big bold typography: She left without saying goodbye.

BEING CHOSEN

I keep this trip to Puerto Rico, the first of many chosen family vacations and spa trips that we took over the years, in a very special folder. It's filed at the front of the drawer, by far my favorite. Edged with a gilded frame, on the front of this folder I've glued a photo of the glimmering Condado shoreline. The water is a sparkling aquamarine. The sand is fine with an occasional smooth rock or pebble. The sky reflects the color of the water, though in the real world, we know it is the other way around. At the top of the file, in gold glitter and very nice penmanship (which couldn't be my own) it says: Magical Puerto Rican Vacation: That One Time Everything Was Perfect.

Kayla had used her vacation planning acuity to secure us a room at a five-star, beachfront hotel. It was the type of place that smelled like old money. Confident that its past riches would endure, the hotel had recently built a sparkling new wing, where we found ourselves in a two-bedroom with turndown service, evening chocolates, and as many clean towels as we could ask for—which we did.

As we walked around the hotel getting acclimated to the glitzy environment, we stopped in the lobby bathroom. It was bigger than many people's houses, each stall encased in white marble. In the center of the room was a marble hand-washing station. And then there were the luxurious disposable hand towels, a half-yard square.

My first Puerto Rican vacation was indulgent in a way Mennonite Humble had taught me to resist. The idea of traveling to a beautiful faraway place, to sit on the beach and fully enjoy the moment of being on vacation, was a dynamically new concept for me. When I walked outside with my beach towel and water in hand, the hotel staff person greeted me and gave me free things. When we ventured to the beach, someone was there to set up our chaise lounges and strategically position (and reposition) the umbrella (for me).

I felt hesitant and uncomfortable with the racial and class dynamics of what it meant to be a white person from the States. It felt uncomfortable to be so diligently waited on by the disenfranchised citizens of a US imperialist territory.* The power dynamics were of course glaring. But in noticing Felicia and Kayla's orientation toward luxury (mainly my perception of their full enjoyment of it: a striking absence of guilt and self-deprivation, a knowingly strategic use of self-care, and the capacity to treat each staff member with the dignity of their full humanity), I began to try on what I had previously considered unnecessary indulgences.

And it worked. I sat on the beach and by the infinity pool and watched the water, surrendering to my being. I bathed in the sun in the mornings and was lulled by the waves under the shade umbrella in the afternoons. I came back feeling much more rested, but also refreshingly relationally secure. The three of us experienced joy together. We experienced rest together. The experience was one of both self- and community care. It was as if our time together had confirmed my deepest dream that maybe I could find chosen family, people with whom I really belonged.

There is a whole history of women of color, and Black women in particular, carving out self-affirming cultures of joy, restoration, and self- and collective care within systems that view them as capital. A legacy of which Felicia and Kayla are inheritors and also cultivators.† I was somewhat aware of this context going into the trip, but especially while there, it highlighted for me the deficiency of community self-care and resilience practices I learned growing up white. Perhaps my family never felt like we needed to fully rest in order to survive. Perhaps that deeply instilled Protestant work ethic kept our middle-classness in check. Perhaps the potentially guilt-laden drive to make the most of our limited (but also relatively expansive) privilege co-opted rest and unconditioned joy for

---

* Residents of Puerto Rico and other US territories do not have representation in the US Congress nor do they have electoral votes for presidential elections.

† This legacy's lines pervade through the threads of womanism, restorative healing work, art, and joy practices, to name only a few (#BlackJoy, #BlackGirlMagic).

the certainty of self-bettering edification. And also, even as I critically examine my family's relationship to white middle-class travel, I remember having fun, a sense of messy togetherness, and the newness of adventure.

That white middle-class messiness was not apparent at the five-star resort. While I sat on the beach and by the infinity pool learning to relax and enjoy being, what I noticed the most was how much the white people around me seemed miserable. In this old-money luxury, in what I supposed might have been a typical March for many of them, I watched parents ignore their children. I saw boyfriends avoid their girlfriends. I especially noticed vacant stares and a seeming disregard for the luxury around them. Perhaps the disassociation of whiteness keeps even the wealthiest amongst us opiated enough to not be able to actually enjoy its materialistic advantages.

When our last night arrived, I didn't want the vacation to end. We were strolling along the massive hotel deck, watching a cruise ship float by, lit up in the distance. Our favorite astrologer had just posted weekly horoscope affirmations. "Let's read them aloud!" one of us said. We found a place to sit on the plush porch furniture. Listening to astrologer Chani Nicholas's words together and making the occasional connection or self-observation, I felt peaceful bliss.

Feelings: joy, peace, connection, affirmation, belonging.

* * *

The cute little ice cream store in our neighborhood was a leisurely twenty-minute stroll from the home we shared. After several months of separation, my partner had officially moved out. Felicia and I had given Kayla a grand send-off to an actual big city, and so now there were only two of us cohabitating in the huge three-story Victorian. I remember it as a joyful time.

Felicia and I walked to get ice cream in the sunshine, commenting on the changes in the neighborhood with a mix of sorrow, anger, and acceptance. "I remember when this used to be all Black-owned small businesses," she said as we crossed the bridge to the whiter side of the tracks. But this day, as in many others, she was not going to let the greed of white supremacy steal her joy.

The cool pink and white interior greeted us cheerfully as soon as we pulled open the door. That day, they had an exceptionally large selection of dairy-free flavors. Felicia was thrilled and of course wanted to try them all.

The white people ahead of us in line watched the pair of us curiously as we discussed flavors, laughing, our heads intimately close together. As so often happened when we were in public, one of them came over to interrupt our conversation and give unsolicited advice.

I know in general as white people we've been socialized to copiously confer our opinions and to feel comfortable imposing our bodies, words, and energies on others, especially People of Color, but I do wonder how much my presence encouraged these random white strangers even more. *See! This Black woman is approachable; she likes white people.* I imagined this subconscious reel moving through them as the white stranger eagerly approached.

This particular white person, ice cream in hand, moved into our interpersonal bubble to absolutely insist that we get their chosen flavor, even offering us a try. Although we mentioned that their selection contained dairy and thus wouldn't be an option, they kept insisting this flavor was the best one and we should order it, too.

They tried to spark up other conversation, curiously looking at us both as if they were trying to decipher our relationship. Felicia smiled back and nodded, not saying much. Eventually they sauntered out of the building still murmuring about how their flavor was the tastiest.

I already knew what I wanted (chocolate) but tried the cherry flavor just for fun. After her third or fourth taste, Felicia was also ready to order and insisted on paying. She ordered for me, "and my daughter will have a chocolate cone," she told the ice-cream scooper with playful sincerity.

I responded to this new development with my usual poker face as I frantically tried to analyze the meaning of her words on the inside.

It felt a little strange. I'd heard her describe our relationship in various terms in the past. Typically, she introduced me as "my very dear friend." Occasionally, depending on the context, she would share more details, like that we were housemates, or that we had a "neat" mentor/mentee, teacher/student, coworking relationship. And while she had referenced having maternal protective feelings toward me (and also every other human she encountered who was at least ten years younger than her), this was the first time she explicitly called me daughter and claimed me as her child.

I'm retrieving the files now, the ones related to my yoga teacher. On this one I wrote on the top tab: Ice Cream Parlor: She called me daughter. It's a special one. I put it in a pink-and-white-striped folder to match the memory and drew a little ice cream cone icon in the corner with a silver glitter pen. Years later and thousands of miles away, I am finally ready to pull out the files for another, closer look.

DECONSTRUCTING FAMILY

The file reads, feelings: flattered, giddy energy, honored to be claimed by her in this way. I felt chosen, loved, and seen. But also strangeness, a sense of the unknown, discomfort. What did this mean for our relationship—especially, what did it mean for me and my responsibilities to her? Was it an upgrade? Had it come with new expectations? It felt precious, like something I never could have fathomed would exist. But now that I know it could and it does, I had become aware of the possibility of losing it.

I, too, have harbored an idealistic view of family. Unlike the one that conservatives imagine, though, the picture in my mind does not resemble the household in which I grew up with one mother, one father, two children (a boy and a girl), plus a dog. In my dreams it doesn't live within a fenced-in yard. Instead, I envision a thriving ecosystem of interconnectedness in which I feel emotionally safe and I belong. Within that sense of family, I feel connection. I am taken care of while taking care of others. When I dream of *family*, I feel a sense of community, intentionality, mutual availability, collaboration, and interdependence.

I was first exposed to the term "chosen family" in the context of queer community, with friends who had faced distancing, abandonment, and excommunication from their families of origin, and whose cultivation of chosen family centered the values of healthy love and self-determination. Much of what I've learned about navigating consent, relational communication, and boundaries comes from the work of radical queer communities, including strategies to prevent, address, and break cycles of child abuse. As someone who has often felt like a misfit in my birth family, as someone who has yearned for deep, honest intimacy, and as someone who has been in and out of other people's families (as exchange student and nanny), chosen family was a concept I embraced wholeheartedly. And as I mentioned before, my idealism has also been influenced by a Mennonite subculture in which family overlaps and overflows into every sphere of one's life.

Our emerging chosen family dynamic overlapped and overflowed in all of those ways. Felicia became a mother/auntie/mentor/teacher/sister/friend during a disorienting time. As someone who had been nurtured by strong Black women throughout my life, I knew the script of following her lead, valuing her lessons, and gratefully receiving her care. The anti-racist spaces we were organizing in constantly reinforced the notion of following Black leadership and listening to Black women, which felt comfortingly familiar to me.

Yet at the same time, I wonder how within the occasion of our living arrangement I may have begun to conflate the idea of family with that of the household—one that historian Elizabeth Fox-Genovese explicitly differentiates in the book *Within the Plantation Household.* Fox-Genovese intentionally uses the term "household" to describe "a basic social unit in which people, whether voluntarily or under compulsion, pool their income and resources."[1] Conceptualizing household in this way allows for an acknowledgment of differences in power that the warm fuzzies of using the term "family" might conceal. Household, Fox-Genovese continues, "has no necessary relation to family, although members of households may be related and many households may be coterminous with family membership."[2]

I can see how my assumptions and expectations of deep familial relationships in living arrangements are connected to the convenient amnesia of power for white members of the plantation household, a sentimentalizing of relationship that ignores the realities that constructed the household in the first place.

Or, to flip that sentiment, as Painter points out:

> Hierarchy by no means precludes attachment. Just as enslaved youngsters attached to the adults closest to them, white as well as black, so the white children and adults in slaveowning households became psychologically entangled with the enslaved people they came to know well.[3]

And having been raised in part by a Black woman, Ms. Sylvia, I find these considerations of the plantation household particularly relevant to my Mistress Syndrome.

Occasionally, Ms. Sylvia put down firm boundaries (more so with me after my little brother was born), but I mostly remember her as lenient, generous, and very clear about certain protocols—she would never eat my family's food and always left a room cleaner than she entered. I also remember hours and hours of story time, playing outside, and day trips to neighborhood spots within walking distance because she never learned to drive.

It was Ms. Sylvia who would take us up the block to the corner store, where Mr. Williams chain-smoked behind the counter, and the rickety aisles bulged with plastic-covered treats. She would spend her paycheck on goodies we were not allowed to eat at home, then advise us not to tell our mother. Somehow Mom always found out.

Though there were many other—and much better educated—Black women who would become my teachers, Ms. Sylvia was the first to foster my love of books. There's a photo of the two of us that I hold very dear. In it, she is reading *The Real Mother Goose* to me on the questionably hued (peach? beige?) living-room couch. With its black-and-white checkered back cover, the book is as big as me, but you can still see my fresh, paunchy cheeks poking over top. My wide blue eyes fixate on the page as she supports my wobbly little frame.

I remember, as well, a moment when my sense of her began to change. If I were to pull out that folder today, it would smell slightly of shame, although it didn't at the time. I must have been seven or so. Thanks in no small part to Ms. Sylvia's patient hours of story time, I whizzed through the reading levels at school and had read practically all the books in the school's library. I found the library's chapter books at the beginning of second grade, which is when my written vocabulary really took off. I remember Ms. Sylvia reading one particular book aloud, if not to me, then to my brother. I remember a rupture in the cozy moment as she unexpectedly stumbled over a word, one I knew from school. I noticed her stumble with it and was taken aback, and a bit confused: weren't adults supposed to know these things?

Of course, this wasn't the only moment that encouraged feelings of paternalism toward Ms. Sylvia. There were snippets of the conversations between my parents I overheard while they discussed loaning her money. Countering the positive reinforcement of examples of well-educated, institutionally powerful Black women who ran the classrooms of my life was the classist negative stereotype of poor Black neighborhoods that pervaded the local news hour and my mother's reminders to lock the doors and her admonishment of my father to take the back way to avoid the projects. If someone were to give Ms. Sylvia a ride home at night to the much poorer, much Blacker neighborhood barely three miles from my family's home, it would most surely be my father, and we would not have accompanied him.

As I grew older, the distance between Ms. Sylvia and I grew, too. No longer a constant presence in my life, the opportunities for interaction revolved around my family and me supporting her. My mother gets the credit for doing the work of maintaining the relationship. She made sure that we would visit and bring a gift on birthdays and holidays. As a teenager, those interactions were an uncomfortable obligation, but as I got older (and began to unpack my own stuff), I began to more deeply appreciate all that Ms. Sylvia had been and done in my life.

At this point my life was mostly far from Atlanta, but whenever I traveled I sent her postcards, ending each one writing that I loved and appreciated her. Once, when I was back in town, my mom asked if I could take Ms. Sylvia to a doctor's appointment. It was a rare moment of what felt like rekindled intimacy. She shared about her health problems. I shared about my school problems. Then a few years before she passed, we began to talk on the phone.

In our last conversation we talked about my marriage. If I remember correctly, she and Mr. Jimmy had just celebrated their wedding anniversary. Things had become rocky within my own marriage. My partner and I had just started couples therapy. I will never forget her advice, a foreshadowing of what was to come. "Stay," she said. "Whatever you do, stay."

In my life I have consistently had older Black women mentoring, teaching, and caring for me. In many ways, these relationships have prepared me and continue to support me on a trajectory of anti-racism. That Ms. Sylvia had input in my most formative years meant I had opportunities to understand whiteness in ways many white children have not. The countless examples I had of Black women in roles of authority as school educators, nurses, counselors, administrators, and politicians meant that as a white child I learned to respect, listen to, and defer to Black women's wisdom. The years I had of navigating relationship with Felicia as a yoga teacher/mentor/advisor/co-conspirator/cofacilitator/supervisor/housemate/older sister/neighbor/friend has meant that I have had intimate access to the harmful impacts of racism—and impact of *my* racism—on someone I love.

BEING UNCHOSEN

Costco is not the first place that comes to mind for a lesson on self-agency, but it was where Felicia and I were shopping one spring day in the midst of a global pandemic. Our carts quickly piled up with frozen veggies and (at last!) toilet paper.

I was half an aisle ahead of her, focused on checking off my list, when an older Black man approached and expressed his interest in me. I felt a creepy energy in the exchange, a feeling I had been working on noticing and honoring after so many years of suppression. But despite the last several years of strengthening my voice, I responded sheepishly and quietly that I wasn't interested—twice. Yet he persisted. After his third advance, I began to feel even more uncomfortable, and vulnerable, and overwhelmed.

The creepy haze of the moment slightly lifted, and I remembered that Felicia was somewhere in the aisle behind me. I awkwardly backed my cart around and repositioned myself behind her, peeking out to see his response. If you have ever seen a toddler activate their sense of stranger danger and scramble to hide behind their parents' legs, then you have a pretty accurate mental image of what happened—just swap out the toddler for an adult me and add an unwieldy, sizeable shopping cart.

Thinking about it now, I find some humor in the memory (I mean, really, with the shopping cart?). Although when Felicia brought it up later to hold me accountable, I mostly felt shame. These were the moments she needed me to stand up for myself, she told me sternly and, most likely, tiredly. I interpreted her words as meaning this was a moment I had failed (her).

Of course, in unpacking this "teachable moment," she wasn't only talking about Costco. So I heard her, although she didn't explicitly say it, to mean that she needed me to invoke my agency, always. My white woman hiding, my overreliance on her initiative, my expectation that she would expend valuable energy fighting for me when I was certainly capable of doing that myself, was me inappropriately leaning on her to fight my battles for me. It was me asking her to play mammy and protector.

By this point, I had experienced enough examples of how race sets us up for interpersonal failure. Racism divides and conquers our relational spheres as much as it does the systemic. The foundation of the plantation emerged in our relationships even as we were intending to dismantle them.

On my clearest most confident days, I was striving to be her peer, as she once requested. Yet because of age, race, lived experience, and our teacher/student dynamic, it was usually unclear how I would ever be able to do that. Besides, Felicia was incredible. Even when she was wrong, she was right. She'd express her emotions and tell you what she thought. She took responsibility when she realized she messed up. She'd fight with you and then be able to somehow give an unresentful full-on hug by the end of it. I admired those qualities immensely and was trying to cultivate them within myself, but honestly, they seemed unattainable.

Besides, wasn't following Black women's leadership a foundational tenet of anti-racism? Sometimes I deferred because I didn't know what the other options were, and I had absolutely no idea how to get there.

These dynamics sometimes feel impossible to unpack. The many layered and often contradictory messages and experiences cyclone around in my head. I find myself trying to categorize them as either bad (racist) or good (anti-racist). In an effort to sort through the whirling thoughts, I make an overly simplistic list:

BAD/RACIST

- Stereotype: Mammy

    - Message: (Desexualized) Black women—especially those who are older, darker in complexion, and fat—primarily exist to nurture and defend white children (= me).

- Stereotype: Magical Black Character

    - Message: Black folx (…and Indigenous and Asian and other People of Color) have a deeper connection to traditional/cultural/exotic spiritual practices and primarily exist to advise, protect, educate, and confer spiritual guidance to well-intentioned white people embarking on spiritual, often world-saving quests (= me).

GOOD/ANTI-RACIST

- Rule: #TrustBlackWomen

    - Message: Because Black women have the lifelong, constant experience of intersectional racism, they know the solutions best. The people closest to the problems are closest to the solutions.

- Rule: Center Black Leadership

  - Message: Because white people don't experience racism, are ignorant/oblivious/in denial, and are racially conditioned to be in charge, white people (= me) need to talk less, listen more, make space for, and unquestionably follow Black leadership.

Then I make another one:

SOMETHING ELSE ASPIRATIONAL/POSSIBLY LIBERATION?

- Messy Truth

  - Black women are human and are also navigating the traumas of the wicked webs in all the ways and layers and stuff that gets put on them all the time.

- Messy Truth

  - White people (= me) are human and are also navigating the traumas of the wicked webs in all the ways and layers and stuff that gets put on us all the time.

That was perhaps less helpful than I intended. But maybe what I'm trying to say is that in my story (and most likely in yours) there exists both embarrassing clichés and also nuanced insights. Were there things an anti-racist lens was missing? Were there dynamics my application of it just couldn't see?

At least some clear information has emerged in the process of sifting through memories of these life-shaping relationships: I find a level of comfort and care within the emotional extension of Black women. I always have. And I also feel a deep sense of responsibility to that extension of care, to the people and the relationships no matter how they arrived. I feel this deeply, that my life's work is in the reciprocity of working to end the injustices that established the realities that constructed those relational arrangements in the first place.

There is a personal question floating around in that messiness, too. One that asks, What am I looking for and why have I so often sought out Black women's support?

There is a layer to this question that has to do with alleviating the shame of Mistress Syndrome, with proving my enoughness to anti-racism and the communities that racism—and my Mistress Syndrome—has harmed. Perhaps receiving love from Black women has mitigated the guilt, shame, and bad feelings that being an inheritor of Mistress Syndrome might bring. Perhaps I have sought out validation, approval, and the gold stars of anti-racism from Felicia and others because of my insecurities.

And also, I think this question goes deeper than the want of approval or the need to soothe shame. It has something to do with a mother wound. And I don't mean one that has to do with my own, specific mother—she has just as many flaws and gifts as any other human navigating this mess. No, this mother wound is greater and deeper than the actions of any one person. This maternal void has just as much to do with the white childhood of the plantation, the witch hunts, and the banishment of Eve. Beneath the shame is an epigenetic and historical reality. If I stand up to my father, if I lose the conditional love of white supremacy, then where will I go? Who will love me? It has just as much to do with filling a void within myself.

LEAVING THE MASTER'S HOUSE

Whiteness in many ways is a form of amnesia. The spiritual and emotional void it has left us with is a result of a profound communal disruption, one that facilitated white people's identification with their oppressors and one that was likewise built on generations of European matricide.

There is a powerful short story written by Langston Hughes in his collection *The Ways of White Folks* called "Cora Unashamed," which we sometimes read in White Women's Groups. The story is told from the voice of Cora Jenkins who, much like Ms. Sylvia decades before, has been hired to care for the household and children of a white family. To briefly summarize what is much better experienced through Hughes's own words, when the white family's daughter is found out to be pregnant, her parents force her to have an abortion that ultimately results in her emotional and then literal death.

When I first read this story, I felt it in my bones: the violence of the white family to its children, and girl children in particular. That they would rather kill off their own daughter and grandchild rather than hear any rupture to their performance of white upper/middle-class patriarchy; the way Mrs. Cora narrates her experience of having extended herself and her heart to raising someone else's child, only to have them destroy that child; and the funeral scene where Mrs. Cora accuses the family in front of their white guests and then in finality removes herself from the whole situation in the acceptance that there is no saving white people and no place for her in that impossible irredeemable task. Even now in rereading it, I feel the story's heavy truths in between my ribs. My connective tissue begins to ache.

These feelings of grief have me recalling Audre Lorde's words, "For the master's tool will never dismantle the master's house. They may allow us temporarily to beat him at his own game, but they will never enable us to bring about genuine change." However, the last part of this social justice diatribe usually gets left out: "And this fact is only threatening to those women who still define the master's house as their only source of support."[4]

What sense of community and belonging is left for those of us who still define the master's house as our only and—I would add—primary source of support? What ways of knowing and being have we forfeited in order to manage the (plantation) household and raise its inheritors? What psychic damage of slavery (as Painter describes) have we inflicted "upon [ourselves], [our] white families, and, ultimately on [our] whole society?"[5]

Going further, Painter contrasts this description of psychic damage by naming "two crucial means of support"[6] that helped enslaved people in resisting permanent damage from the daily abuses of enslavement: Firstly, this support emerged through the development and practice of spiritual, religious, and ideological beliefs, "a slave religion," that not only opposed "the masters' religious and social ideology of white supremacy and black inferiority," but also created a countersystem of beliefs that proclaimed "equity would ultimately prevail in God's world."[7]

Secondly, this support manifested through the intentional cultivation of community made up of "actual or fictive kin."[8] Enslaved women were the main actors in weaving and maintaining their chosen family networks, as Painter refers to Deborah White's work: "Enslaved women forged 'their own independent definition of womanhood' through their own web of women's relationships, which functioned as an antidote to slavery's degradation."[9]

Black women carried, and continue to carry, the disproportionate amount of communal, relational, emotional, and spiritual labor in the cultivation of alternative family, co-creating belief systems that repudiated what was proselytized in the master's house. This historical revelation tells me something about why I have gravitated toward chosen family with Black women and why that invitation exists—why it has even had to exist at all.

The codependency that whiteness enabled/s has resulted in a messy enmeshment—Black women's labor sustained their community's resistance while they were simultaneously being forced to sustain their white charges; the plantation's white children were dependent on their Black caretakers who also provided perhaps their only entrée to support beyond the master's house; the high majority of white children grew up to replicate the violence of the master's house despite their earliest and most constant attachment figures; and white women, in particular, were rebranded (and refashioned ourselves) as dependent on that which brought us harm. These make up some of the sticky threads I am working to untie.

I am especially struck by Painter's interpretation of what all this meant for white women who lacked collectively held alternative ideologies, such as slave religion, and whose positionality granted them immense power in certain spheres (such as with enslaved people in their homes), while stripping them of access in most other ones. Painter notes, "Of all the people living in slaveholding societies who might have benefited from an alternative system of values, rich white women were least likely to forge one. In the words of Catherine Clinton, plantation mistresses, unlike plantation slaves, 'had no comparable sense of community.'"[10]

For those of us who have had "no comparable sense of community," it is no surprise that we gravitate to those who have centuries of experience forging self-determined identities and networks of kin. There are reasons why our movements need leadership from those who have been most impacted.

It makes sense that I would seek out mentorship from someone I admired, that I would look for guidance from someone with emotional intelligence, courageous truth-telling, and a spiritual practice to back it all up. And as someone still licking the wounds of my home culture, it's no surprise that I began to idealize another, that I found a special pedestal for Felicia and her life's work.

Given the rejection of the wicked webs, given the lack of safety I felt in my home community (whether real or perceived), given plantation mistresses having "no comparable sense of community," it is no wonder I attached so completely. Given the mother wound, it is no wonder I repressed my truth so diligently. Is it safe to express anger at the one who is keeping you alive?

Self-abandonment is, after all, at Mistress Syndrome's core. Self-abandonment is, after all, one of the master's most effective tools. Self-abandonment brought my concept of chosen family to its knees.

Since the era of glitzy beach vacations and ice-cream parlors, I have learned more information that has both poked holes in my understanding of chosen family and also reinforced the goodness of that time. I am learning to hold both the heartbreak and the joy, the hardships and the triumphs of trying to untie the wicked webs and co-create something new.

And despite the heartbreak and the rocky endings, chosen family was and has been a lifeline for me. It was because of this lifeline, because of the respite and the work I have risked within chosen family that I have been gradually more able to reflect upon, move closer toward, and more authentically reengage with the traumas and healing within my own.

IT'S TIME TO CHECK IN

CHECK IN WITH YOUR BODY:

Where in your body do you notice tension or stress?
Where in your body do you feel ease or pleasure?

CHECK IN WITH YOUR HEART:

How are you feeling?
What emotions came up for you as you read the past chapters?
What emotions are coming up for you now?

CHECK IN WITH YOUR MIND:

Notice your thoughts.
Notice them again.
Notice again. And again.

CHECK IN WITH YOUR SPIRIT:

What is giving you life?
What is bringing you joy?
How are you nurturing your creativity and imagination?

CHECK IN WITH YOUR BREATH:

Inhale.
Exhale.
Repeat.

PART IV

POST-TRAUMATIC GROWTH

CHAPTER TWELVE

TAKE (ONLY) WHAT YOU NEED

A woman should learn in quietness and full submission.
I do not permit a woman to teach or to assume authority
over a man; she must be quiet. For Adam was formed first,
then Eve. And Adam was not the one deceived; it was
the woman who was deceived and became a sinner.

—1 Timothy 2:11-14, NIV

We abolition women are turning the world upside down.

—Angelina Grimké

Among the thousands of pages of the Christian Holy written word, there are none credited to be written by women. The canon of both Old and New Testaments selected by Church Fathers in fifth-century Europe were presented to me as the literal words of God, a belief still upheld by many in my family and community. Since the invention of the alphabet, men have been the scribes of his-story, law, religion, and moral code.

We were sitting in an Austrian museum café when I pointed out the gender politics of biblical canonization to my father with the desperate hope that he would hear my plea to see the divine equally present in me. His commitment to biblical literacy held strong. His faith was unchallengeable, even in the face of his daughter's spiritual trauma.

We were driving in a minivan on I-85 when I brought up the sickening feeling in my gut each time we sang to God as he, him, and father in the familiar hymnal tunes I loved. My mother and her friend dismissed my intuition. They too had felt that when they were my age but had since realized those words were just a vestige of tradition and not something to dwell on.

I was sitting in a bed in France reading parts of the New Testament when I arrived at the words of Paul condemning women for our existence. I put down the book and threw up in the toilet.

The withholding of divinity from some and over-associating it with others is both impetus and explanation for why we are in this mess. It has taught us to forget the divinity of the rock and the river, the divinity inside each and every one of us. This omission gives us permission to violate and permission to be violated. In a rejection of the pain, it is tempting for me to intellectualize spiritual violence as a basic means of social control. I move to analyze rather than feel.

I see myself circling eloquently around the pain rather than diving in fully. It feels awkward to talk directly about my spiritual journey. The historical trauma of my ancestors screams through my DNA that to be spiritually visible as different is to be in danger. I feel the residual witch hunts warning me to tread cautiously around outing my beliefs. I notice the fear of exclusion crawl on my skin as my body remembers my community's practice of shunning as pre-enactment of hell on earth. With sadness, I receive the tug on the edges of my heart as I recall the way my father responded in one of our latest intense exchanges. What I shared in that conversation confirmed his suspicion that I was not Christian—according to his definition at least. In that moment, I saw clearly that had this been 1535, he would have turned me in.

I've had a bone to pick with my dad for a very long time. This bone has motivated me tremendously in my life. Sometimes I have been motivated by my rage at the dehumanizing ideology he represents and the injustices his belief systems perpetuate. Sometimes I have been fueled by incredulous disbelief that makes it quite personal: How could he not see how his convictions hurt and erase me? How could he not care or love me enough to change them? At other times I have been driven by a slightly more open curiosity to understand where he is coming from. Those questions have propelled my studies in Sociology and Conflict Transformation and inspired me to work for social justice.

Justly or not, my dad has served as a representation for patriarchy's thousand-years rule. His politics, beliefs, and position have served as a target for my pain in coming to terms with spiritual abuse.

I tend to my wounds in litany:

That of the 1,426 people given names in the Hebrew Bible, only 111 are women[1] (and these named characters were usually portrayed as supporting the work of men).

Lord have mercy.

That in the creation story most upheld, Eve is fashioned from Adam's rib (reversing tens of thousands of years of cosmology in which creation is birthed by people who have wombs, like in real life).

Christ have mercy.

That the story of Lilith, Adam's rebellious first wife, was not accessible to me until I was in my thirties.

God have mercy.

That the Gnostic texts recovered in 1945 and rejected by Christian denominations as equally divinely inspired were not part of my biblical indoctrination (the Gnostic texts are laden with language of the divine feminine).

Holy Spirit have mercy.

That the selected and canonized Pauline letters that promote God-given male authority were and are upheld as proof that wives should submit to their husbands and that women should not preach to or teach men. (My childhood church debated the question of whether or not a woman should even be considered during the pastoral search process. To date, they have never had a non-cis male pastor.)

Sophia have mercy.

That communion, that the giving of the eucharist, that "my body broken for you" has been historically and still is in many traditions the exclusive terrain of men as priests and ministers (even though the feeding of people and breastfeeding in partic-ular—the literal breaking of one's body to provide sustenance—has been the act of those who birth[2]).

Goddess have mercy.

Have mercy.

We were sitting around my kitchen table during one of my dad's brief visits to Pittsburgh when I relinquished the idea that I could ever change his heart, mind, and soul. It was another argument that wasn't changing anything. "You should pray to God," my dad told me. So I did: I surrendered the work of changing my father to the divine. I released the belief that I am responsible for changing him, or that I even can.

TRANSFORMATIVE GRIEF

I have a bone to pick with myself for (still) believing the lies of white patriarchal Christianity. Even though I am relearning the voice of the divine within me, self-doubt sneaks in. It is the voice of fear. It tells me my intuition is not trustworthy. It lies to me that there is safety in confor-mity. It whispers that I am not enough. And so I diligently practice replacing its angst with the grace and abundance of trusting my Self.

I have a bone to pick with my ancestors who let their unhealed trauma fester and mutate into the scabs of whiteness. I resent my lineage for leaving me such a shameful legacy and with a lack of liber-atory cultural and spiritual tools. Sometimes I feel overwhelmed by the task of exhuming that which has been buried for generations. I feel incapacitated by the buildup of silenced trauma, disoriented by the chosen traumas/chosen glories that we've deliberately proclaimed.

My journey is disturbing the peace of my ancestors' lies. The public nature of my digging is disrupting the myth of peace in my family and community. This process of transformative grief is uncomfortable and terrifying work. There are days when I feel encouraged and days when I just shut down.

In the article "Grieving the White Void," Abraham Lateiner asks what it means to grieve that which white culture has taken from us:

> Grief is usually thought of as a product of losing something or someone. But what happens if parts of myself were tied off at the stump with the fine threads of White culture, never allowed to develop in the first place? What is the absence of humanity inside of me created by Whiteness? And what would it mean to fully grieve that absence?[3]

I am grieving the cultural and spiritual wellness my ancestors forfeited to become white. I am grieving their choice to compartmentalize Jesus's words "Blessed are the peacemakers,"[4] to mean only certain kinds of violence, like serving in the military, but not others, like stealing land. I am grieving the denial and dissociation that's piled up over generations proclaiming it was possible to be "in the world but not of it"* as a way of washing our hands of the violence from which we benefited. I am grieving the ways we assimilated into white American Protestantism, pacifying our radical Anabaptist roots to gain white status and privilege.†

I am grieving the cultural and spiritual wholeness misplaced by my ancestor's embrace of patriarchy. I am grieving their affinity

---

* "In the world but not of it" is a Christian expression that's derived from John 15:18–19: "If the world hates you, know that it has hated me before it hated you. If you were of the world, the world would love you as its own; but because you are not of the world, but I chose you out of the world, therefore the world hates you." Various Anabaptist traditions have interpreted this to mean not engaging with politics, media, and other aspects of mainstream culture and society.

† See also "How Mennonites Became White: Religious Activism, Cultural Power, and the City" by Philipp Gollner.

toward puritanism, their disdain of dance, their fears of the body, the feminine, queerness, and sexuality. I am grieving because the traditions I've inherited are marred and distorted through lenses of oppression and I am grieving the ways I was taught to disconnect from my felt sense and intuition as a result. Perhaps most of all, I am grieving the ways I learned to not see the divine in me.

What would it look like for those of us who have come to be called white to fully grieve?

I know this at least: that in order to grieve, we must slow down, be still, and feel.

There is the idea of "post-traumatic growth,"[5] which certified yoga trauma therapist Dr. Gail Parker defines as "the ability to find the growth opportunity in whatever traumatic event you have experienced."[6] Dr. Parker also reminds us that the avoidance of pain inhibits healing. We have to go through (temporary) pain in order to heal. And yet the paradox of the oppressor is that the luxury of grieving from a place of privilege often creates more injustices.

Sometimes in pain and desperation, we rush to replenish our spiritual closets with a quick fix to fill the empty space. We see the spiritual deadness in the mirror and long to be fulfilled. This makes sense. We are spiritual beings. We yearn for connection and meaning. And indeed, our wisdom traditions have been compromised. Our practices were burned at the stake. Our intuition has been silenced and our connections severed.

PRACTICING YOGA WHILE WHITE

I know this too: our search for spiritual renewal is not separate from histories and systems of oppression. Our healing traditions have been so compromised that we end up seeking the wisdom of cultures people who look like us have historically sought to eradicate. Our bodies practice other people's traditions while representing and perpetuating the violence we seek to heal. Like white women bulldozing over people on the way to the yoga studio, the road to cultural appropriation is paved with good intentions.

I first began practicing yoga in college, although I had been somewhat aware of its existence in high school. My school's yoga class was offered at the fitness center once a week by a very kind yet suspiciously thin middle-aged white woman. The class was primarily focused on *asanas*, or physical poses, with no mention of yoga's origins or philosophy.*

In the midst of my collegiate overachievement with my deeply internalized perfectionism, eating disorder relapses, and general social insecurities, the brief moment of *shavasana*, or final relaxation at the end of every class, revolutionized my life. Along with the immediate stress relief following each class, I noticed my increased capacity to access a sense of peace when I attended yoga consistently. It provided moments of internal respite from the daily toils of Mistress Syndrome.

In retrospect, it is no surprise that a small private Christian school neglected to include the full scope of the practice and history of yoga, especially in relation to colonization, imperialism, and spiritual associations with Hinduism and Buddhism.† Like many yoga spaces, my school preferred the exercise genre popularized in the West, which secularized the practice for finicky Christian audiences. It is also no surprise that I neglected to ask questions about its origins; a part of me didn't want to do the work of curious inquiry, which might disturb my newly found peace. In this way, I first started practicing yoga ignorant to its origins and depth. And as part of the initial wave of millennial yoga students, I was no exception.

In their article "Yoga and the Roots of Cultural Appropriation," Shreena Gandhi and Lillie Wolff consider yoga's history in the West and how yoga has been refashioned for US consumption:

---

* The lineage of yoga I've studied under is Raja Yoga, which has eight limbs. *Asana*, or physical postures is one of those eight limbs. The others as I learned them include *yama* (restraints), *niyama* (observances), *pranayama* (breathing techniques), *pratyahara* (sensory withdrawal), *dharana* (concentration), *dhyana* (meditation), and *samdhi* (enlightenment).

† According to Susanna Barkataki in *Embrace Yoga's Roots*, yoga "developed alongside Sramana traditions that emerged as Jain and Buddhist as well as Vedi and Hindu traditions and later was influenced by Islam and Christianity" (13). In addition to the dangers of whitewashing yoga is over-associating yoga with Hinduism, since yoga has been misused to promote a Hindu Nationalist agenda and oppress others.

The reasons why yoga became popular, and why various Indian yogis started traveling to England and the United States to "sell" yoga, is also tied up with colonialism. Yoga was often used as a tool to show the British that Indians were not backwards or primitive, but that their religion was scientific, healthy, and rational. This was a position they were coerced into, and unfortunately reified colonial forms of knowledge—that knowledge must be proven or scientific to be worth anything.[7]

New and improved! The answer to life's problems! Selling is what US capitalism does best. I am struck by how this approach to yoga mirrors the consumption of evangelical Christianity. The industry of yoga reminds me of the performative pop-Christian worship concerts of my youth. Replacing *Jesus is the answer* with *Yoga is the answer* does little to address the deeply embedded belief that someone or some*thing* will show up to fix us. Replacing one form of consumerism with another does little to loosen our codependency with capitalism.

Yet like the evangelicals, I too believe our dominant culture is desperately spiritually malnourished. The culture of whiteness prioritizes time and task over relationship, comparison and competition over collaboration, and perfectionism over holistic acceptance. In its single-minded thirst for coercive power and profit, white culture razes our organic interconnected humanness. Its hunger is bottomless, fueled by chewing up life-giving cultures and spitting out the assimilated bones.

The irony is that white culture feeds off the cultures of those it marginalizes in order to perpetuate itself. The more white culture oppresses, the more resisting cultures evolve to sustain life and to rehumanize what white culture has attempted to dehumanize. Like white suburban kids growing up to make money off of hip-hop—or teaching Nepalese refugee children mindfulness practices—the machine of imperialist white-supremacist capitalist patriarchy would see this as a simplified chain of supply and demand: the feedback loop of oppression.

Author Maisha Johnson describes this dynamic of cultural appropriation as "a particular power dynamic in which members of a dominant culture take elements from a culture of people who have been systematically oppressed by that dominant group."[8] As the

Native Governance Center notes, "Cultural appropriation involves profit, too. Members of the dominant culture almost always have the ability to profit off of what they've stolen, providing no compensation to those from whom they've stolen."[9] In addition to dynamics of power, author Susanna Barkataki includes "doing emotional and psychological harm"[10] as a criterion for cultural appropriation.

While I was organizing around anti-racism in Pittsburgh schools, mindfulness began trending in education. White-led organizations, nonprofit and for profit alike, marketed mindfulness as a tool for student well-being, but also student compliance. One local egregious example involved a white-owned nonprofit that taught mindfulness devoid of its historical, philosophical, and spiritual context to Nepalese refugee children in public schools with the stated goal of addressing trauma. While this situation was exploitative on many accounts (mindfulness practices come from spiritual lineages of Buddhism and the region of the world in which Nepal is located; white people were making money teaching Nepalese children a whitewashed version of their own traditions; there were qualified Nepalese Buddhist practitioners who weren't being sought after and compensated to do this work), perhaps the most painful irony is that a practice that could have helped young people navigate systems of oppression through a deeper connection to their own cultures was being used instead to help them better assimilate into the trauma of oppression's institutions.

As Ron Purser and David Loy detail in their article "Beyond McMindfulness," this perversion of the practice reinforces oppression. In describing mindfulness in corporate settings, they write:

Up to now, the mindfulness movement has avoided any serious consideration of why stress is so pervasive in modern business institutions. Instead, corporations have jumped on the mindfulness bandwagon because it conveniently shifts the burden onto the individual employee: stress is framed as a personal problem, and mindfulness is offered as just the right medicine to help employees work more efficiently and calmly within toxic environments....Mindfulness training has wide appeal because it has become a trendy method for subduing employee unrest, promoting a tacit acceptance of the status quo, and as an instrumental tool for keeping attention focused on institutional goals.[11]

The term "cultural appropriation" is a pacified way of saying stealing. And stealing only exists if we think we can own. Ironically, one of the precepts of yoga is *asteya*, or non-stealing.

The danger of white culture is that it has convinced us that we own, that we have owned, and that we can own. It has tricked us into believing it is possible to own a thing, the earth, the truth, a practice, and other people. White culture spiritually starves us, so we think we have no choice but to join in its hunger games. But we always have choices even when they are not obvious or easy. The spiritual malnourishment is real, but how we go about pursuing nutrition is a practice we can choose and adjust along the way.

Our ancestors forfeited their cultures in order to access whiteness in a society in which not being white was to experience insidious violence. Perhaps there's a message here about believing that comfort is the opposite of violence. Our ancestors assimilated into whiteness in order to be more comfortable within systems built on violence.

The yoga studio has become a symbol of white-woman comfort—a moment of respite *before* returning to the drudgeries of the fluorescent cubicle, our never-ending to-do lists, and the busyness of life—but not necessarily a space for liberation. In recent years, waves of people have come forward about decades of sexual abuse by revered yoga teachers and in yoga spaces, which tells us something about the false safety of spaces built on reifying white womanhood.* Mainly that the illusion of comfort is usually a cover up for more insidious harm.

---

* Yoga in the US has a long history of abuse going back to some of the earliest "gurus" to popularize yoga, including Paramahansa Yogananda, the "founding father" of yoga in the West; Pattabhi Jois, founder of the Ashtanga tradition; Amrit Desai of kundalini; and Bikram Choudhury of bikram yoga among many others. These spiritual leaders used their power, position, and access to those looking for spiritual leadership and to sexually harass, abuse, coerce, and manipulate students over many decades (Beck, "Power and Prana").

Which has me asking myself, Why have I been so drawn to yoga? And, moreover, what has kept me coming back? At this point, it is certainly not the feeling of comfort.

Practicing yoga while white-aware is uncomfortable. Recognizing my connection to cultural theft is distressing. Being held accountable to this information is awkward. Committing to a practice I've accessed through imperialism feels both problematic and humbling. It feels uncomfortable to practice something that could never be my own. It feels disturbing to notice I thought I could own something in the first place. And that dynamic tension, that icky awareness of imbalanced relationship, that dissonant ongoing discomfort is precisely where I need to be.

I am thinking about the many times I have practiced yoga with the goal of being a gold star anti-racist practitioner. I was intentional about studying Raja Yoga through an explicitly anti-racist lens and from a teacher who integrates Raja philosophy and acknowledges its South Asian origins. I have applied the Raja yoga framework of self-study daily. I have committed to examine my whiteness every single day. But my intentions, commitment, and practice are not a pass from reality. I am a white person using a colonized cultural and spiritual practice to improve my well-being. And practicing yoga has benefited me tremendously. It has supported me in gaining the spiritual strength to engage my family and faith community of origin in healthier and more life-giving ways. It has offered me community, status, a sense of my purpose and worth, and, at times, some income. The contradiction of whiteness is that even as I seek healing and liberation, I am nevertheless connected to oppression's tools.

These are some of the questions that keep me up at night: Given cultural appropriation, is it even possible to divest from the violence of white culture while studying BIPOC wisdom traditions? What are the pathways for white folks to heal and reclaim our humanity without perpetuating harm? Can I practice (and teach!?) yoga without automatically embodying more harm?

My fear of being bad fuels angsty spirals. I distance and shut down. Maybe I shouldn't engage with yoga at all? But if I quit, am

I opting out? Maybe I'll take a break from yoga and take up dance instead. I run away. I gravitate toward the Latin dance community in my new home.

Oh wait.

Perhaps I am slowly understanding that practicing yoga might not be so much about finding a right way toward embodied peace nor realizing a path that preemptively atones for my connection to harm. Perhaps it is more about engaging with these messy discomforting contradictions.

And the messy discomforting contradictions are plentiful.

NEW ROOTS, NEW FRUITS

My concerns about facilitating a South Asian wisdom tradition in a white body initiate a host of other questions about the impact of my body's movement within and throughout BIPOC spaces. This line of inquiry interrogates my occupation as a white settler on stolen Indigenous land. Do settlers have the right to exist here? Do I believe that I have the right to exist here?

Kimmerer asks a related question: Can settlers become indigenous to place? She is telling the story of the plantain, known by its Latin name as *Plantago major* and known by Indigenous peoples as "White Man's Footstep" because it followed European settlers to the lands they colonized:

> At first Native people were distrustful of a plant that came with so much trouble trailing behind. But Nanabozho's people knew that all things have purpose and that we must not interfere with its fulfillment. When it became clear that White Man's Footstep would be staying on Turtle Island, they began to learn about its gifts.[12]

Kimmerer notes that plantain is so abundant on Turtle Island, it has become "naturalized." She suggests that the teachings of White Man's Footstep might offer a way for settlers "to throw off the mind-set of the immigrant," "to live as if this is the land that feeds you," to "give your gifts and meet your responsibilities," "to live as if your children's future matters," and "to take care of the land as if our lives and the lives of all our relatives depend on it. Because they do."[13]

Plantain grew all over my former Pittsburgh home, popping up in the garden beds, nesting inconspicuously between the roots of the maple trees, and emerging between the sidewalk cracks and potholes in the middle of the street.

As an avid gardener, I pulled them out with spite, treating them like an annoying scourge. But to hear that they've learned to exist harmoniously, even helpfully: now, this is something I want to pay attention to.

Perhaps I've spent so much energy weeding out the violent roots of my settler colonialist past/present that I've neglected to proportionately nurture the ways my existence might contribute to the health of our ecosystems. That it might be possible to not do colonized harm while also existing on these lands challenges my internalized dualism. I'm not sure I'm ready to agree it's possible, but I'm willing to try it on. I hear Kimmerer's invitation not as an invitation to forget history, but as a possibility to breathe into the future of a both/and.

I notice my feelings of dependence on Kimmerer, a member of the Citizen Potawatomi Nation's permission and invitation. But I'm also recognizing that it's an invitation for me to do my part, to move into the responsibility Indigenous frameworks* remind us of, to release the rights-based ideologies that imply entitlement, ownership, and "divinely"-appointed hierarchies.

An image of the plantain flashes across my mind. It's an illustration done by Austrian botanist Lore Kutschera and other researchers at the Pflanzensoziologisches Institut in Austria. I see the elaborate root system of White Man's Footstep. Each root hair has been carefully recorded and observed. The root systems are intricate and vast, often

---

* In addition to scholars like Robin Wall Kimmerer, Eve Tuck, Leanne Betasamo-sake Simpson, and Linda Tuhiwai Smith, Abenaki elder Jamie Bissonnette Lewey's work has greatly informed my understanding of decolonization and Indigenous frameworks: https://www.abbemuseum.org/blog/tag/Jamie+Bissonnette+Lewey

spreading much beyond the reaches of the part of the plant above the soil. I remember how much we don't see. Our roots are deeper and wider than we may ever know. Perhaps we white settlers have more of a basis for (inter)connection than we've realized.

I am reminded that there are resilience and resistance practices within my roots, too.

MOVING BEYOND WHITENESS

There is much about our legacies not to love. But what then are the parts we can?

One resource that has been helpful for me to begin moving toward a more solutionary approach is a document by Kenneth Jones and Tema Okun titled "White Supremacy Culture."* In the original document, they identify culture as "powerful precisely because it is so present and at the same time so very difficult to name or identify."[14] To make the often invisibilized culture of white supremacy visible, they chronicle thirteen main characteristics with detailed descriptions of how these characteristics show up in workplace settings. Since this document first came out, Okun has reenvisioned the work into a vibrant multimedia website that embraces the feeling and spirit of moving toward collective liberation.

What I've appreciated about the document and website is that in addition to identifying white supremacy culture, they also offer concrete antidotes. These antidotes, like "understand that discomfort is at the root of all growth and learning" (to address entitlement to comfort) and "separate the person from the mistake"[15] (as an antidote

---

* I was first introduced to this document via a PDF that cited "Dismantling Racism: A Workbook for Social Change Groups," by Kenneth Jones and Tema Okun (2001). According to an article from The Forge, "Originally, Okun listed her co-trainer and mentor, Kenneth Jones, a Black man, as a co-author, but he asked to be removed since he did not co-author the paper." The panelists featured in the article offer an interesting and nuanced critique around the limits of Okun's piece (Diaminah, Nakagawa, Sen, Thomas-Breitfeld, and Villarosa, "How (Not) to Dismantle White Supremacy").

for perfectionism), likewise encourage us to identify elements from our own cultural traditions that already support "divorcing white supremacy culture."[16] This both/and approach doesn't bypass the harm and it doesn't forfeit our imaginations for whom we could become.

This solutions-based approach is an invitation to hold the imperfections of our cultural legacies alongside their values. Given the violence of our oppressive histories and our collusion with white supremacy, what from our traditions and histories (or their-stories) are worth holding on to? What about them are worth fighting for? Which parts hold nutrition and which parts are poisonous? Which are the rhubarb stalks, and which are the leaves? The path toward healing from Mistress Syndrome includes taking what we need and composting the rest.

I consider Alice Walker's words often: "Take what you can use and let the rest rot."[17] Also, Biss's: "Whiteness is not who you are. Which is why it is entirely possible to despise whiteness without disliking yourself."[18]

Despising whiteness is not the hard part, though liking ourselves may be.

Who am I beyond whiteness? Who are you? Culturally, spiritually, who are we? What from our traditions do we want to re-claim? Which narratives need to be re-storied? Which ingredients are worth re-membering? Which seeds do we want to save?

RE-CLAIMING

Growing up, Sunday morning church service was an integral part of my family's routine. We went every week. Rare exceptions were made for travel or, as I got older, soccer tournaments, but definitely not for the day after birthday party sleepovers or for catching up on homework.

When I was in middle school, one of the church ladies put up a quilt frame in the back of the sanctuary. From then on, while the (mostly) men were at the pulpit, the (mostly) women were humming away at the quilt frame, listening or not listening to the sermon, silently agreeing or disagreeing with what was preached.

As I became more uncomfortable with what I was hearing from the pulpit, I started to think of the busy quilters in the back of the sanctuary as the Subversive Sunday Sewing Circle. These were Mennonite women undermining patriarchal sermons with practical, comforting, communal, life-nourishing acts. Here they were maintaining the fiber art traditions that are some of humanity's oldest technology.* The quilt tops that appeared at the back of my home congregation's sanctuary were intended to be auctioned at the Mennonite Relief Sale.† These quilts were not just works of art; they would provide food and services (and possibly some dry latrines) for people all over the world. These quilts were practical. These quilts supported life. It was nice that the sermons would still be preached and the scriptures continued to be read, but sermon or no sermon, a quilter's work must go on.

Of course, like my queering of Aunt Amanda, this is a perspicuous projection on my part. I doubt that the quilters' intent was to undermine a status quo in which all eyes, ears, hearts, and minds were supposed to be fixated on the white cis male speaker by organizing a collaborative sewing circle in the back of the sanctuary. But also, maybe it was.

However, the impact, at least on me, was the slightest waft of subversion. Wafts of subversion have been existing even within the innermost chambers of the wicked webs.

Where, then, is our potential for subversion from within? What are the liberatory threads awaiting our reclamation? Where are the quilters in your lineages, quietly subverting as they get on with nurturing life?

---

* Feminist scholars have pointed out the bias built into historical references, including identifying the Bronze or Iron Age in ways that highlight technologies related to weaponry rather than those related to textiles, such as weaving and spinning, which are some of the oldest technologies on the planet and have had major influence. Weaving looms, for example, are the predecessor of contemporary computers (St. Clair, "What If We Called It the 'Flax Age' Instead of the 'Iron Age'?").

† Mennonite Relief Sales raise money for Mennonite Central Committee. Think county fair with lots of baked goods and a quilt auction.

RE-STORYING

The stories we tell ourselves are a source of our power. Just as the stories we neglect and the silences we protect have often been used against us, the wicked webs want us to abandon our pasts as shameful, to leave our histories neglected for others to misuse. As status quo and passing white ladies, there is much to reclaim and work with; we have much to re-story.

In a world replete with white people upholding racism, projects like the Anne Braden Anti-Racist Organizer Training Program, the Legacy Quilt Project, and The White Antiracist Ancestry Project help us access and tell other stories. Going deeper with these stories can support us to get clearer about how our white anti-racist ancestors learned and unlearned their racism, leveraged their power and access, navigated solidarity and healing, and reclaimed their humanity and interconnected ways of being.

Once upon a time, nineteenth-century sisters Sarah and Angelina Grimké refused to forfeit the God territory. Serious about reclaiming spiritual integrity from both racism and patriarchy, they created theological arguments for the abolition of slavery while also refusing to silence their voices when they were told to shut up by white men. The Grimké sisters grew up as part of the Charleston slaveholding aristocracy and were some of the only (if not the only) Southern white women to condemn the institution of slavery and fight for real racial equality, a politic even many abolitionists were opposed to.

Once upon a time, Jessie Daniel Ames from Texas organized other Southern white women against lynching. After first organizing as a suffragette, Ames realized the failures of (white) women's organizations in addressing racial issues. In 1930, she founded the Association of Southern Women for the Prevention of Lynching, bringing attention to the hypocrisy of justifying lynching based on the supposed rape of white women by African American men, which very seldom actually occurred. Ames wrote two books on anti-lynching and petitioned law enforcement to take an anti-lynching pledge. Ames offers us lessons from her powerful and courageous organizing of white women and also from her missteps: her organization excluded African

American women and ultimately opposed federal anti-lynching laws in favor of state ones.

Once upon a time, Southern writer Lillian Smith used her words and actions to fight against segregation and analyze the pathological disease of whiteness. In addition to her acclaimed works, *Strange Fruit* (a 1944 novel) and *Killers of the Dream* (a 1949 autobiographical work), she wrote in support of *Brown v. the Board of Education*, and, along with her lifetime partner Paula Schnelling, began a literary magazine that invited both Black and white writers to be critical of Southern injustices. Smith also leveraged her inherited wealth as a white person, becoming the owner and director of Laurel Falls Camp for Girls, founded by her father. As director, Smith created a progressive space for white girls to critically examine the status quo.

Once upon a time, Virginia Foster Durr was not deterred. The fact that one of Durr's grandfathers had been a member of the Ku Klux Klan and the other had enslaved people did not dissuade Durr from becoming a skilled, strategic anti-racist organizer. Her long legacy began in support of FDR's New Deal and in helping found the Southern Conference for Human Welfare, an interracial group before interracial was cool. In the 1940s she lobbied to abolish the poll tax, ran for US Senate on the Progressive ticket, supported SNCC,* and housed and fed Freedom Riders. Perhaps most significant is the legal, financial, and moral support she and her husband, attorney Clifford Durr, contributed to the Civil Rights Movement. Along with representing Claudette Colvin,† the Durrs arranged for Rosa Parks to attend Highlander Folk School where Parks was trained in strategic nonviolent action. The Durrs stayed in relationship with Parks, bailing her out of jail after she was arrested in the act that

---

* SNCC stands for the Student Nonviolent Coordinating Committee, which was the student-led arm of the Civil Rights Movement Encouraged by organizers such as Ella Baker, the SNCC was a key player in the Freedom Rides of the 1960s.

† Before Rosa Parks, fifteen-year old Claudette Colvin refused to give up her seat to a white woman on a bus in Montgomery, Alabama. However, Colvin's courageous activism and subsequent court case was dropped by civil rights campaigners because Colvin was pregnant and unmarried during the time of the court proceedings.

initiated the Montgomery bus boycott. Durr understood the function of white saviorism and paternalism and believed that white activists should be cautious of assuming leadership in case it be seen as whites "giving" rights to Black people, who were only claiming what already belonged to them.

Once upon a time, Joan Trumpauer Mulholland staunchly rejected the racism of her upbringing in Virginia, even to the point where it is purported that she was examined for mental illness. In her late teens and early twenties, Mulholland was part of a wave of Black-led youth activism. Her commitment to solidarity as a Freedom Rider saw her and her compatriots arrested and sent to the infamous Mississippi Parchman Penitentiary, where she served two months on death row. Her challenge to Southern social norms included integrating the historically Black Tugaloo College and participating in the 1963 Woolworth lunch counter sit-ins in Jackson, Mississippi, along with thirteen other activists.

Once upon a time, Anne Braden embraced her white Southern identity for anti-racism. She didn't let herself off the hook and she didn't let others off either, using her journalistic skills and insider status to advance the anti-racist cause. Born in 1924, Braden held a deep love and compassion for white Southerners. Despite being cut off and despised by family, friends, and most of her beloved community in Louisville, Kentucky, she remained committed to the Southern struggle and to organizing white people within multiracial efforts. Over her long life, she made numerous contributions to anti-racism, economic justice, labor organizing, peace work, civil rights, and civil liberties and worked closely with many historically renown civil rights activists including Ella Baker and Fred Shuttlesworth, among others.

Braden, along with her husband Carl, is perhaps best known for undermining racist institutions by buying and selling a house in a white neighborhood to Andrew and Charlotte Wade, a Black family, during 1950s Southern segregation. After the house was bombed (thankfully no one was harmed), presumably by white neighbors who had already unleashed threats and violence on the Wades' home, Anne and Carl Braden were accused by the county prosecutor of being

masterminds of a communist plot to incite race wars. These insinua-
tions followed them for the next two decades, but Anne Braden was
undeterred, continuing her anti-racist activism up until three days
before her death in 2006. Her mentorship of younger activists links
to my life. In the 1980s, she was one of several civil rights elders who
encouraged PISAB's founders Dr. Jim Dunn and Ron Chisom, the
organization that helped to mentor me in my analysis of racism.

Once upon a time, Mab Segrest, an anti-racist, lesbian, feminist
writer, and activist chronicled her work with North Carolinians
Against Racist and Religious Violence in *Memoir of a Race Traitor*.
Segrest challenged and expelled elements of the North Carolina Ku
Klux Klan in the 1980s. A Southerner originally from Alabama,
Segrest's intersectional approach understood and named the ways
sexism, racism, homophobia, and classism work together long before
other white folks were embracing intersectional praxis. Particularly
poignant to me is how she unpacks her family's racist legacy as well
as the tender interpersonal relationships with family members as she
evolves within anti-racist queer organizing.

The stories we tell ourselves matter. And it matters that we take
responsibility for both our greatness and our flaws.

Catherine Fosl, in *Subversive Southerner: Anne Braden and the
Struggle for Racial Justice in the Cold War South*, writes about Braden's
internal dilemma. As a newspaper editor, Braden went back and forth
about how much to focus on the contributions of white folks. To what
extent should she publish the examples of a very small number of
white Southerners, especially in the midst of large-scale Black leadership? While highlighting Black struggle and resistance was never a
question, ultimately Braden decided that celebrating even the smallest
acts of resistance by white people was important to give other white
people examples and encouragement.

I have come to a similar conclusion. My predecessors never acted
in a vacuum, and their work was constantly impacted by the Black,
Indigenous, and other People of Color they worked with, for, and
alongside. Mine isn't either. This book would not have been possible
without the generosity, wisdom, and, criticisms of the many Black

and Brown folks I've lived, worked, and played besides. Their work and stories are valuable (Support them by investigating the Resources for Further Support and researching local BIPOC-led organizing in your context). Yet, those are their stories. We need more examples of white settlers trying and failing and trying again. We need more stories of anti-racist white folks staying with the fight despite the steep obstacles and temptations to opt out. We need more stories of us standing in solidarity by those who realize that harm to another is also harm against ourselves.

I certainly hadn't known the above white activists' names and stories while growing up white. I am hopeful that this is changing, just as I am hopeful that my story can contribute to change. For all my faults and failures, for all the ways I have and continue to uphold the things I say I want to dismantle, for all my questions and fears, for all the ways I will want to rewrite this text in the future, there is incredible value in sharing our imperfect, ever-evolving stories. We all have things to learn and things to teach. I look forward to the day when there are more books and history lessons about white people dismantling imperialist white-supremacist capitalist patriarchy than books and history lessons about us upholding it.

And you don't have to be a writer who spent eight years and way too many pages to re-story white womanhood. We can re-story as we tuck our children into bed. We can re-story as we decide how we want to talk about and celebrate holidays. We can re-story with our genealogical research and at happy hour with our friends. We can re-story in the workplace and with our neighbors. We can re-story in our heads.

RE-MEMBERING

The first time I learned to reprogram my mind I was sixteen.

When I was at the height of my disordered eating and body dysmorphia, I drew myself back to a healthy self (body) image. In my high school art classes, in self-portrait after self-portrait, I drew and redrew versions of myself. I experimented with what came up for me when I made myself smaller or curvier. I put all that I hated and detested about myself on the page. I drew to externalize my worst fears and emerge from the distortions of my mind. I made likenesses of myself beautiful on the pages until I slowly began to believe it more on the inside. In drawing and redrawing myself, I was able to try on many possibilities. The repetitive act gave me a container of sorts, within which to practice loving my body and to begin regaining some trust in it.

When I was twenty, I recreated my internal image of God.

I was inspired by a sermon preached about Jesus representing the most marginalized. I think they quoted Matthew 25:40: "Whatever you do to the least of these..."

At the time, I was rageful at white men and particularly suspicious of father figures. Whenever an image of an old white muscular Santa-god appeared in my mind, I resentfully pushed it away. At some point I realized that if I wanted to hold on to any shred of my faith, I would need an image of the divine that was less triggering.

I remembered a laminated poster of acclaimed author Toni Morrison displayed on one of my school's walls. Probably first placed there by an English teacher with pride and care, it often became subject to the casual disregard of adolescents and the haphazard energy of the hallways, typically leaning more to one side than the other. Despite its frequent tilt, Toni Morrison still appeared upright, stately with warmth. Her long gray locks testified to a deep soulful wisdom.

At chapel services in college when I heard "God" invoked and the uninvited muscular Santa image appeared, I began to reach for a different picture. The stately poster of Toni Morrison I had passed every day in the hallways of adolescence reemerged. At first, I had to re-member this new visual for God every time, but eventually Mrs. Morrison's image began to organically appear to me.

That one New Testament bible class I took in undergrad re-membered too. My professor Nancy Heisey suggested replacing the word "kingdom"—historically preferred by the European ruling class for its association with royal hierarchy—with "kin-dom." Kindom, she said, calls us into a horizontal society based on interconnected relationships, in which all of creation holds the potential of becoming kin.

I remember how that concept of kinship felt so different than that of ownership. Heralding in the kinship of God felt quite different than ushering in God's kingdom. Similar to Kimmerer's description of Indigenous worldviews, this slight shift in perspective, the dropping of one letter, has helped me to re-member, to bring back together, to reintegrate bodies and communities, to reunite my body with my communities.

* * *

I had not been to a Mennonite service, or any Christian service for that matter, in years. The last time I made an attempt, I made it halfway through. The scripture readings had felt like a personal attack. With each "he" or "Lord" reference to the divine, a little shot of pain went through my spine. The congregational singing was more palatable, but once the preacher started talking, his words filled with assumptions about me and "our" shared beliefs, I ducked out.

It was seven or eight years into studying Raja yoga that I reluctantly returned to a worship service. This time, I was less concerned about the usual triggers. It was a service coordinated by Pink Menno—a group organizing to make the Mennonite Church an open, inclusive, and welcoming place for LGBTQ people—so I felt an added sense of safety as I arrived. My nervous system calmed as I received a warm welcome at the front door. But as I slid into the pew, a string of filing cabinet moments hit me hard. Perhaps it was something about the wood under my bum or the angle of the rigid seat. My body was remembering the reasons why we left and was making sure we were forewarned. I noticed my urge to bolt and the thoughts that followed, *dharana* (concentration); I took a grounding breath, *pranayama* (breathing techniques); I stayed with the discomfort, *dhyana* (meditation), like my yoga practice reminded me to do.

I wept through congregational singing, even though I wanted to join in. It was the absence of harm in the hymns that sparked the tears, each song mindfully selected with attention to language and theology, or rewritten with inclusive language and an invitation I could feel. As the service continued and several faith leaders shared their perspectives, I was surprised by the lack of hardness. The brick wall that typically appeared for me as I tried to get at some spiritual meaning just wasn't there. Instead, a stream of energy and insights flowed. I noticed a slight buzz around the crown of my head, an unclenching of my fists. I checked in with my body. She was tired, but wanted to stay.

I am reminded of words from *The Living Gita* about the limitations of scripture. "If you want to keep the story, you can, but just for fun. You don't need it anymore. Until you get the truth, you need the story."[19] Sort of like scaffolding, Sri Swami Satchidananda advises, once you've built it and you've learned the thing, you can throw it all away.

There of course remain many complexities and complications of practicing (and teaching) yoga while white. Practicing an East Indian–embodied spiritual tradition imparted to me through Black womanism as a white-bodied Mennonite is not void of tensions and the potential to cause much harm. I am reminded of Gloria Anzaldúa and Cherríe Moraga's anthology, *This Bridge Called My Back*, the complexities of appropriating and appreciating, of needing to feel pain in order to heal. Who is harmed by my healing? Is it possible to find healing if we are causing more harm?

I am wondering about many other things: Whatever could be ours to practice and teach? Are there embodied practices not sacrificed on the altar of whiteness? Or their remnants, at least? I think of the cultural practices from my own lineages: quilting; singing; cooking; storytelling; laughter.

Perhaps these practices and antidotes offer those of us who have come to be called white the potentiality to re-member our long neglected indigeneity. Perhaps, as Kimmerer encourages us to consider, they can support white settlers to begin to feel (again) what it is to honor the knowledge of the land and care for its keepers. Perhaps they are Sri Swami Satchidananda's scaffolding and problematized by Moraga and Anzaldúa's bridge. Perhaps they require discernment and attunement and harm reduction. Perhaps they can help guide a group of well-intended white ladies on the path of collective liberation.

CHAPTER THIRTEEN

WE WHITE LADIES LOVE A GOOD PLAN

For the master's tools will never dismantle the master's house.
They may allow us temporarily to beat him at his own game,
but they will never enable us to bring about genuine change.
And this fact is only threatening to those women who still
define the master's house as their only source of support.

—Audre Lorde

The most common way people give up their
power is by thinking they don't have any.

—Alice Walker

The historic library classroom's air was dusty. I watched a density of particles float in front of a window as the spring sunlight split through the glass at a sharp angle, coming in low. One of the white women in the group sat slouched, her arms folded tightly across her chest. She was not the only one. Of our circle of white people at this three-day workshop, only a handful were not embodying this self-protective stance.

Though it hadn't really been on our agenda, somehow the conversation had veered onto the topic of white women's tears. "So, when is it okay to cry, then? Are we not allowed to be ourselves?" one white woman asked defensively. "You want us to be vulnerable and human," another chimed in, "but also not show sadness. If I cry, I'm wrong. If I don't cry, I'm not vulnerable enough."

A conversation about the difference between weaponized tears and authentic emotion ensued. Our facilitation team named the long history of white women's tears signaling danger for Black communities. We talked about how context matters. For example, in this caucusing space we welcomed a full range of emotions, as they were doing. That's the value of affinity spaces, we said. It's part of the reason why we split into groups.

Despite this reasoning, mostly those who crossed their arms stayed that way. *They probably didn't really want a nuanced consideration of white women emoting*, I thought skeptically. *More likely, they were searching for a rulebook.* Well, that was an illusion I was used to shattering.

So, I did. "There's no such thing as a rulebook in this work. There's no checklist. There's no how-to manual. If you're looking for one here, you won't find it." My comments were met with mixed responses. Well, mostly more defensiveness. The arms-crossed white ladies slouched further in their metal folding chairs. I had offended a few others, too. *If you can't tell us the way it should be done,* I imagined them thinking, *then why are we here?*

In the language of evangelism, I did not win over many converts that day. I can report that my approach to white-lady defensiveness has shifted, most days. But and also, I am me, and the temptation to cut through the bullshit is hard to resist. I have prided myself on my agility to deftly analyze, clearly name what needs to be named, and pointedly reply. Except the scalpel in me has not always furthered my hopes and dreams. Speaking caustic truth to power is not always strategic, especially when the goal is to move power to your side.

In all honesty, the there's-no-how-to-manual speech had become a touchstone of comfort for me. Although somewhat aspirational—I still had my own anti-racist rulebook moments—I loved the call to imagine something else. It felt open and freeing to think that we could make it up as we go along. This kind of expansive thinking got me excited about possibilities.

Though usually there was also a comedown. I got frustrated when the daily realities of anti-racist organizing showed up: The white ladies' defensiveness reminded me that we weren't there yet. Perhaps we'd never be. (Heavy sigh.) Why were these white ladies holding on to their illusions so tightly? If they'd just accept the problem then we could get to work, instead of arguing over the emperor's nudity. I'd rationalize my frustration with urgency: People are dying. People are suffering. And here we are debating the degrees of the emperor's clothing. *I can see that he's lost his gloves,* I imagine a white lady conceding, *but he still has his hat.* Meanwhile, I watch as frostbite sets in.

It turns out that most humans don't want their whole sense of themselves in the world to be shattered by one clever facilitator's speech.

Okay. Okay. It has taken me a while and many unscripted lessons to begrudgingly accept this as true.

RETURNING TO THE 4DS: DEFENSIVENESS

In returning to what we know about embodied trauma and the 4Ds, the defensive posture of Arms Crossed and Slouch tells us as much about what we are going through in the moment as what we have been through before it. And this information is key, especially if we are going to unlock the plantation doors of Mistress Syndrome.

The perception of threat felt by those arms-crossed white ladies in the hard metal folding chairs was happening in their bodies. As impossible as it might sound, in that very safe library, perhaps their bodies were sensing a threat to their lives. So why might a racialized correction incite such a severe physiological response? Why might a white lady having her tears critiqued react as if rejecting that information means preserving her life?

Let's return to the work of trauma healing and somatics practitioners who offer insights about the 4Ds, toxic shame, and other adaptive responses in the body, and who say our bodies have learned to respond in these ways for a reason. Dr. Porges's work examines "how our nervous system either supports our ability to co-regulate with another's or supports defense."[1] To paraphrase, defensive behavior is not necessarily voluntary, but a result of how our nervous systems have encoded violations of trust and interpretations of threat. People who have histories of trauma are prone to go into a fight response. Just by correcting their language, for example, their bodies can go into this involuntary defense mode. Or as Dr. Porges notes, "If you are in the mode of detecting a predator, you can't even hear what another person is saying."[2] When our bodies are in a state of heightened activation, we can lose our capacity to connect. And clearly, defensiveness makes it difficult to have reciprocal interactions with another person.

Relatedly, somatic therapist Karine Bell examines the role of shame and, specifically, toxic shame in the body. The wicked webs are fueled by this toxic shame. Specifically, Bell links toxic shame to white-body supremacy and its cultural ethos (white supremacy culture) noting that toxic shame is "reflective of a structural hierarchy that's inherent to white-body supremacy,"[3] which includes a hyperfocus on individuals by pathologizing individual behaviors and then identifying people with them. Essentially, white-body supremacy uses shaming for control and coercion.

So it is within cultures of toxic shame, within these wicked webs, that our bodies perceive being confronted about a racist behavior as an actual threat to our lives. Understanding this now, it feels pretty incredible that, for all the hundreds of white ladies I've confronted within the years of my anti-racist organizing, the damage hasn't been more severe.

But, also, maybe it has.

Given our voting record and extremist conspiracy theory candidates, given my own reactions and responses, given the trials and tribulations of the past eight years of White Women's Groups, it seems that we have been indeed experiencing these corrections as "life threat."

It's worth asking, though, about the actual threats. As in, what is the danger in a group of white women coming together to organize?

* * *

The first WWG cohort after our total reset was actually the third.

The group of white ladies and I sat around my dining room table. Mostly folks were eager and excited, if also a bit nervous. I know I was. To start us off, I gave a little speech.

"White Women's Group is dangerous," I said. "On one hand, we are in danger of continuing what white women have done for centuries. In our organizing, we could accidentally reinforce white supremacy. In ignorance, we could end up shoring up our own power as white women while believing that we are working against it. We could easily end up as dangerous to People of Color as a chapter of the WKKK*—perhaps even more dangerous because our racism is hidden beneath calling ourselves "anti-racist."

"Or, if we really get our act together, if we hold ourselves and each other accountable to ending racism not only out there but also within our group and within ourselves, if we hold our attachment to privilege loosely, if we organize others to do the same, we could be one of the most dangerous threats imperialist white-supremacist capitalist patriarchy has ever seen."

Or in other words, the choice is ours. We will be dangerous either way.

RETHINKING "EQUALITY": DENIAL

I learned how to facilitate restorative circles from white woman Kay Pranis who learned from the First Nations people of Yukon and had been sent with their blessing to teach circle processes to non-Indigenous people.† Though the practice and philosophies of restor-

---

* The Women's Ku Klux Klan emerged after the suffrage movement as a way of building white Protestant women's rights and upholding white supremacy especially in the South. In an interview, Kathleen M. Blee, author of *Women of the Klan: Racism and Gender in the 1920s*, notes how the WKKK advocated for "an eight-hour day for mothers, pay for housewives, and all these kinds of agenda that are similar to what progressive women are arguing for in the 1920s, but in the case of the women's Klan, a very racially defined set of rights" (Bragg, "First Came Suffrage. Then Came the Women of the Ku Klux Klan").

† I had the opportunity to study with Kay Pranis while at Eastern Mennonite University's Center for Justice and Peacebuilding. Kay Pranis first learned how to facilitate peacemaking circles from the First Nations people of Yukon. For more on Circle processes, see the book *Peacemaking Circles* by Kay Pranis, Barry Stuart, and Mark Wedge.

ative justice come from many Indigenous cultures and communities, contemporary adaptations have become increasingly distanced from their origins. Like the growing appropriative mindfulness movement, a restorative justice "field" has sprung up—its original transformative potency in jeopardy of becoming another technical tool of whiteness. Now there are more jobs administering decontextualized Indigenous ways of being, more (white) folks who have become certified to do so, and more programs to answer the demand.

A restorative circle in its very structure gives every human an equal seat and an equal voice. But how can an hour of circle process restore five hundred years of racial oppression?

A few years into working for the peace and justice nonprofit, I received an email from a group of older white women peace activists who were growing in their awareness of racial injustice. In their increasing concern, they urgently wanted to do something. They had learned about a popular film on racism and reached out to Felicia and me for facilitation support.

Because white people and organizations so often expect People of the Global Majority to offer this education for free, we responded to their email with a question. Would the group be able to compensate Felicia? (My time was also already compensated through my job.)

The email turnaround was quick. In their response, the group brusquely clarified. They didn't have a budget, and they wanted us to understand that they were all volunteers. Before Felicia and I were able to draft a response, I had already been copied on a second email from them. Now they were asking another white facilitator if they would volunteer to cofacilitate with me.

In this new email thread, which Felicia was not on, they didn't mention their previous email request to us. They neglected to share with the new potential facilitator how they had already asked Felicia, how we had named the connections between racial and economic justice, and how they had so swiftly declined and moved on. Foregoing an opportunity to creatively problem-solve issues of compensation together, they prioritized their urgency of task over tending to relationship.

This group of activists may have had the best of intentions, yet their actions communicated that they didn't value Felicia enough to work through the situation *with* her. Since they were all volunteers, they felt justified in asking other people to do work for free. They ignored—or perhaps weren't in touch with—the important details of how centuries of forced labor brought Felicia's ancestors to this land. They failed to realize how they were summoning that history within their request for her free labor. They overlooked the potential emotional stress for a Black woman to facilitate a discussion about racism for a room full of white people. Whatever the group heard through that brief email exchange, it made them uncomfortable enough that they ran to the next closest white facilitator who was willing to do this work for free.

Though the email exchange had been infuriating in an unsurprising sort of way, we decided it had potential. Felicia and I brainstormed how it might become an opportunity for a "teachable moment," to use Felicia's words. We strategized: How might we support them in understanding that their actions reinforced the racism they were now so interested in fighting? The exciting thing about this moment is that you are getting to hear the debrief of this dynamic and glean its wisdom. Unfortunately, the group of white women peace activists did not.

In considering how we could address the interpersonal harm while also transforming power dynamics, Felicia and I requested an unconventional restorative circle process. With the support of a local (also white lady) restorative justice practitioner, we designed a process that would center Felicia's voice, opening with space for her to share about the impact of the group's actions and for me to follow up by making historical connections. In our proposed agenda, and unlike more typical restorative circle processes, we offered them only one opportunity for response within the circle, and then allotted Felicia the final words.

As you may have anticipated, our proposed restorative circle process was not to their liking. They emailed back that the agenda was unlike any restorative process they had ever experienced. It would not give them equal voice. That's not how circles work, they said. They wouldn't feel safe with our agenda, they said. And so, they refused to engage, again.

The irony is that the second time around, Felicia was offering her work for free.

In reflecting on this incident, I am struck by how quickly their flight response was engaged, how fast their denial appeared. It is hard to hear what someone is saying when your back is turned. It is impossible to listen if you are running away. It is difficult to be in right relationship if the slightest discomfort activates a full-on sprint.

But could an hour of circle process restore five hundred years of racial oppression? And what might it have to offer those of us conditioned to flee?

In her chapter "Who's In & Who's Out? Problematizing Circles in Diverse Classrooms" in the powerful and much-needed book *Colorizing Restorative Justice: Voicing Our Realities*, Christina Parker writes that although circle processes can challenge privileged ways of communicating, "when race cannot be discussed openly...the possibility for marginalization still exists." Parker implores those working with restorative justice to consider histories and cultures of oppression and reflect on how, even within circle processes, marginalized people remain dispossessed "because the colonial oppressor is unable to hear."[4]

Likewise, in their chapter "Burn the Bridge" in *Colorizing Restorative Justice,* Erica Littlewolf, Michelle Armster, and Christianne Paras, with Lorraine Stutzman Amstutz discuss how restorative practices tend to function on white liberal colonized assumptions such as: "Everyone is equal," "This is a safe space," "Circle symbolizes community," and "Facilitators are impartial/neutral/detached."[5] While we may pretend that everyone comes to a circle equally, the wicked webs know otherwise.

White democratic liberalism is supposed to give every human an equal seat and an equal voice. But is it helpful to give equal credence to every perspective? Do we want to give hate the same legitimacy as love? Do we want to give greed the same validity as equity? Giving these views equal weight without addressing power doesn't actually balance the scales; it validates oppression. And a critical moment with democratic liberalism begs the question: Why is balancing the scales of oppression a celebrated goal?

Perhaps we validate oppression because we are afraid of losing control. Perhaps we flee because we are afraid of having to choose. Perhaps we deny because choosing solidarity might have us realize that we, too, are a target. Perhaps we run because deep down our bodies remember this. Despite the shield of whiteness, perhaps we still feel our bodies under threat.

The circle story also has something to say about our good intentions and deeper motivations. It has something to offer us about the difference between solidarity and saviorism.

As a reader of this book, you are obviously concerned about racism and want it to end, just as I do. In taking the time to delve into such a long and complex text, you are most likely serious about doing your part. Good intentions are important. They are a great place to start. They are the entry point to change.

But intentions can also be fragile, especially when they're new. Like the peace activists trying to do a new anti-racist thing, sometimes when our intentions are fragile, perhaps still a little unclear and aspirational, we try to protect them with the 4Ds. And if we can notice them, we can get clearer about our motivations.

We can ask ourselves why we're trying to protect our intentions. We can ask if our actions, our impact, and the feedback we receive is lining up with our initial intent. We can test out our true motivations. Are we doing this on behalf of others or on behalf of ourselves? My answer may surprise you. I think in order to shift from saviorism to solidarity, we need to be more focused on being motivated on behalf of ourselves. A shift from saviorism to solidarity relocates the core of our motivation internally as we seek to be true to ourselves rather than strive to externally justify our role and value to white supremacy. And being true to ourselves supports us in being true with others, to listen better, and to move from places of integrity and alignment.

CONTENDING WITH SHAME: DISTANCING

Somatic therapists talk about our nervous system's window of tolerance. When we feel uncomfortable, our nervous systems get activated and that activation can push us up against the edges of our tolerance. Practicing feeling discomfort along those edges can help us learn and grow. But when we are under extended stress and/or have our core fears triggered, our nervous systems can become dysregulated. In our dysregulation we may move toward the hyperarousal responses of fight or flight, or, if those aren't accessible to us, we end up in the hypoarousal responses of freeze. Here we can also add fawn.

So what causes us to flee? Or, perhaps, more importantly: What causes some of us to stay? While there were white ladies who fled White Women's Group, the majority who signed up stuck it out.

My former colleague and I first came up with the name as a placeholder, but then kept it when we realized its clarity. As white women, we were used to gathering with each other. In book groups and knitting circles, at happy hours with friends, with fellow teachers in the break room, and within spaces of "doing good," we were pretty good at seeking each other out. Mostly though, all this self-organizing has served to reinforce a racialized status quo. At WWG, our goal was different. Our goal was explicit. We were coming together, aware of our whiteness with the strategic goal to challenge said status quo.

Perhaps like you, the white women of WWG were not new to thinking and talking about race or their racism. Though they may have crossed their arms defensively in a library three to five years before or fled an uncomfortable teachable moment in the past, by the time they arrived at WWG, these white ladies had a sense of their racialized windows of tolerance, and they had committed to keep coming back.

It was months after Covid had put an end to the WWGs that were held around my dining room table, when we had been able to share home-cooked meals and the chaos of children happening up or down the stairs. On this night, the virtual WWG space was tense. I could feel the tightening vibrations through our high-speed highly privileged internet connection. As a group, we had been investigating white-lady ego and describing how we saw it happening in us. We were looking at how it showed up in our notions of body image, how it surprised us within our most intimate relationships, and how it infiltrated our sense of agency.

In a breakout room, one of our members was on a downward spiral of self-loathing, a ride that was not unfamiliar to me. The WWG member had been sharing about how her internalized intersectional racism was showing up that week. As she was telling us about it, she noticed that she was manifesting more racism even now in her debrief. She was telling us about her perfectionism in a performative way. She was describing her need for control as she controlled the narrative for our fellow anti-racist white-lady ears. She was talking about her competitive drive competitively.

Being able to identify and apply these manifestations was one of WWG's foundational objectives, so as the facilitator I should have been thrilled. But as I listened to her express pain in noticing how her racism had harmed others and herself and watched her become devastated in her awareness that she was responding to her racism with more internalized racism, I began to question our entire theory of change.

My former cofacilitator and I had assumed that working with white ladies to build an awareness of self, contextualized by history and an understanding of our power, would lead us to interrupt harmful patterns in our families, communities, and within ourselves. However, this member's increased awareness was leading her to increased despair.

Rather than feeling a sense of agency to change what was most within her control (thoughts, beliefs, and emotions), she was getting stuck in an exhausting pattern: she applied the anti-racist analysis to her thoughts; saw how her internalized patterns of racism were present; judged herself for having the patterns; realized she was judging herself; applied the analysis toward her own judgment; and then once again she noticed her internalized patterns of racism and got angry at herself. In short, her self-criticism was only leading to more self-criticism. Of course, she felt exhausted, frustrated, and despairing. I get tired just trying to describe the fateful pattern here.

For all our ups and downs, WWGs have been an important space to practice anti-racist affinity organizing. I am grateful for Black organizers' calls to organize my own. I am grateful to myself for being courageous and trying and failing and trying again. I am grateful for the white ladies who came and went and stuck around through its many iterations. The WWG member's fateful spiral moment reinforced for me a commitment to cultivate space with other white folks to hold our own and each other's pain, to practice what it is to love each other.

I am grateful that this one white lady was willing to share her process with so much vulnerability. I am especially grateful because the moment gave me an opportunity to see how I had been doing, and modeling, that very same cycle.

I am typically a confident student. But when I was first introduced to the concept of internalized oppression, I felt daunted by the task of identifying the specific ways I had acted out racism. It helped that other white anti-racist facilitators shared how they saw it in their lives. But it was the swift push to facilitate that really motivated me to work the analysis. I was often the white person in the room with the most experience, and, after only attending a few trainings, was urged to take a leadership role.

Despite (or maybe because of) the jolt of panic that shot up my spine when asked to share about my internalized oppression, I quickly embraced the formulaic aspects of the analysis. I entered these trainings intending to vulnerably talk about my internalized racism, but when I tried, my distancing emerged. I gravitated toward the long list of manifestations, ticking off the boxes one by one as I went down the list, tracing each historical thread. After a couple months, I could tell you which familial patterns this form of my racism was linked to and which historical events had inaugurated it. In fact, I have. These pages contain many of those reflections. Noticing these manifestations in myself was easy (since there are many). Noticing them in other white people was even easier.

This self-criticism was not a new skill. I had been honing an analysis of what was wrong, what was wrong with other people, and especially, what was wrong with myself for decades before I ever set foot in an anti-racism workshop. The workshop's intent was not to shame or chastise white folks. Yet, that was the toxic shame culture in which my anti-racist analysis took hold. The tools meant for liberation provided new words with which to judge myself and others. I still believe that identifying the ways we uphold harmful systems has incredible value, but I am also learning how, when planted as a monocrop, honing a critical analysis can yield paralyzing despair.

A downward spiral of despair might not appear as distancing on the surface. A well-articulated critique might not seem like a dissociative response. We might not interpret self-criticism as a way of checking out, especially if we are doing the anti-racist thing of naming our racism.

Or, of naming the racism of other white people.

In discussing toxic shame, Bell describes the policing of other white bodies by those "in the work." Bell notes that toxic shame within anti-racism "can produce perfectionism and policing of others (judgment): elitification, virtue signaling and performative gestures." This form of blaming ultimately cuts us off from "staying present to the experience with what's happening."[6]

We can extend this policing to self-blame as well. The policing of our own white bodies, the internal distancing from parts of ourselves we don't like, and the identification and judgment of our internalization of oppression further disconnects us from our Selves and each other. Those clear-cut anti-racist critiques were what we thought—what I thought—liberation work was supposed to be for white people. But now, I am aware of how the monocrop of critical analysis might not have been as transformative as I once presumed. I have become more sensitized to my replication of harm, more attuned to compassion.

After I closed out the WWG video call, I sat for a moment feeling responsible and questioning my leadership. How had I modeled self-awareness in a way that led to such intense despair? I felt responsible to make a change, but wasn't sure how to shift it. What could we do to shake it up? How could we get out of the downward spiral of self-loathing critique?

Then an idea came quickly. What if I asked the group to write love letters to their internalized white supremacy? What if we could embrace our racism rather than trying to eradicate it? What if we tried to love all the parts of our Selves?

These questions may sound odd, even like a contradiction to what you've read thus far. And in total honesty, they felt risky to pose. But in that moment of downward spiral, I realized one way WWG had been using the master's tools. We had been going after our internalized racism with more internalized racism, trying to root out the violent parts with the tools of violence. We had been afraid of our fear. We had been loathing our aversions. As a testimony of how deeply we have internalized oppression, we had been using its tools to try to make it go away. And I had been modeling it all.

What had been missing in my fellow white lady's spiral and in my own self-criticism was practicing self-compassion for all aspects of ourselves, even those parts which are racist.

Perhaps this was the moment I started to truly love other white ladies. Perhaps this was the moment I began to practice deep compassion for myself. What had I cut off in order to police other white people? From which parts of myself did I have to disconnect?

The white ladies and I ended up writing a series of blog posts in response to the prompt. I appreciate their honesty—not everyone was convinced that white people loving our internalized racism will move us away from racism. Mostly, I think it's the edgy uncomfortable contradiction we need to be working within, though some days I have my doubts. It could also be a terrible idea that encourages white people to spiritually bypass the embodied realities of harm.

Even as I still have my doubts, I can see the fruits of holding my flaws—and my racism—with compassion. Compassion offers me the spacious adaptability to get curious about the harm I've been a part of rather than to judge and resist it. Compassion is helping me to differently enter relationships in which I have felt responsible for identifying another white person's racism or for identifying my own.

And for all of WWGs' flaws, we had been trying to unlearn our racism together. It turns out that it's the interpersonal ways of staying present that help keep our nervous systems online. According to Dr. Porges, it is through our social interactions that we, as humans, have evolved to alleviate defense-based trauma responses. We are deeply physiologically attuned to each other's facial expressions, muscle tension, and vocal tones. We are designed to emotionally regulate together, to help each other move out of defense and into connection.

In examining our internalized racism, perhaps we have been attuning to each other's despair, but could we also use it to attune to each other's love?

Shame is likewise a physiological evolutionary trait, which, as Bell notes, evolved to alert us to potential danger. Unlike toxic shame, healthy shame presents a temporary rupture within human relationship and is always met with swift relational repair. Within a healthy shame dynamic, we can receive correction. Or as Bell says, "I can take it if you have something you need to say or if there's a behavior in me that you need to point out because it's potentially causing harm."[7]

Within this healthy shame paradigm, there is no need to get defensive, run away, or self-loathe. There's no reason to deflect correction at all costs, because on the other side of correction is deepened secure relationship. The healthy shame response and repair actually strengthens our ability to coregulate and our ability to be in solidarity together.

COMPLICATING SUPPORT: DEFERENCE

Which brings us again to the fourth D, deference. Like those other Ds, deference has served a purpose. As a white kid who was sometimes in all Black spaces, it kept me safe in contexts in which I didn't know the rules. As an exchange student, it helped me forge protective social connections as a stranger in a foreign land. Within systems and institutions, it signaled to authority figures that I was someone to protect. Just as it has for white women since the invention of race.

But my application of deference (often subconsciously) in contexts in which I've had a lot of social and positional power has offered some fraught lessons in the ways of Mistress Syndrome. Let me explain.

In the slightly musty office room with its dark wood paneling and trim, I was sitting at my desk preparing for the afternoon youth organizing gathering. It had been a year since I became the program's director and turnout had been extraordinary.

The program had originally focused on more traditional (white) peace movement concerns. But through the organization's national network, I was introduced to powerful anti-racist organizing happening in Seattle and other parts of the country.* When we were invited to become a part of this anti-racist youth-focused organizing network, I jumped at the opportunity and—despite some resistance from our local advisory board—we pivoted to refocus our programming.

This was in 2014 and 2015, in the aftermath of Mike Brown's murder by police. The youth attending the program were hungry to talk about race. They brought their friends and their friends' friends. This rapid and ultimately unsustainable expansion proved challenging, but for now I want to consider the interpersonal dynamics within a program led by one paid white lady and a burgeoning number of youth, especially youth of color, and, mainly, Black youth.

I entered the role quite aware of the systemic harm these young people were experiencing in their relationships with white women as their teachers, counselors, and family members. In fact, the analysis the program used centered the lived experiences of Black youth and invited, encouraged, and affirmed the naming of racialized harm especially in the education system with its many white-lady gatekeepers.

Now that we were doing anti-racist organizing with Black youth, I was becoming increasingly uncomfortable in the sole leadership role. While the support team and I worked on a long-term plan to shift the leadership to be more representative of the youth, in the short term it meant building relationships in ways that did not replicate the daily racialized harm they experienced.

---

* In partnership with PISAB, Youth Undoing Institutional Racism is a program of the American Friends Service Committee with past and ongoing organizing in Seattle, St. Louis, Minneapolis/St. Paul, West Virginia, and Pittsburgh. Seattle's anti-racist organizing at the time included work happening through Ending the Prison Industrial Complex (EPIC) and European Dissent.

One afternoon, one of the young people walked into the office. They were early, as this particular young person often was. They casually flopped down in one of the hard, heavy wooden chairs, dropped their backpack on the table, and flung their legs over the armrest. "Ugh, I'm so tired of the bullshit…" They shared yet another story of a white woman in their life who had hurt and harmed them.

I listened and affirmed their experience, hyperaware of my own white-ladyness and slightly distracted by the ways I did not want to be like the white lady they were describing. I most certainly did not want to recreate that harm.

On this day, I listened and affirmed as I did on so many occasions when young people shared vulnerably about hard things. While I fully agreed they had been wronged by their (white lady) teacher and their rage justified, and while I did not judge them for the way they responded, I also saw a missed opportunity in their situation. In my mind, a more calculated response would have helped them get what they wanted. Perhaps there were more options than their rage was allowing them to perceive?

After they vented and processed intense emotions, there was a moment when I could have shared my thoughts and questions. But as I paused to make sure they were finished, the self-doubt of my anti-racist analysis kicked in: Who was *I* to advise *them* on their lived experience? And then, fear: What if my perspective invalidated their feelings and experience? I'd just be another white lady inflicting harm.

Rather than asking or advising, I decided to defer to their (adolescent) judgment. I did not encourage them to take responsibility for their part of the dynamic—as I probably would have done with one of the white youth. Ultimately, I did not challenge myself to take responsibility either. I didn't question their perspective out of my own fear of getting it wrong.

There is a diagram popular in restorative justice that examines ways of cultural relating. This diagram, called "Impact of Social Environments on the Brain" by Chuck Saufler,[8] charts "boundaries/limits" on one axis and "nurture/support" on the other; it describes a relational dynamic that has high nurture and support but low boundaries and limits as "permissive." In the "permissive" quadrant, one is "doing FOR" another, using excuses and reasoning to passively enable negative behaviors.

Deference dwells in the "permissive" quadrant. In its unquestioning, supportive stance, it avoids the tensions that might build connection, accountability, or long-term trust and the risks that come along with that. Even though the intention of deference may be to support, the permissive approach can end up dismissing the wisdom we may have to offer. Deference's fear of engagement short-circuits authentic trust building. It prevents us from learning that relationships can still exist on the other side of open conflict. In this way, it moves us away from deepened relationship. This makes it very hard to learn from one another and especially, to learn from those leaders among us who know something about the things we want to change.

I get why deference is so attractive. In Saufler's diagram, opposite the permissive quadrant sits a "punitive" one, one that uses authoritarian tools including stigmatization and shame. This punitive "doing TO" quadrant especially describes how our relationships have come to function under the wicked webs. The punitive model is all too familiar in our family histories, dominant culture, and politics. Our leaders have been widely imposed on us and ethically compromised. I am highly suspicious of authority figures too.

The opposite of bad can seem pretty good. Yet, similar to the paternalism of white saviorism, doing FOR is also about taking matters into one's own hands—even if those hands are perceived as supportive—rather than engaging the awkward discomfort that may come from doing WITH and the potential relational risks involved.

While the 4Ds may have been the last options available for the bodies of our European grandmothers and white-lady forerunners, while the 4Ds may have tried to keep us safe as children, it is worth reexamining how they serve us today. Is defending our tears helping us to grow? Is denying our power doing (us) justice? Is distancing from self-compassion supporting anti-racism? Is deferring to anti-racist leadership helping us to get free? At this point, what do we think they are protecting us from?

One of the problems with relying on deference in relationships is that when it comes time to set a boundary, it can come as a surprise.

* * *

Over a year earlier, when I first officially proposed shifting our work to center anti-racist youth organizing, we had been working to get the advisory committee up to speed. It had been a jam-packed and tumultuous process. In just over a year's time, we had done internal workshops on diversity, equity, and culture, hosted a preview event open to the community, and kicked off our first weekend-long youth anti-racism workshop. Through all this, we continued with weekly youth programming. More and more young people were showing up to organize with us. We had begun a youth-led campaign to replace punitive school culture with restorative anti-racist alternatives and were actively engaging with representatives from the public school system.

In the midst of the programmatic shifts, two-thirds of the committee resigned, so I took it as an opportunity to invite people who would be more racially representative of our youth group, and, as importantly, who shared a deep understanding of the anti-racist analysis. The youth organizing was growing more rapidly than I anticipated and I was desperate for more (aligned) adult support.

That year, at the request of the youth, we skipped the summer break. They wanted to keep meeting, they said. This space was important to them. Even though I was already exhausted, I obliged. I rationalized our work's importance, pushing through my exhaustion.

The youth were tired, too. I saw glimpses here and there, especially in how mental health issues began showing up in the space after our summer session ended. It was the fall of 2016 when election coverage was heating up and 45's toxicity had been increasingly indulged by the media. The young people were on the defensive against the racism of their schools and peers. We were preparing for our next big youth training, doing outreach and lots of prep. Despite all the evidence, despite my own exhaustion and that of the leadership team, it took a crisis incident—and Felicia's adamancy—to put the program on pause so we could rest up for the big event. I was learning lessons of self- and collective care alongside the youth. A critique one of the youth leaders made later was accurate: we talked a lot about self-care, but didn't really model the tools.

The first boundary I set was pausing the programming; the second when the youth leaders weren't fulfilling their leadership roles. Given my past leniency, these boundaries probably came as a complete surprise.

When I enforced the second boundary in the middle of our big event, the reaction was disproportionate, but also developmentally appropriate. I can see that now, but in the middle of the event, as the youth leaders organized their peers to shut the training down, I had no idea what was going on.

I'm still not sure I totally understand. Their discontent was clear, but their reasons less so. After one particularly tense confrontation during break, we decided to have a circle to discuss their complaints. They felt that a grant was being misused (it turned out they had the wrong information). They wanted the space to be more youth-led (though we had just added new paid youth leadership positions). But mostly, they were upset that I was a white lady in charge (that fact at least was right).

I wish I could say that the circle process resolved the issues, but it hadn't. We ended up putting the entire program on pause, and some of the messiness from that weekend followed our organizing for years.

In reflecting on my responsibility in the mess, I know my deference and distancing got in the way. Along with the lessons on self/ community care and sustainability, there were protocols, boundaries, and developmentally appropriate education I should have put in place. In the heat of the moment, both at the training and after, there were times where I froze and over-relied on Felicia and our other Black advisors to assess the situation and decide what to do next. I even used her words once to describe what had happened without fully discerning what it might mean for me, a white woman, to repeat something that came out of the experience of a particular racialized context. I later realized that in repeating that description to young Black people, I caused harm.

It is this part of the story that brings me the most sadness, because the relationships with the young people that were damaged in the process were relationships close to my heart.

My biggest regret is that in all the fallout, I let one very important relationship go. I was hurt, still feeling confused and betrayed. In the aftermath of putting everything on hold, one of the youth leaders sent me a text wanting to meet with me and explain. This incredible young person took the risk of reaching out, but I wasn't ready to receive them. I was still angry and hurt and their text still didn't acknowledge the impact of their actions. Felicia had advised a complete shutdown because the conflict was beginning to take on a life of its own. By being put in the position of having to prove and defend against information that wasn't true, we were giving it fuel. I agreed we needed a reset, but my heart still tugged in the direction of this one young person.

Even though to this day I think Felicia's advice was sound, I regret not following my heart. My actions may or may not have caused a different outcome, but at least it would have been my mistake to make. At least I would have taken full responsibility for my own heartbreak.

Despite the messy fallout and the heartbreak, I look back on that time with some pride. After all, the youth put their anti-racist organizing skills to use, though perhaps not in the most strategic way. The program had taught them to hone critical analyses and push together for change, and that's precisely what they tried to do.

I still wonder what could have been. If we have been able to do WITH, if I had been able to balance clear boundaries with strong support, what Pittsburgh could we have had?

Both the WWG and youth organizing were replete with many lessons. For one, none of the 4Ds—deference included—would stop me from going through hard and painful things; they wouldn't keep my chosen family from leaving; they wouldn't prevent my foundational sense of self from crumbling beneath my feet.

CHAPTER FOURTEEN

CHOSEN FAMILY: TAKE TWO

We can learn from what lurks in the shadows.

—Rachel Held Evans

It's about how you recover.

—Felicia Savage Friedman

It was Halloween of 2019 when Kayla came home. After that, everything changed.

I was excited for her to move back in, remembering the warmth of the last time we had lived together. I was also a little nervous. Much had changed.

Since Felicia had married and moved out, I had become used to living on my own and surprised myself by liking it. Initially terrified to live alone, I became grateful for my own space. Although I was having some white guilt about being the single occupant of a large space in a gentrifying neighborhood, I was also feeling good about how the space supported our organizing. Kayla's soon-to-be bedroom had become my home office, while her other future room was devoted to WWG. The first floor hosted countless meetings, dinners, and workshops as a revolving door for strategizing and community. The outdoor space, once a playground for the neighborhood kids, had since become a thriving garden and a sanctuary for me to rejuvenate and tend to my relationship with the earth.

Felicia still lived close by and checked in regularly. Though we were seeing each other gradually less and less, we still overlapped frequently in our work lives. After the reset, the youth organizing had made a slow and steady comeback and we were debating whether to stay with the nonprofit that sponsored it. Her yoga teacher trainings had taken off, with a new flight beginning each year. I was involved in supporting those and regularly taught her classes.

Although since she had moved out, there had been opportunities for roommates and an increasing financial pull to do so, I did not want a housemate just because. My standards had shifted; I only wanted to live with people I knew well and shared compatibility. Since Kayla and I had lived together in the past, she fit the bill. I was little anxious that we hadn't discussed all the details yet, but figured it could wait until she arrived.

I spent weeks preparing her space. Plugging holes in the closets while realizing these potential (and probably well-used) rodent passageways must have scared the bejesus out of Felicia. I tried to do better this go-round, even enlisting Karriem's support to help me use the power tools left by my former partner to rodent-proof the house.

Despite my reservations about having a housemate again, I was glad that Kayla still felt like she had a home in Pittsburgh, and with me. Her mom was beside herself. Feeling exuberant on that drizzly Halloween morning, the two of us drove to meet Kayla at the truck rental. We hopped out of the car and ran toward her. There were hugs from the huggers (Felicia) and the non-huggers (Kayla and me). For a moment the sun peeked out from between the clouds, and I felt the same contented sense of belonging that I had on our last day of Puerto Rico vacay.

It took a week for that illusion to be shattered.

My memory of those moments is selectively vivid. I reach for my emotional filing cabinet for help in describing a sequence of events for you. The front of one folder has melted and become misshapen. Like plastic accidentally in contact with hot metal, there's a waft of pungent after-smell. Its petroleum colors have fused in places, some of them bright compounds and others muddled into murky pools.

At least the first two memories are clear.

The three of us were in her mother's Jeep, leaving a business meeting. I was in the front seat, Kayla in the back. We were talking about our plans for the week. "I have a meeting with my sperm donor," Kayla said with a glint of humor. "What?" I was confused. *Is Kayla trying to get pregnant?* I thought, keeping my confusion to myself. *Eventually it will become clear.* And it did. "With my father," she clarified. *Oh,* my internal dialogue continued, *I've never heard that term used that way.* I added it to my vocabulary and used it days later, when she got home late from meeting up with her dad.

She was quiet as she came through the front door and walked up the stairs. I passed her in the hall on the way up to my room. The energy felt heavy, so I went for levity. "How was your meeting with your sperm donor?" I asked. She didn't want to talk about it and said she was going to bed.

I didn't think much about our interaction until I received a text message from her the next day. I was about to leave (or perhaps had already left) for an out-of-town workshop, when I received her abrupt text.

Then things get fuzzy in my mind. I glance at the file for help. The top is labeled: **Kayla Had an Epiphany and We Were No Longer Sisters.** I've jotted down a list of the things I remember. My notes read: "She said not to ever talk to her unless we set up a meeting ahead of time. She said don't knock on her door or talk to her in passing. She said she's tired from processing all of this and doesn't want to talk further. She said it was racist for me to call her father that."

I try to process it all again. Well, at least that last one makes some sense. I didn't mean it that way, but I can see how, given racism's treatment of Black fatherhood, those words were inappropriate coming from me. I can hold that she might want to vent about her relationships, but not have other people reflect them back to her using her words. I've felt that, too: I'm allowed to complain about my family, but that doesn't give anyone else permission to do so. Although I felt the defensiveness push on my window of tolerance, at least this one piece made sense to me.

The rest was a very stressful mystery.

Feelings: fear, confused, hurt, silenced and shut out, trapped, angry, upset.

Though to say I was upset is an understatement. At some point after my return from the out-of-town workshop, I spent one particularly undignified afternoon bawling on the bathroom floor. It was beyond ugly cry. The deepest wave of grief hit me while I was standing at the sink. Its upswell started in my toes and consumed my entire body. I found myself shaking on the cold floor, the tiles hard beneath my shins, my body quaking in a snotty pile. I felt incredibly alone. Later I was able to name these episodes as panic attacks.

It was on that cold, tiled floor that I fully knew, though for months and in many different ways still tried to deny, the pending demise of my chosen family. I didn't yet have the information, which would later be revealed: Kayla didn't want a friendship or a sisterhood with me, but a transactional tenant/housemate relationship. I didn't yet have a full understanding of my truth: I absolutely did not want to live in that arrangement. I did not yet allow myself to connect with the scariest reality of all: my relationship with Felicia would be impacted, and maybe it already had, though I was refusing to acknowledge that scary truth. But my body knew. My body knew all that and more, long before my mind caught up.

ANTI-RACIST COPING STRATEGIES

That was a difficult time. The sun had left us, gone to visit the penguins in Antarctica. Everything outside my home was dying, the leaves had fallen, and the skies were a plummeting gray. With this shift, it appeared that everything inside would be dying, too.

There is a second folder file I manage to pull out: The Moment I Asked Her to Leave. We were in the living room, me in the white Ikea chair; her in the red one my former partner and I bought as a joint Christmas gift one year, carefully researched as having been manufactured in the USA.

I said, shakily at first, "This arrangement isn't working for me." Then I stated my meaning more clearly: "You need to leave." She outright refused. "No," she said. "I'm not moving again."

I stood up, unsure what to do. I couldn't evict her. I mean technically, I could, but I wasn't going to. My values would not allow it. I saw the options for honoring myself slowly recede into the distance, impossible to reach. I knew this newly recalibrated dynamic was not a healthy one for me. It was also not one I had wittingly agreed upon.

In that moment in the living room, when she refused to leave, it was as if I let all the air get sucked out of me. I deflated myself. I got small. I deferred. Even though my name was on the mortgage, I felt like I had no other choice but to make it work. I distanced myself from my feelings and my body. I shut my systems down. I rationalized it as a hard thing I'd just have to make work.

Besides, I told myself, I was working on my Pittsburgh exit strategy. I could make anything work for a year, I tried to psyche myself up. Besides, I rationalized again, we were figuring out a way for Felicia to buy the house.

At some point, Felicia had asked that we handle our conflict between us and not involve her. I was committed to honoring her wisdom and request. Kayla was her daughter after all.

In the weeks and months following Kayla's refusal, there were moments when I spoke my truth freely, when I let myself be less censored in my expressions of anger, when I admitted what I wanted and asked for it, when I did conflict bravely and said what I was thinking as we tried to figure out what it meant to share a roof, but not secrets (or pillow fights).

But at some point—really, at many points—I repressed emotions that were "inconvenient." I prioritized a superficial harmony over upending conflict.

On the inside, I refused to relinquish the righteousness of victimhood (I spoke my truth and she did not honor it, I told myself, so there's nothing else to do but make the most of it). I neglected to tell her those feelings were still present for me. On most days, I neglected to acknowledge those feelings to myself. I felt so hurt and angrily justified: my fears of abandonment had come to pass. I was correct to hold my cards tight. I was justified in not sharing or giving of myself vulnerably, since abandonment would be the inevitable result, as it already had.

But on many days, I also genuinely tried to do and be my best given the challenges of the situation. I know on many days she tried her best as well.

I see now, but was not in touch with then, how much my Mistress Syndrome was triggered within the context of the dynamic. I see now, but was not in touch with then, how much I leaned on my internalized white supremacy to cope.

Trauma therapists talk about how traumatized people often seek out similar situations to the site of their trauma. Yoga teaches that the lessons we get in life are the ones our souls are calling out to learn. Kayla's rejection regurgitated my ancestral trauma of being shunned in my own home, of being cast out of the community, of being condemned to eternal damnation. The world I had believed in was crumbling; the house I had relied on was being dismantled even as I lived in it. No wonder I was bawling on the bathroom floor.

The tools of white supremacy whispered the rules of anti-racism in my ears. *Don't be a victim*, it said. *Anti-racism is uncomfortable. It's okay for you to feel uncomfortable.*

The tools of white supremacy minimized my experience and told me to ignore my gut. In my desperation I grasped for a list of shoulds and supposed tos. Its (self)control told me I should suffer in silence. Its individualism told me to shoulder the burden alone. Its martyr complex told me I'm supposed to sacrifice for a Black woman's comfort. Its saviorism told me I should prioritize her requests even if it meant suppressing my own. Its violence told me that having all these feelings were bad and therefore, I was bad.

It took seven months, a global pandemic, a text exchange, and several nights of insomnia for me to make a move. After months of feeling a grating discomfort in my own home, I moved to move... out. I reached out to Kayla and her mom for a conversation about how this could be achieved.

In order to describe the next scenes to you, I have leafed through the filing cabinet for days. This memory is stubbornly buried. It does not want to be found. I am seated on the floor, surrounded by manila folders and scribbles on the backs of torn envelopes and old receipts.

Screw this filing system, for it does not show you how, in trying to write this all down, my forearms have broken out in hives and now the rash has spread to my chest and neck above my sternum. Maybe I've been looking in the wrong places, spending my time searching through the messy folders of my mind when I should be searching my body instead.

* * *

It was June and I was trying to move out.

"We think you are running," Felicia said. Or maybe it was Kayla. The details are hazy, but this was the main theme: "You need to stay and work it out. If you leave, you are a white lady opting out."

As you probably can imagine, that conversation didn't go the way I had planned. And even in trying to unpack it for you, I am struggling to release my sense of victimhood. I am noticing how the words that come to mind still center the hurt that was done to me—I was in the hot seat; I received hard feedback, and later, hard feedback about how I was receiving the hard feedback; I had to list all the ways my internalized racism was showing.

And also, I felt hurt and was silenced when I tried to name the harm I felt had been done to me. There wasn't space to name how the dynamic was unhealthy for me. There wasn't space to share that I was having panic attacks on my bathroom floor.

Initially, I played with describing the scene this way:

The community held incredible and very patient space for me to express my emotions. My housemate and her mom shared vulnerably of themselves. I had moments of vulnerability as well and practiced open conflict in ways I had avoided before. There were both tears (mine) and laughter (shared and toward the end). They both expressed an openness to continue to share

space with me, even concluding that I was not allowed to move out, at least not yet, and not by leaving behind an aftermath of having generated such dishonest negativity (my words, not theirs). Personally, I slept excellently that night and woke up feeling relieved.

But now rereading my words, I'm not so sure that that is what I actually experienced. In its retelling, I see myself superimposing the good, anti-racist white-lady analysis onto the turn of events. I see my feelings of indebtedness, obligation, and guilt about Black women's emotional labor come through. I see myself rushing for dualistic clarity. In the moment, I was defensive, but in its aftermath, I rush to name the ways I was racist and wrong as a white lady. I rush to internalize the corrections Felicia and Kayla named for me.

I may have believed it when I wrote it. But now another layer emerges. Perhaps it's because I am extending grace to myself and because I am beginning to take Felicia off the pedestal I put her on. I am beginning to humanize us both.

Sure, I can write a neatly wrapped-up anti-racist analysis, but is it my truth?

The theme of that conversation, the three of us triangulated in the living room, was fear, specifically my fear. Felicia said she could smell it the moment she opened the door. Fear was the monster I had been feeding as I tiptoed around Kayla in a melodramatic show of appeasement. The house was in my name. The racial advantage on my side. So why couldn't I engage my agency?

When I think back on the situation with more distance, I realize I had been trying so hard not to fail them, when ultimately, I had been failing myself.

Former therapist and personal coach Mollie Birney differentiates between authentic and inauthentic compassion. "True compassion," she writes, "is on the other side of our difficult feelings, and comes as a result of validating our reactions and skillfully communicating." While "compassion that requires us to invalidate our own feelings" is not only inauthentic, "it's self-manipulation."[1] She lists some of the ways we can force ourselves into inauthentic compassion, such as by judging, intellectualizing, rationalizing, and excusing someone else's behavior, which are all paths toward self-abandonment.

Well, that is a list I identify with. In trying so hard to be in right anti-racist relationship with my chosen family, I did all those things. I rationalized Kayla's behaviors and my feelings about them. I responded to Felicia's corrections by judging my feelings and trying to think them into an anti-racist shape. Perhaps I had been practicing self-abandonment in these relationships all along.

I have my regrets, but they aren't necessarily that I was afraid or that I tried to leave the situation. Instead, my regrets are about how I abandoned myself. I regret not pushing back on Kayla's initial refusal to leave. I regret not standing up more for myself in June after I'd summoned enough courage to initiate the second conversation. I wish I had been able to validate my own truths while still being open to receiving the hard truths of their feedback. I imagine that had I fought harder for my Self, I might have been able to move from a place of authentic compassion.

Certainly, as Felicia named, fear and my internalized racism had been present—even my move to move out was, in some ways and unavoidably, me opting out. But also, it was me opting in to a loving acceptance of what was and where I was at the time, an acknowledgment of my very human limitations.

I see parallels between that messy living situation and the ruptures that happen for white people upon realizing our racial ignorance, when we realize we haven't known what we haven't known. Maybe it arrives as a big aha moment, an epic call-out or call-in, but equally as likely it forms slowly, like a series of small seismic murmurs, the sand sinking out from under us, granularly.

That rupture is in many ways a rupture within ourselves. How had we not known? How have we been so ignorant? How is it that something so pervasive, so obvious to so many others has been hiding in plain sight our entire lives?* Race and racism have been embedded

---

* Hiding in Plain Sight is also the name of a workshop series on anti-racist and white culture I collaborated on with educator Ivonne Ortega for white parents, educators, and child caregivers.

in our social structures and laws and schools and hospitals and yet, we have not really known. It has influenced our lives, our families' lives, the lives of our ancestors. It has been in our thoughts and bodies, and we had no idea. We hadn't known that we needed to watch out for the racism inside of us. We hadn't known to be afraid.

That moment of rupture can feed a particular form of self-doubt, especially for those of us who navigate a sense of internalized inferiority based on other aspects of our identities. I wonder how much the calls to follow Black and Indigenous leadership, the calls to humble ourselves as people who have been taught to be in charge, are getting co-opted by our self-doubt. Perhaps our unhealed Mistress Syndrome is appropriating #TrustBlackWomen and channeling it into a deep distrust of our Selves.

Why is it that I have been nurturing a deep distrust of my Self? What is it that I'm so afraid of? Perhaps it is my own power that has me so afraid. Like the collective power that provoked the witch hunts, the embodied power that had the puritans crack down, the feminine power that sent my dad scrambling for biblical justifications of patriarchy, these forms of power wouldn't have been targeted if they hadn't posed a threat.

I am seeing that in many ways I have been deeply afraid of my own power. I have been afraid of me.

A SEED PLANTED

A few years before Kayla moved back in, a small group of us gathered around the dining room table. Felicia was still living with me during this time, but wouldn't be for much longer. She had met the love of her life but did not know it yet.

We had just wrapped up our second major youth event. There was one particular moment in the workshop that stood out: a "come-to-Jesus moment," Felicia called them. These pivotal moments—in which (most usually) a white person enacted a micro-aggression and/or argued with the facilitator and/or resisted participating (as everyone had agreed to do)—usually included some sort of confrontation, a call-out, or a call-in, depending on your perspective, when the person and dynamic presented itself to the group as an opportunity for everyone to learn.

Addressing such behaviors in the moment was important and part of what made this workshop's style both unique and difficult for many people. These moments also provided incredible opportunities to shift the space from a heady, intellectualized discussion about racism to working with actual, palpable examples in the moment as they happened. Such confrontational moments offered the white folks in the room clear examples of how racism was showing up and how to name and interrupt it. For the participants who were of color, it affirmed their experiences; unlike in white organizations, in this space, racism would be explicitly addressed and named.

This time the moment happened with a white woman who had been invited as a guest. She had said a problematic thing. Felicia addressed it. There was pushback and an exchange. I remember the young people leaving that day energized. As they walked out the door, a couple of youth discussed with a mixture of glee and disbelief that a white woman had been openly corrected in their space.

I remember a familiar feeling, too, a mixture of disappointment (in myself), gratitude, and guilt. Again, I had figured out what was going on "too late," realized the racism after it had appeared and been addressed. It was impossible to catch up with what these Black bodied folks have had to attune to their whole lives—racism's facial expressions before the words came, its subtle posture and posturing, the almost imperceptible energy of white supremacy that radiated from across the room.

While I struggled to attune myself to covert racism's body language, I was finding it much easier to attune myself to the energetic subtleties of the Black women I knew. *I may never be able to pick up on the problematic thing in enough time to intervene*, I thought, *but at least I could attune myself to its impact.* I may not be able to trust myself enough to sense it directly, but I could trust those around me with their lifetimes of experience to pick up on the vibes.

In the days after that youth workshop, Felicia convened a follow-up meeting with the white committee members, which is how we ended up around the dining room table, smiling at each other, anxious on our insides.

In advance of the meeting, Felicia had sent us an article for prereading. I frantically skimmed the article looking for a clear reason she had sent it: What was the lesson? The takeaway? The hidden script I was supposed to pick up on and more deeply understand? The article was interesting, but I wasn't getting its application. I had a vague feeling I had done something "wrong." I wished again that I'd confronted the white lady. Felicia once again had had to do the emotional labor on behalf of us all…on behalf of me.

Tucked away in the folder of this memory are some quickly scribbled notes:

- A debrief of what happened
- A question to assess our understanding
- A reflection question about our whiteness
- A desire to also be held accountable

Then she said, "One day, you will all be able to hold me accountable, too."

I was skeptical, dubiousness sculpted all over my face. She noticed and looked me in the eye. "Yes, I want you to hold me accountable," she said firmly. Then with compassion, she suggested, "Start to try with the little things."

Ha! I thought on the inside. *Now, this was a ridiculous expectation.* There's no way I, her student who was twenty years younger and still learning—and always would be—about what my whiteness meant, would ever be able to hold her accountable…and *as a peer.* I breathed in the idea for a moment but refused to let it take hold, though the idea lingered in my consciousness, descending like a dandelion seed every now and then before drifting off in the wind.

DECONSTRUCTING ACCOUNTABILITY

Throughout our years of collaborating, Felicia gave out more of my business cards than I did. Many other friends and colleagues sent their confused white people my way. Which is how a year or so after that dining room debrief a friend and colleague's white coworker emailed me for support, asking about accountability.

"Thank you for sharing vulnerably and naming some of the difficulties in building accountable partnerships in organizing," I responded in my email. "Your dilemma sounds familiar. Right now with White Women's Groups, we are getting requests to start new groups. Even though I have a committed, clear accountable organizing relationship with Felicia and YogaRoots On Location, I recognize for this work to be sustainable, those accountable relationships can't only exist through me as the facilitator. I think a lot about how to support and challenge WWG members to build their own personal relationships in addition to and beyond our group accountability. Centering the relational aspect means I prioritize building authenticity and—when I'm able—grounding within ongoing relationships."

Ah, accountability...This was something I obsessed over. Of all our organizing principles, accountability was the one that felt most important. It was nonnegotiable. It was the ultimate measure of integrity. To lose accountable relationships was to lose the legitimate ability to do the work.

I can, on occasion, downplay my work (it's the Mennonite Humble coming through), but this was one aspect of anti-racism organizing I did not mask with humility. I was honored to be in accountable relationship with Black organizers I respected. I believed that the effectiveness of the work ultimately depended on it.

Yet now I write this, three thousand miles from the Pittsburgh communities I worked so hard to be accountable to. I am no longer in the same relationships I deemed so crucial to "the work." I am questioning my interpretation of accountability. I am remembering my rigidity and dogmatism around it. I am reflecting on how my deference created an unsustainable power dynamic. How did my fear of doing and being wrong ultimately forfeit my self-agency and, moreover, my accountability to myself? Experience is a bitch.

Let me be more specific as I go back in time.

We were only a few months in when I asked WWG to share back their Anti-Racist Family History Projects. We were investigating how our family lineages became white, what we had lost because of it, and what harm was done to Black, Indigenous, and other People of Color as a result. I had invited Felicia and her husband to join us for the WWG shareback.

To say it went disastrously would be an understatement. I facilitated a movement exercise. "That's white people stuff," Felicia said, raising her eyebrows. I began to notice something was off as soon as the first WWG member shared about how her family had built a rural PA town. Okay, I pushed the initial uncomfortable feeling aside, noting what I'd need to address later. We still needed to get through six more presentations. After the second presentation had the group, including our Jewish guest, sing "O Christmas Tree" in German, Felicia stood up and left. Her husband followed.

The white women who had courageously gone first were left with an intensity of emotions. Well, we all were. I felt responsible for having curated harm in the space. I had been the one who set the questions, guided their approach to family history, missed important corrections that might have prevented what our guests had endured in their brief visit to the WWG space.

Miraculously—and moreover to the credit of the people who stayed engaged—repair was on the other side. I penned apology letters to Felicia and her husband, taking responsibility, apologizing for my ignorance and oversights. Her husband said it was the best apology letter he'd ever received. Felicia dealt with it in stride; clearly, we had more work to do. Some of the white women left in the aftermath, but the remaining small group proved to be a committed and courageous force.

The next year's shareback was an open house. WWG members invited friends and family. It was an organizing opportunity. No one left in distress. People's moms attended with curiosity.

Then the following year, Felicia proposed we engage some of the Black women from her yoga teacher training as accountability partners. The idea was to expand the accountability partnership so that WWG didn't so entirely rely on her as our only advisor.

We assembled once again at my place, the group now consisting of five white women, myself, five accountability partners, and Felicia. I've filed this story away in a folder marked Someone Else Was in the Hot Seat, though I don't remember for what. It was uncomfortable to witness though, the intensity for my fellow white woman, the emotional extension of our accountability partner. I have no doubt that what our accountability partner had said was valid, relevant, and helpful, yet what I mostly remember was the flush of my face, my anxiety in sharing, the relief that this time it wasn't my racism that was being so publicly addressed.

Afterward, we apologized for our racial ignorance and causing harm. We committed to do better. Our accountability partners left feeling disappointed. They had expected more from the white ladies of WWG who had so diligently been working to undo our racism. With nervous optimism, they had suspended their skepticism for this one moment, out of relationship to Felicia and me. Yet, we again had disappointed them, perhaps proving their suspicions correct: giving of themselves for white ladies had indeed been a waste of their energy and time.

Yet, Felicia continued to read every WWG email. She made herself available to debrief WWG quandaries. She supported me when yet another member left the group. She advised when it was time to shut down the fourth iteration and then insisted on the creation of a fifth. Her yoga business was growing, which meant there were more white women to support. How could WWG grow to meet this demand? How could those who'd been part of WWG for the past three years be part of that expansion?

Over a year after our last accountability meeting, after lots of mapping and swirls and charts, we were ready to present our ideas to a newly assembled group of accountability partners identified by Felicia and invited by me. Once again, these were Black women I had relationships with and whose perspectives I valued.

Though this time we were on Zoom.

My armpits had sweated through the outfit I'd carefully chosen to instill self-confidence and boost my mood. My laptop sat on the top of Aunt Amanda's cedar chest. I opened the Zoom Room and immediately all the accountability partners appeared. The energy was high. We joked and laughed and waited for the white ladies, which was not the usual order of things. The white ladies were typically punctual. Their absence made me nervous. My stomach sank at the thought of having to do it all on my own.

Eventually the paler faces popped up on the screen. We continued to laugh and joke until an offense shifted the mood.

One of our accountability partner's life partner had a growing business selling baked products. "I saw their cookies at the co-op!" I said, excitedly. "Have you tried the stone fruit hand pies?" another person chimed in. "Yums" and "Mmmmms" came from everyone who had.

"Oh, I love to bake," said one of the white ladies, in an effort to connect. "Do they share recipes?" The laughter became stilted, awkward. My smile froze and the distance between my eyebrows became shorter.

"No," the baker's partner said, firmly. "It's their business."

There were stern nods of agreement all around. Okay, it was addressed, I thought. And the meeting moved forward, the tone noticeably more somber, as I presented a vision for WWG expansion, an anti-racist pyramid scheme of sorts.

I remember feeling the weight of my fellow white ladies' silences. I remember wishing we had prepared more for how we would present. I remember wondering where all their enthusiasm had gone; our last WWG planning meeting ended upbeat, positive, and energized. I remember feeling responsible again for having convened all these fabulous advisors, and once again, having so little to show for it.

One of our accountability partners asked a question, which was met with silence. Eventually, we eked out a couple responses. The answers weren't sufficient. She expressed how disappointed she felt, especially that not a single one of us had held our white sister accountable earlier when she asked such a disrespectful thing. It had been on our accountability partner to do that. Our advisor left the call.

More silence.

I didn't know what to do or say. A huge wave of sadness overcame me. *Speak your truth. Name what you feel,* I heard Felicia's voice say in my head. So, I did. I named what I felt.

"I feel sad…" I began to say.

Felicia cut me off abruptly. "Enough of your sadness, Amanda. I am tired of your sadness. That's the problem." She was frustrated. She wanted to know about joy. "What is bringing you joy?"

I was shocked, then angry. *Is she telling me how to feel?* I wondered, frustrated and confused.

"Well, now I feel angry that you're telling me how to feel."

It was my truth.

The rest of the meeting was a short blur. Eventually the white ladies rallied enough to share some joy practices. Felicia facilitated the process. I ended it awkwardly.

Immediately following there was a call from Felicia with all the accountability partners on it: the meeting after the meeting. She was surprised when I answered. "Did you mean for me to be on this, too?" I asked. It seemed she hadn't.

But the universe had.

Once again, I was privy to the insights of Black women whose opinions I trusted. "It's a beautiful expansion plan," one advisor said, "but they aren't ready." Silently, I wondered if I was the one who wasn't ready.

Our accountability partners expressed disappointment, anger, rage…another misuse of their energy. They had hoped for more. They had hoped for different. But here we were, a group of white ladies disappointing them again. "They're not even trying!" one person exclaimed, exasperated. "They are trying," Felicia corrected. "They're trying very hard."

Hmmm, I thought later, *maybe that's the problem. We're trying too hard.*

After we hung up, I thought about the many apologies I had written each time after the accountability moments of the past. It had taken six years for me to notice the pattern, the many WWG accountability meetings, the emails and texts from Kayla, the corrections in the living room. I stared at the nineteenth-century cedar chest.

It's a setup, I thought. I may have even said this aloud.

In the meeting, I had done precisely what Felicia had asked of me in the past. I expressed in the moment my honest feelings and she had rejected it. She was dismissive of the truth she had worked so hard to have me say. She didn't hold space for me.

"She's just human," I told Aunt Amanda's cedar chest.

It was a revelation of sorts. I mean, I knew Felicia was human, but somehow as my teacher, mentor, and accountability partner, I had carved out an exceptional space for her perspective and wisdom. I had weighed the value of her perspective more than others and even more than my own. I had trusted her to have the collective well-being, including mine, in mind. I never considered that I would need to stand up for myself with her, that I might adamantly disagree.

I thought back to the moment in June a few months before when I knew the living arrangement wasn't healthy for me. I had tried to leave. "You need to stay and work it out with Kayla," she had said then. *She must know better*, I thought, as I gave up trusting what my body had been screaming at me for months.

I had given my trust and agency away, and that was on me.

It was as if suddenly I put on the glasses I reserve for night driving. Perhaps all these accountability meetings had been setups, too. Ultimately, we were creating a dynamic of codependency, a self-fulfilling prophecy of sorts. Of course our accountability partners found something wrong with our work—that's what we were asking them to do. Our accountability partners came each time, hopeful that the white ladies wouldn't be racist, and of course we still were. The white ladies came each time fearful that our racism would still be there and that it would show, and of course it still was and did.

For years, I've had a little story in my head about all the things that are wrong with me, including my inability to be vulnerable enough. Few things clam me up more than being instructed to "be vulnerable," "act authentically," "just be yourself." When I hear that advice,

I search my mind for how to do it. My body freezes. I can't feel my arms. My shoulders constrict. I am just now coming to terms with how difficult and challenging anti-racism spaces have been for me.

Moreover, contriving a culture of dependency in which only Black women (or BIPOC individuals and communities) can hold white people accountable uses the same tired hierarchy dynamics of imperialist white-supremacist capitalist patriarchy; it just switches out the players. In the name of anti-racism, I was reinforcing a racist dynamic that the burden of ending racism must ultimately reside with those most impacted—be it for their approval or critique.

I'm not saying that white people should take the lead or single-handedly make strategic plans, nor am I saying that white people shouldn't put energy and resources into BIPOC-led movements and campaigns or establish long-term relationships of accountability with BIPOC organizers. Those are all important and strategic ways to organize (and we'll go into it more in the last chapter). But what I am pointing out are some of the pitfalls of unquestionably following really anyone's leadership. I am naming how my own internalization of white cultural models led me to contribute to this dynamic. I'm saying that if my liberation is tied up with yours, then the (co)dependency that's been created in many of our anti-racist organizing models is not helping us to get free.

And even more specifically, what I'm saying is that Mistress Syndrome has made me deeply distrust myself, that the guise of antiracist dogma gave me another external structure to hold onto when taking responsibility for constant discernment felt too overwhelming. It gave me a rulebook when trusting my gut was too scary. It gave me a roadmap to appease my fear of my own power and agency. The "there's-no-rulebook" talk is really one I've needed to give to myself.

I have wanted there to be a right, anti-racist way to be in these messily human relationships, but there isn't. There are only the ways I choose, the ways others choose, and the ways we choose (or don't choose) to be in them together.

Felicia was my teacher and mentor and accountability partner. I learned from her in many ways, but there was also a point where I started to try to emulate. I thought I was learning how to be true to myself in mimicking her leadership, but I was only learning another way to not be me.

This accountability aha moment and the subsequent deterioration of our relationship has asked big and scary questions of me: What would it mean for me as a white woman to do this work without the backing and legitimacy of an accountability partner? What would it mean to relocate the core of my accountability within myself?

* * *

It was the last moment. The moving truck was packed. Kayla still had the house keys, so I was sure she, Felicia, and Felicia's husband—or Felicia at the very least—would swing by on their way out to say goodbye. After all, I was only a block away.

I was upstairs getting ready for my own move. I could still see their moving truck through the sparsely leafed autumn trees as I sorted through thirteen years of my Pittsburgh life. When I looked up again the truck was gone, but there was a text on my phone from Kayla. She had dropped off the keys in the mailbox. *Oh*, I breathed in sharply, *I guess that was the goodbye*.

A month later I left too, driving to Mexico for sunshine, distance, and perspective.

Though we still had one shared piece of work, or rather, I had promised Felicia some workshop support.

I tried it out the first week, even though my gut was grumbling "no." The session moved in slow motion. My facilitation flowed with surprising ease, probably because by this point I had nothing to lose. But my heart wasn't into it. I felt the integrity of my work slipping away.

I fought with myself about it at first using the old tools. I rationalized that I shouldn't go back on my word, fearful it would place further distance between me and my organizing community. Besides, it was my main source of income. I tried to rally myself.

But deep down I knew it was not to be. I listened to my body. I changed my mind. I remembered those were lessons Felicia had taught me. I moved from a place of grounded grief. I extended myself compassion and space.

When I told Felicia on the last day of the week, I offered to finish out the month until she had someone else in place. We left the call with her suggesting I sleep on it, but the next morning she sent out a text to the team saying it had been my last day. I guess none of us want to be the one who gets left.

I thought back to the many times after we had been through something together. "You can put this in your tell all," she'd say, half-jokingly, half-sincere. Which I suppose I have, although I had no intention of writing any such book at the time.

CHAPTER FIFTEEN

BURYING THE LEDE

This is hospice work. We are watching these folks pass away.
We just have to hold space gracefully and save our energy
for the advocates already letting themselves be known.
—Conly Basham

But you don't have to take my word for it.
—Levar Burton

I'm not so convinced about endings.
—Donna F. Henson

C ovid got my great-uncle Samuel when he was 101 and a half
years old.

My first memory of him was at his wife's viewing. I was seven,
maybe eight years old. This was my first encounter with the formal
drapes of funeral homes. I remember shiny end tables with carefully
placed floral displays. The vibrance of the fresh-cut bouquets disagreed
with the stiff, heavy furniture and uncomfortable seating that made
me squirm. My mosquito-bitten legs dangled off the hard cushions,
which threatened to confine the slightest urge for play. *Dying meant*
not growing anymore, I thought. My great-aunt Elizabeth, who I
had not really known, would no longer grow. Neither would these
bouquets of flowers, cut for the consolation of human impermanence.

In this, my earliest memory of my great-uncle Sam (in his later years, he would ask to be called by his full given name, Samuel), he is ancient yet warm and kind and not at all frightening like the old people in German fairy tales. On that day at the funeral parlor, next to his wife's casket, he greeted me with an easy sincerity. He leaned forward, and, undeterred by our difference in age, deeply thanked me for the condolences my mother had reminded me to say.

I made him a card after the viewing. It was handmade, probably decorated with one of the flower motifs I had been practicing during that era. I don't remember all the specifics of how our relationship emerged, but I do recall that of my grandma's seven brothers, he was the one I felt closest to. I was one of dozens (hundreds?) of grand-nieces and grand-nephews and he consistently remembered my name. Later, when I was in college, I had the occasional privilege of visiting with him and his second wife at the Mennonite retirement center down the road from the Mennonite school I attended.

I have a vague memory of my father speaking fondly of Uncle Samuel; perhaps he was referencing the era when my parents lived in that same town while attending the same school as I had. My parents were freshly partnered then, married at the ages of twenty and twenty-one and inhabiting a trailer that my father had wired to give you a little *zing* every time you reached for the metal front doorknob. The story went that the bonus shock was an accident, proof of why he did not become an electrician. Sometimes my mother told the story to explain why she called repair people rather than ask my dad to fix things around the house.

My great uncle Samuel, who had stark white hair, a beard, and an uncanny resemblance to the Uncle Sam of settler colonial lore, passed away on January 6, 2021, the same day a highly organized mob of armed insurrectionists stormed the US Capitol building in an attempt to overthrow the government.

Uncle Samuel had lived his life in accordance with Anabaptist nonviolence yet taken a vocal stance in politics and racial justice unusual for white Mennonites of his generation. It was after I hung up from a heavy phone call with my dad that I first remembered, and then doubted my memory of, his expression of fondness. In my own sentimentality, perhaps I was misremembering. Maybe I had inserted the fondness expressed by my aunt's husband into the mouth of my dad. Maybe my father and my great uncle Samuel hadn't gotten along after all. Maybe they had actually had heated political debates? I couldn't imagine my father having any political disagreement with ease. Over the past thirty-some years, he and I certainly hadn't.

That same heavy phone call with my dad just days after the attempted insurrection didn't include any of the fiery political debates that had shaped the past decades of our exchanges. Remarkably, talking to him about politics couldn't have been further from my mind. I was calling him out of sincere concern for his well-being.

My mother had frantically texted me hours before, snapping me out of a leisurely morning on the western coast of Baja, Mexico. "We should talk soon," she texted. "Not going back to the condo with dad."

My parents had been in a stalemate for several months now. On top of some very significant transitions in their lives (selling my childhood home, my dad's retirement, moving into a small condo while buying and renovating a second home in a different state), the pandemic had been concretizing the political into daily consequences in ways America usually reserves for People of Color and the poor, though my parents still had the privilege of their outs. My dad was refusing to observe the Covid social distancing practices my mother requested, so for several months they had been trading living arrangements, metaphorically waving at each other on I-85 as they exchanged destinations.

I called my mom. "He agreed to wear a mask and apologized for how he acted about it," she shared. I winced, knowing how difficult it must have been for my stubborn father to openly take responsibility for a stance he'd been doubling down on for months. This turn was significant, unprecedented even.

I winced, too, and my heart hurt because his shift was too little too late. The final straw was his support of the insurgents. "He believes the conspiracy theories, that the election was rigged. I can't be around him." My mother was devastated, disgusted, done with it all, and also worried about him. "It'd be good if you reached out."

I texted my brother, who was already upset. I assumed he had engaged my father about the insurrection. "He's impossible to talk to, he just gets defensive," he texted me back.

Which is how I ended up on the phone with my election-doubting father, deeply concerned for his emotional state and reassuring him I would not ostracize him for his political beliefs.

He may have been paranoid about fake news and the left-wing media, but my father's fears of familial ostracization were well-founded. Over the past decades, our political bickering had led to several stretches of distanced silence. I would call home from college to talk with mom. "Tell dad I say hi," I ended the conversation with no intention of telling him myself. Long gone were the days of daddy-daughter dates at Atlanta greasy spoons, for pancakes and conversation and quality time.

He was responsible for some of the distance, too, for sure. Gradually at first, and then seemingly rapidly, he filled his bookshelves with right-wing ideological propaganda, as if building a fortress of protection in the midst of what he perceived as a bastion of liberalism, specifically Atlanta and our family. He stacked his shelves with selections from Christian bookstores about the natural differences between men and women. He filled his ears with Rush Limbaugh and other conservative sound waves, which demonized a "certain kind" of poor person. Either you were with my father and his God or against them both. His walls seemed to get higher and more rigid as I developed an analysis of power. The more I expressed my developing political beliefs, the more solidified he became in his.

One trip home from college, while looking for a casual read, I skimmed his library and stumbled upon a how-to book of theological arguments against feminism. I probably should have kept it moving, but ultimately, the pull to have my rage validated was too strong. Already cynical, I pulled the antifeminist literature off the shelf. The book was not a quick and casual read. Instead, it was a lengthy treatise that suggested feminist rhetoric and then debunked each idea with

multiple talking points and biblical annotations. Its basic format went
something like this:

"If a feminist says…
what they really mean is…
and you should disagree with them by saying…"

About half of the described feminist ideals were misinterpretations
bent to fire up a reaction for the book's target audience, but the other
half were actual basic tenets of feminism, like how thinking that men
should be the spiritual head of the household is a problematic and
sexist idea. Those blatant sexist arguments were the ones that most
fueled my anger.

Enraged at his treason to my humanity, I opened his desk drawer.
I grabbed the first pen I could find. I crossed out phrases and wrote
out my disagreements in the margins. I was furious, steaming. I placed
the now newly annotated book back on his shelf to decide whether I
wanted to address it with him in person or leave my passive-aggressive
markings for him to discover later. With twisted glee, I imagined him
reaching for the book one day when faced with a real-life encounter
with "scary" feminist ideology. Just in his time of need, I saw him
opening the book to a page of redactions. Rather than rely on the
patriarchal propaganda, he would have to come up with his own
words.

He probably wouldn't even have any, I thought bitterly.

Sometimes, in my mind, I see my father as a caricature of right-
wing talking points. From Reagan to W to 45, my father has been
line in step. At night using my parent's cable, I would watch the late-
night talk shows' video reels of five to seven Republicans repeating
the exact same phrases my father had uttered that evening at dinner.

Mostly, my idea of him and his ideologies have fueled my rage.
But lately, I have been feeling more sadness, softness, and even the
inklings of compassion. When I pull out the file labeled Antifeminist Bookshelf Incident: feelings: hurt, rage, smugness (that
my suspicions had been confirmed), I feel less emotionally impacted

by the violence of the book itself. Instead, I am struck by how fearful he must have been to have surrounded himself with such shields. I am struck by how deep his insecurities must be for him to seek being propped up by others' words, rather than access his own critical thinking.

This recent softening toward my father has prompted me to reflect on myself. I wince, because there's a parallel here in my reliance on anti-oppression terminology and dependency on the opinions of Black, Indigenous, and other People of Color whom I respect and regard as "authorities."

It feels tender to admit that I, too, have surrounded myself with books, articles, and singularly vetted perspectives. At times, my inquiries have been out of genuine curiosity to learn, grow, and love better. But, at many other moments, I have been compelled by my insecurities. I've used shelves of history books and pages of diligently taken notes to buffer anxieties that my experience, emotions, and intuition are no match for the structural legitimacy of rational scientific ways of knowing and the words of politically backed religious men. I have spent hours preparing for debates on other people's terms. I have invested energy in the rote memorization of the "right" words and followed other people's strategies without being honest with myself about mine.

In our father-daughter dynamic, I have felt insecure about my ability to coherently articulate my beliefs. I, too, have felt threatened by the slightest challenge. I have felt the desperation of proving and defending my perspective at all costs. I have been afraid that opening myself up even a little bit to others' critiques would threaten everything I believe in, or at least everything I believe about myself.

I'm not equating our circumstances and certainly I'm not insinuating that our ideologies or lived experiences are in some way equivalent; to do so would be to follow the mistakes of white liberalism, which in striving for equality flattens out very real power dynamics and thus continues disproportionate impact. It would be unhelpful to erase these distinctions in a search for a vague humanized commonality, to view us as polar opposites on a linear continuum of "The

Left" and "The Right," to pretend our differences could be mediated without the accountability of justice, repairing of harm, and an earth-moving shift of power.

However, we are also not unrelated. We share the same DNA. Post-Traumatic Master and Mistress Syndromes come from the same virus. The uncomfortable fact is that he and I have similarities in our insecurities and responses. Our worldviews may be incommensurable, but our processes—the need to be "right," defensiveness as a trauma response, and an underlying motivation of fear—are all learned behaviors of white supremacy culture and ones that we share.

But I am digressing into the comfortable orbit of analysis, mostly because I am avoiding much more complex emotional galaxies. Like an amateur magician, I am distracting you (well, mostly me) with my showy comparisons while the real magic happens in my other hand. It is the hand I am not comfortable with you seeing. As Karriem gently asked after listening to me name that I felt concern for my father's alienation, "Do you feel guilty that you contributed to your father's situation?"

The short answer is yes.

I don't remember all the details of the heated conversation that followed the antifeminist bookshelf incident. But I do remember that I was unable to keep my rage to myself. As soon as my dad came home from work, I exploded. If not at the door the moment he entered the house, the confrontation most certainly occurred at the dinner table over my mother's lovingly cooked food. I remember expressing my anger to him, and then my underlying hurt. I remember it not going well. I remember—a repeat of so many times before—I argued first the facts and then, after watching him get defensive, laid bare my heart in a desperate plea that he acknowledge me: "Can't you see how your views hurt me?" I eventually got at my underlying pain. I remember that we left even more entrenched than when we started.

I had called Karriem a few hours after I hung up the call with my dad.

"I don't know that I feel guilty," I replied to Karriem's question, contradicting parts of myself. I shifted back and forth on my bed, trying guilt on like a new pair of jeans. Even though it resonated, the word "guilt" wasn't an exact fit, too loose in the waist. "I don't feel like I had the skills to do it differently. I don't regret naming things and expressing my feelings all those times. No one else was holding him accountable, and silencing myself certainly wouldn't have been the answer. I am proud I chose to use my voice. But I do feel bad that he felt alienated and that he feels that way now. I guess I feel a sense of responsibility to him and to my family…and to the world."

The world certainly knows how dangerous an alienated-feeling white man can be.

RESPONSIBILITY WITH VS. RESPONSIBILITY FOR

This sense of responsibility has been an undercurrent throughout most of my life, especially showing up when I contemplate my vocation and life's purpose on this earth. In moments of unhealth, I've conflated my sense of responsibility with the more punitive concept of obligation. I have at times allowed myself to get bogged down by the burden of my ancestors' sins. I've been motivated, sometimes unconsciously, by the duty to make right the (collective) wrongs of the past. I have taken on the task of repairing multigenerational trauma on behalf of my entire family line. Even the name I chose for my work, Mistress Syndrome, invokes the violence, trauma, and illness of millions of people.

I have also at times felt responsible for my father's politics. It's not that I feel responsible for him having those views in the first place: I don't. But I have believed it was up to me to challenge his behavior, or who else would? I have taken the call from anti-racist organizing spaces to "organize your own" very seriously. Those spaces challenged me to collect my family members, and—overachiever that I am—I set out to collect them all.

And while I am thrilled for recent shifts toward anti-racism within my family and the conversations we've been able to have, I am painfully aware of the ineffectiveness of my actions to support my father in moving away from harmful ideologies. In these cases, my motivations have been mixed. At the same time that I deeply desired collective liberation, I have also been impatient for others—mainly and especially my father—to change. Willing people to change, I'm learning, is incompatible with unconditional love.

But I also think, and I am realizing, that this sense of responsibility is one of my superpowers. In its healthy form, it's less of an I-am-responsible-for-the-behaviors-of-others-and-therefor-obliged-to-fix-them attitude. It's less of an ancestral burden and more of a knowing sensitivity. A slight prepositional shift has made all the difference. The sense of being responsible *with* and not *for* others invites me to attune to them and the quality of our relationships, but not take on the baggage of their actions. Being responsible with others also challenges my individualism when I am tempted to wash my hands of uncomfortable relationships. A sense of responsibility in this way encourages me to notice relational fibers and the whole of the familial fabric. Perhaps it tells of a form of collective accountability that is rooted in myself.

Most importantly, I'm learning that the superpower of my sensitivity emerges when I am sensitive to myself. In its healthiest form, responsibility asks me to respect both interconnectedness and boundaries, to see the similarities in our reactions at the same time as the differences in our orientations. Within this sensitivity, there is the possibility to hold my father accountable for egregious behaviors, and interrelatedly, to hold his humanity as sacred, just as I am learning to do so for myself.

The possibility for this both/and is invigorating and fuzzy like a gust of cool air on a warm sunny day, suddenly alerting my forearm hairs to its presence. I can feel that it exists. I know it's here, but I have no idea what it is to manifest. When I look around for white people who have practiced this both/and before, especially with their family members, I find few mentors. Instead, I keep encountering those on a similar search. Mostly, I find people who ask me to be their guide. Sure, brisk air is invigorating, but I would much prefer to bask in the consistent shine of the sun.

Sometimes, I get grouchy that I do not yet know how to be both honest and to genuinely love. I get mad at the confused fuzziness that comes when I try to imagine visionary yet reality-based alternatives. Really, I am irritated that I must try and err and work for what I am looking for. I am annoyed that I can't Google-search my way to transformation, that I can't order it online, that the how-to manual will not arrive on my front doorstep via next-day delivery and by punching in the numbers from my credit card. I am annoyed at myself for this as well: beneath its tranquilizing convenience, capitalism has been disappearing my creativity.

Yet, even as I grumble about the hard work (privately to myself and rarely aloud), I am feeling the potential of both its futurism and its here-and-nowness. During those early 2021 days of family and nation-state upheaval, I began feeling a concern and compassion for my dad in a way I had not felt before, or at least not in a long time.

When I shared the scope of these feelings with Karriem, he asked a second and even stickier question: "What has caused you to have compassion for him in this moment and not before?" This is the question I've been sifting through.

The most obvious answer is that I am accessing more compassion for him because I have been practicing more compassion for myself. Perhaps working to love all parts of me, including the nooks and crannies where my white supremacy hides, is helping me have compassion for my dad and even the parts of him that embrace white-supremacist thinking.

"What has caused you to have compassion for him in this moment and not before?"

I scroll my mind for more possible answers. On that phone call, my dad seemed so vulnerable, so afraid of being alone. I felt sympathetic. When my dad shared that he was afraid of being isolated from the family, his voice slightly cracking as he did so, I was reminded of the many instances when I had felt that way too. My directness has also repulsed others. I remembered the contracts I didn't get, the friendships that fell apart, and the times family members stopped speaking to me. In a family and culture that has preferred superficial harmony to uncomfortable conflict, a part of me has always respected my father's blunt honesty. Even though his truths can be devastating to hear, I know the courage required to speak an unpopular opinion and the energy of a dissenting crowd.

But along with my growing empathy and self-compassion, there is something else happening caused by a ripple effect in our family patterns. The silver lining of this recent era of US politics is that its overt white supremacy is compelling white folks who have been quiet(er) to engage in the struggle, my mother and brother included.

THE WORK CONTINUES

That summer, after the murders of Breonna Taylor and George Floyd, after the murders of so many other Black and Brown people by police and vigilantes in a violent pattern that spans centuries, my brother called me to talk about racial justice.

Although we connect easily when we're in person, long-distance telecommunication has never been our forte.

He called me. To talk. About racial justice.

And so did my mom.

It's not that I never had conversations with my mom and brother about such things. We've been having these conversations in many different ways for years, occasionally on the phone, or around the dining-room table. More often than not, I've been the one initiating the discussions, sharing my opinions or strategically weaving in something related to my work; but not always. Sometimes my brother, and even more often, my mother, have brought up genuine questions about current events and wanted to share their thoughts.

But the phone calls of 2021 felt different. For the first time, I was hearing my mother and brother strongly express disgust, anger, rage, frustration, and fear. They weren't just holding space for me to vent or listening respectfully as I shared about my work. They weren't just thinking critically about the issues or mulling over electoral politics; they were feeling it.

They were feeling.

And they weren't only talking to me. Between the lines of texts, I realized they were talking to my dad and talking to each other. My family was talking about racism without me.

My family. Was talking about racism. Without me.

(!)

In my mind I see shooting stars and draw the cutest little rainbows around the folders that will mark these telephone calls. This is the organizer's dream, that the work will continue without their constant support and motivation. Am I living that dream?

I've left the file **My Family was Talking About Racism Without Me!** out on my desk for a month now. It is decorated in glittery rainbow stickers and unicorns reminiscent of my Lisa Frank phase. Each time I glance at it, I feel a sense of immediate physiological release. My shoulder blades drop down the back of my ribcage. My gut expands. My jaw unclenches. My lungs exhale. I am filled with instant relief. I am no longer the only one. It is not all on me. I can share the responsibility. I let out an audible sigh. We can be in this together.

I am reminded of the connection between body and imagination, how constrictions in the body restrict our abilities to imagine an abundance of choices.* Between the self-compassion work and the elastic expansion of my body, I am finding new pathways. The expansion of my thoracic cavity reflects the openings in my relationships. I am inviting new choices in and breathing old patterns out. As I feel less threatened, I am opening more to creative response.

When my father and I talked on that day in early January of 2021, I didn't feel the bubbling rage of the antifeminist bookshelf incident. I didn't feel the press of our previous boundary wars. I didn't feel the burden of thousands of years of European patriarchy heavy on my chest. And I wasn't fueled by a need to correct him. I didn't move toward fight or flight. Instead of being focused on the need to protect myself and others, I felt surprisingly secure…and soft. In that moment on the phone, I realized I could trust myself to be safe enough to be tender with him.

After hanging up, I searched for the familiar feelings of frustration that usually followed our interactions. They weren't there. I didn't feel

---

* Conflict mediation forerunner Paul Wahrhaftig's Tension Triangle model notes that "the higher your level of tension, represented by the vertical line on the side of the diagram, the less options you perceive yourself to have" ("Tension Triangle," 15).

like I needed to abuse my body on the treadmill or eat carbohydrates to fill the void. Instead, there was a feeling of satisfied emptiness in the center of my gut. I sat suspended by the absence of guarded resentment. I felt an initial distrust of the lack of stress. Like waiting for an arriving visitor, I peered at the edges, expecting that eventually they would be there.

Ohhhh, I thought after sitting still for a while. *Maybe this is what healing feels like.*

Just as white ladies have attempted to compete within patriarchy's rules, I have been desperate for my dad to fully see and accept me. I am seeing even more clearly how the past several years' process of letting go of wanting to change him has corresponded with these seismic shifts. There is a yoga dharma talk in here somewhere, a message about surrendering to the divine. Perhaps the biggest reasons for our relational shifts are due to dynamics far beyond my control. Far beyond my reach, his changing life circumstances—the upending of his home, identity, life's work, and family structure—have made him vulnerable. Not anything I did or didn't do.

That phone call was tough and tender. I've covered the folder in a soft cloth case and embroidered gently around its edges. I've redacted a lot of the dialogue with a silver Sharpie because it is sacred.* But I do want to share one other thing. At one moment on the call, my father asked for help. "Maybe you could help me out?" he spoke softly. "Be my guide? Since you've been through divorce before…"

My father asked for help. He reached out. To me.

I apologize; I have totally buried the lede.

On the phone, I was stunned. I hesitated, unprepared for his request. Self-consciously, I mumbled something about being there for him. I wouldn't know what it's like to end forty-eight years of

---

* Eve Tuck and K. Wayne Yang's article "R-Words: Refusing Research" (2014) has helped me to challenge my previous interpretation of sacrificing myself and my family in order to expose every aspect of our whiteness. Considering the Indigenous origins of refusal and the white settler context of my family members' stories, I discerned what to include and what to withhold in this book through an application of Abolitionist Ethics, and, when possible, as part of an ongoing dialogue.

marriage, but I would do my best. Here was the opportunity of a lifetime. In all of our years together, I have never once recalled my father genuinely asking for my help. Here he was acknowledging my experience with something tender and scary. It was my chance to do the dance I've been preparing a lifetime for and all I could do was shuffle my feet.

I buried the lede on the call with Karriem, too. "That's huge!" he said, after I finally got around to the real news. "He asked for your help."

I agreed. It was huge and momentous and earth-shattering, or at least worldview-shattering. But I was also a little apprehensive to celebrate. As in, I didn't quite trust it to be real. As in, the unfamiliarity inspired self-sabotage. This was what I've always thought I wanted and never received: his validation, his acknowledgment of what I've been through, a nod to the work I've done and risks I've taken. To be fully seen.

Why then was I so reticent to believe it to be true? Why was I not elated? The tenderest parts of me felt deeply touched, humbled by his request.

I teared up with Karriem when he acknowledged the significance of my dad's words. I put the phone on mute to retrieve a tissue from the box on the bathroom sink. He noticed my sniffling anyway. "Are you crying? That means it's important." But although I was touched, I was also a bit disoriented, shaken, a little scared to discover that the inflated, wizard of Oz is merely a mortal behind a curtain.

I take full responsibility for placing him there. In my rage and reactionary habits, I've been giving the wizard all this power (over me). I have been fighting for him to see me. What if his power over me has been an illusion this whole time? What if the ways I've been gearing up to fight have been a severe waste of energy? What if the only person my rage is exhausting is me?

I had reached the limits of good guy/bad guy, of villains and saviors. Or rather the limits of dualism had reached me. The mortal behind the curtain, my stand-in for the wicked webs, my motivation to fight for justice was just as fragile and just as flawed. The spiritual teacher/

mentor/mother/auntie/heroine was too. Within the pedestals and curtains of my psyche I had been giving away my agency, fueling the power over dynamics I hoped to resist, exceptionalizing and demonizing, reinforcing unhuman expectations, applying anti-racist rules that skipped over the messier realities of humanity. After all, both my father and Felicia contain multitudes; they could be both dangerous and fragile, both powerful and vulnerable, just like me.

There are parallels here with how easy it is to blame white men for the evils of the world. Yet such a villain archetype facilitates an untruth about both his power and ours. We blame the fascist leader, but not the systems that facilitated his rise. We blame the white men who voted for him, but not the white women who made up the deciding demographic. We, too, give up our power to the wizard of Oz. We are a part of the systems that facilitated it. We are a part of that deciding demographic.

What if we recognized that even our perspectives are within our power to change? As Kaba writes, "We have all so thoroughly internalized these logics of oppression that if oppression were to end tomorrow, we would be likely to reproduce previous structures."[1] The curtains in our psyches are there for us to pull down, the pedestals within our reach to dismantle. The internalization is inside us.

What a gift to do the healing work my ancestors couldn't. What a gift to have the spaciousness to retrieve the filing cabinets of their lingering wounds. What an honor to go further and deeper than they could, to be safe enough to feel again, to be safe enough to extend compassion.

And what an incredible opportunity we have to attend to the psyches of oppression. It is the work we have before us. It is work we can do here and now. What an inspiration and motivator to have the capacity to connect. "Under oppression," Dr. Nieto says, "every single action should be really deadly—and most of them are, but sometimes they're not. Why?…That we connect at all is an absolute miracle."[2] That even after centuries of racism and capitalism, even after colonization and the devaluation of our labor, even after millennia of patriarchy, that we still have the potential to connect at all signals potent possibilities.

Like the illusions of curtain and pedestal, the personal healing work is not separate from our collective liberation. Our wounding is interconnected; our healing is too. Healing from Mistress Syndrome is an interdependent part of healing our collective trauma. Our healing work disrupts patterns and opens pathways for post-traumatic growth. Moreover, our healing is connected to our collective power.

This healing work supports a practice of right relationship with each other, with our Selves, and with the earth. It can help us take responsibility for ourselves as part of a whole, to acknowledge and reclaim our power, and to further discern what is ours to contribute and what is our work to do. Healing from Mistress Syndrome is intrinsic to co-creating different ways of being with each other, to dismantling the master's house together, and it informs how we show up in our movements and how we shift our cultures, psyches, and imaginations for all that will become.

UNCONCLUSION

GOING BACK THROUGH

In order to untie a knot, you have to go back through.
—Felicia Savage Friedman

NO ONE WAY WORKS, it will take all of us shoving at the thing from all sides to bring it down.
—Diane di Prima

The "Revolution Will Not Be Televised,"[1] and this book won't have a conclusion.

I do hate to disappoint you. You have read through so many pages to get to this point. I have tried for a tidy ending, but this is not that. After all, I am still figuring it out. We all are.

Also, I don't want to leave you thinking that white women feeling our feelings will end racism. I mean, that is a part of it. But how is it a part? How might this internal healing work help us co-create different ways of being together on the outside? How does awareness help dismantle the master's house? How do we move from our tissues to protest signs to rewriting legislation? How can we alchemize our grief into meaningful change?

As we learn to feel again, as we become further sensitized to the pain and suffering of our ancestors, of ourselves, of our neighbors, and of our world, what do we do with it? How do we mobilize our embodied realizations and use them to effectively organize?

Moreover, how can we wade into the waters of solidarity and take back our stake in dismantling the wicked webs? How do we reclaim ancestral trauma and transform the impositions of Good Plantation Wife, Vixen Mistress, Damsel in Distress, Great White Mother, and White Savior? What happens when we take responsibility for our power and our impact? How do we leverage our incredible access to networks of power for meaningful change?

How do we get our collective act together so these wicked webs won't stand a chance?

While the focus of this book has been about disrupting our internalizations of Mistress Syndrome, in these final pages, I share a few more examples of how I have been part of collective organizing to disrupt the racist status quo.

ORGANIZE YOUR OWN

You don't have to start a White Women's Group to find a group of white ladies. Unofficial white women's groups are everywhere. Book clubs, prayer circles, play groups, PTAs…you may already be part of one, which is fabulous news. These are the social spheres where white-lady influence is leveraged and ideas are spread. These are spaces where we can enforce, challenge, or maintain the racist status quo. In recommending a book to read, questioning language, sharing about our struggles and dilemmas with the wicked webs, and inspiring groups to imagine how we might do life differently, these spaces become regular relational opportunities to organize.

These spaces also offer containers to practice showing up in courageous love, failing, and imperfectly trying again. I repeat: there is no one right way to do this work.

In the messy aftermath of the first WWGs, there was plenty to learn from. Always the teacher, Felicia advised a rubric* for moving

---

* We called these rubrics "FRubrics," as in Felicia + Rubrics. The FRubric was developed in partnership with YogaRoots On Location (see the copyright page for the full attribution.) Visit https://www.mistresssyndrome.com/resources to find out how to access these tools.

forward so the white women could better understand the continuum of our anti-racist growth. We also made changes to how WWG members would be invited. Now recruits would be welcomed in from the pool of Anti-Racist Yoga Teacher Training graduates. They would already have developed a shared foundational anti-racist analysis (part of the training's curriculum) and had a year of relationship building—with themselves, with Felicia as an account-ability partner, and with me.

While these changes didn't necessarily prevent tensions, conflicts, and fallouts, they helped to deepen and widen our ways of being together. Honestly, it was still painful every time a white woman left the group. Each time, I mourned the loss of relationship and the potential for what could have been. Each time, I had to refocus on who was still showing up. When I think about WWG through that lens, I realize there have always been those who do show up—no matter how few—ready and willing to get our collective act together.

Among other things, in the WWG space we examined our power within our institutions, social spheres, and families. We developed a gatekeeping workbook to help us get specific about the positional and cultural power we held on the job and within other spheres of influence. As part of a grassroots organizational assessment, WWG members engaged their colleagues to listen to their perspectives, build organizing relationships, and advocate for workplace change.

As I learned from PISAB, a good organizer can leave and the work will continue. One WWG member was so energized by the gatekeeping workbook that she wanted to develop it further. A few years later when the next iteration of WWG was formed, it was she and not I who facilitated the gatekeeping sessions. This was one of our many leadership development wins in which members from earlier WWGs mentored and supported newer ones.

In addition to the gatekeeping work, WWG mobilized in response to requests for support from Black organizers in our networks. We showed up by sharing resources, writing letters to institutions, volunteering at events, and canvassing in white neighborhoods. Our affinity work was not in isolation, but in relationship to BIPOC-led organizing, which was mobilizing in response to harm and building alternatives to violent systems.

But perhaps most impactful (at least for me) was the work we began regarding our families through the Anti-Racist Family History Project. Existing beyond and outside of a white cultural timeframe, the ancestral healing work has demanded that we, and especially me as the facilitator, consider the whole human, take a more embodied approach, and courageously engage our families in the work of healing justice.

In addition to the WWG work, I have offered versions of it to the general public. These white affinity workshops use a sliding payment scale in the spirit of mutual abundance, and consider participants' access needs. The family history project greatly informed my own dissertation research and the editing of this book, which I will detail in the Afterword.

There have been many moving parts to offering anti-racist affinity spaces like WWG and out of it has come many resources, but in WWG and in the white affinity spaces I've been a part of, I've come to realize that the cultural shifts of how we are together are as important as the content of any readings or discussion. It has taken me a while, many attempts, and much unlearning to come to this awareness. In answering Black organizers' longtime call to organize our own, our reorientation toward humanizing relationship, community care, and embodied attunement matters as much as the anti-racist analysis. It is the attention to co-creating healthy anti-racist culture, as Menakem likewise tasks white-bodied folks, that will sustain us for long-term engagement, de-center whiteness, and guide us toward alternative paths forward.

To date, WWG has had five iterations. I dream of many more, including ones that may form in response to this book! At times I have yearned to scale up the work and become more visible. Yet, for all my efforts and intentions over the past decade, WWGs and Mistress Syndrome have continued mostly underground.

For those of us who have been working under the radar, there are benefits of keeping low to the ground. There are seasons when tender, fresh things need to be incubated and protected from the critical energies that a more visible expression might bring. Staying close to the ground can also be an effective organizing strategy.

Karriem first introduced me to the concept of tunneling, or "tunnel building," which he learned during his involvement in local community development. This is an old organizing strategy and one that certainly does not belong to us white ladies, but it is one that can teach us a lot. It speaks to the work that needs to be done slowly, methodically, wisely. It speaks to the work that needs to be done undercover and without acclaim. It speaks to leveraging the access we have within systems and institutions because we are perceived as status quo and not a threat.

When I think of tunnel building, I think of a coordinated effort to dig a complex underground maze of connections. The tunnels are hidden to the powers-that-be who rush busily above in their skyscrapers and pollution machines. The tunnel network can be used to pop up and disrupt, but it also creates a protected collectively held space for practicing how we want to be with each other, to collaborate on alternatives, and to build relationships, community, and our collective power. At some point, the skyscrapers and pollution machines above will no longer be able to continue. When they crumble under the weight of their own oppression, an intricate web will emerge. Some call this abolitionism.

I think about this underground organizing as soil work. Soil work is unseen and often happens in darkness. Soil work involves composting rotting matter, balancing the browns and the greens, waiting, turning, testing and testing again, and partnering with others (like sunflowers!) to remove the heavy metals and ready the dirt for the hope of future plants. Soil work is critical for plant health and their fruits. Yet soil work, just like cultural work, might not involve planting seeds, especially if the dirt needs more time. It is patient, humbling, and often messy work. Sometimes a soil worker readies the dirt for someone else to plant, for someone else to water the seedlings, harvest the fruit, and preserve the nutrition.

#LANDBACK AND REPARATIONS

To be honest, the first time I heard scholar and founder of the Community for the Advancement of Native Studies, Waŋbli Wapȟáha Hokšíla (Dr. Edward Valandra) talk about land return, I felt a sense of existential dread. To paraphrase his words, all white settlers are equally complicit in stealing Indigenous lands and thus need to return them. Intellectually I agree with this reasoning—of course stolen lands should be returned—but the fleshy survival mode of my body struggled with how to metabolize the possibility of nonexistence.[2]

The 4Ds were present for sure, and, as I stayed with it, I wondered why was it so existential for me. What was I so afraid of—or attached to—about land return? When I thought about getting rid of the wicked webs, I felt excitement, not fear. When I imagined what our world would be like with Indigenous leadership and the wisdom of bodies of culture, I felt energized, not stuck. When I released the fear of the unknown, when I released my attachment to the very known wicked webs, I felt relief and release.

As I learned from Abenaki elder Jamie Bissonette Lewey, the restorative justice process includes: 1) acknowledgment of harm; 2) apology; 3) acceptance of apology; 4) repair; 5) restoration/transformation of relationship.* As Hokšíla points out, reparations as a part of restorative justice's repair is not an abstract concept. Likewise, Tuck and Yang remind us that decolonization is not metaphorical.[3] There is no symbolic #Landback. Decolonization includes the actual return of land.

When my home congregation was considering selling their church building and land, I floated the idea of land return to the peoples indigenous to Atlanta.† While they ultimately decided not to sell,

---

* My understanding of restorative justice has also been greatly influenced by my studies with Dr. Howard Zehr while at Eastern Mennonite University's Center for Justice and Peacebuilding.

† Depending on which part of Atlanta, these include the "Mvskoke (Muscogee)" and the "ᏇᏣᎳᎫᏤᏘᏱ Tsalaguwetiyi (Cherokee, East)," according to https://native-land.ca.

it offered me an opportunity to dream. What would it mean for Mennonite settlers to actually restore and repair? What could it mean for Mennonite institutions to organize widespread land return? What are the relationships and solutionary arrangements that might come out of an attempt to restore the "property" that built European Mennonite wealth and secured white existence here? How might this be done while simultaneously acknowledging the advantage that has been derived from the disadvantages of Black, Indigenous, Latine, Asian, and other People of the Global Majority, including those who are also Mennonite, and in conversation with those who are also Mennonite? Can you imagine the message this would send to other denominations and institutions? Can you imagine the conversations we could begin?*

And while we can continue to advocate for reparations and land return by our institutions and governments, there are opportunities to do this at the individual and interpersonal levels. When my parents were ready to sell their house and side lot in the city neighborhood in which I grew up, I encouraged them to get creative. At Felicia's suggestion, I made a cost-benefit analysis. The cost-benefit analysis compared the money they'd pocket against the potential generational wealth building that could happen for a family if they donated the lot to Habitat for Humanity, for example.

They declined for many reasons, but when it was time for me to leave Pittsburgh, I got a chance to try again, this time with land that was under my name.

Felicia had lived in the zip code almost her entire life. Her grandparents had lived on the same street as us. Yet like many others impacted by systemic racism, in this zip code she had only ever paid rent to a landlord. For her, as for many others, this had to do with

---

* Some congregations have begun to ask these questions. Columbus Mennonite Church takes the amount they would be paying in property tax if they weren't exempt as a church and donates it each year to local Black- and Indigenous-led social justice organizations. The congregation remains engaged in ongoing work to recognize and dismantle their internalization of racism, settler colonialism, and the Doctrine of Discovery.

things like student loan debt, racist credit scores, family commitments, and a vocational path that was not (until recently) so eagerly funded by capitalist institutions. By contrast, within a year of moving to that same zip code, as a married white person with little to no savings or income, I was able to finance and purchase a newly renovated home and adjacent lot.

When I started to think about leaving Pittsburgh and selling the house, I asked myself what reparations could be within the context of our interpersonal relationship. How could we both benefit? What might help balance some of the wicked webs' disparities? This was an opportunity to choose differently, to get creative in our involvement with racist economic systems, and to do so in a relational way.

After several months of brainstorming, Felicia, her husband, Kayla, and I gathered to get specific. We planned for me to sell the house to Felicia by self-financing over several years. In addition, I would leverage my home equity to complete some much-needed repairs. We consulted with a real estate agent, home inspector, attorney, and bank to ensure feasibility and gather more info. We had an attorney draft an initial agreement, outlining the renting-to-own arrangement. Either party could opt out at any time; Felicia could cash out her equity and I would retain the property.

We consulted ourselves, too, to make sure it felt right. And at some point, it didn't anymore. As our relationships shifted, as I tried to move out of my uncomfortable and painful living arrangement with Kayla, as Felicia realized she also wanted a change, the energy around the arrangement shifted, too. "I don't think I want to be in relationship with you in this way," she eventually said, backing out. And I agreed. So, we regrouped and came together a second time to consider other options.

In our mutually agreed upon plan B, I sold the house and shared the sale with her (and others). This was a nod toward the equity she had been paying into by renting in this neighborhood for four decades, a small attempt at regaining some of the wealth lost in her lifetime due to racism, a small attempt to rebalance some of the wealth gained in my lifetime due to the same.

While my last season in Pittsburgh was an emotionally tumultuous time for me, I never wavered about redistributing those resources. Sure, I had moments when I felt angry and hurt. There were moments when I gave myself permission to reconsider our plan B, to check in and feel out if sharing these resources in such a big way still felt aligned. And even though resource sharing at this level no longer accurately reflected a chosen family dynamic, my gut told me it still aligned with my values, goals, and the dream that I wanted to be a part of.

We carried out our plan B. I sold the house and shared the sale, but decided not to sell the adjacent lot. Something about selling the land didn't feel right. How could I privatize and monetize a space the community had used in so many ways, where children played and a garden continued to grow?

In learning more about the land return movement, I searched online to see if there were Indigenous nations in Pittsburgh accepting land donations. While I was in this research phase, a friend and colleague called me to talk about something unrelated. She was a connected Pittsburgh activist, so it occurred to me that I should ask her if she knew of any groups looking for land donations. "We are," was her response. "My organization is looking for land to garden."

Active in Pittsburgh-area communities for over a decade, their organizing has sought to celebrate the contributions of Black women and queer people through creative acts of community care, education, mutual aid, and, more recently, gardening.

We consulted with a real estate agent and made a plan. Before leaving Pittsburgh, I sold the land to them for $1. These new fruits are just beginning, but their seeds have a history. Faithfully, on that same land where healing herb plants and flowers grow, Black children will feel the invitations of play, welcome, and love.

In some ways at least, the intention my former partner and I originally made to be in right relationship with the neighborhood has been sustained. Despite the real and persisting threats, and the challenges and ongoing struggles, at least this space is in the hands and wisdom of Black femmes who are committed to healing and liberation work.

While my organizing relationships have shifted, especially after leaving Pittsburgh at the end of 2020, I continue to organize in different ways. One way I think about leveraging my access is to ask: Who else could I bring with me? When I get a contract with an institution, and especially if it's to do facilitation with a multiracial group, I ask: Who else's skills and perspectives are needed? Who else's platform could I promote? What other BIPOC-created resources could I link to? What networking connections could I make?

At the end of 2021 I moved to Western North Carolina on the homelands of the ᏣᎳᎩ Tsalaguwetiyi (Cherokee). This move has brought me closer to my mom's family and the southern organizing culture of my childhood. As a new community member in a very white place, I still have much to learn about the history and organizing work that precedes me. As I ask what my role is as a white woman who's new to this place and community, I have been met with opportunities to contribute in ways that feel supportive and in solidarity with local Black- and Brown-led organizing.

In 2020, the City of Asheville became the second municipality in the country to pass reparations for Black residents and was followed by its surrounding county, Buncombe, in passing reparations. The city and county acknowledged the harm done from enslavement, segregation, and, most recently, urban renewal policies that displaced Black residents, demolished Black neighborhoods, and had a major economic impact on Black businesses. Asheville had the most urban renewal/removal of any city in the Southeast. As part of the process, the city and county created a Community Reparations Commission to provide recommendations for how to go about reparations including allocating an annual reparations budget. Local organizations such as the Asheville Racial Justice Coalition have been organizing locally to support this innovative and important process. White volunteers have been tasked to help educate and mobilize fellow white community members to advocate and protect the reparations process so it centers the experiences of Black residents and gives the Community Reparations Commission the time, space, and resources requested to attempt something that—with the exception of Evanston, Illinois*—to date, no municipalities have ever done.

In part as a result of the outrage that was mobilized in 2020, Asheville's reparations process offers an example of the important change that can happen in moments of upswell and outrage. However, since that original commitment, it is unclear if the city and county are going to fulfill their commitment to meaningful reparations. For example, in not fully supporting the Community Reparations Commission's request for an extension, they have potentially undermined an opportunity to do the important repair work that's never been done.

Moments like these test our soil. They ask: Has our soil work created the nutrition we need to grow resilient movements? Are our underground grassroots infrastructures wise and adaptable enough to outlive the systems above? What is the quality of our movement cultures? Are they solutions-based life-sustaining connections? Are they holding us together in new ways?

When I meditate on these above questions, there is no lingering existential dread. The more I learn about alternatives to the wicked webs—cooperative economics, embodied relational cultures, honoring eldership and wisdom, mutual aid and abundance, reconnection with the earth—the less the uncertainty feels scary. Instead, the unknown of reparations and land returns feels invigorating; it becomes a path on which I am determined to go.

FAMILY WORK

Perhaps the biggest area of influence we white ladies occupy is in that domestic realm which we've been instructed to maintain. Despite the patriarchy embedded in our family systems, we have tremendous

---

* In November 2019, the Evanston City Council committed the first ten million dollars of the Cannabis Retailers' Occupation Tax to fund housing reparations and economic development programs for Black residents (City of Evanston, "Evanston Local Reparations").

influence in our family cultures and relationships, and especially within our access to other white family members.

The ancestral family systems work is where much of my work has landed. This family work has kept me accountable to keep coming back to my own. It is the deepest, hardest, and most personally impactful work I have done.

As you may remember from chapter seven, when my cousins took a stand against racism and transphobia in the family email thread, it disrupted the status quo of silence around harm. Given all my training, I knew such open conflict was an opportunity, but I wasn't sure at first how to show up for it. It was one thing to navigate conflict anywhere else, but a whole other to consciously move toward it within my family system.

Let's just say I did not craft my most skilled reply in my first response to the fear that conflict was Satan's division. But I stayed with it and tried again:

Hello All,

As I sit here reading through the email thread and anxiously waiting for the jury to share its verdict in the trial of the police officer Derek Chauvin for the murder of George Floyd, I keep coming back to the ideas of abolitionism. In my understanding, Abolitionism is an orientation that is unapologetically opposed to violent structures and ideologies. Abolitionism opposes what bell hooks calls "imperialist white-supremacist capitalist patriarchy" in all its forms and recognizes that not only do our systems (of policing, of imprisonment, of militarization, of family, etc.) not adequately address the harms they claim to address, but they also cause more harm and violence, especially to Black, Brown, and LGBTQ folks.

Abolitionism, (sometimes called Abolitionist Futures), is also unapologetic in striving for accountability processes that do not replicate the violence of our systems. Mariame Kaba talks about how in this society, we've so deeply internalized colonized, violent ways of being in relationship with each other that even if all our systems were done away with, we would still likely replicate their

punitive models. Our transformation has to happen in disman-
tling violent systems, ending harm, and tending to healing, and
also in transforming our replication of structural violence. She also
talks about her experiences with accountability being conflated with
punishment and says an Abolitionist model embraces accountability
but does away with punishment.

Too often, especially in the white Mennonite communities I've
experienced, naming a harm or conflict gets associated with causing
the harm or conflict. The courageousness of family members to name
harm and violence is not causing additional harm. It is bringing
attention to what many of us, especially white family members,
myself included, were not previously aware of or tuned in to. There
is important and specific work, especially for those of us in the family
who have been racialized as white to do. I have been in conversation
with a few family members about opening up a white affinity space
specifically for anti-racist education and I continue to be open and
committed to supporting our family's growth in this way.

I don't presume that most of you on this thread will share an
Abolitionist orientation, but nevertheless, I am faithful to practicing
accountability processes that move beyond the replication of punish-
ment models. I am faithful to the co-creation of new ways for us to
be in relationship. I deeply believe that we can both uncompromis-
ingly prioritize the safety of marginalized family members while
also manifest accountable processes that honor each of our potential
for deep transformation.

Sending love and care on this difficult day,
Love, Amanda

After my reply, an email appeared in my inbox.

It was from a second cousin, who I met as a child, but had not seen since. She, her sister, and their cousin, white people of my generation, were reaching out, citing the wisdom that came through between the lines of the emails. How could we help our family? they wanted to know. How could we do this together?

The email threads led to awesome new relationships, as we grieved the harm together and considered how we might engage our family members. We ended up offering a white affinity educational space for interested family members. Twenty people attended the three-part series. Our collaboration led to a small healing justice fund for our BIPOC family members. Some of the conversations started then have continued to this day.

Doing this work with family is perhaps an organizer's biggest fear and deepest dream. I know it has been mine. The healing part keeps me coming back. Each time I speak a silenced truth, I have more options for how to speak that truth. The second time I can hold back. The third time I can go slow. The next times I can discern and attune to the relationship and set boundaries when I need to.

The practice of trying even while feeling afraid has yielded some profound results. After that uncomfortable car conversation during the too-cold spring, my mother did not in fact abandon me. Rather, she has become one of my staunchest supporters, a co-conspirator in embodying anti-racist change.

After the email exchanges had subsided, we had our first extended-family white affinity group. Twenty of us popped up on the screen. I asked my white family members: Who wanted to start our circle? Who wanted to share why they had come? No longer so afraid to engage in conflict, no longer the silent in the land, my mom was the first to raise her hand. And she shared with a depth that set the tone for others to do the same.

Her shifts have caused life-changing ripple effects. My parents' eventual divorce has opened up new and different spaces for my relationship with my dad. It has helped me to humanize him and pull back that curtain. Though the chasm of our worldviews continues to prevent deeper intimacies, I am feeling safe enough to engage more genuinely, while also respecting the chasm's limitations.

As with White Women's Groups, as I focused less on my anger at the people who leave, I have ended up moving toward those who have been moving toward me.

When I confided in my brother and sister-in-law about my childhood molestation, they believed me the first time.

And they remembered.

They offered me affirmation and support. "That shouldn't have happened to you," they said. "How does it feel when we mention their family?" They checked in to better understand impact. My brother reflected on how oblivious he had been: "I guess as a boy, I didn't have to be aware." My sister-in-law considered her role and how to disrupt the patterns. "What can I change in my parenting?" she asked. "How can we make our family safer?" we asked each other.

My family continues to ask and reflect. We continue to make mistakes and we continue to make adjustments. We are doing it. And we are doing it together.

I now have two niblings by birth and many others via community. My auntie energy is fierce. I am determined that the silence and secrets and embodied violence that happened to me will not be their story. As a family, we have been making plans, sharing resources, and educating ourselves and the older generations so children of all genders are allowed to express anger and rage, softness and tenderness—and to wear pink dresses (if they want to). In my family, on purpose, we have been learning about the cycles of abuse and releasing the toxic shame stories about ourselves and our bodies.

Most of all, we are no longer being silent. My youngest nibling, the loudest of us all, is leading the way.

AFTERWORD

Sue Monk Kidd writes, "When you can't go forward and you can't go backward and you can't stay where you are without killing off what is deep and vital in yourself, you are on the edge of creation."[1] For those of us who have come to be called white and who are committed to the hard, uncomfortable, and messy unknowns of ending oppression, we find ourselves in a similar predicament. If we can't move forward with our whiteness in the lead, if we can't go back in time and change the wrongs of our ancestors as the physics of space and time currently indicate, and if whiteness has been "killing off what is deep and vital" in ourselves, as the many chapters of this book have hopefully illuminated, then we are poised for momentous transformation.

When I began drafting this book and preceding blog entries, I had not thought deeply about how my writing might impact my family members and our relationships. I felt convicted about my responsibility as a person who had been racialized as white to make our whiteness visible as both a form of accountability and a model for others. It wasn't until that phone call in the car with my mom that I realized my family relationships might be jeopardized by my actions..

When I started my doctoral studies in 2020, I knew I wanted to use my research to help me finish writing this book. I entered with a big question that I hoped would help me move beyond critical analysis and toward a more solutions-based approach. How can arts and culture support white settlers in sustaining a long-term commitment to anti-racism and decolonization? I honed my question: How could I engage family members and others whose relationships I unpack in this book? How could I do this in ways that maintain integrity, are relational, and align with anti-racist and decolonizing methodologies for multigenerational trauma healing, transformation, and collective liberation?

As I engaged my family members, new pathways for accountability emerged.

With my mom, siblings, and other extended family members, this meant inviting and initiating intentional spaces for dialogue. Through these openings, I have been able to listen more deeply to my family, respond from a less reactionary space, and approach them with more curiosity and less judgment.

These new ways of listening have opened me up to surprises. For one, my family members surpassed my expectations in their courage and willingness to engage with what I'd written. They shared in ways that helped me to learn and reconsider my own perspectives about our shared family culture, histories, and cultural connections. During one of these conversations I learned that my parents paid for my childhood caregiver Ms. Sylvia's social security and covered her vacation expenses.* I am learning that despite the depths of work we still have to do, my family has also been contributing to healing and liberation work, particularly through multigenerational care, addressing and repairing harm, and relational ways of being together, which actively create alternatives to white culture's individualism, historical amnesia, and erasures of harm.

Coming back to family relationships through my doctoral research helped me to clarify anti-racist boundaries. As I thought about whether and how to include my father, I ultimately decided that his participation might derail its focus. I also sensed that navigating our interpersonal dynamic would require an overwhelming amount of energy, ultimately distracting me and potentially others

---

* While paying any employee's social security should be the norm, it isn't. It especially wasn't in the 1980s and '90s.

from opportunities to align with anti-racism, co-create, and do things differently.

Inspired by Tuck and Yang's work on refusal,[2] setting this boundary with him helped me get clearer about my own authorial and narrative power as a gatekeeper for anti-racism. Whereas oftentimes the role of an anti-racist gatekeeper means opening gates to support the flow of information, resources, and access (as I learned from PISAB), in this instance using my anti-racist gatekeeping power meant that I not open the gate to begin with. Getting clear about my power likewise helped me get clearer about how I wanted to use it, both in moving toward right relationship and in recognizing those in which there were certain limitations.

As my publishing date neared, I reflected on the many relationships I've unpacked throughout these pages. I asked myself in which relationships might there be possibility for repair and reconciliation. Did I even want that? What was my responsibility with my father, with Felicia, with Kayla, given where things had been left?

Ultimately, I decided differently with each relationship. I extended an invitation to Felicia to read and have conversation around this book's draft. She declined to read it in advance of its print date, but was open to a conversation. Our conversation led to the idea of her writing the Foreword. My father and I have had conversations about the book, but whether or not—and to what extent—he will read it is still TBD. I have shared with others who appear throughout the pages, including Kayla, very generally about what I've written. I've extended an invitation for conversation, but am working to release my expectations and anxieties about how those might go.

BUILDING AT THE SPEED OF TRUST

As I continue to interrogate the ways I grasped for an anti-racist rulebook, my approach to accountability has shifted as well. This has been part of my healing from Mistress Syndrome, part of acknowledging and reclaiming my own power. Kaba says, "You can't force somebody into being accountable for things they do. That is not possible. People have to take accountability for things that they actually do wrong."[3] I'm realizing accountability is not so much needing someone to call me out as it is being able to listen deeply to others, and moreover, to myself. At the end of the day and no matter other people's perspectives, I am ultimately responsible for discerning when I've done wrong as well as when I haven't, for opening to the possibility of having caused harm and seeking repair, and for choosing whom and what I want to be responsible to and with.

A few years into facilitating White Women's Groups, I was attending a different white affinity space. The facilitators offered a list of shared agreements. As in many other organizing spaces, these shared agreements were not just about how we wanted to be together in the group, but also a reflection of how we wanted to be with each other in the world, or at least how we aspired to be. The facilitator read down the list. "Build at the speed of trust,"* they said. Inside, I felt a twinge of resistance. I crinkled up my nose. Something about it felt a little too hand-holdy, a little too focused on white comfort.

But now in writing those words, "Build at the speed of trust" feels very relevant. I want to bring it closer; I'm attracted to it and am curious.

In my accountability relationships with Felicia and others, I thought there was a lot of trust. I trusted her and my accountability partners immensely. I believed them, I listened deeply, and I followed their lead. But now I'm wondering which parts were trust and which were deference? Had I trusted myself? Could mutual trust even be built without me trusting myself? For me, that has been the work of healing from Mistress Syndrome. It has been about rebuilding that trust with myself, reclaiming my Self from the wicked web's lies, and taking the risks to be vulnerable with myself so that I can be vulnerable, courageous, and stand in solidarity with others.

hooks writes:

---

* While not directly attributed in the space, this shared agreement may have been inspired by adrienne maree brown's concepts in *Emergent Strategy*.

Solidarity is not the same as support. To experience solidarity, we must have a community of interests, shared beliefs and goals around which to unite...Support can be occasional. It can be given and just as easily withdrawn. Solidarity requires sustained, ongoing commitment.[4]

This healing justice work is about moving us from more shallow support into the deeper, life-sustaining waters of solidarity.

* * *

Maybe by reading this book you are just beginning to dip your toes into the waters of solidarity. Maybe you have waded in them for a long time. Maybe you've been in and out and are ready to test the waters once again. But wherever you're at and wherever you've been, you are welcome here.

There are countless ways for white women to get ready. There are so many things that are within our personal and collective power to change. I hope these words have supported you in reflecting and feeling, in grieving and healing, and in further embodying your own stories. As we continue the collective work of liberating our minds and our bodies, I hope they support further pathways toward solidarity and meaningful action so we can more effectively contribute to the health, safety, and well-being of us all. I offer these words as both invitation and imperative.

White women, get ready.

ACKNOWLEDGMENTS

This book is a manifestation of contributions by many individuals, organizations, communities, movements, and ecosystems. I offer acknowledgment and deep gratitude to my teachers, community, and collaborators, to those who poured into me as a human and an organizer, and to those who have poured into social justice movements in countless ways, both known and unknown to us.

To the lands and ecosystems that held me in process and practice, to their Indigenous peoples, to the Lenape of Pennsylvania, the Haudenosaunee of Pittsburgh, the Monacan, Shawnee, and Manahoac of Harrisonburg, the ᎠᏍᎩᏯ Tsalaguwetiyi (Cherokee) of Asheville and Ashe County, and the Mvskoke (Muscogee) of Atlanta, to the cultures, lives, and wisdoms that existed before my ancestry arrived on Turtle Island and still exist today. Thank you for the reminders to stay unsettled and honor relationship to place.

To the diverse legacies of Black and Indigenous-led movements that have shaped and continue to shape this work, to the scholars who have taught me to think critically and make connections, to bell hooks, Patricia Hill Collins, and Imani Perry, to Audre Lorde, Grace Lee Boggs, and Mariame Kaba, to Eve Tuck and K. Wayne Yang, to Dr. Joy DeGruy, Rev. Angel Kyoto Williams, and Robin Wall Kimmerer. To the legacies of Rev. Dr. Martin Luther King Jr., Ella Baker, and civil rights organizing in the South that helped shape the cultural landscapes of my youth. Thank you for teaching me that change is possible and that I have a role as one small but important part of a much bigger interconnected whole.

To my Anabaptist ancestors who embodied their values in the face of flames, spoke truth to power, and committed to following Jesus's way within community, thank you for the inheritance of grounded faith. To the many strongly rooted Mennonite women in my lineage, to my Great-Great Aunt Amanda Buckwalter (for whom I am named), to Elsie, Katie, Marion, and Orpah Mae, who taught me love through action and that there is much power in the kitchen. Thank you for the lessons of courage, roots, and belonging.

To my mom, who navigated having a memoirist for a daughter with astounding patience and courage, who has read and reread, asked and listened, discussed and recounted, supported me and nurtured my body, spirit, and ever-evolving work through dynamic discomfort and deep love. Thank you for teaching me how to grow, care, and thrive. I am so grateful to be your child.

To my father who has modeled generosity, passion, and faith alongside confounding politics. Thank you for teaching me how to stand up for what I believe in, stay true to my values, and seek paths of righteousness.

To Sylvia Wheeler, who read me book after book, took me on walks to the park, snuck me junk food, and helped raise me from infancy to adolescence. Thank you for initiating me into womanism, grounding me in relationship, teaching me about the ways of white folks, and extending depths of love and care.

To my brother Conrad who survived my sibling schooling and has become an incredible human, friend, and supporter. Thank you for teaching me how to play nicely with others. To my sister-in-law Morgan and the niblings. Thank you for your enthusiastic support, curiosity, and the reminder to laugh, cry, and have fun.

To my Aunt Becky for your lifelong mentorship and modeling, to my Kurtz and Horst family, many of whom read excerpts, bravely engaged with my autoethnographic research, and helped co-create spaces for risk taking, difficult dialogue, humility, and relational repair. Thank you for teaching me about openness, intentionality, and grace.

To Karriem, without whose emotional and material support this book would most certainly not have been published. Thank you for your generosity, carefully attuned listening, and tenacity. Thank you for teaching me so much about myself and about my capacity for vulnerability and healing.

To those who have emerged throughout my life as chosen family, to the Masts, Troyers, Wilkersons, and Shalom and AMC families, to the Kingsley Center, Knit the Bridge, YogaRoots On Location, my Solidarity Circle, RJC's Reparations Are Due team, and Asheville's Latin dance community. To my academic communities of EMU, CJP, and EGS, to Jenna, Chuan, Darci, Conly, Helena, Mari, Ofir, Cynthia, Bee, Shabrae, and Chelsea, who artfully and enthusiastically encouraged my process when I was at an impasse. Thank you all for the offerings of community and support.

To those of you who have been brave enough to embrace the role of teacher and mentor me in the ways of collective liberation and of life. To Felicia Savage Friedman, who supported me in reclaiming my intuition, pushed me to go deeper, and whose lessons are still revealing themselves, to the People's Institute for Survival and Beyond for the grounding in anti-racist analysis and practice, to Dustin Washington for telling me I should write a book that didn't yet exist, to Jamie Bissonette Lewey, Amy Springer, Kirsten Ervin, Penny Mateer, Dr. Howard Zehr, and Dr. Christine Brooks, who have supported these words beyond the pages. Thank you for your guidance, questions, assessments, encouragement, and support as I continue to learn how to learn and unlearn.

To my awesome colleagues, friends, and collaborators, to Sheba, Cythera, Sandra Luise, Kit, Kaoly, Bethany, Shelly, Jeannie, Ivonne, Dale, Jill, Jennifer, and Cassie. Thank you for the many ways you accompanied this book's long gestation and helped me to form and birth it. Thank you for your kindness, friendship, and the enticements to emerge from my writing cave. To Valerie, Cole, R/B, Bekezela, Dr. Ari, Esther, Liza, Caryn, Mariah, Pam, Emily, Lena, Hayley, Maria, and Tasha. Thank you especially for your input, time, and care in reading various iterations of the book and giving valuable feedback.

To those who have been my students, to the youth of YUIR, to the white ladies of WWG, to YROL students, to the many people who have attended my workshops, trainings, and classes. Thank you for the lessons in slowing down and bringing humanity and care to spaces of learning. You shaped these pages in so many ways.

To Taia Pandolfi, who had her hands in almost every draft. Thank you for lending your dexterity, diligence, and discernment to eight-plus years of process (whew!). I am so grateful for you. To Rebecca Rudel, who encouraged me to get out of my comfort zone and put myself out there. Thank you for your skillful cheerleading, embodied listening, and comms expertise. To my cousin, Margaret High, who arrived on the scene to help edit and discern in a moment of need. Thank you for helping me move hard truths forward. To my editor, Amy Reed, who took on a too-long book and helped me make it longer, stay true to its emotional spine, and reminded me to extend compassion to myself and my readers, and to Saeah Lee Wood and the expert staff at Otterpine. Thank you for guiding this book through and out the birth canal.

To the hundred-plus generous souls who helped turn 140,000 words into a shiny object. To Rhoda and Jon and the Frame Factory and Gallery, to Nancy and my mom's book groups, to St. John's Episcopal in Haw Creek. Thank you for believing in the purpose of this book and inviting others to share space to consider these words. To each and every one of you who contributed through GoFundMe, shared on social media, told your neighbors and friends, asked how the book was coming, and offered words of encouragement. I so deeply appreciate you.

RESOURCES FOR FURTHER SUPPORT

In addition to the abundant scholarship referenced in the Bibliography, here are some organizations and colleagues that have been in relationship with and influenced the work of Mistress Syndrome. I encourage you to seek out and support their work!

Collective Trauma and Healing Resources

Dr. Joy DeGruy (*Post Traumatic Slave Syndrome*): https://www.joydegruy.com/
Embodied Social Justice Summit: https://www.embodiedsocialjusticesummit.com/
The Rooted Global Village: https://www.rootedglobalvillage.com/

Reproductive Justice

New Voices for Reproductive Justice: https://newvoicesrj.org/
Sister Song: https://www.sistersong.net/
Mountain Area Abortion Doula Collective (MAADCO): https://mtnabortiondoula.co

Anti-Racist White and White Woman-Focused Organizing

Catalyst Project and the Anne Braden Program: https://collectiveliberation.org/
White Antiracist History Project: https://burnett-lynn.medium.com/white-antiracist-history-white-antiracist-mobilization-the-vision-statement-for-the-white-1a6ff4f86d43
We Are Finding Freedom: https://www.wearefindingfreedom.org/

What's Up with White Women?: Unpacking Sexism and White Privilege in Pursuit of Racial Justice by Ilsa Govan and Tilman Smith

White Women: Everything You Already Know About Your Own Racism and How to Do Better by Regina Jackson and Saira Rao

Against White Feminism: Notes on Disruption by Rafia Zakaria

"White Women: Maintainers or Disruptors of Racism?": http://www.ntl-psc.org/archive/white-women-maintainers-or-disruptors-of-racism/

Me and White Supremacy: Combat Racism, Change the World, and Become a Good Ancestor by Layla Saad

Assimilation into Whiteness

Critical Family History by Christine Sleeter: https://www.christinesleeter.org/critical-family-history

How the Irish Became White by Noel Ignatiev

How Jews Became White and What That Says about Race in America by Karen Brodkin

Are Italians White? How Race Is Made in America by Jennifer Guglielmo and Salvatore Salerno

"How Mennonites Became White: Religious Activism, Cultural Power, and the City" by Philipp Gollner

Kinship Concealed: Amish-Mennonite & African-American Family Connections by Sharon Cranford and Dwight Roth

Parenting, Early Childhood, and Resources for Educators

Anti-Racist Early Childhood Network: https://www.antiracistece.com

Raising White Kids: Bringing up Children in a Racially Unjust America by Jennifer Harvey

Parenting Beyond Power: How to Use Connection & Collaboration to Transform your Family and the World by Jen Lumanlan

Landing Places: https://www.lizagleasoncoaching.com

What White Parents Should Know about Transracial Adoption: An Adoptee's Perspective on Its History, Nuances, and Practices by Melissa Guida-Richards

Reparations

Racial Justice Coalition Asheville, Reparations Are Due: https://www.rjcavl.org/reparations-are-due/

Reparations Stakeholder Authority of Asheville: https://www.rsaasheville.org/

Congregational Reparations: https://healingmnstories.wordpress.com/2021/03/14/one-churchs-path-towards-reparations-donating-its-property-tax-equivalent-to-black-and-indigenous-lead-organizations//

The Cost of Inheritance (film): https://www.pbs.org/video/the-cost-of-inheritance-bdzmlq/

The Big Payback (film): https://www.pbs.org/independentlens/documentaries/the-big-payback/

Cousins by Betty Kilby Baldwin & Phoebe Kilby: https://walnutstreetbooks.com/titles/cousins/

Coming to the Table: https://comingtothetable.org

Morgan Curtis, Ancestors & Money Coach: https://www.morganhcurtis.com

Land Back and Decolonization

Indigenous Land Map: https://native-land.ca/

Land Back: https://landback.org/

Indigenous Environmental Network: https://www.ienearth.org/

The Auntie's Dandelion Podcast: https://www.theauntiesdandelion.com/podcast.html

Coalition to Dismantle the Doctrine of Discovery: https://dismantlediscovery.org/

Circleworks: Transforming European Consciousness by Fyre Jean Graveline

Intersectional Social Justice, Education, and Abolition

The People's Institute for Survival & Beyond: https://pisab.org

Building Bridges Asheville: https://www.bbavl.org

Highlander Research and Education Center: https://highlandercenter.org/

Southerners On New Ground: https://southernersonnewground.org

Let's Get Free: https://linktr.ee/womeninprison; Instagram: @womeninprison

Jewish Voice for Peace: https://www.jewishvoiceforpeace.org/

Boycott, Divestment, Sanctions (BDS): https://bdsmovement.net

Christians for a Free Palestine: https://christiansforafreepalestine.com

Youth Undoing Institutional Racism Pittsburgh: https://issuu.com/yuirpgh

Stop Cop City: https://stopcop.city

Center for Justice and Peacebuilding: https://emu.edu/cjp/

Zehr Institute for Restorative Justice: https://zehr-institute.org/

Barnard Center for Women: https://bcrw.barnard.edu/home/

Congregational Abuse and Prevention

Into Account: https://intoaccount.org/

Congregational Sexual Abuse Response and Prevention (Mennonite Church USA): https://www.mennoniteusa.org/resource-portal/resource/sexual-abuse-response-and-prevention/

Resistance: Confronting Violence, Power, and Abuse within Peace Churches edited by Cameron Altaras and Carol Penner

Yoga

YogaRoots On Location: https://www.yogarootsonlocation.com/

Yoga is Dead: https://www.yogaisdeadpodcast.com/home

Critical Yoga Studies: https://crityogastudies.wordpress.com/on-critical-yoga-studies/

YogaMotif: https://www.yogamotif.com

Diarra Imani: DiarraImani.com

Solutionary Examples and Inspirations

How We Show Up: Reclaiming Family, Friendship, and Community by Mia Birdsong

YES! magazine: https://www.yesmagazine.org/

Dreams of Hope: https://www.dreamsofhope.org

The Legacy Quilt Project: https://www.aaronrosestudio.com/

The Black Unicorn Library and Archive Project: https://www.theblackunicornlibrary.org/

WHEAT (Winnipeg Holistic Expressive Arts Therapy) Institute: https://www.wheatinstitute.com

The People's Place: https://peoplesplaceavl.com

Dr. Ariana Brazier: https://linktr.ee/ari.brazier

Ujamaa Collective: https://www.ujamaacollective.org

Cutting Root Farm and Apothecary: https://www.cuttingroot.com

Autoethnography and Memoir

Memoir Magazine: https://memoirmag.com/

The AutoEthnographer: A Literary & Arts Magazine: https://theautoethnographer.com

Handbook of Autoethnography by Tony E. Adams, Stacy Holman Jones, and Carolyn Ellis

R/B Mertz: rbmertz.com

NOTES

INTRODUCTION

1. DeGruy, Post Traumatic Slave Syndrome, 4.
2. DeGruy, 121.
3. DeGruy, 66.
4. MacNair, Perpetration-Induced Traumatic Stress, 9.
5. MacNair, 9.
6. Richards in Dawson, "Beah: Thus a Black Woman Speaks."
7. DeGruy, Post Traumatic Slave Syndrome, 4–5.

CHAPTER ONE

1. "STAR: Strategies for Trauma Awareness and Resilience," Center for Justice and Peacebuilding, 4.
2. Langholtz, foreword to Perpetration-Induced Traumatic Stress, by Rachel MacNair, vii.
3. MacNair, Perpetration-Induced Traumatic Stress, 3.
4. Yoder, The Little Book of Trauma Healing, 14.
5. Yoder, 14.
6. "STAR," Center for Justice and Peacebuilding, 11.
7. "STAR," 11.
8. "STAR," 11.
9. "STAR," 11.
10. Center for Action and Contemplation, "Transforming Pain."
11. Nerenberg, "Why Are So Many Adults Today Haunted by Trauma?"
12. Menakem, My Grandmother's Hands, 5.
13. Menakem, 138.
14. Yellow Bird, "Decolonization: Seeking Symbols of Hope," 40:10.

CHAPTER TWO

1. Allen, Hubain, Hunt, Lucero, and Steward, "Race Matters." 5.
2. Vaid-Menon, "Book Report: Making Sex: Body and Gender from the Greeks to Freud by Dr. Thomas Laqueur," slide 3.
3. Vaid-Menon, slide 3.
4. hooks, The Will to Change, 66.
5. The New School, "Teaching to Transgress: bell hooks Returns to the New School."
6. Shlain, The Alphabet Versus the Goddess, 50.
7. Shlain, 87.
8. Shlain, 152.
9. Federici, Caliban and the Witch, 75.
10. Federici, 171.
11. Federici, 76.
12. Roper, The Witch in the Western Imagination, 142
13. Federici, Caliban and the Witch, 169.
14. Federici, 88.
15. DiAngelo, "White Women's Tears and the Men Who Love Them."
16. Deahl, "Countries Around the World Beat the U.S. On Paid Parental Leave."
17. Gonzalez, Guo, Romer, and Kesler, "Baby's First Market Failure."
18. Roper, The Witch in the Western Imagination, 71.
19. Federici, Caliban and the Witch, 11.
20. Federici, 13.
21. Kurlansky, as quoted in Federici, 189.

CHAPTER THREE

1. Federici, 97.
2. Federici, 92.
3. Morgan, Laboring Women, 3.
4. Reese, "What Is Emotional Labor, and Why Does It Matter?"
5. Reese.
6. adrienne maree brown, Pleasure Activism, 231.
7. adrienne maree brown, 231.
8. Reese, "What Is Emotional Labor, and Why Does It Matter?"
9. Gallant, "Fuck You, Pay Me: The Pleasures of Sex Work," in Pleasure Activism, edited by adrienne maree brown, 177.
10. Gallant, "Fuck You, Pay Me: The Pleasures of Sex Work," in Pleasure Activism, edited by adrienne maree brown, 177.
11. Gallant, "Fuck You, Pay Me: The Pleasures of Sex Work," in Pleasure Activism, edited by adrienne maree brown, 180.
12. Federici, Caliban and the Witch, 75.
13. Porges, "Demystifying the Body's Response to Trauma—A Polyvagal Perspective," 47:00.

14. Porges, 47:00.
15. Federici, Caliban and the Witch, 88
16. Vaughan, "Patriarchal Capitalism vs. a Gift Economy," in The Rule of Mars, edited by Cristina Biaggi, 266.
17. Federici, Caliban and the Witch, 139–40.
18. Buck, "The Reason You Answer Work Email on the Weekend Is Actually 500 Years Old."
19. Buck.
20. Johnson, Nieto, and Williams. "PANEL — What is Embodied Social Justice with Rev. Angel Kyodo Williams, Dr. Rae Johnson, Dr. Leticia Nieto." 59:55
21. Kimmerer, Braiding Sweetgrass, 6–7.
22. The Gilder Lehrman Institute of American History, "The Doctrine of Discovery, 1493."
23. Oyěwùmí, The Invention of Women, 123.
24. Oyěwùmí, Kindle Location 120 of 5709
25. Oyěwùmí, 124.
26. Oyěwùmí, 125.
27. Biss, "White Debt."
28. Biss.
29. Personal communication, January 17, 2024.
30. National Labor Relations Board, "Unfair Labor Practices Charge Filings Up 16%, Union Petitions Remain Up in Fiscal Year 2023."
31. Shierholz, Poydock, and McNicholas, "Unionization Increased by 200,000 in 2022."

CHAPTER FOUR

1. Kathleen M. Brown, Good Wives, Nasty Wenches, & Anxious Patriarchs, 249.
2. Painter, The History of White People, 42.
3. Painter, The History of White People, 43
4. Painter, The History of White People, 54.
5. Painter, The History of White People, 55.
6. Painter, The History of White People, 111–12.
7. Kathleen M. Brown, Good Wives, Nasty Wenches, & Anxious Patriarchs, 369.
8. Battalora, Birth of a White Nation (book), 4.
9. Battalora, Birth of a White Nation (book), 6.
10. Battalora, Birth of a White Nation (book), 7.
11. Kathleen M. Brown, Good Wives, Nasty Wenches, & Anxious Patriarchs, 118.
12. Kathleen M. Brown, 119.
13. Kathleen M. Brown, 125.
14. Kathleen M. Brown, 122.
15. Kathleen M. Brown, 128.
16. Battalora, Birth of a White Nation (book), 10.
17. Battalora, Birth of a White Nation (book), 22.

18. Battalora, Birth of a White Nation (book), 25–6.
19. Battalora, Birth of a White Nation (book), 11.
20. Alexander, "Tarana Burke."
21. Rossetto, "The Trauma of Privilege."
22. Rossetto.
23. Carnes, Sexual Anorexia, 56.
24. Battalora, "Birth of a White Nation" (conference proceedings, The White Privilege Conference), 7.
25. Battalora, "Birth of a White Nation" (conference proceedings, The White Privilege Conference), 7.
26. Tippett, "Bessel van der Kolk – How Trauma Lodges in the Body, Revisited," 19:50.
27. Hozumi, "The Key to Healing Whiteness Is Understanding Cultural Somatic Context."
28. Menakem, My Grandmother's Hands, 47.

CHAPTER FIVE

1. Glymph, Out of the House of Bondage, 2.
2. Glymph, 3.
3. Glymph, 4.
4. Glymph, 35.
5. Glymph, 28.
6. Glymph, 7.
7. Glymph, 13.
8. Glymph, 20.
9. Glymph, 3–4.
10. Desmond-Harris, "What Exactly Is a Microaggression?"
11. Smith, Bentley-Edwards, El-Amin, and Darity, "Fighting at Birth," 1.
12. Glymph, Out of the House of Bondage, 6.
13. Glymph, 19–20.

CHAPTER SIX

1. Dorr, White Women, Rape, and the Power of Race in Virginia: 1900–1960, 137.
2. Hodes, White Women, Black Men: Illicit Sex in the 19th Century South, 175.
3. Allain, "Sexual Relations Between Elite White Women and Enslaved Men in the Antebellum South: A Socio-Historical Analysis."
4. Young as quoted in Allain.
5. Allain.
6. Allain.
7. Dorr, White Women, Rape, and the Power of Race in Virginia, 150.
8. Weaver, "Why White People Keep Calling the Cops on Black Americans."
9. Weaver.

10. Weaver.
11. Allain, "Sexual Relations Between Elite White Women and Enslaved Men in the Antebellum South."
12. Dorr, White Women, Rape, and the Power of Race in Virginia, 141.
13. Dorr, 141.
14. Hodes, White Women, Black Men: Illicit Sex in the 19th Century South, 193.
15. Buroughs, as quoted in Hodes, 198.
16. Kaba, We Do This 'til We Free Us, 59.
17. Livingston and Brown, "Intermarriage in the U.S. 50 Years after Loving v. Virginia."

CHAPTER SEVEN

1. Hodes, White Women, Black Men: Illicit Sex in the 19th Century South, 3.
2. Hodes, 96.
3. Davis, "The 'Orphan' I Adopted from Uganda Already Had a Family."
4. Davis.
5. Glymph, Out of the House of Bondage, 64.
6. Glymph, 29.
7. Glymph, 220.
8. Newman, White Women's Rights, 41.
9. Carter, "Manitoba History: 'Your Great Mother Across the Salt Sea': Prairie First Nations, the British Monarchy and the Vice Regal Connection to 1900."
10. Carter.
11. Newman, White Women's Rights, 40.

CHAPTER EIGHT

1. Newman, 52.
2. Newman, 123.
3. McRae, Mothers of Massive Resistance, 7.
4. Aizenman and Gharib, "American with No Medical Training Ran Center for Malnourished Ugandan Kids. 105 Died."
5. Aizenman and Gharib.
6. Aizenman and Gharib
7. Aizenman and Gharib.
8. Aizenman and Gharib.

CHAPTER NINE

1. Painter, Southern History Across the Color Line, 29.
2. Painter, Southern History Across the Color Line, 29.
3. Glymph, Out of the House of Bondage, 69.
4. Painter, Southern History Across the Color Line, 29.
5. Painter, Southern History Across the Color Line, 33.
6. Painter, Southern History Across the Color Line, 32.

7. California Newsreel. "Race - the Power of an Illusion."
8. hooks, The Will to Change, 66.
9. Kathleen M. Brown, Good Wives, Nasty Wenches, & Anxious Patriarchs, 140.
10. Kathleen M. Brown, 40.
11. Kathleen M. Brown, 154.
12. Kathleen M. Brown, 149.
13. Kathleen M. Brown, 140.
14. Kathleen M. Brown, 166.
15. Kathleen M. Brown, 164.
16. Kathleen M. Brown, 162.
17. Kathleen M. Brown, 170.
18. Kathleen M. Brown, 140.
19. Kathleen M. Brown, 140.
20. Kathleen M. Brown, 371.
21. Despart, "'Systemic Failures' in Uvalde Shooting Went Far beyond Local Police, Texas House Report Details."
22. U.S. Senate Committee on the Judiciary, "Fact: Arming More People Doesn't Make Us Safer."
23. Everytown for Gun Safety, "Stop Arming Teachers."
24. CBS News, "'Shame on You': Uvalde Parents Lash out at School Board after Release of Scathing Report on Police Response to Shooting."
25. Kathleen M. Brown, Good Wives, Nasty Wenches, & Anxious Patriarchs, 320.
26. BBC, "How Many US Mass Shootings Have There Been in 2023?"
27. Curtin and Hedegaard, "Suicide Rates for Females and Males by Race and Ethnicity: United States, 1999 and 2017."
28. King, Smith, and Gracey, "Indigenous Health Part 2: The Underlying Causes of the Health Gap."
29. Parker, Horowitz, Igielnik, Oliphant, and Brown. "The Demographics of Gun Ownership in the U.S."
30. Siegel and Rothman, "Firearm Ownership and Suicide Rates Among US Men and Women, 1981–2013."
31. Frakt, "What Can Be Learned from Differing Rates of Suicide among Groups."
32. McRae, Mothers of Massive Resistance, 3.
33. McRae, 4.
34. Painter, Southern History Across the Color Line, 29–30.
35. Painter, Southern History Across the Color Line, 33.
36. Painter, Southern History Across the Color Line, 34.
37. Coalition to Stop Violence Against Native Women, "MMIWG2S – Missing and Murdered Indigenous Women, Girls, and Two Spirit."
38. RAINN, "Children and Teens: Statistics."
39. Painter, Southern History Across the Color Line, 25.
40. Smith, Decolonizing Methodologies, 23.

CHAPTER TEN

1. Bieber, "Revealing Divorce Statistics in 2024."
2. Battalora, Birth of a White Nation (book), 8.
3. Battalora, Birth of a White Nation (book), 12.
4. Battalora, Birth of a White Nation (book), 13.
5. Battalora, Birth of a White Nation (book), 38.
6. Kathleen M. Brown, Good Wives, Nasty Wenches, & Anxious Patriarchs, 249.
7. Bergen and Barnhill, "Marital Rape: New Research and Directions."
8. Jacobson, "13 Legal Benefits of Marriage."
9. The Journal of Blacks in Higher Education, "The Significant Racial Gap in Marriage Rates in the United States."
10. Bieber, "Revealing Divorce Statistics in 2024."
11. Bieber.
12. Substance Abuse and Mental Health Services Administration, "Harm Reduction."
13. Frankenberg, White Women, Race Matters, 1.
14. Cohn, "How U.S. Immigration Laws and Rules Have Changed through History."
15. Hodes, White Women, Black Men: Illicit Sex in the 19th Century South, 7–8.

CHAPTER ELEVEN

1. Fox-Genovese, Within the Plantation Household, 31.
2. Fox-Genovese, 31.
3. Painter, Southern History across the Color Line, 31.
4. Lorde, Sister Outsider, 112.
5. Painter, Southern History Across the Color Line, 27.
6. Painter, Southern History Across the Color Line, 27.
7. Painter, Southern History Across the Color Line, 28.
8. Painter, Southern History Across the Color Line, 27.
9. Painter, Southern History Across the Color Line, 28.
10. Clinton, as quoted in Painter, 29.

CHAPTER TWELVE

1. Kidd, The Dance of the Dissident Daughter, 70.
2. Kidd, 15.
3. Lateiner, "Grieving the White Void."
4. Holy Bible: NIV: New International Version, Matthew 5:9.
5. Psychology Today (website), "Post-Traumatic Growth."
6. Parker, "Rest, Reflect, Renew."
7. Gandhi and Wolff, "Yoga and the Roots of Cultural Appropriation."
8. Johnson, "What's Wrong with Cultural Appropriation?"
9. Native Governance Center, "Cultural Appropriation and Wellness Guide."
10. Susanna Barkataki, Embrace Yoga's Roots, 46.
11. Purser and Loy, "Beyond McMindfulness."
12. Kimmerer, Braiding Sweetgrass, 213–14.

13. Kimmerer, 214–15.
14. Jones and Okun, "White Supremacy Culture from Dismantling Racism: A Workbook for Social Change Groups."
15. Jones and Okun.
16. Okun, "(Divorcing) White Supremacy Culture."
17. Walker, In Search of Our Mothers' Gardens, 59.
18. Biss, "White Debt."
19. Satchidananda, The Living Gita, 100.

CHAPTER THIRTEEN

1. Porges, "Demystifying the Body's Response to Trauma—A Polyvagal Perspective."
2. Porges.
3. Bell, "Developmental Trauma and Anti-Racism Work with Karine Bell."
4. Parker, "Who's In & Who's Out?" in Colorizing Restorative Justice, edited by Edward Valandra, 69.
5. Littlewolf, Armster, Paras, and Amstutz, "Burn the Bridge," in Colorizing Restorative Justice, edited by Edward Valandra, 93–4.
6. Bell, "Developmental Trauma and Anti-Racism Work with Karine Bell."
7. Bell.
8. Saufler, Chuck. "Impact of Social Environments on the Brain" (diagram), from Restorative Approach Facilitator Training by Ima Gomez, https://slideplayer.com/slide/16282470/, slide 16.

CHAPTER FOURTEEN

1. Birney, "molliebirney," slide 6.

CHAPTER FIFTEEN

1. Kaba, We Do This 'til We Free Us, 4.
2. Nieto, "Looking into the Well: Action Practices for Sustainable Justice."

UNCONCLUSION

1. Scott-Heron, "Gil Scott-Heron - Revolution Will Not Be Televised (Official Version)."
2. Zehr Institute for Restorative Justice, "Restorative Justice and the First Harm: Indigenous Land Acknowledgments and Beyond."
3. Tuck and Yang, "Decolonization Is Not a Metaphor."

AFTERWORD

1. Kidd, Dance of the Dissident Daughter, 83.
2. Tuck and Yang, "R-Words: Refusing Research."
3. Kaba, We Do This 'til We Free Us, 87.
4. hooks, Feminist Theory, 64.

BIBLIOGRAPHY

Aizenman, Nurith. "U.S. Missionary with No Medical Training Settles Suit Over Child Deaths at Her Center." NPR, Goats and Soda, July 31, 2020. https://www.npr.org/sections/goatsandsoda/2020/07/31/897773274/u-s-missionary-with-no-medical-training-settles-suit-over-child-deaths-at-her-ce.

Aizenman, Nurith, and Malaka Gharib. "American with No Medical Training Ran Center for Malnourished Ugandan Kids. 105 Died." NPR, All Things Considered, August 9, 2019. https://www.npr.org/sections/goatsandsoda/2019/08/09/749005287/american-with-no-medical-training-ran-center-for-malnourished-ugandan-kids-105-d.

Alexander, Kerri Lee. "Tarana Burke." National Women's History Museum. Accessed February 17, 2024. https://www.womenshistory.org/education-resources/biographies/tarana-burke.

Allain, J. M. "Sexual Relations between Elite White Women and Enslaved Men in the Antebellum South: A Socio-Historical Analysis." *Inquiries Journal* 5, no. 8 (2013). http://www.inquiriesjournal.com/a?id=1674.

Allen, Evette, Bryan Hubain, Cerise Hunt, Star Lucero, and Saran Steward. "Race Matters: Implementing Racial Identity Development into the Classroom." In *Diversity Summit*, 1–21. 2012 Diversity Summit, May 4, 2012. https://drive.google.com/file/d/1_WxG7t7B6zPgKqMqBNn0pA_ZoXZxuvv9/view.

Allison, Emily Joy. *#ChurchToo: How Purity Culture Upholds Abuse and How to Find Healing*. Minneapolis: Broadleaf Books, 2021.

Anzaldúa, Gloria, and Cherríe Moraga. *This Bridge Called My Back: Writings by Radical Women of Color*. Albany: State University of New York (Suny) Press, 2015.

Arnold, Amanda. "American Woman Accused of Letting Hundreds of Ugandan Kids Die at a Fake Clinic." The Cut, July 18, 2019. https://www.thecut.com/2019/07/renee-bach-pretended-to-be-a-doctor-in-uganda-lawsuit.html.

Atlanta History Center. "Cyclorama: The Big Picture" Atlanta History Center. Accessed February 17, 2024. https://www.atlantahistorycenter.com/exhibitions/cyclorama/.

Barkataki, Susanna. *Embrace Yoga's Roots*. Orlando: Ignite Yoga and Wellness Institute, 2020.

Battalora, Jacqueline. *Birth of a White Nation: The Invention of White People and Its Relevance Today*. Kindle Edition. Strategic Book Publishing and Rights Co., 2013.

Battalora, Jacqueline. "Birth of a White Nation." Conference proceedings. In *Understanding & Dismantling Privilege*, V:1–12. The White Privilege Conference, 2015.

BBC. "How Many US Mass Shootings Have There Been in 2023?" BBC News, December 7, 2023. https://www.bbc.com/news/world-us-canada-41488081.

Beck, Phillipa. "Power and Prana: When Yoga Leads to Abuse." Full Circle Yoga. December 4, 2019. https://www.full-circle-yoga.ca/power-and-prana-when-yoga-leads-to-abuse/.

Bell, Karine. "Developmental Trauma & Anti-Racism Work with Karine Bell." The Embody Lab. Video, 40:53. Accessed January 1, 2023. https://learn.theembodylab.com/products/bonus-embodied-social-justice-2022-early-bird/categories/2149666785/posts/2155287391.

Bergen, Raquel Kennedy, and Elizabeth Barnhill. "Marital Rape: New Research and Directions." National Online Resource Center on Violence Against Women, Applied Research Forum. February 2006. https://vawnet.org/sites/default/files/materials/files/2016-09/AR_MaritalRapeRevised.pdf

Biaggi, Cristina, ed. *The Rule of Mars: Readings on the Origins, History and Impact of Patriarchy*. Manchester, CT: Knowledge, Ideas & Trends, 2006.

Bieber, Christy. "Revealing Divorce Statistics in 2024." Edited by Adam Ramirez. *Forbes Advisor*, updated January 8, 2024. https://www.forbes.com/advisor/legal/divorce/divorce-statistics//.

Billings, David. *Deep Denial: The Persistence of White Supremacy in United States History and Life*. Roselle, NJ: Crandall, Dostie & Douglass Books, Inc., 2016.

Birdsong, Mia. *How We Show Up: Reclaiming Family, Friendship, and Community*. New York: Hachette Go, 2020.

Birney, Mollie. "molliebirney." Instagram, November 27, 2023. https://www.instagram.com/p/C0KIkYopgqu/?img_index=1.

Biss, Eula. "White Debt." *The New York Times Magazine*, December 2, 2015. https://www.nytimes.com/2015/12/06/magazine/white-debt.html.

Blee, Kathleen M. *Women of the Klan: Racism and Gender in the 1920s*. Berkeley: University of California Press, 2009.

Boggs, Grace Lee. "Solutionaries Are Today's Revolutionaries." *The Boggs Blog*, October 27, 2013. https://conversationsthatyouwillneverfinish.wordpress.com/2013/10/27/solutionaries-are-todays-revolutionaries-by-grace-lee-boggs/.

Bond, Shannon. "How Alex Jones Helped Mainstream Conspiracy Theories Become Part of American Life." NPR, Weekend Edition Saturday, August 6, 2022. https://www.npr.org/2022/08/06/1115936712/how-alex-jones-helped-mainstream-conspiracy-theories-into-american-life.

Booker, Brakkton. "Amy Cooper, White Woman Who Called Police on Black Bird-Watcher, Has Charge Dismissed." NPR, February 16, 2021. https://www.npr.org/2021/02/16/968372253/white-woman-who-called-police-on-black-man-bird-watching-has-charges-dismissedd.

Boswell, John. *Same-Sex Unions in Premodern Europe*. New York: Vintage Books, 1994. Kindle Edition.

Bragg, Ko. "First Came Suffrage. Then Came the Women of the Ku Klux Klan." The 19th, December 28, 2020. https://19thnews.org/2020/12/first-came-suffrage-then-came-the-women-of-the-ku-klux-klan/.

Braght, Van, Jan Luyken, and Joseph F. Sohm. *The Bloody Theater or Martyrs Mirror of the Defenseless Christians: Who Baptized Only upon Confession of Faith, and Who Suffered and Died for the Testimony of Jesus, Their Savior, for the Time of Christ to the Year A.D. 1660*. Scottdale, PA: Herald Press, 2012.

Brigham, Katie. "How Conflict Minerals Make It into Our Phones." CNBC, February 15, 2023. https://www.cnbc.com/2023/02/15/how-conflict-minerals-make-it-into-our-phones.html.

brown, adrienne maree. *Pleasure Activism: The Politics of Feeling Good*. Chico, CA: AK Press, 2019.

Brown, Kathleen M. *Good Wives, Nasty Wenches, & Anxious Patriarchs: Gender, Race, and Power in Colonial Virginia*. Chapel Hill: University of North Carolina Press, 1996.

Buck, Stephanie. "The Reason You Answer Work Email on the Weekend Is Actually 500 Years Old." Medium. May 16, 2017. https://medium.com/timeline/invention-of-wasted-time-mercantilism-e11df6f8dfa1.

Burke, Natasha L., Amy H. Egbert, Rowan A. Hunt, Karen Jennings Mathis, and Kayla L. Williams. "Reporting Racial and Ethnic Diversity in Eating Disorder Research over the Past 20 Years." *International Journal of Eating Disorders* 55, no. 4 (2022): 455–62. https://doi.org/10.1002/eat.23666.

California Newsreel. "Race - the Power of an Illusion." YouTube video, 5:13. Posted April 24, 2014. https://www.youtube.com/watch?v=Y8MS6zubIaQ.

Carnes, Patrick. *Sexual Anorexia: Overcoming Sexual Self-Hatred*. Center City, MN: Hazelden Publishing, 1997. Kindle Edition.

Carter, Sarah. "Manitoba History: 'Your Great Mother across the Salt Sea': Prairie First Nations, the British Monarchy and the Vice Regal Connection to 1900." Manitoba Historical Society Archives, *Manitoba History* 48 (Autumn/Winter 2004–2005). http://www.mhs.mb.ca/docs/mb_history/48/greatmother.shtml.

CBS. "'Shame on You': Uvalde Parents Lash Out at School Board after Release of Scathing Report on Police Response to Shooting." CBS News, July 19, 2022. https://www.cbsnews.com/news/uvalde-texas-school-shooting-parents-board-meeting-scathing-report-law-enforcement-response/.

Center for Action and Contemplation. "Transforming Pain." *Center for Action and Contemplation*. October 17, 2018. https://cac.org/daily-meditations/transforming

-pain-2018-10-17/#:~:text=If%20we%20do%20not%20transform,common%20 storyline%20of%20human%20history.

Center for Justice and Peacebuilding. "STAR: Strategies for Trauma Awareness and Resilience." In *Level I Participant Manual*. Harrisonburg, VA: A Program of the Center for Justice and Peacebuilding at Eastern Mennonite University, 2009.

"Chatbooks Commercial." YouTube video. July 15, 2019. Accessed September 1, 2019. https://youtu.be/mF2eKaOc3wo?si=3zmbwRn8mqGy5GMh.

City of Evanston. "Evanston Local Reparations." Accessed February 23, 2024. https://www.cityofevanston.org/government/city-council/reparations.

The Coalition to Dismantle the Doctrine of Discovery. "Timeline of the Doctrine of Discovery." May 11, 2023. https://dismantlediscovery.org/2023/05/11/ timeline-of-the-doctrine-of-discovery/.

Coalition to Stop Violence Against Native Women. "MMIWG2S -- Missing and Murdered Indigenous Women, Girls, and Two Spirit." 2024. https://www. csvanw.org/mmiw/.

Cohen, Arianne. "How to Quit Your Job in the Great Post-Pandemic Resignation Boom." Bloomberg.com, May 10, 2021. https://www.bloomberg.com/news/ articles/2021-05-10/quit-your-job-how-to-resign-after-covid-pandemic.

Cohn, D'Vera. "How U.S. Immigration Laws and Rules Have Changed through History." Pew Research Center. September 30, 2015. https://www.pewresearch. org/short-reads/2015/09/30/how-u-s-immigration-laws-and-rules-have-changed-through-history/#:~:text=A%201790%20law%20was%20the.

Complex Trauma Resources. "Co-Regulation." Foundation Trust, 2024. Accessed Feb 1, 2024. https://www.complextrauma.org/glossary/co-regulation/.

Creative Praxis. "Who We Are." Created 2019. https://www.creativepraxis.org/ about.

Crumbie, Trey. "A Lifestyle of Empowerment." *Inside NKU, Northern Kentucky University Magazine*, February 2022. https://inside.nku.edu/nkumagazine/2022/ February/blackhistorymonth/michaelwashington.html.

Curtin, Sally C., and Holly Hedegaard. "Suicide Rates for Females and Males by Race and Ethnicity: United States, 1999 and 2017." National Center for Health Statistics, Center for Disease Control and Prevention. June 20, 2019. https:// www.cdc.gov/nchs/data/hestat/suicide/rates_1999_2017.htm.

Davis, Jessica. "The 'Orphan' I Adopted from Uganda Already Had a Family." CNN, October 13, 2017. https://www.cnn.com/2017/10/13/opinions/adoption-uganda-opinion-davis/index.html.

Dawson, Trevon. "Beah: Thus a Black Woman Speaks." YouTube video, 15:00. Posted May 14, 2014. https://youtu.be/RcZntCk_beA?si=50_8G2MMQNUH3TA_.

Deahl, Jessica. "Countries around the World Beat the U.S. on Paid Parental Leave." NPR, All Things Considered, October 6, 2016. https://www.npr. org/2016/10/06/495839588/countries-around-the-world-beat-the-u-s-on-paid-parental-leave.

DeGruy, Joy. *Post Traumatic Slave Syndrome: America's Legacy of Enduring Injury and Healing*. United States: Joy DeGruy Publications Inc., 2005.

Desmond-Harris, Jenée. "What Exactly Is a Microaggression?" Vox, February 16, 2015. https://www.vox.com/2015/2/16/8031073/what-are-microaggressions.

Despart, Zach. "'Systemic Failures' in Uvalde Shooting Went Far beyond Local Police, Texas House Report Details." *The Texas Tribune*, July 17, 2022. https://www.texastribune.org/2022/07/17/law-enforcement-failure-uvalde-shooting-investigation/.

Diaminah, Sendolo, Scot Nakagawa, Sean Thomas-Breitfeld, Rinku Sen, and Lori Villarosa. "How (Not) to Dismantle White Supremacy." The Forge, April 20, 2023. https://forgeorganizing.org/article/how-not-dismantle-white-supremacy.

DiAngelo, Robin. "White Women's Tears and the Men Who Love Them." The Good Men Project. September 19, 2015. https://goodmenproject.com/featured-content/white-womens-tears-and-the-men-who-love-them-twlm/.

Disabled World. "What Is: Neurodiversity, Neurodivergent, Neurotypical." Updated September 29, 2023. https://www.disabled-world.com/disability/awareness/neurodiversity/#google_vignette.

Donnella, Leah. "2 Teach for America Alums Say TFA Has Big Problems When It Comes to Race." NPR, Code Switch. October 14, 2015. https://www.npr.org/sections/codeswitch/2015/10/14/447217749/two-teach-for-america-alums-say-the-program-has-big-problems-when-it-comes-to-ra.

Dorr, Lisa Lindquist. *White Women, Rape, and the Power of Race in Virginia, 1900–1960*. Chapel Hill: University of North Carolina Press, 2004.

Eisler, Riane. *The Chalice and the Blade*. New York: Harper Collins, 2011.

Evans, Rachel Held, and Jeff Chu. *Wholehearted Faith*. New York: Harper One, 2021.

Everytown for Gun Safety. "Stop Arming Teachers." Everytown for Gun Safety Action Fund. 2024. https://www.everytown.org/solutions/arming-teachers/.

Fausset, Richard. "What We Know about the Shooting Death of Ahmaud Arbery." *The New York Times*, May 11, 2020. https://www.nytimes.com/article/ahmaud-arbery-shooting-georgia.html.

Federici, Silvia. 2004. *Caliban and the Witch: Women, the Body and Primitive Accumulation*. New York: Autonomedia, 2004.

Fieggen, Ian. "Shoelace Knots." Ian Shoelace Site. Updated April 9, 2024. https://www.fieggen.com/shoelace/knots.htm.

Fox-Genovese, Elizabeth. *Within the Plantation Household*. Chapel Hill: University of North Carolina Press, 1988.

Frakt, Austin. "What Can Be Learned from Differing Rates of Suicide among Groups." *The New York Times*, December 30, 2020, The Upshot. https://www.nytimes.com/2020/12/30/upshot/suicide-demographic-differences.html.

Frankenberg, Ruth. *White Women, Race Matters: The Social Construction of Whiteness*. Minneapolis: University of Minnesota Press, 1993.

Gallant, Chanelle. "Fuck You, Pay Me: The Pleasures of Sex Work." In *Pleasure Activism*, edited by adrienne maree brown, 177–88. Chico, CA: AK Press, 2019.

Gandhi, Shreena, and Lillie Wolff. "Yoga and the Roots of Cultural Appropriation." Trauma Sensitive Yoga. April 23, 2021. https://www.traumasensitiveyoganederland. com/yoga-and-the-roots-of-cultural-appropriation/.

The Gilder Lehrman Institute of American History. "The Doctrine of Discovery, 1493." Accessed February 17, 2024. https://www.gilderlehrman.org/history-resources/ spotlight-primary-source/doctrine-discovery-1493.

glennEmartin. "Glenn E. Martin." X, February 6, 2022. https://twitter.com/ glennEmartin/status/1490479496335663111?lang=en.

Goldenberg, David M. *The Curse of Ham: Race and Slavery in Early Judaism, Christianity, and Islam*. Princeton: Princeton University Press, 2009.

Gonzalez, Sarah, Jeff Guo, Keith Romer, and Sam Yellowhorse Kesler. "Baby's First Market Failure." NPR, Planet Money, February 3, 2023. https://www.npr. org/2023/02/02/1153931108/day-care-market-expensive-child-care-waitlists.

Grace to You. "Slavery and True Liberty (John MacArthur)." YouTube video: 2:55. July 17, 2012. https://www.youtube.com/watch?v=HSKj3LQilcI.

Greenhouse, Steven. "'Striketober' Is Showing Workers' Rising Power – but Will It Lead to Lasting Change?" *The Guardian*, October 23, 2021. https://www.theguardian. com/us-news/2021/oct/23/striketober-unions-strikes-workers-lasting-change.

Glymph, Thavolia. *Out of the House of Bondage: The Transformation of the Plantation Household*. Cambridge: Cambridge University Press, 2008.

Hackman, Rose. *Emotional Labor: The Invisible Work Shaping Our Lives and How to Claim Our Power*. New York: Flatiron Books, 2023.

Healing Minnesota Stories. "One Church's Path Towards Reparations: Donating Its Property Tax Equivalent to Black- and Indigenous-Lead Organizations." March 14, 2021. https://healingmnstories.wordpress.com/2021/03/14/one-churchs- path-towards-reparations-donating-its-property-tax-equivalent-to-black-and- indigenous-lead-organizations/.

Higginbotham, Leon. *In the Matter of Color: Race and the American Legal Process: The Colonial Period*. New York: Oxford University Press, 1980.

Hill, Roger B. "History of Work Ethic: 5. Two Perspectives of the Protestant Ethic." Workethic.coe.uga.edu. UGA, 1996. http://workethic.coe.uga.edu/ htpp.html#:~:text=Max%20Weber%2C%20the%20German%20economic.

Hochschild, Arlie Russell. *The Managed Heart: Commercialization of Human Feeling*. Third Edition. Berkeley: University of California Press, 2012.

Hodes, Martha. *White Women, Black Men: Illicit Sex in the 19th-Century South*. New Haven: Yale University Press, 1999.

Holy Bible: NIV: New International Version. 1973. Durbanville: Christian Media Bibles.

hooks, bell. *Feminist Theory: From Margin to Center*. Boston: South End Press, 1984.

hooks, bell. *All About Love: New Visions*. New York: Harper Perennial, 1999.

hooks, bell. *The Will to Change: Men, Masculinity, and Love.* New York: Washington Square Press, 2004.

hooks, bell. "Understanding Patriarchy." Accessed January 22, 2024. https://imaginenoborders.org/pdf/zines/UnderstandingPatriarchy.pdf.

Hozumi, Tada. "The Key to Healing Whiteness Is Understanding Cultural Somatic Context." *The Selfish Activist* (blog). January 18, 2019. Accessed March 1, 2020. https://selfishactivist.com/the-key-to-healing-whiteness-is-understanding-cultural-somatic-context/ (site discontinued).

Hughes, Langston. *The Ways of White Folks.* New York: Vintage Books, 1990.

In Our Own Voice: National Black Women's Reproductive Justice Agenda. "Reproductive Justice." Accessed February 23, 2024. https://blackrj.org/our-causes/reproductive-justice/.

Jackson Lee, Sheila. "H.R. 40 Is Not a Symbolic Act. It's a Path to Restorative Justice." American Civil Liberties Union, News & Commentary, May 22, 2020. https://www.aclu.org/news/racial-justice/h-r-40-is-not-a-symbolic-act-its-a-path-to-restorative-justice.

Jacobson, Ivy. "13 Legal Benefits of Marriage." Theknot.com. Accessed February 17, 2024. https://www.theknot.com/content/benefits-of-marriage.

Janney, Caroline E. "United Daughters of the Confederacy." Encyclopedia Virginia, 2020. Accessed March 1, 2023. https://encyclopediavirginia.org/entries/united-daughters-of-the-confederacy/.

Johnson, Maisha Z. "What's Wrong with Cultural Appropriation? These 9 Answers Reveal Its Harm." Everyday Feminism, June 14, 2015. https://everydayfeminism.com/2015/06/cultural-appropriation-wrong/.

Johnson, Rae, Leticia Nieto, and Angel Kyodo Williams. "PANEL - What Is Embodied Social Justice with Rev. Angel Kyodo Williams, Dr. Rae Johnson, Dr. Leticia Nieto." The Embody Lab, 2021. Video, 59:55. Accessed February 24, 2024. https://learn.theembodylab.com/products/summit-collection-embodied-social-justice-summit-2021/categories/4404821/posts/14783738.

Jones, Ellen E. "From Mammy to Ma: Hollywood's Favourite Racist Stereotype." BBC, May 31, 2019. https://www.bbc.com/culture/article/20190530-rom-mammy-to-ma-hollywoods-favourite-racist-stereotype.

Jones, Kenneth, and Tema Okun. "White Supremacy Culture: From Dismantling Racism: A Workbook for Social Change Groups." Minnesota Historical Society, Department of Inclusion and Community Engagement. 2001. https://www.thc.texas.gov/public/upload/preserve/museums/files/White_Supremacy_Culture.pdf.

The Journal of Blacks in Higher Education. "The Significant Racial Gap in Marriage Rates in the United States." November 21, 2022. https://jbhe.com/2022/11/the-significant-racial-gap-in-marriage-rates-in-the-united-states/.

Kaba, Mariame. *We Do This 'til We Free Us: Abolitionist Organizing and Transforming Justice.* Chicago: Haymarket Books, 2021. Kindle Edition.

Kelly, Makena. "Inside Nextdoor's 'Karen Problem.'" The Verge, June 8, 2020. https://www.theverge.com/21283993/nextdoor-app-racism-community-moderation-guidance-protests.

Kendi, Ibram X. *How to Be an Antiracist*. New York: One World, 2019.

Kidd, Sue Monk. *The Dance of the Dissident Daughter: A Woman's Journey from Christian Tradition to the Sacred Feminine*. New York: Harper San Francisco, 1995.

Kimmerer, Robin Wall. *Braiding Sweetgrass: Indigenous Wisdom, Scientific Knowledge and the Teachings of Plants*. Minneapolis: Milkweed Editions, 2013.

King, Cody. "Chaotic Video Shows Parents Pleading with Law Enforcement to Enter Uvalde School, Save Children from Gunman." *KSAT,* May 26, 2022. https://www.ksat.com/news/local/2022/05/26/chaotic-video-shows-parents-pleading-with-law-enforcement-to-enter-uvalde-school-save-children-from-gunman/.

King, Malcolm, Andrea Smith, and Michael Gracey. "Indigenous Health Part 2: The Underlying Causes of the Health Gap," *Lancet* 374, no. 9683 (July 4, 2009): 76–85. doi: 10.1016/S0140-6736(09)60827-8.

King, Marshall V. *Disarmed: The Radical Life and Legacy of Michael "MJ" Sharp*. Harrisonburg, VA: Herald Press, 2022.

Koren, Marina. "Telling the Story of the Stanford Rape Case." *The Atlantic*, June 6, 2016. https://www.theatlantic.com/news/archive/2016/06/stanford-sexual-assault-letters/485837/.

Lakoff, George. *Don't Think of an Elephant!: Know Your Values and Frame the Debate*. White River Junction: Chelsea Green Publishing, 2004.

Langholtz, Harvey. In *Perpetration-Induced Traumatic Stress: The Psychological Consequences of Killing* by Rachel MacNair, (vii–ix). New York: Authors Choice Press, 2005.

Lateiner, Abraham. "Grieving the White Void." Medium, March 7, 2016. https://abelateiner.medium.com/grieving-the-white-void-48c410fdd7f3.

Lawal, Shola. "A Guide to the Decades-Long Conflict in DR Congo." Al Jazeera, February 21, 2024. https://www.aljazeera.com/news/2024/2/21/a-guide-to-the-decades-long-conflict-in-dr-congo

Levin, Bess. "Dr. Oz Is Sorry You Were Offended by His Comment That It's Fine for 2–3% of Schoolchildren to Die." *Vanity Fair*, April 17, 2020. https://www.vanityfair.com/news/2020/04/dr-oz-school-children-non-apology.

Library of Congress. "Homestead Strike: Topics in Chronicling America." Library of Congress Research Guides. Accessed February 17, 2024. https://guides.loc.gov/chronicling-america-homestead-strike#:~:text=In%201892%2C%20the%20Carnegie%20Steel.

Library of Congress. "Born in Slavery: Slave Narratives from the Federal Writers' Project, 1936 to 1938." Digital Collection: Born in Slavery: Slave Narratives from the Federal Writers' Project, 1936 to 1938.. Accessed February 17, 2024. https://www.loc.gov/collections/slave-narratives-from-the-federal-writers-project-1936-to-1938/

articles-and-essays/introduction-to-the-wpa-slave-narratives/wpa-and-the
-slave-narrative-collection/.

Littlewolf, Erica, Michelle Armster, Christianne Paras, and Lorraine Stutzman Amstutz. "Burn the Bridge." In *Colorizing Restorative Justice: Voicing Our Realities*, edited by Edward Valandra, 87–100. St. Paul: Living Justice Press, 2020.

Livingston, Gretchen, and Anna Brown. "Intermarriage in the U.S. 50 Years after Loving v. Virginia." Pew Research Center. May 18, 2017. https://www.pewresearch. org/social-trends/2017/05/18/intermarriage-in-the-u-s-50-years-after-loving-v-virginia/.

Lorde, Audre. *Sister Outsider: Essays and Speeches*. Berkeley: Crossing Press, 2012.

MacNair, Rachel. *Perpetration-Induced Traumatic Stress: The Psychological Consequences of Killing*. New York: Authors Choice Press, 2005.

Mathieson, Iain, Iosif Lazaridis, Nadin Rohland, Swapan Mallick, Nick Patterson, Songül Alpaslan Roodenberg, Eadaoin Harney, et al. "Genome-Wide Patterns of Selection in 230 Ancient Eurasians." *Nature* 528, no.7583 (2015): 499–503. https://doi.org/10.1038/nature16152.

McLaughlin, Eliott C. "State Prosecutors Mostly Avoided Race in Trying Ahmaud Arbery's Killers. Feds Won't Have That Option as Hate Crimes Trial Begins Today with Jury Selection." CNN, February 16, 2022. https://www. cnn.com/2022/02/06/us/ahmaud-arbery-killers-hate-crimes-trial-walkup/ index.html.

McRae, Elizabeth Gillespie. *Mothers of Massive Resistance: White Women and the Politics of White Supremacy*. New York: Oxford University Press, 2018.

Menakem, Resmaa. *My Grandmother's Hands: Healing Racial Trauma in Our Minds and Bodies*. Las Vegas: Central Recovery Press, 2017.

Miller, Chanel. *Know My Name: A Memoir*. New York: Penguin Books, 2020.

Mistress Syndrome. "Resources." Accessed February 17, 2024. https://www. mistresssyndrome.com/resources.

Mitchell, Margaret. *Gone with the Wind*. S.L.: Pan Books., 1936.

The More Up Campus. "Anarcha, Lucy, and Betsey | The Mothers of Gynecology." 2023. https://www.anarchalucybetsey.org.

Morgan, Jennifer L. *Laboring Women: Reproduction and Gender in New World Slavery*. Philadelphia: University of Pennsylvania Press, 2004.

National Alliance to End Homelessness. "Racial Inequalities in Homelessness, by the Numbers." Data and Graphics. June 1, 2020. https://endhomelessness.org/ resource/racial-inequalities-homelessness-numbers/.

National Center for Education Statistics. "Data Point: Race and Ethnicity of Public School Teachers and Their Students." September 2020. https://nces.ed.gov/ pubs2020/2020103/index.asp.

National Institute for the Clinical Application of Behavioral Medicine. "How to Help Your Clients Understand Their Window of Tolerance." Accessed

February 1, 2024. https://www.nicabm.com/trauma-how-to-help-your-clients-understand-their-window-of-tolerance/.

National Labor Relations Board, Office of Public Affairs. "Unfair Labor Practices Charge Filings up 16%, Union Petitions Remain up in Fiscal Year 2023." News & Publications, April 7, 2023. https://www.nlrb.gov/news-outreach/news-story/unfair-labor-practices-charge-filings-up-16-union-petitions-remain-up-in.

Native Governance Center. "Cultural Appropriation and Wellness Guide." Resources. Accessed February 1, 2024. https://nativegov.org/resources/cultural-appropriation-guide/.

Native Land Digital. "Native Land Digital." Accessed February 23, 2024. https://native-land.ca.

Nerenberg, Jenara. "Why Are So Many Adults Today Haunted by Trauma?" *Greater Good* magazine, the Greater Good Science Center at the University of California, Berkeley. June 8, 2017. https://greatergood.berkeley.edu/article/item/why_are_so_many_adults_today_haunted_by_trauma#:~:text=Trauma%20is%20not%20terrible%20things.

The New School. "Teaching to Transgress: bell hooks Returns to the New School." The New School News, October 7, 2014. https://blogs.newschool.edu/news/2014/10/bellhooksteachingtotransgress/.

Newman, Louise Michele. *White Women's Rights: The Racial Origins of Feminism in the United States.* New York: Oxford University Press, 1999.

Nicholas, Chani. "Chani Nicholas ~ Horoscopes, Astrology Workshops & More." Accessed February 17, 2024. http://chaninicholas.com.

Nieto, Leticia. "Looking into the Well: Action Practices for Sustainable Justice." The Embody Lab. Video, 1:21:26. Accessed February 24, 2024. https://learn.theembodylab.com/products/summit-collection-embodied-social-justice-summit-2021/categories/4404820/posts/15632170.

Nocella, Anthony J. "An Overview of the History and Theory of Transformative Justice." *Peace & Conflict Review* 6, no. 1 (2011). http://www.antoniocasella.eu/restorative/Nocella_2011.pdf

O'Toole, Elisabeth. *In On It: What Adoptive Parents Would Like You to Know about Adoption: A Guide for Relatives & Friends.* St. Paul: Fig Press, 2011.

Okun, Tema. "(Divorcing) White Supremacy Culture." White Supremacy Culture. August 2023. https://www.whitesupremacyculture.info.

Oyěwùmí, Oyèrónké. *The Invention of Women: Making an African Sense of Western Gender Discourses.* Minneapolis: University of Minnesota Press, 1997. Kindle Edition.

Painter, Nell Irvin. *The History of White People.* New York: W. W. Norton & Company, 2010.

Painter, Nell Irvin. *Southern History across the Color Line, Second Edition.* Chapel Hill: UNC Press Books, 2021. Kindle Edition.

Parker, Christina. "Who's In & Who's Out?" In *Colorizing Restorative Justice: Voicing Our Realities,* edited by Edward Valandra, 65–86. St. Paul: Living Justice Press, 2020.

Parker, Gail. "Rest, Reflect, Renew." The Embody Lab. Video, 1:11:28. Accessed February 23, 2024. https://learn.theembodylab.com/products/summit-collection-embodied-social-justice-summit-2022/categories/2149274739/posts/2155890172.

Parker, Kim, Juliana Menasce Horowitz, Ruth Igielnik, J. Baxter Oliphant, and Anna Brown. "The Demographics of Gun Ownership in the U.S." Pew Research Center's Social & Demographic Trends Project, Pew Research Center. June 22, 2017. https://www.pewresearch.org/social-trends/2017/06/22/the-demographics-of-gun-ownership/.

PBS. "The Roman Empire in the First Century: Early Christians." pbs.org. Accessed March 1, 2020. https://www.pbs.org/empires/romans/empire/christians.html -:~:text=In 313 AD, the Emperor.

PBS. "Why Does 'Straight' Mean Heterosexual?" *Origin of Everything*, season 3, episode 4. Video, 8:07. pbs.org. PBS Studios, January 30, 2020. https://www.pbs.org/video/why-does-straight-mean-heterosexual-mz0kp2/.

PISAB. "About Us." Undoing Racism: The People's Institute for Survival and Beyond. Accessed February 17, 2024. https://pisab.org/about-us/.

Porges, Stephen. "Demystifying the Body's Response to Trauma—A Polyvagal Perspective." The Embody Lab, 2022. Video, 1:21:37. Accessed February 23, 2024. https://learn.theembodylab.com/products/bonus-embodied-social-justice-2022-early-bird/categories/2149666785/posts/2155287385.

Pranis, Kay, Barry Stuart, and Mark Wedge. *Peacemaking Circles: From Conflict to Community*. St. Paul: Living Justice Press, 2003.

Psychology Today. "Post-Traumatic Growth." Accessed February 17, 2024. https://www.psychologytoday.com/us/basics/post-traumatic-growth#:~:text=Post%2DTraumatic%20Growth%20is%20the.

Purser, Ron, and David Loy. "Beyond McMindfulness." HuffPost, The Blog, July 1, 2013. https://www.huffpost.com/entry/beyond-mcmindfulness_b_3519289.

Quart, Alissa. *Bootstrapped: Liberating Ourselves from the American Dream*. New York: HarperCollins, 2023.

RAINN. "Children and Teens: Statistics." Accessed Feb 27, 2024. https://www.rainn.org/statistics/children-and-teens.

Rayworth, Melissa. "This Innovative Program Is Bringing Tomorrow's Teachers of Color to Pittsburgh Today." PublicSource. October 30, 2021. https://www.publicsource.org/this-innovative-program-is-bringing-tomorrows-teachers-of-color-to-pittsburgh-today/.

Reese, Hope. "What Is Emotional Labor, and Why Does It Matter?" *Greater Good* magazine, the Greater Good Science Center at the University of California, Berkeley. April 5, 2023. https://greatergood.berkeley.edu/article/item/what_is_emotional_labor_and_why_does_it_matter#:~:text=Hackman%20describes%20emotional%20labor%20as.

Róisín, Fariha. "Why Hollywood's White Savior Obsession Is an Extension of Colonialism." *Teen Vogue,* September 14, 2017. https://www.teenvogue.com/story/hollywoods-white-savior-obsession-colonialism?mbid=social_facebook.

Roper, Lyndal. *The Witch in the Western Imagination.* Charlottesville: University of Virginia Press, 2012.

Rossetto, Harriet. "The Trauma of Privilege." *Jewish Journal,* May 21, 2015. https://jewishjournal.com/commentary/opinion/171298/.

Satchidananda, Swami. *The Living Gita: Commentaries on the Bhagavad Gita.* Yogaville, VA: Integral Yoga Publications, 1985.

Scott-Heron, Gil. "Gil Scott-Heron - Revolution Will Not Be Televised (Official Version)." Ace Records. YouTube video, 3:06. Posted October 7, 2013. https://www.youtube.com/watch?v=vwSRqaZGsPw.

Sharpe, Susan, and Edmonton Victim Offender Mediation Society. *Restorative Justice: A Vision for Healing and Change.* Edmonton, Alberta: Edmonton Victim Offender Mediation Society, 1998.

Shierholz, Heidi, Margaret Poydock, and Celine McNicholas. "Unionization Increased by 200,000 in 2022: Ten of Millions More Wanted to Join a Union, but Couldn't." Economic Policy Institute. January 19, 2023. https://www.epi.org/publication/unionization-2022/.

Shlain, Leonard. *The Alphabet versus the Goddess: The Conflict between Word and Image.* New York: Penguin/Compass, 1998.

Siegel, Michael, and Emily F. Rothman. "Firearm Ownership and Suicide Rates Among US Men and Women, 1981–2013," *Am J Public Health* 106, no.7 (July 7, 2016): 1316–22. doi: 10.2105/AJPH.2016.303182.

Smith, Imari Z., Keisha L. Bentley-Edwards, Salimah El-Amin, and William Darity, Jr. "Fighting at Birth: Eradicating the Black-White Infant Mortality Gap." Duke University's Samuel DuBois Cook Center on Social Equity and Insight Center for Community Economic Development. March 2018. https://socialequity.duke.edu/wp-content/uploads/2019/12/Eradicating-Black-Infant-Mortality-March-2018.pdf.

Smith, Lillian. *Killers of the Dream.* New York: W. W. Norton & Company, 1994.

Smith, Linda Tuhiwai. *Decolonizing Methodologies: Research and Indigenous Peoples.* Ventura, CA: Content Technologies Inc., 2012.

Sonneville, K. R., and S. K. Lipson. "Disparities in Eating Disorder Diagnosis and Treatment according to Weight Status, Race/Ethnicity, Socioeconomic Background, and Sex among College Students." *International Journal of Eating Disorders* 51, no. 6 (2018): 518–26. https://doi.org/10.1002/eat.22846.

St. Clair, Kassia. "What if We Called It the 'Flax Age' Instead of the 'Iron Age'?" Literary Hub, November 19, 2019. https://lithub.com/what-if-we-called-it-the-flax-age-instead-of-the-iron-age/?fbclid=IwAR2kY2ghGWAQJFng0c_4pnY686Mjlo3agGp-oZEoGMXPsqxlA5W1g9w-HYg.

Stein, Marc Eliot. "Diane Di Prima's Revolutionary Letters." Literary Kicks, October 26, 2020. https://litkicks.com/RevolutionaryLetters/.

Stone Mountain Park. "Memorial Carving." Accessed Feb 27, 2024. https://stonemountainpark.com/activity/historynature/memorial-carving/.

Substance Abuse and Mental Health Services Administration. "Harm Reduction." Updated April 24, 2023. https://www.samhsa.gov/find-help/harm-reduction.

Sue, Derald Wing, and Lisa Spanierman. Microaggressions in Everyday Life: Race, Gender, and Sexual Orientation. Hoboken, NJ: John Wiley & Sons, 2020.

Thompson, Derek. "Three Myths of the Great Resignation." The Atlantic, December 8, 2021. https://www.theatlantic.com/ideas/archive/2021/12/great-resignation-myths-quitting-jobs/620927/.

Tippett, Krista. "Bessel van der Kolk – How Trauma Lodges in the Body, Revisited." The On Being Project. Original air date July 11, 2013, last updated November 11, 2021. https://onbeing.org/programs/bessel-van-der-kolk-how-trauma-lodges-in-the-body-revisited/.

Torres-Spelliscy, Ciara. "Blood on Your Handset." Slate, September 20, 2013. http://www.slate.com/articles/news_and_politics/jurisprudence/2013/09/conflict_minerals_from_the_congo_is_your_cellphone_made_with_them.html.

Tuck, Eve, and K. Wayne Yang. "Decolonization Is Not a Metaphor." Decolonization: Indigeneity, Education & Society 1, no. 1 (2012): 1–40.

Tuck, Eve, and K. Wayne Yang. "R-Words: Refusing Research." In Humanizing Research: Decolonizing Qualitative Inquiry with Youth and Communities, edited by M.T. Winn, 223–48. Los Angeles: Sage Publications, 2014.

Turner, Meagan. "Purity Culture: Repercussions & How to Heal." Choosing Therapy. November 28, 2023. https://www.choosingtherapy.com/purity-culture/#:~:text=What%20Is%20Purity%20Culture%3F,the%20same%20across%20the%20board .

U.S. Senate Committee on the Judiciary. "Fact: Arming More People Doesn't Make Us Safer." September 23, 2019. https://www.judiciary.senate.gov/press/dem/releases/fact-arming-more-people-doesnt-make-us-safer.

United Nations. "Indigenous Peoples: Background." Accessed February 17, 2024. https://www.un.org/en/fight-racism/vulnerable-groups/indigenous-peoples#:~:text=Common%20historical%20continuity.

United Nations Human Rights Office of the High Commissioner. "Intersex." Free & Equal: United Nations. https://www.unfe.org/know-the-facts/challenges-solutions/intersex

United States Census Bureau. "Race." Census.gov. 2023. https://www.census.gov/quickfacts/fact/note/US/RHI625222#:~:text=OMB%20requires%20five%20minimum%20categories.

Vaid-Menon, Alok. "Book Report: Making Sex: Body and Gender from the Greeks to Freud by Dr. Thomas Laqueur (Harvard University Press, 1990)." Instagram, July 20, 2023. https://www.instagram.com/p/Cu61YoNur0T/?img_index=3.

Valandra, Edward Charles, ed. *Colorizing Restorative Justice: Voicing Our Realities.* St. Paul: Living Justice Press, 2020.

Vaughan, Genevieve. "Patriarchal Capitalism vs. a Gift Economy." In *The Rule of Mars,* edited by Cristina Biaggi, 263–71. Manchester, CT: Knowledge, Ideas & Trends, 2006.

Vedantam, Shankar, and Maggie Penman. "Remembering Anarcha, Lucy, and Betsey: The Mothers of Modern Gynecology." NPR, February 16, 2016. https://www.npr.org/2016/02/16/466942135/remembering-anarcha-lucy-and-betsey-the-mothers-of-modern-gynecology.

Villanueva, Edgar. *Decolonizing Wealth: Indigenous Wisdom to Heal Divides and Restore Balance.* Oakland: Berrett-Koehler Publishers, Inc., 2018.

Wahrhaftig, Paul. "Tension Triangle," in "Respectful Listening and Dialogue Curriculum," edited by the American Friends Service Committee. Pennsylvania Project. Pittsburgh, PA. Accessed January 10, 2024. https://afsc.org/sites/default/files/documents/Respectful%20Listening%20and%20Dialogue%20Curriculum.pdf

Walker, Alice. *In Search of Our Mothers' Gardens: Womanist Prose.* New York: Harvest/Harcourt Brace Jovanovich Publishers, 1983.

Weaver, Vesla Mae. "Why White People Keep Calling the Cops on Black Americans." Vox, May 29, 2018. https://www.vox.com/first-person/2018/5/17/17362100/starbucks-racial-profiling-yale-airbnb-911.

X, Malcolm. "Malcolm X on the Black Revolution." ICIT Digital Library. April 8, 1964. https://www.icitdigital.org/articles/malcolm-x-on-the-black-revolution-april-8-1964.

Yellow Bird, Michael. "Decolonization: Seeking Symbols of Hope." Omega Institute for Holistic Studies. 2024. https://www.eomega.org/videos/decolonization-seeking-symbols-of-hope?itm_source_h=search&itm_source_s=search&itm_medium_h=tile&itm_medium_s=tile&itm_campaign_h=searchcr&itm_campaign_s=searchcr.

Yoder, Carolyn. *Little Book of Trauma Healing: When Violence Strikes and Community Security Is Threatened.* Intercourse, PA: Good Books, 2005.

YogaRoots On Location. "Embodied Antiracist Organizing." Accessed May 15, 2024. https://www.yogarootsonlocation.com

Zehr Institute for Restorative Justice. "Restorative Justice and the First Harm: Indigenous Land Acknowledgments and Beyond." October 19, 2022. https://www.facebook.com/Zehr.Institute.Restorative.Justice.EMU/videos/1113299369298515.

ABOUT THE AUTHOR

Amanda K Gross is an intersectional anti-racist organizer, educator, and director of Mistress Syndrome, from which she organizes with fellow status quo and passing white ladies to heal from, disrupt, and transform the legacies of white womanhood. Certified at the 200-hour RYT level by YogaRoots On Location's AntiRacist Raja Yoga School, Amanda has an MA in Conflict Transformation and has a PhD in Expressive Arts. Her autoethnographic research investigates how arts and culture can support white settlers in sustaining anti-racist and decolonizing efforts.

Amanda recently relocated to the Appalachian South on the stolen lands of the ᏣᎳᎫᏪᏘᏱ Tsalaguwetiyi (Cherokee) and is reconnecting with the Southern racial justice organizing traditions within which she was raised. Other writings include contributions to *Resistance: Confronting Violence, Power, and Abuse within Peace Churches* and *Bodies & Beliefs: Purity Culture and the Rhetoric of Religious Trauma*.

Find out more about Mistress Syndrome and other resources at mistresssyndrome.com.

For further resources, group discussion guide, upcoming events, and other ways to mobilize for anti-racist change, visit mistresssyndrome.com or scan the QR code below.

www.ingramcontent.com/pod-product-compliance
Lightning Source LLC
Chambersburg PA
CBHW022042020426
42335CB00012B/500